THE TRANSFORMATION
OF PALESTINIAN POLITICS

OTHER BOOKS BY BARRY RUBIN

The Arab States and the Palestine Conflict

Assimilation and Its Discontents

Cauldron of Turmoil: America in the Middle East

The Great Powers and the Middle East

Islamic Fundamentalism in Egyptian Politics

Israel, the Palestinian Authority, and the Arab States

The Israel-Arab Reader: A Documentary History of the Middle East Conflict
(with Walter Laqueur)

Istanbul Intrigues

Modern Dictators: Third World Coupmakers, Strongmen, and Populist Tyrants

The New Middle East: Opportunities and Risks

Paved with Good Intentions: The American Experience and Iran

Revolution Until Victory? The Politics and History of the PLO

Secrets of State: The State Department and the Struggle over U.S. Foreign Policy

THE TRANSFORMATION OF
PALESTINIAN POLITICS

FROM REVOLUTION TO STATE-BUILDING

BARRY RUBIN

HARVARD UNIVERSITY PRESS
Cambridge, Massachusetts
London, England
1999

LIBRARY OF CONGRESS CATALOGING-IN-PUBLICATION DATA

Rubin, Barry M.
The transformation of Palestinian politics :
from revolution to state-building / Barry Rubin.
p.   cm.
Includes bibilographical references (p.   –   ) and index.
ISBN 0-674-00071-4 (cloth : alk. paper)
1. Palestinian National Authority. 2. Arab-Israeli conflict—1993– —Peace.
3. Palestinian Arabs—Politics and government.   I. Title.
DS119.76.R83   1999
321.09'095695'309049—dc21   99-34447

Designed by Gwen Nefsky Frankfeldt

TO GABRIELLA RUBIN

CONTENTS

Preface   ix

1 The Rulers, the Ruled, and the Rules   1

2 The Palestinian Legislative Council   27

3 Democracy, Stability, and Human Rights   45

4 The Polity and the People   71

5 The New Palestinian Political Elite   88

6 The Palestinian Opposition   114

7 The Palestinian Authority and the Middle East   138

8 Thinking about Israel and the United States   162

9 Recognizing Facts, Creating Facts   187

Appendixes:
  1. Palestinian Authority Cabinets, 1994–1999   203
  2. Membership of the Palestinian Legislative Council (PLC)   206
  3. The Fatah Central Committee   213
  4. The PLO Executive Committee (EC)   216
  5. Middle East States and the Palestinian Authority   219

Notes   221

Glossary   267

Bibliography   269

Index   279

PREFACE

This book's subject is the Palestinian Authority (PA) phase of Palestinian political history, a transitional era between the revolutionary movement and the achievement of an independent state. It analyzes the PA's structure as a governmental institution; the dynamics of Palestinian state-building; the new Palestinian political elite; and the PA's relationship with foreign governments, the opposition, and its own people.

The study is part of a long-term research project on this subject. I dealt with some aspects of the pre-1948 era of Palestinian politics in an earlier book, *The Arab States and the Palestine Conflict*, while the second, 1948–1993, era of Palestinian politics I covered more comprehensively in *Revolution Until Victory? The Politics and History of the PLO*.

The focus of the current study is on post-1993 Palestinian politics, though obviously what went before remains important and influential. Since the book concentrates on the areas where the PA ruled, it deals only briefly with East Jerusalem; neither does it analyze the complex details of Israeli-Palestinian negotiations and the peace process or Israeli policy and debates—subjects covered in many other studies. These are worthy topics that are indeed interconnected with this book's subject. But to include these matters, which have been written about far more extensively than the issues which preoccupy me here, would reduce the space for considering the PA's composition, history, and so on. The lack of discussion of the Jerusalem issue—as with the limited amount of space spent on several other points—is not intended in any way as a political statement on that question.

All available sources in Arabic, Hebrew, and English have been used and compared. My goal here is to seek the most accurate possible approximation of truth. My conclusions have been influenced by my research far more than the reverse.

Despite all efforts, it is often difficult to ascertain certain matters of fact that might be easily verifiable in other circumstances. The Palestinian journalist Muna Hamza-Muhaysan wrote a memorable case study on this dilemma in *Palestine Report* (September 25, 1998) about her difficult, ultimately unsuccessful quest merely to discover the population of the Bethlehem district.

There is a whole range of semantic issues that often seem to have political implications, which I wish to avoid. I do not refer to a state of Palestine, since that polity did not yet exist in fact during the transitional period led by the PA. Palestinians sometimes refer to the Palestinian National Authority (PNA), which is a reasonable substitution for PA. But I use PA because that is the name in general international usage and official documents.

Some Palestinian writers refer to the PA as incorporating the Palestinian parliament (Palestinian Legislative Council, PLC). Consequently, they speak of the PA executive branch. In this book, though, for clarity, the term PA is confined to the executive branch. Again, this is not intended as a political judgment. For example, in American usage, the term "U.S. government" usually refers exclusively to the executive branch, though technically it includes Congress as well.

I favor the creation of a Palestinian state. Criticism of the PA does not imply its illegitimacy or any belief that it would be unable to govern such an entity. Similarly, positive statements about the PA are not meant to imply any apologetic intent. Understanding a situation can result only from incorporating a well-rounded analysis of complex realities. In short, sympathy does not exclude criticism and vice versa.

This book presents in detail the failures and misdeeds of the PA within the framework of the tremendous pressures and limitations it faces. It is important to document every instance of antidemocratic practices and corruption, but it is also necessary to put them in some kind of context of Palestinian political history, comparative Arab polities, other state-building experiences, or genuine alternatives. On balance, in this context, and despite very great shortcomings, the PA's successes are more impressive than its failures. This needs to be stressed because it has often been overlooked in other writings about this subject.

The book is deliberately structured to show the cross-references between topics. Chapter 1 discusses the background and some key issues in the transformation of Palestinian politics, governance, and leadership. Chapter 2 examines the PLC's role, and Chapter 3 the questions of democracy and human rights. Chapter 4 considers a number of civil society institutions as well as the economy, educational system, and media. Chapter 5 looks at Fatah and more broadly at the PA political elite. Chapter 6 analyzes the opposition. Chapter 7 considers the relationship between the PA and the Arab states, including Palestinians living in those countries. Chapter 8 looks at PA views of Israel and the United States, and Chapter 9 raises a number of questions regarding the future of the PA and the transition to a state.

The transliteration system used—devised with the generous help of Dr. Ofra Bengio—aims for simplicity and consistency. The names of authors of English-language works cited in the notes, as well as the spelling of words in direct quotation from those materials, have been left unchanged even when inconsistent with that system. In some cases, people mentioned in the text have written articles in English using a different transliteration of their name. In such cases, I have used a consistent transliteration in the text but have given the spelling used in the English publication in the bibliography and notes. After the entry in the bibliography and the first appearance of the name in the text, I have put my transliteration in brackets. The main examples are Abu-Amr [Abu Amr], Shikaka [Shiqaqi], and Sourani [Surani].

I have benefited from the assistance of people too numerous to be named here, especially scores of Palestinians who have given me off-the-record interviews over many years. Special thanks are owed for the research assistance of Cameron Brown, Malaika Martin, Amir Rom, and Gilad Tsur. As always, Judy Colp Rubin has given excellent editing advice, as well as encouragement for which I am always grateful.

But if the enemy incline toward peace, do thou also incline toward peace, and trust in God.

—Koranic verse frequently cited by Yasir Arafat

Interviewer: Has the revolutionary era ended? Has the state era begun?

Yasir Arafat: The revolution will go on until an independent Palestinian state is established with Jerusalem as its capital . . . We will struggle on all fronts to prove that this land is Arab, Arab, and Arab; we will defend every particle of Palestinian soil; and we will wage the battle of building a Palestinian state as we waged the liberation and peace battle.

—Interview in *al-Wasat,* January 9–15, 1995

1

THE RULERS, THE RULED, AND THE RULES

"We have transferred from a revolution to a state," exulted Ahmad Khuri (Abu Ala), speaker of the Palestinian Legislative Council (PLC), in defining the new era in his people's political history.[1] Yet with equal accuracy Sufyan Abu Zayida of the Palestinian Authority (PA) Planning Ministry noted the enterprise's difficulty: "We are having a hard time making the transition from an underground movement to the building of national institutions," he said. "I am very disappointed by our inability to create the basis for our future state."[2]

A remarkable transformation was indeed taking place for Palestinians after their historic 1993 agreement with Israel and the PA's establishment as interim government in the following year.[3] Under the leadership of Palestine Liberation Organization (PLO) chairman Yasir Arafat, the PA became the ruler over about 2.5 million Palestinians in the Gaza Strip and West Bank. Starting from scratch, it took on the tremendous burdens of maintaining stability, promoting economic development, creating social institutions, and reaching a peace agreement with Israel.

But achieving a Palestinian state proved to be a very difficult, relatively slow process for two reasons. First, the PA was still engaged in tough, complex, and lengthy negotiations with Israel over how, when, and even whether such a state might be created at all.[4] Second, Palestinians themselves were in the midst of one of the world's most difficult state-building processes, simultaneously constructing a new country's foundation and a new society's structure under tremendous pressure of time and from a seemingly endless series of turbulent events.

To succeed in negotiations, the PA had to prove its ability to fulfill its commitments to Israel. To succeed in state-building, the PA had to maintain popular support both by making steady progress toward independence and by meeting constituents' needs.

This transitional epoch between revolution and state was the era of the PA, created as a unique structure for a unique situation. The PLO and the majority of Palestinians, despite reservations and suspicions, had accepted a compromise agreement to end the long, bitter conflict with Israel. Still, a significant minority of radical Islamic and nationalist forces rejected any deal and were determined to wreck it. Within Israel, too, there was heated debate over whether peace could be achieved and what form a solution should take.

Thus, while the two peoples' objective relationship was quickly transformed, subjective views and internal political balances underwent a far slower change. The peace process's architects had expected this result, believing that new facts would create new relationships, making transfigurations thought impossible a few years or even months earlier. Often this perspective proved accurate. Yet while everyone knew it would be a difficult endeavor, the obstacles proved even greater than expected.

The PA had far fewer assets and far more problems than other newly created states. It did not have full power over its own territory or any control over its borders. Five years after the Oslo agreement was signed, the PA ruled almost all Palestinians in the West Bank and Gaza but still controlled only part of the West Bank, with Israel having a right to supervise security in most of that area. There were Israeli checkpoints that could close traffic between West Bank towns. With few natural resources and little help from Arab states, the PA was dependent on donors who were made more skeptical by reports that the PA was misusing funds. Most PA administrators lacked appropriate training and experience. The PA shouldered a heavy burden in trying to overcome a history of violence, extremist ideology, and undemocratic structures.

It was no exaggeration for Palestinian administrative expert Muhammad Dajani to write that "creating a Palestinian political system is a Sisyphean task." After all, the PA-ruled territories had a "crumbling infrastructure, high unemployment, lack of revenues and violent underground political opposition. Crippled by economic crisis, and locked in tough negotiations with Israel, which places high priorities on its security needs, the PA can hardly spare the energy to tackle this crucial problem. Nevertheless, this task is being performed and a viable political system is being created."[5]

Given this critical situation, the PA's supporters had a credible argument in urging Palestinians to put the priority on maintaining unity. State-building, they argued, would succeed only if led by a strong leader and government with full control over resources, decision making, and popular loyalty. Democracy's requirements, they insisted, might contradict those of national reconstruction.[6]

Yet the radical Palestinian opposition branded the PA's most basic policies as treasonous, directly challenging the very premise of recognition, negotiation, compromise, and peace with Israel. It claimed that a Palestinian state could be created only through violence, as well as a thorough change in the PA's strategy and leadership. The PA's more moderate critics insisted that democracy and respect for human rights must be built into the new polity from the very beginning. Not only were these values precious in their own right, they argued, but without them a state would not come into existence at all.

While the Palestinian case held many parallels to other state-building experiences, much of the process and many of the problems involved were quite distinctive. Usually countries become self-governing and formally independent at the same time. The state has clearly defined national boundaries, and with all conflicting claims at least temporarily resolved, the government can rule this national territory free of outside interference while enjoying internal legitimacy. The type of political system is already decided. The majority of the people whom the state claims as citizens live in that territory. When one of these elements is not in place, a common result is war or, at least, a crisis threatening that state's very existence.[7]

In the Palestinian case, however, none of these factors was fully resolved. The PA had come into existence and ruled a partial-state polity. The tenants were moving in while the property was still being surveyed, the purchase price and conditions of occupancy were under negotiation, the architects continued to argue over the blueprints, renovations were under way, and the buyers were still trying to raise the money.

The tasks of political construction faced by the Palestinians were thus more difficult than those confronting new states in Africa, Asia, and elsewhere in the world. For the projected state of Palestine, one might say, existence preceded essence. The outbreak of war or breakdown of the peace process would signal the abortion, not birth pangs, of a new state. Indeed, the special paradox for the PA was that a determined struggle to obtain a state had to be waged both internally and externally while it simultaneously proved its moderation and stability.

Arafat, veteran leader of both the PLO and its main group, Fatah, now also became the PA's head. His overwhelming command over policy, decisions, and appointments was the regime's dominant feature. As a Palestinian magazine put it: "Arafat is the chairman of the PLO, the president of the PA; he holds all the reins, he controls all the money, he takes all the decisions . . . and he, by and large, is the only law, whose authority is respected, established and enforced."[8]

His refusal to delegate power was so complete that PA decision making stopped when he was abroad or even away from his office for a day. The democratic institutions created remained subordinate to the chief executive. Two of Arafat's Palestinian Legislative Council (PLC) critics summed up the point admirably. "Arafat is individualistic to an abnormal degree . . . he prefers to make decisions on his own," said Abd al-Jawad Salah.[9] Ziyad Abu Amr wrote, "If there is an embodiment of institutionalization, Arafat's style of leadership is the antithesis."[10]

The main problem was not that Arafat was a fearsome dictator but rather, as Salah and Abu Amr had pointed out, his anti-institutional, impulsive decision-making style. Arafat's hesitant, compromising approach was quite different from the dominating, centralizing technique of other Third World revolutionary leaders. "Every hero has his flaw," a Palestinian journalist noted. "Arafat's is indecisiveness."[11] Arafat did not have the personality of a ruthless tyrant systematically imposing his will. Rather, his style was one of ceaselessly maneuvering, balancing, and juggling factions and options.

This approach had often worked well during his more than a quarter-century as PLO leader. Perhaps there was no alternative, since Arafat had been constantly constrained in the PLO era by having to please non-Fatah groups, unruly leaders within Fatah itself, and sponsoring Arab states. As Jamal al-Surani, a PLO leader, explained this system, some might think that Arafat "issues the orders and must be obeyed." But he "is not the head. He and we are partners. We are not his employees . . . [Arafat] does not decide what is right and what is wrong on his own personal whim."[12] Arafat himself grumbled, "I am not at the Cannes Film Festival where I can choose the best movie."[13]

Spread over a dozen countries, often having limited contact with the Palestinian masses, and with no totally reliable base of support, the PLO had been a bureaucratic nightmare. Arafat could not simply give orders. He had to cajole, manipulate, and threaten to resign. In his own words: "We are the flying carpet revolution, we are treading on burning coals.

Tonight I am seeing you in Baghdad. I don't know where I will see you tomorrow."[14]

Thus, the PLO had been neither a dictatorship nor a democracy. As Hatim Abu Ghazala, a leading Gaza activist, noted, the Palestinians were "the only nation in the world that has to govern itself by consensus and not majority rule." He might equally have added that consensus also supplanted one-man rule. In this situation, the primacy on maintaining PLO unity at all costs had often given veto power to extremists and thus damaged Palestinian interests.[15]

The PA's creation, on the one hand, partly liberated Arafat to act more on his own wishes. The Oslo agreement itself had been made possible only because Arafat acted decisively and autonomously, willing even to split the PLO to seize this opportunity. In the PA era Arafat had more of a chance to make himself a dictator. Impatient with criticism, convinced that he was the only one who could lead Palestine to independence, and determined to limit dissent, Arafat could be high-handed and repressive.

But on the other hand, a real dictatorship was not his style or preference, and suited neither the PA's situation nor its limited power. If Arafat was not constrained by laws, courts, or parliament, he was certainly restricted by a need to maintain his political base, national unity, international backing, and internal peace. Moreover, Arafat's popularity showed that his decisions usually did represent what most Palestinians wanted. Arafat remained committed to pluralism and sensitive to public opinion. The way to control a diverse Palestinian political spectrum, he believed, was by avoiding confrontation and building a united front. As he had once mollified PLO factions, he now tried to co-opt the Islamic opposition, unite former exiles with indigenous people, and bridge gaps between wealthy notables and young activists.

Such a leader was not going to institute a Western-style democracy. Yet he was also less likely than most Third World leaders to foreclose the possibility of democracy by creating authoritarian institutions and a monolithic society. Since Arafat, as the Palestinian movement's "founding father" and the movement's leader for decades, had such huge legitimacy and leverage, he could afford to give more latitude to critics and opponents than might be granted by a less secure ruler.

Arafat felt it his unique duty and sole ability to create a state and set it on firm foundations. Most Palestinians agreed, as even his opponents acknowledged. It was hard for anyone to compete with what Ziyad Abu

Amr, a pro-democracy advocate and frequent critic, called Arafat's "dominant and charismatic personality . . . and the multiple sources of legitimacy he enjoys in exercising his individualistic style of leadership. Many people argue that the more difficult the Palestinian situation becomes, the more the Palestinians need him, despite all the problems they have with his leadership."[16]

Equally, Arafat himself embodied the complex nature of PA politics. Despite the establishment of governmental structures resembling a state, Palestinian fortunes were now tied to Arafat's decisions and character more than ever. As if to make up for all those years he had spent trying to direct the anarchic PLO, Arafat closely managed every PA decision and appointment. He could do this more easily than other Middle East leaders because his domain was smaller and his sphere of control more limited than that of a fully independent state's leader. Still, as Abu Zayida noted sadly: "Arafat busies himself with small details, which he should not be handling. He should not be issuing building permits for another house or floor. He should not be holding meetings with all and sundry. He is having a bad influence on the behavior of his ministers. He constantly interferes with their work and the work of the senior bureaucracy."[17]

The relationship between Khuri and Arafat illustrated both the Palestinian leader's high-handedness and his tolerance. Long director of the PLO economic department, Khuri was elected to the Fatah Central Committee in 1989 and became chief Palestinian negotiator for the 1993 Oslo agreement with Israel. When the PA was established, Arafat appointed him economics and trade minister in May 1994. But Khuri resigned that post in September 1994 to protest Arafat's policies, then also quit his job as chief of the ill-fated Palestinian Economic Council for Development and Rehabilitation (PECDAR), which was supposed to—but never did—control incoming aid funds.[18]

Despite their clashes, Arafat put Khuri on the Fatah ticket for the January 1996 elections, and he proved the biggest vote-getter in East Jerusalem. Two months later, the PLC's first session elected Khuri as the parliament's speaker. In that job he continued to criticize Arafat and PA policies while fighting for a strong parliament to balance the leader's power. Yet after all this, Arafat still included Khuri in his highest councils and even used him as a negotiator with Israel.

The proposed Palestinian constitution—passed by the PLC but never ratified—named the PLC speaker as Arafat's interim successor if anything should happen to him. This made Khuri in theory, though not in practice, the number two Palestinian leader. Khuri's multiple, seemingly conflicting roles illustrated the incongruities of Palestinian politics. He was both member of the new political elite and its resolute opponent; an aristocrat turned revolutionary, then architect of a negotiated peace; and a loyal PLO and Fatah man battling the esteemed leader of both groups.

Such contradictory situations were built in to the dramatic turn of events which had transformed the revolutionary movement into a government, with Arafat's leadership an indispensable element of continuity. The PA existed as a result of the 1993 Israel-PLO agreement and the process set in motion by it and subsequent accords. In turn, that outcome capped a long, slow, difficult evolution for Palestinian politics toward something dramatically new, often totally contradicting fervent beliefs and cherished practices held during the preceding half-century. A mere list of key changes shows how complex a transformation took place as the PLO moved:

• From a revolutionary movement toward a state trying to meet the needs of 2.5 million citizens. The PLO had always engaged in a wide range of welfare, economic, diplomatic, and other activities. But its motive power had been armed, radical guerrilla groups that fought Israel and sometimes one another. Now the PA had to become an administrative body, building roads, collecting garbage, and running huge education and health systems.

• From a loose coalition of independent groups to a government needing to impose some discipline and monopolize certain services and functions. Arafat had never made a serious effort to impose his will on a PLO splintered by ideologies, fiefdoms, and loyalties to different Arab states. He often conceded veto power over PLO policy to the most militant. While this pattern continued in the new era in the form of Arafat's pluralist style, the PA needed to reduce that anarchy. Indeed, it had to do so in order to survive and make progress in building a state.

• From dependence on violence, which often meant striking at Israeli civilians, to responsibility for stopping Palestinian terrorism against Israel. The goal of total war aimed at eliminating Israel had been replaced by that of negotiating toward peace and coexistence. After 1993 there were virtually no armed attacks on Israelis by Fatah members or PA supporters. People who had believed their whole lives that no compromise was possible and almost any tactic was acceptable against a totally evil enemy were now cooperating with those whom they blamed for all their problems and sufferings.

• From the dream of total victory—a Palestinian state encompassing everything between the Jordan River and the Mediterranean—to a new goal of creating a Palestinian state in the West Bank and Gaza with its capital in East Jerusalem.

• From dispersed exile to restoration in its claimed homeland, reuniting a people scattered for almost a half-century. While the PLO had won support from the vast majority of West Bank and Gaza residents, its leadership and policy had always come from people who, in 1948, fled areas now part of Israel to many different countries. Returning PLO cadres were a small minority among local people whose leaders also had to be integrated and interests taken into account.

• From viewing the United States as a chief enemy which was inevitably anti-Palestinian to becoming a virtual American client. The PLO had seen itself as part of a world struggle against Western imperialism, allied with the USSR and seeking to expel U.S. influence from the region. Now Arafat visited Washington, shook hands with members of Congress, and depended on Western donations mobilized by the United States. The situation's irony was embodied by the résumé of a senior PA official handling U.S. aid at the Ministry of Planning and International Cooperation which listed his "educational experience" as "explosives engineer."[19]

• From relying on Arab countries and Pan-Arab nationalist ideology to implementing a separate Palestinian nation-state nationalism. While Palestinians still believed in Arab solidarity, they now explicitly embarked on building their own small independent state, rather than trying to add one province to an Arab realm stretching from the Atlantic Ocean to the Persian Gulf. Moreover, their expectations were constantly disappointed by the limited help or aid received from their "brothers" in the Arab states.

• From expecting to create a utopian society that would be a shining model of Islam, socialism, democracy, and rapid development to facing the unpleasant realities of slow progress, limited resources, and accommodation with an imperfect situation.[20] So long as building a Palestinian state was just an idea, it was possible to imagine that all problems would be solved and all dreams fulfilled. Now no one could avoid confronting the reality of the nation's small size, poverty, and relative weakness, as well as the human elements of corruption, incompetence, and greed in the Palestinian movement.

Each Palestinian individual, institution, and group was located at a different point on this evolutionary progression between the old and new situations. If the shock entailed by such shifts contradicting the movement's entire history were compressed into two sentences, these might be what Arafat told the 1996 session of the Palestine National Council (PNC, the PLO's parliament): "All revolutions end in agreements. Do you think you can get everything you want?"

The interminable time span, emotional pain, and political difficulties needed for persuading Palestinians to alter their national program proved that this was not easily or spuriously done. How had this transformation taken place at all?[21]

First, the PLO's new circumstances were a result of its own long-term experiences and maturation, as well as pressure from external forces and new opportunities. A key factor in this mutation was the PLO's failure over thirty years to progress in its goal of destroying Israel. The PLO had tried a wide range of methods, including goading Arab states into war and seeking an Arab hero to defeat Israel for them; promoting revolution in the Middle East, international terrorism, guerrilla war, and strikes against Israeli civilians; and aligning with the USSR to subvert Western influence in the Middle East. Nothing worked, and the Palestinians' strategic position had worsened over time.

While the PLO suffered defeat and even lost ground on achieving its goal, the organization did succeed in keeping the Palestine question alive, winning hegemony among Palestinians, building their morale, intensifying their struggle, and gaining some international support. Yet the PLO's ability to respond successfully to those experiences had been constrained by the demands of Palestinian public opinion, ideological assumptions, threats from radical groups and regimes, a powerful belief in ultimate total victory, inability to comprehend Israel's strength, and many other factors.

In the end, most of the PLO leadership had to conclude that any solution or even material gains required a compromise diplomatic settlement with Israel. As the veteran PLO leader Hani al-Hasan candidly admitted in 1989, "It took us a hell of a long time to come unambiguously to terms with reality."[22]

A second factor in this process was the PLO's worsening circumstances. It steadily lost support from Arab states weary of the conflict and pressed by other issues. The PLO's Soviet ally collapsed while U.S. leverage increased in the region. Israel became socially and militarily stronger rather than weaker, bolstered by almost 1 million immigrants from the Soviet Union starting in the 1980s.

The Palestinians' hope that Iraqi President Saddam Husayn would be their savior was crushed by his 1991 defeat in Kuwait. Gulf Arab rulers angry at the PLO for backing Iraq expelled several hundred thousand Palestinians and cut off donations, pushing the PLO toward bankruptcy. The Palestinian uprising (intifada) which began in December 1987—whatever its achievements—did not force Israel's withdrawal from the West Bank and Gaza. Local Palestinians there demanded that the PLO negotiate to end Israeli occupation. The threat to its supremacy posed by Hamas (the Islamic Resistance Movement) also gave the PLO an incentive for achieving a breakthrough.

The third main factor was a change in Israeli policy motivated by changes in the PLO, combined with weariness at the conflict and costs induced by the intifada. In 1974, then–Prime Minister Yitzhak Rabin had declared that Israel would negotiate with the PLO only when that organization was ready to recognize Israel and abandon violence. Now, as this was happening, a new government led by Rabin came to power in 1992 ready to talk to the PLO and perhaps accept an independent Palestinian state in the West Bank and Gaza.

Secret Israel-PLO talks in Norway reached an agreement, signed on the White House lawn in September 1993, redefining Palestinian goals as seeking an independent state alongside Israel and creating a new political dynamic on whose success Arafat and his colleagues staked their future.[23]

The agreement was structured as a five-year, three-stage process, a complex and gradual approach required by the high degree of mutual mistrust and large number of difficult issues to be resolved. Throughout this five-year transition period, while Israel relinquished territory and released hundreds of Palestinian prisoners, it was also to retain control of international borders, overall security, East Jerusalem, and Jewish settlements. In exchange, the PA was to put an end to Palestinian terrorism against Israel, change its Charter calling for Israel's destruction, and cease hostile propaganda.

During the first stage, in 1994, Israel withdrew from, and the newly formed PA took over 90 percent of, the Gaza Strip and also the town of

Jericho in the West Bank. Details for implementing this step were set down in a May 1994 agreement signed in Cairo.[24]

In stage two, the PA expanded its rule to almost all Palestinian-populated areas of the West Bank (September–November 1995), held elections (January 1996), and gained control over most of Hebron (January 1997). The basis for these steps was the September 1995 Interim Autonomy Agreement, which was delayed by a series of terrorist attacks and took nine months to negotiate.[25] The West Bank was divided into three parts. Area A, the towns, was under full PA control. Area B, the 450 West Bank villages, would be under PA political control but with shared security responsibility. Area C, which remained under Israeli control, included unpopulated areas, key roads, and Jewish settlements. Three further Israeli deployments were supposed to take place at six-month intervals.

By late 1998, the PA partly or fully controlled about 30 percent of the West Bank. But only 3 percent of this territory was in Area A. The further withdrawals mandated by agreements were delayed until the October 1998 Wye Plantation agreement. It designated another 12 percent of the West Bank to be transferred from Area C to Area B, and 15.2 percent to be moved from Area B to Area A. Thus, the PA was supposed to control 43 percent of the West Bank, including 3 percent set aside as a nature reserve. In exchange, the PA restated earlier commitments and promised to implement more effectively its security arrangements against attacks on Israel.[26] The Wye agreement, however, ran into paralyzing delays, culminating in the government of Israeli Prime Minister Benjamin Netanyahu's stopping implementation and his coalition's collapse over the issue.

During the third stage, originally scheduled to begin in May 1996 and be completed by May 1999, "final status" negotiations were supposed to produce a treaty resolving all remaining issues. These included the fate of East Jerusalem, Palestinian refugees outside the territories, and Jewish settlements in the West Bank and Gaza Strip, as well as the shape of the Palestinian polity, security arrangements, and borders. But these talks had barely begun by the time they were supposed to be reaching their successful conclusion.

Throughout all these negotiations, the PA had to carry out the staggering job of nation-building. Arafat's list of the tasks required showed how much there was to be done. These tasks included building "a legal system, infrastructure, job programs, economic production, agriculture, a social security and educational system; finding export markets; attracting capital from abroad for investment; rehabilitating freed prisoners; developing health and childhood and women's projects; and organizing village councils and city government." The PA also needed to complete "establishment of the main institutions such as the judiciary, the monetary authority, the development bank, the housing bank, the water authority, the energy authority, and the land authority."[27]

The PA began its effort in May 1994 when, after missed deadlines for reaching agreements—a problem that would characterize the peace process thereafter—it moved into the Gaza Strip and Jericho.[28] From that day on, Arafat complained that the aid promised by mostly Western donors was slow in arriving and too hedged by conditions.[29] From the very start, too, dissident Palestinians challenged the new arrangements. On May 20, Hamas killed two Israeli soldiers in the Gaza Strip. In response, Israel imposed the first of many border closures, demanding that the PA police find the culprits.[30]

Although the police failed to catch the killers, the closure was soon lifted because both sides perceived that advancing the peace process was the only or best way to deal with the problems of delays, security, and funding. On July 1, 1994, Arafat finally set foot for the first time in twenty-seven years on the territory he had claimed. Four days later he was sworn in as the PA's leader and his first cabinet began to function.[31] One week after that, Arafat moved into his new home in Gaza.[32]

Israel withdrew from Jericho and most of Gaza in 1994, from West Bank Palestinian towns and villages between September 1995 and January 1996, and from Hebron in January 1997. Palestinians held joyous celebrations as PA forces entered each new place.[33] These agreements were reinforced by January 1996 elections renewing Arafat's mandate as the PA's head and choosing an eighty-eight–member PLC.[34]

Despite each side's constant complaints about the other's behavior, bitter exchanges over even the smallest details, and deadlines repeatedly missed, both parties met their commitments to a far greater extent than was recognized. During the 1994–1996 period, steady progress was being made, and if this situation had continued, a successful final agreement would probably have been worked out within the five-year timetable, despite all the difficult issues remaining to be tackled.

A series of terrorist acts in 1995 and 1996, however, diverted the course of events and slowed progress. Hamas fiercely opposed the peace process. Using concepts endorsed by the PLO until a few years earlier, it argued that Israel must be eliminated and replaced by a Palestinian

Islamic state, that there could be no compromise with Israel, and that Israel had no intention of yielding territory. The PA's policy, it claimed, was simultaneously treasonous and doomed to failure.[35]

For Arafat, handling Hamas's challenge was a very difficult task requiring a delicate mix of pressure and accommodation, of suppression and persuasion. He genuinely wanted to co-opt the movement in exchange for a share of power and patronage both to strengthen his own regime and to prevent Hamas's violence from so threatening Israel's security as to endanger the peace process itself. But he also wanted to avoid a Palestinian civil war and not to antagonize non-Hamas Palestinians by appearing too eager to "appease" Israel.

Consequently, he alternatively arrested, intimidated, complimented, and freed Hamas leaders. He also let them maintain their institutions and even military networks, praised their martyrs, and constantly offered conciliation. This was a delicate game, and Arafat somewhat miscalculated the balance. Most immediately, attacks by Hamas or other radical groups brought months of Israeli closures of the territories and declining employment for Palestinians in Israel in 1995. Arafat's soft policy gave Hamas the opportunity and the confidence to blow up the peace process itself in a series of bloody bombings in Israeli cities during February and March 1996.

Arafat tried and failed throughout 1995 to persuade Hamas to stop attacks on Israel and participate in elections. Hamas would neither abandon its aims nor obey Arafat's authority. Still, as the PA consolidated power, Hamas knew it was in trouble, losing public support and even some members to a rival apparently succeeding in fulfilling its promises. Hamas's chance for taking over and establishing an Islamic regime was fading away. This desperation gave Hamas an additional incentive to go on the offensive with a series of terror attacks during most of 1995 and, after a brief pause, in early 1996.

The incessant bombings and shootings undermined the process's all-important confidence-building element. Many Israelis believed that Palestinians still sought to destroy their country or to continue terrorism. The PA, they thought, was either unwilling or unable to stop the attacks. At the same time, many Palestinians thought that Israel had no intention of relinquishing the territory or accepting a Palestinian state. When Israel postponed negotiations or closed the territories in response to attacks, Palestinians saw this as Israel's way of avoiding its commitments. By mobilizing people to action, extremist ideas had become—at least partly and temporarily—a self-fulfilling prophecy.

At the same moment when Palestinians were claiming that Rabin was giving up nothing, Jewish extremists accused him of giving away everything. The Israeli right was horrified by Rabin's concessions. Insisting that the PA was merely using the pretense of compromise to be better able to destroy Israel, many of its members feared that the country's survival was in jeopardy. Some of its supporters believed that the government was acting directly contrary to God's will. On November 4, 1995, a right-wing Jewish fanatic assassinated Rabin as he was leaving a peace rally in Tel Aviv. Although Rabin's successor as prime minister, Shimon Peres, pursued the same policy, he was a less popular and effective politician.

The combination of events and doctrines led to a dramatic change. Likud Party candidate Benjamin Netanyahu won the May 1996 election by the narrowest possible margin, and so instead of final status negotiations commencing that year, the process became bogged down. Renegotiating Israel's withdrawal from Hebron took nine months until success was achieved in January 1997. No new deal or other progress in the peace process was achieved between the Hebron agreement of January 1997 and the Wye accord of October 1998. Palestinian morale plummeted.

Many Palestinian leaders had miscalculated in arguing that Netanyahu would be the same as or even better for their interests than Rabin or Peres. As *Palestine Report*, a publication of the respected Jerusalem Media Communications Center (JMCC), noted, "Some viewed the Likud victory as a catastrophe for the peace talks; others were more optimistic, expecting the Likud to send clearer messages than the former Labor government which, behind the peace curtain, continued its policies in violation of this very process."[36]

Arafat tried to hope for the best and stuck with the peace process. After his first meeting with Netanyahu, on September 4, 1996, he pledged "our commitment to pursue the cooperation with Israel . . . in all aspects in accordance with the agreement" and declared, "We and Mr. Netanyahu . . . will walk together to advance the peace process." Arafat claimed a victory on the grounds that Netanyahu had met him only under international pressure and that even the conservative Likud had now recognized the PA.[37]

But this was one of Arafat's few successes with the new prime minister over the following two years. The Netanyahu government increased support for building in existing settlements, began new efforts to ensure future Israeli control over East Jerusalem, and made much stricter demands on the PA to prove compliance with its prior commitments. For example, Peres had hailed the PLO's repeal of its Charter as a big step toward peace, while Netanyahu denied that any change had been made at all. At most, the prime minister was willing to offer the Palestinians something more than autonomy, far less than the whole of the West Bank, and none of East Jerusalem.[38]

As mistrust intensified, clashes broke out on September 25, 1996, two days after Netanyahu ordered the opening of a tourist tunnel near the Jerusalem holy sites. This was a step toward tightening Israeli control over East Jerusalem which was somewhat provocative in its own right, but Palestinian extremists spread the inflammatory rumor that Israel was planning to destroy the al-Aqsa mosque, the most important Muslim shrine there. Eighty-six Palestinians and fifteen Israelis were killed and many more people were wounded in the ensuing riots, which included some gun battles between PA and Israeli troops.[39]

Rising tensions united Palestinians against Israel and intensified support for Arafat, which had been falling owing to dissatisfaction with the PA's performance as well as economic hardships. Arafat told a PLC emergency session that Palestinians had chosen a "just peace, and not surrender," and would refuse to "change a letter or even a comma" in the previously signed agreements.[40]

But the danger of confrontation encouraged both sides to return to serious negotiations over Hebron. In January 1997 an agreement was finally reached, and the PA took over 80 percent of the city. When Arafat visited on January 19, sixty thousand cheering Palestinians came out to welcome him.[41] But talks again soon stalled over the small size of Netanyahu's next proposed redeployment on the West Bank and his approval for building a new Jewish neighborhood at Har Homa in East Jerusalem. The Israeli government complained that the PA had not kept its commitments regarding anti-terror efforts and other matters. The rest of 1997 and most of 1998 were spent in endless talks, failed initiatives, and fruitless recriminations. Many observers and participants declared the peace process to be near death.

Yet what was most remarkable in light of these problems was both sides' refusal to abandon the process or return to violent confrontation. The leadership of both sides needed progress to show their citizens, followers, and the rest of the world that they were able to achieve peace and security. Whatever Netanyahu's personal feelings about the Oslo agreement, his career would be destroyed if he led Israel into a conflict with the Palestinians and international isolation while also being unable to provide a reasonable level of security. Consequently, while Netanyahu stalled for time, he had to show periodic progress despite serious opposition inside his own ruling coalition, as with the 1997 Hebron and 1998 Wye agreements. Indeed, right-wing criticism of the Wye accord brought the collapse of his government in December 1998.

For his part, Arafat knew that the PA might continue to exist only within the framework that had created it. The Palestinians were likely to lose any all-out violent conflict, which would result in the PA being driven from the territories and Arafat's leadership being totally discredited. Moreover, the PA saw any breakdown of the peace process as a victory for Netanyahu, since this would freeze a situation in which Israel still controlled most of the land, the PA was vulnerable to Israeli pressure, and there was no Palestinian state.

After waiting so long, then, the PA was determined to fulfill the process and complete its state-building effort. Having refused to make peace with Israel for so many years, Palestinians now demanded that Israel make peace with them. Arafat told a Gaza rally in January 1997: "We need to find a mechanism . . . to face Israel's refusal to fulfill what has been agreed upon . . . [But also] we have no choice but to adhere to reason, wisdom and courage as well as to the option of peace."[42]

Concurrently with the tough negotiations, the PA had to handle a wide range of domestic Palestinian issues. Talks with Israel dealt with the question whether there would be a Palestinian state. Inter-Palestinian politics revolved around the kind of state and society to be created. The PA's structure certainly gave hints and influences for that ultimate outcome, but did not necessarily predetermine it.

Even though Arafat monopolized key decisions, he actually led in conjunction with three groups which together constituted the PA's leadership: the cabinet; executive branch personnel (including the security services); and the top leadership of the PLO (its Executive Committee) and Fatah (its Central Committee). These circles were the PA's real high command, and their weekly meetings were the PA's most important policy forum. The PLC, which was left out, complained that this unelected body subject to no legal control was wrongfully acting as the PA's real government. Nevertheless, a number of its own members, including Khuri, participated in those sessions.[43]

The cabinet as an institution was weakened by the leadership meetings and Arafat's centralization of decision making in his own hands. Still, some individual members had real power as part of the inner circle, most did run their own departments, and Arafat rarely interfered with several ministers, particularly those who were experts in their field. Moreover, the PA's structure in this respect was like that of most Western democratic nations, where strong chief executives have overwhelming authority and power to run the government.

The ministers also embodied the alliance of forces backing the PA. Many of them were Fatah members, but there were a lot of independents (often longtime Fatah sympathizers), leaders of smaller parties Arafat wanted in his coalition, individuals close to Hamas, and even critics being at least temporarily co-opted. In cases where Arafat did not completely trust non-Fatah appointees—as with Labor Minister Samir Ghawsha and Agriculture Minister Abd al-Jawad Salah—he installed his own director general, authorized to bypass the boss in reporting to Arafat and in choosing key junior officials.

Nabil Amr, a strong supporter of Arafat named parliamentary affairs minister in 1998, accurately defined the cabinet's makeup as reflecting Arafat's need to satisfy various interests, including "regions, religion, political loyalty, competence and [the PLC's] membership."[44] The PLC sometimes complained that Arafat did not pick enough of its members as ministers. But when he expanded the cabinet to include far more of them in 1998, PLC critics claimed—not inaccurately—that he was trying to buy legislative support by giving so many such gifts.

There was, then, little overall continuity between the historic PLO or Fatah hierarchies and the cabinet. Aside from Arafat, who always kept the Interior Ministry for himself, only six of those ever appointed as ministers had served on the PLO's highest body, the Executive Committee. Moreover, only two of them—Yasir Abd al-Rabbu, head of the Palestine Democratic Party (FIDA), and Muhammad Nashashibi, an experienced administrator—lasted very long.[45] Only four ministers— Khuri, Intisar al-Wazir, Nabil Sha'th, and Ghawsha's replacement, Rafiq al-Natsha—had belonged to the Fatah Central Committee in exile, all only briefly or very late in the movement's history. Of twenty-three individuals in the 1996 cabinet, only Arafat and Abd Rabbu could truly be called PLO political leaders.[46]

The "Outsiders," abroad since 1948 or 1967, had dominated the PLO and Fatah hierarchies.[47] Most of them had fled their homes in areas now located inside Israel during the 1948 war; some left the West Bank or Gaza Strip after Israel captured those territories in the 1967 war. Still, remarkably few important PLO figures had originated in the West Bank or Gaza, the places the PA now ruled, though many had relatives there. The Outsiders' life experiences during a quarter-century or more of exile, along with their psychological orientation as 1948 refugees, were somewhat different from the perspective of the "Insiders," who had always stayed in the West Bank and Gaza and lived those twenty-five years under Israeli rule.

Arafat used the cabinet largely to ensure top-level representation for these Insiders. In general, they were not career revolutionaries but business or professional people who had long supported Fatah without being members, or at least had never been underground cadres. While about half the ministers in the 1994 cabinet were returning Outsiders, over two-thirds of the 1996 and 1998 cabinets were Insiders who had skills the PA required, such as Minister of Health Dr. Riyad al-Za'nun, a physician; Minister of Economy and Trade Mahir al-Masri, an industrialist and PLC member from Nablus's leading family; and Minister of Justice Frayh Abu Midayn, former head of the Gaza lawyers' association. While Arafat respected Masri's ability to negotiate with foreign banks and investors, Abu Midayn was more of a figurehead in the onerous task of handling the court system. Arafat did not accept his July 1997 resignation despite angry complaints from the attorney general and judges about Abu Midayn's meddling. Minister of Local Government Sa'ib Arikat, from Jericho's most prominent family, was one of Arafat's favorites among the Insiders.

The Palestinian business and professional elite was important to Arafat not for its money, but because it had the polish and expertise he needed for handling diplomatic and financial matters. In addition, those belonging to powerful Insider families had a broad support base of relatives from all social strata, which gave them a detailed knowledge of local conditions and lots of votes in elections. These assets also explained why Arafat chose so many mayors from that group.

Another important category was that of Outsider technocrats with long records as PLO officials. Minister of Finance Muhammad Zuhdi al-Nashashibi had been the Executive Committee's secretary and was elected as a full member in 1993. Minister of Planning and Economic Cooperation Nabil Sha'th was trusted by Arafat for his international connections and expertise.

While revolutionaries were largely absent from the cabinet, they entered the leadership as Fatah leaders, military commanders, heads of PA agencies, and advisers to Arafat.[48] One of the two main exceptions, and another of those appointed to the cabinet three times, was Minister of Social Affairs Intisar al-Wazir, the sole woman in the entire PA power elite (and the only one on the Fatah Central Committee). Arafat did not seem to like her. Still, she had a long record as a Fatah activist, and her late husband, Abu Jihad, assassinated by Israel in 1988, was the man Arafat most respected among all the PLO leaders. A large photo of Abu Jihad hung prominently in Arafat's office, and he was the only other Palestinian leader whose image was permitted to be displayed widely in PA territory.[49]

The other cabinet member with impressive revolutionary credentials was Minister of Supply Abd al-Aziz Ali Shahin. He was a founder of Fatah's military wing in 1965 and commanded it in the West Bank's southern part until the Israelis captured him in 1967. Released in 1982 after fifteen years in prison and deported shortly thereafter, Shahin went to Lebanon, where he commanded Fatah troops in battle against anti-Arafat rebels. He then went on to PLO headquarters in Tunis, where he helped organize the intifada in the West Bank and Gaza.[50]

Since it was important politically to show that the PA was more than just a Fatah regime, Arafat also named several ministers from smaller parties or Islamic groups in order to broaden the coalition. Yet precisely because they were not Fatah members, they had far less influence. The only exception was Yasir Abd Rabbu (Information, Culture, and Arts), who backed Arafat in the 1980s so energetically that many considered him a virtual Fatah member. He left the Democratic Front for the Liberation of Palestine (DFLP) to form his own group, FIDA.[51] Ghawsha was picked for a similar reason. Bashir al-Barghuti, secretary general of the Palestine People's Party (PPP, Communist) and minister of industry in the 1996 cabinet, represented another group basically supportive of Arafat, though it often criticized specific PA policies.[52]

Arafat was especially eager to bring Islamic figures into the coalition. Two ministers close to Hamas were prized despite problems they brought Arafat. Tallal Sadir (Minister of Sports and Youth, 1996 cabinet; without portfolio, 1998 cabinet) was, to judge from the large amounts of funds his office misplaced, one of the most corrupt or incompetent ministers. Minister of Telecommunications and Post Imad al-Faluji (1996 and 1998 cabinets) was the most significant Hamas figure Arafat won over, though he also continued to criticize PA policies. In addition, the Ministry of Waqf and Religious Affairs gave the PA influence in the religious sector by exercising some control over sermons, employment of clerics, and funding of mosques and religious schools. Many of its employees were Hamas supporters who had switched loyalty to ensure that they kept their jobs.

Arafat also used ministries as gifts to strengthen supporters' loyalty and to co-opt opponents, especially PLC members. This was a major reason why the number of ministers grew from fourteen in the May 1994 cabinet, to twenty-three in 1996, and to thirty-three in August 1998.[53] To critics of the PA offered a cabinet post, patriotism was either a motive or a rationale for taking the job. Thus, Hanan Ashrawi justified accepting the position of higher education minister in 1996 by saying, "With the new [Netanyahu] government in Israel, the PA needs a good, strong and professional cabinet."[54]

Of course, resigning was a way to show dissent. But only four people actually did so during the PA's first five years. Khuri quit the 1994 cabinet over economic policy.[55] Ghawsha left in 1998, complaining about corruption and Arafat's bullying of the PLC and courts, though others attributed his departure to Arafat's bypassing him on ministry appointments.[56] Hanan Ashrawi and Abd al-Jawad Salah quit the new 1998 cabinet just after it was announced to protest Arafat's failure to fire several ministers accused of corruption.

Salah was virtually the sole minister who criticized PA policies while still in office. A former elected mayor of al-Bira who had been close to the radical nationalist PFLP (Popular Front for the Liberation of Palestine) and DFLP, Salah had his own political base and was less dependent than most others on Arafat's support. Deported by Israel during the 1980s, Salah was one of the relatively few people with solid experience in both the Outsiders' and Insiders' worlds. He combined good contacts and knowledge of West Bank conditions with comprehension of PLO exile politics, having been one of the few post-1967 West Bank residents who served on the PLO Executive Committee.

Running as an independent in the 1996 PLC election, he was the top vote-getter for the Ramallah/al-Bira constituency. After accepting a cabinet post, Salah pledged that he would not "keep silent about the negative aspects of the [PA] . . . If Arafat doesn't like my positions, he can tell me good-bye."[57] But Arafat hardly ever fired anyone, and when he presented his new 1998 cabinet to the PLC, Salah quit, shouting that corruption had "become an institution in the Palestinian system."[58]

Salah also charged that Arafat's decision to add ten new ministers who also sat in parliament was "an attempt to buy the [PLC]." That assessment was true, but the PLC itself had demanded that Arafat choose more of its members. Indeed, the strategy worked very well for Arafat. The PA leader was able simultaneously to disarm critics and gain legislative endorsement.[59] As of 1999, over one-quarter of all PLC members had served in one of Arafat's cabinets.

One of the few others who both sat in the cabinet and retained a strong independent base was Faysal al-Husayni, responsible for Jerusalem affairs, who served as both PA and Fatah leader in East Jerusalem.[60] Since the Oslo agreement prohibited PA activities in East Jerusalem, and Israel frequently objected to violations, Husayni had to keep a low profile in terms of his PA activities. Husayni headed Orient House, a mansion serving as unofficial PA headquarters. Working to lay a foundation for a future Palestinian capital in the city, he hosted foreign officials, mobilized popular support, and expanded PA presence there.[61]

But while Husayni was a loyal veteran Fatah member, Arafat also mistrusted him as a potential rival and wanted to limit his role. After all, Husayni was heir to history's most prominent Palestinian political family (of which Arafat was a poor, distant cousin), a man of great ability, and the most important Insider leader before Arafat arrived. He sometimes showed independence, trying for example to organize his own local united front list for the 1996 PLC election.[62] Senior Fatah officials showed great respect for him.[63]

To ensure that Husayni did not become a rival, Arafat gladly reduced his power when he had a chance to do so. The most notable such occasion was when Arafat cut Orient House's budget by a large margin, forcing Husayni to lay off a number of his staff members.[64] Keeping Husayni in the important but somewhat off-to-the-side Jerusalem office and cabinet slot suited Arafat's interests.

The second group in the PA leadership was Arafat's advisers and the heads of executive branch agencies. These were usually veteran PLO functionaries carrying on the same tasks they had performed in exile. For example, the Palestinian National Fund, headed by Jawad al-Ghusayn, raised money for the budget and projects. Three PLO specialists who led key departments were Hasan Asfur, head of the Negotiations Directorate and also a PLC member; Abdallah Hurani, an Executive Committee member who ran refugee affairs; and Major General Abd al-Razzaq Yahya, a former Executive Committee member who headed the Security Liaison Committee.[65]

The PA's secretary general was Tayyib Abd al-Rahim, a Fatah Central Committee and PLC member who had served as PLO ambassador to four countries. Ahmad Abd al-Rahman, the cabinet secretary and an Executive Committee member, had also worked with Arafat for many years as his chief public spokesperson. There were several loyal officials running the media, of whom the best known was the Insider journalist Radwan Abu Ayyash. The top officials in the many security agencies were closely tied to Arafat and were a tremendous asset to him.[66]

The leadership's third cluster were those members of the PLO Executive Committee and the Fatah Central Committee who now lived in the PA-ruled territories.[67] In practice, Arafat always had a large degree of control in choosing members, except for those representing smaller PLO member groups on the Executive Committee. The majority of the Executive Committee was nominally nonpartisan independents, but they were usually reliable Fatah supporters.[68]

Aside from Arafat himself, the Executive Committee member most important in PA decision making was Mahmud Abbas (Abu Mazin), whom many saw as Arafat's most likely successor. Abbas was an intelligent man and a moderate in PLO terms but a far less charismatic or effective politician than Arafat. He had played a key role in formulating the Oslo agreements but sharply criticized Arafat's policy thereafter and refused to move from Tunis to the PA-ruled area until Arafat gave him a suitably important job. He finally accepted posts as head of the PA election commission and nominal leader of its team negotiating with Israel. Still, Abbas had no direct authority over PA institutions.

Almost half the Executive Committee members in 1993 rejected the Oslo agreements, and most of those adversaries remained abroad. Others representing non-Fatah groups either did not support the PA or (except for Abd Rabbu) gained no important position in it. Consequently, membership on the Executive Committee by itself was not such an important credential for achieving status in the PA power elite.

The Executive Committee and Fatah Central Committee had always been the domain of Outsiders and rarely included any members who had lived in the West Bank or Gaza after 1967. Of course, those PLO cadres residing in Israeli-ruled areas could not be open or active members. But barely any deportees were included either, nor were people ordered by the PLO to leave the territories in order to take up such seats. Indeed, when the Fatah Central Committee decided in 1989, during the intifada, to add some members more representative of Insiders, the two chosen (Sha'th and PLO ambassador to Germany Abdallah Franji) had not been there for decades.

With the PLO's return, five Insiders were added to the Executive Committee, most notably Husayni; Zakariyya al-Agha, Arafat's choice to head Fatah in Gaza; and Nablus mayor Ghassan Shaq'a. But it was still an Outsider-dominated body, a fact rationalized by its continuing responsibility for representing all Palestinians and not just those living in the West Bank and Gaza Strip.

The Fatah Central Committee had also always been overwhelmingly an Outsider body. In contrast to the Executive Committee's declining influence as an institution, however, the Fatah Central Committee took on added significance now that it was the leadership of the PA's ruling party. The members included Arafat and Abbas along with others holding top-level positions and PLC seats: Khuri (PLC speaker); Wazir (minister of social welfare); Sha'th (minister of planning and international cooperation); Rahim (PA secretary general); Hakim Bal'awi (a close Arafat confidant from his days as PLO ambassador to Tunis); and Sharif Ali Mash'al (Abbas Zaki, PLO director of Arab and foreign relations and now in charge of mobilization and organization for Fatah). Nasir Yusuf (Public Security Police commander and the PA's most important military officer) was also in the Central Committee.

Only two men, Zakariyya al-Agha and Faysal al-Husayni, were added to be new members representing Insiders. Although these leaders of Fatah in Gaza and East Jerusalem were on the Central Committee, notable by his absence was the group's West Bank chief, Marwan Barghuti, because he was so critical of Arafat.[69]

While all those in the leadership had credentials as veterans of the nationalist cause, this was not by itself sufficient to gain status in the PA. In general, the PA political elite was also defined mostly by an individual's close relationship with Arafat, and largely by being a Fatah member or supporter. Insiders gained access by possessing special skills—in finance, diplomacy, medicine, or law—which Outsiders could not supply. Although there was a conscious effort to strike a balance between these two groups, Outsiders enjoyed a disproportionate level of power.

But all power came ultimately from Arafat himself. As frequently happens in politics, a strong leader prefers lieutenants with a plodding loyalty over those whose brilliance and ambition seem to threaten his own position. As William Shakespeare so accurately had Julius Caesar say:

> Let me have men about me that are fat;
> Sleek-headed men and such as sleep o' nights;
> Yond' Cassius has a lean and hungry look;
> He thinks too much: such men are dangerous.

Only a few boldly independent-minded individuals—Abbas, Husayni, and Khuri—played a leading role. This did not mean, however, that the rest were simply "yes-men." They had simply worked alongside Arafat for years and were prepared to defer to his judgment, believing his strong leadership necessary for the Palestinians to survive and achieve a state. But they did not live in fear of Arafat and could talk to him frankly. Indeed, Arafat himself was always ready to conciliate critics and address—at least verbally—the grievances of those around him.

The rule of Arafat, the new political elite, and the PA rested on three pillars: legitimacy, patronage, and repression, with the last often being the least important in mobilizing support. In terms of legitimacy, Arafat had a huge political asset from his decades at the helm, his role as founder of an independent Palestinian nationalist movement, and his status as internationally recognized ruler of the Palestinian state-in-the-making. Most Palestinians saw him as their leader, even though his image was tarnished by the PA's slow progress, corruption, and inefficiency. And many—though by no means all—Palestinians argued that a failure to unite behind Arafat would only help Israel and might bring a civil war and catastrophic defeat, as fratricidal splits had done in the 1937–1939 uprising and during the 1948 Arab-Israeli war.

Even Hamas and the democracy advocates were restrained either because they feared that these arguments were true or knew that much of Palestinian public opinion accepted them. Confronting Arafat or appearing to undermine Palestinian interests could destroy a movement's popularity. A case in point was Hamas's temporary retreat from terrorism in late 1995, when the PA warned it that violence was slowing Israel's withdrawal from West Bank Palestinian towns and thus damaging Palestinian interests. Similarly, even Arafat's strongest critics within Fatah, such as Khuri, drew back from conflict to avoid splitting the movement or challenging Arafat personally.

In sharp contrast to many other Third World state-building processes, Palestinian politics was not based on a one-party system. Opposition groups functioned legally even when they ridiculed the PA's political line and endangered its very existence. Hamas, Islamic Jihad, the PFLP and DFLP continued to advocate Israel's destruction, engaged in terrorism, and rejected the peace agreements. The PPP and FIDA parties accepted the peace process's framework but claimed that Arafat made too many concessions to Israel and was too undemocratic toward Palestinians.

Furthermore, there was no viable alternative leadership to Arafat, Fatah, and the PA. The opposition's ideological, policy, and personal conflicts prevented its factions from uniting or even cooperating to compete with the PA. Critics insisted that Palestine could be free only by first being Islamic or democratic. But the PA was far more successful in mobilizing popular backing by arguing that only support for itself could achieve a Palestinian state. In general, then, opponents were held back not by fear of repression so much as by knowledge that they would be politically obliterated if they went too far.

Arafat's control over patriotism and patronage gave him power to reward or punish every Palestinian. Those who cooperate got jobs, contracts, and permits for themselves and relatives; opponents might face sanctions against their businesses, families, and careers. Many people had too much to lose if they antagonized Arafat and a lot to gain by supporting him. Aside from Hamas leaders, most PA critics could not resist the lure of high office and other gifts Arafat could offer them. Apart from careerism or greed, they could not face the prospect of being excluded from a real role in building the state they had desired for decades. Such rewards were a natural seedbed for corruption, but for the PA, as for many governments throughout history, they proved an effective tool in political base-building.

Given the regime's legitimacy and patronage, repression was an important though secondary priority. Still, Arafat was ready to use force against those who had formerly cooperated with Israel or were currently attacking it by terrorism. Arafat had thousands of police to enforce his will. And he knew that the most powerful deterrent was a threat of punishment to discourage disobedience. For every individual tried and sentenced in court, a dozen were questioned, physically abused, or intimidated to show them what might happen if they persisted in their activities or at least crossed certain permissible limits.

Yet PA repression was also sporadic and incomplete. The PA alternated between freedom of action for political competitors and pressure against them. Opponents were not lined up against a wall and shot, nor were many leaders kept in prison very long. Violent activists might be sentenced, then quietly released. Few democratic critics were held for any length of time.

Large opposition groups did, however, continue to use violence and maintained that they had a right to do so no matter how much it damaged the PA's situation. Israel reacted to attacks with border closures that imposed suffering and economic costs. On the one hand, Arafat wanted to do enough toward stopping violence to keep Israel satisfied and ready to advance the peace process. On the other hand, he did not want to be so tough as to set off a Palestinian civil war or reduce his own popularity by appearing to be Israel's policeman. Yet it was very difficult to find the proper balance in handling Hamas. Israel complained that those who promoted violence were either not stopped, not caught, or not kept in jail. The Palestinian opposition complained that the PA arrested and held hundreds of Hamas and Islamic Jihad supporters without warrants or trials.

The PA's survival in the face of these problems and disruptive events was a real achievement. It kept the peace process going, fulfilled most (though by no means all) of its commitments, steadily expanded its powers and territories, preserved good relations with the West, and integrated disparate elements in its population. The task of balancing between domestic radicals, Palestinian public opinion, and Israel was very hard, but one for which Arafat's previous career had well prepared him.

Arafat could claim a number of successes in this effort: "the establishment of the [PA], the return of the leadership and the Palestinian security forces, and the beginning of the march of building and reconstruction [and of] a long peace process with a complicated and knotty struggle." Those who had expected anarchy or a Palestinian civil war were proved wrong. He argued that the PA had given citizens more security than they had possessed for decades. There was "the beginning of the process of building institutions . . . Thousands of our trained personnel in various fields have joined . . . ministries and departments [which] began their work and assumed responsibilities."[70]

Even given his narrow margin for maneuver, however, Arafat and the PA also made costly mistakes of emphasis and priority. By being somewhat too soft on Hamas and Islamic Jihad, they let terrorism drive events, destroying the peace process's momentum. Failing to understand Israeli politics, they wasted opportunities in the 1993–1996 period and unintentionally helped bring to power there in 1996 a government whose interpretation of agreements and opposition to a Palestinian state was quite different from those leaders with whom Arafat had made the original deal.[71]

2

THE PALESTINIAN LEGISLATIVE COUNCIL

On January 20, 1996, 670 candidates from 16 districts in the West Bank, Gaza Strip, and East Jerusalem competed for 88 PLC seats as mandated by the September 1995 Israel-Palestinian Interim Agreement.[1] About 1 million Palestinians, 88 percent of Gaza's and 70 percent of the West Bank's eligible voters, participated.[2] Any Palestinian over the age of thirty could run. In Gaza, there were 295 candidates—including 229 independents and 33 from Fatah—campaigning for 35 PLC seats. In the West Bank, 375 candidates competed for 53 seats. Six places were reserved for Christians and 1 was allotted to the 300-member Samaritan Jewish sect living near Nablus.[3]

That moment's high enthusiasm and sense of expectation was well expressed by Mahmud Abbas, head of the PA Election Commission: "The elected council has brought us five minutes away from independence, and this council will be the one to declare this independence during its reign."[4] Ziyad Abu Amr wrote: "The campaign period saw almost the whole of Palestinian society become involved in the electoral process. Debate was wide-ranging, covering the peace process with Israel, democratization, human rights, economic conditions, the problem of corruption, and other topics . . . Everyone who voted was conscious of participating in a historic event."[5]

While traditionally powerful families put a few able heirs in the PLC, there were not many of them compared to the number of Fatah politicians and independent or pro-Fatah middle-class professionals. Those elected from the traditionally powerful and wealthy families—Shawwa

(Gaza), Masri (Nablus), and Arikat (Jericho)—were Palestinian patriots though not social radicals or advocates of violent upheaval. There were also several self-made figures who had built up strong local bases over the years, such as Jamal al-Tarifi (Ramallah) and Abd al-Jawad Salah (al-Bira), who were their towns' first choices in the election.

The number one vote-getter in many places was a Fatah official: Hebron (Sharif Ali Mash'al), Tulkarm (Tayyib Abd al-Rahim), Khan Yunis (Nabil Sha'th), Jerusalem (Ahmad Khuri), and Bethlehem (Asad Abd al-Qadir). In Dayr al-Balah, Frayh Abu Midayn, a lawyer whose parents were illiterate bedouin, came in first. In Gaza, the largest district, popular veteran leftist Haydar Abd al-Shafi was first, followed closely by Fakhri Shaqura, PA military intelligence chief in the Gaza Strip.

Yet, the election also represented a clear transformation of Palestinian leadership, compared to the traditional elite as well as to those political figures who had run the PLO for decades. Of the PLC's eighty-eight members, no more than ten had been important PLO figures in exile. And even of those, several did not join the leadership until 1988 or 1990, very late in the movement's history.[6]

On March 7, 1996, the successful candidates took their places in the first session, held in Gaza.[7] The ceremony was opened by PNC chairman Salim al-Za'nun, symbolizing the transmission of authority from that old, transnational PLO parliament to a new, territorially organized PA legislature. In his speech, Arafat emphasized his determination to continue the peace process. Afterward, the PLC chose as speaker Khuri, an economist and veteran Fatah official from a wealthy Jerusalem family who had been a key negotiator of the Oslo agreement and the PA's first minister of economic affairs, over the independent leftist Abd al-Shafi by a 57–31 vote.[8] In his inaugural speech, Khuri said that the PLC would be the factory of democracy in Palestine and that its mandate was to ensure a separation of powers between legislative, executive, and judicial authorities.[9]

Khuri's claim expressed the PLC's sense that the Palestinian people had given it authority to balance the power of the executive branch. The PLC's general view was that its ability to control Arafat and create a framework of laws regulating PA behavior would be the measure of democracy. This approach would be enshrined in both the PLC's own Standing Orders (bylaws) and the Basic Law (constitution) that it would also pass.

While this was an understandable position in terms of political philosophy, it was also an institutionally self-interested strategy. The executive branch had prerogatives which it was unwilling to surrender. Arafat was the PLC's eighty-ninth member and claimed to be its chief as well. When attending PLC meetings, he sometimes sat in the speaker's seat to assert this status.

The PLC's proposals went well beyond anything existing in the Arab world and, indeed, tipped the balance toward the legislature even more than did the American system. By reaching so far, the PLC made it inevitable that Arafat would perceive the legislature as a rival that must be curbed. The conflict's origin, then, was due not merely to Arafat's dictatorial tendencies but also to the PLC's confrontational stance.

While the PLC considered itself to be fighting a noble battle to defend democracy, this was a competition it could not win. Not only did it have to compete with Arafat's high prestige and overwhelming power, but also the PLC's majority—while willing to criticize and challenge him—backed down on patriotic, personal, and partisan grounds when Arafat resisted them. Even Ziyad Abu Amr, one of Arafat's severest critics, recognized the leader's irresistible appeal. The PLC tried to pressure Arafat "while avoiding a showdown at a time when the peace process suffers from serious deadlock and deterioration, a situation that compels the Palestinians and the PLC to turn their attention to the external Israeli challenge."[10]

Within the PLC there were no well-organized parties or even factions, and it was hard to define precisely many members' views. Of the eighty-eight people elected, fifty-one were official Fatah candidates. But since many Fatah members had run as independents because they were not on Arafat's official list, the total number of Fatah members or nominees was around sixty-two.[11]

Fatah was not interested in organizing itself as a formal party, and its parliamentary discipline for voting was weak. Fatah veteran and PLC member Nabil Amr warned that creating a Fatah bloc within the council would cause resentment and fear that it was seeking to monopolize power.[12] Thus, one could find people elected as "Fatah" who acted like independents in condemning the government, alongside independents who behaved like the most loyal Fatah members in backing Arafat.

Consequently, the PLC members could be divided politically into four groups.[13] First, there were reliable Arafat supporters who tended to be PLO, PA, or high-level Fatah officials (Nabil Amr, Asfur, Bal'awi, Rahim, Sha'th, Wazir, Za'nun), some wealthy people (Mahir al-Masri, Shawwa), and insider leaders long close to Fatah (Arikat, Midayn, Tarifi). Most ran on the official Fatah slate, but some were independents. This group included about sixty people. While perhaps also motivated by personal advantage in backing the ruling party, most were movement veterans genuinely convinced that only Arafat's strong leadership could keep Palestinians united and lead them to a state. As Rawiya Shawwa, an independent member from Gaza who was sometimes critical of Arafat, put it, "Because he is the president [of the PA] . . . he is the leader of the [PLC] members."[14]

Second, there were about a dozen critical supporters of the PA who were current or former Fatah officials and activists (Marwan Barghuti, Khuri, Salah Ta'amri, Khadir) who might publicly, passionately castigate Arafat and champion the PLC's authority but would not break completely with the regime. Ta'amri and Khadir, though veteran Fatah members, had to run as independents because they were too freethinking for Arafat's taste. Resentment at being left out by him may have alienated them further. While focusing on democracy, human rights, and limiting the executive branch's power, this group also tended to be more hard-line than Arafat on the peace process. Though few in number, the Fatah rebels included many of the PLC's most interesting and energetic figures.

Third, there were about a dozen radical opponents, who basically rejected the Oslo agreements, though they might claim they differed only on tactical grounds (for example, Abd al-Shafi),[15] numbering about seven independent Islamists and five leftists, who had run for office despite their groups' decisions to boycott the election.[16]

Fourth, about five PLC members were moderate opponents, independents who supported Oslo but demanded more democracy than the PA would deliver (Ziyad Abu Amr, Salah, Ashrawi). Even some of them were willing to try working with Arafat in his cabinet, though they found the experience frustrating.

The first two groups sometimes joined together to preserve PLC support for Arafat on key issues, providing him with a two-thirds majority. But Arafat loyalists could also join the critical supporters in a coalition promoting the PLC's interests, or combine with the third and fourth groups to muster a majority and pass laws or resolutions which Arafat did not like. This was what happened regarding the Standing Orders and Basic Law.[17] The existence of this large swing vote, made easier by the fact that Fatah was not organized as a party, gave the PLC its special complex character.

Ziyad Abu Amr stressed that Arafat had the ability to mobilize the first two groups and claimed that Fatah functioned as a party despite heated internal disputes and lack of any formal apparatus. "There is no bloc in the PLC," he wrote in 1997, "to oppose the [PA] or hold it accountable for its actions." The opposition was "a disparate group, including sympathizers of Hamas, the PFLP, and Fatah itself."[18] Ashrawi suggested that since the real opposition had boycotted the election, within the PLC there were merely "different degrees of agreement and different perspectives and approaches. We still don't have a crystallized political life where you have political parties that can be considered opposition."[19]

Still, the PLC's votes often gave Arafat enough headaches to qualify the legislature as an opposition on internal policy and, less directly, on the peace process. One of the PLC's first acts, on April 4, 1996, was to formulate Standing Orders giving itself a powerful oversight over the executive branch. This document traced the PLC's authority through the elections to the Palestinian people, who wanted it to establish "the principle of separation of powers[,] . . . the independence of the legislative authority and its right to legislate and to control and inspect the works of the PA." This would ensure achieving "national independence[,] . . . an advanced democratic society, and the exercise of sovereignty on the homeland."[20]

The Standing Orders established the PLC's structure and procedures. The speaker presided (Article 5) over February–May and September–December sessions (Article 12), alternating sites between Ramallah and Gaza. This required the construction of offices and meeting halls in both places. PLC members needed an Israeli permit to travel between the West Bank and Gaza, leading to frequent complaints about being detained at Israeli military checkpoints. For example, several members, refused entry to Gaza, never arrived at the PLC's opening session.[21]

Essentially, the Standing Orders asserted parliament's power over the executive. The PLC must approve the budget (Article 68) and might force changes to it. Members could submit questions to ministers, demand they respond to any complaint (Articles 69 and 95), or require them to testify at committee meetings (Article 55). But ministers who were PLC members could not be on committees or the council's ruling body (Article 47).[22] The PLC had its own security force, with no other police allowed to enter without the speaker's permission (Article 99).[23]

Especially noteworthy was the system for passing laws. According to Article 64, proposed laws would undergo two readings, with the second for the purpose of considering amendments. The cabinet or any PLC members could request a third reading. But once a simple majority passed a bill, according to Article 66, it "shall be forwarded to the President . . . for assent and publication." There is no mention of any presidential veto power.[24]

The power struggle between the PLC and Arafat—and its repeated resolution in Arafat's favor—often revolved around votes of confidence for the government. The pattern was for the PLC, led by dissident Fatah members, to threaten Arafat. Next, Arafat might promise improvements but never produced concessions. After several months the PLC would eventually give way to him without receiving any reciprocal compromise. Members were usually persuaded by pleas that Arafat must be supported to ensure a strong Palestinian position in negotiations with Israel or because the Fatah organization pressured its members in the PLC to back the PA.

In 1996, for example, PLC critics such as Salah Ta'amri, a Fatah veteran chairing the Land and Settlement Committee, demanded that Arafat release one thousand Hamas and Islamic Jihad supporters, arrested after their groups conducted a bloody bombing campaign against Israeli civilians, in order to get a vote of confidence for his new cabinet.[25] At the June 5–6, 1996, session in Gaza, debate became especially heated. Marwan Kanafani, who had switched from being Arafat's spokesman to become one of his critics, accused Arafat of breaking the PA's own Election Law mandating that at least 80 percent of cabinet ministers must be PLC members. In Arafat's new cabinet, only twelve of twenty ministers—60 percent—were from the PLC. Kanafani also demanded that some ministers be fired for poor performance.[26]

When PLC member Fakhri Turkman then ridiculed some of the PA's positions, Arafat angrily warned that critics would have to prove everything they said, "or else I will ask the Council to take measures against them."[27] On June 20 the PLC formed a committee to meet with Arafat to demand that he implement PLC resolutions.[28] Arafat did respond to PLC pressure by starting to release some of those who had been arrested.[29] But he also went on the offensive against the PLC. On June 30, 1996, the Fatah Central Committee cautioned ten Fatah members who opposed giving Arafat a vote of confidence that they faced suspension or expulsion unless they changed their stand.[30]

A month later, the PLC approved the cabinet by a 50–24 vote.[31] Hours after thanking the PLC, Arafat met Netanyahu's adviser Dore Gold, the first official contact between the new Likud-led Israeli government and the PA.[32] It seems likely that Arafat's supporters insisted the PLC show support in order to get talks going again.

Soon, however, the PLC was threatening another no-confidence vote against the government in response to Arafat's failure to approve PLC decisions—including its draft constitution, the Basic Law; resolutions demanding the release of prisoners held by Israel; and budget revisions. Of twenty-eight bills the PLC had passed in recent months, Arafat endorsed only the Local Committee Councils Law and the Local Committee Councils Election Law. Among other items, he had not yet ratified such major legislation as the Basic Law, Monetary Authority Law, and Civil Service Law.[33]

"I don't know why they bothered to elect us," one prominent member complained. "We have no effect anyway." More combatively, Ta'amri urged, "We must not reach a point where we as [PLC] members can . . . do nothing but complain."[34] But outspoken PA Justice Minister Frayh Abu Midayn blamed the PLC for the impasse, claiming it preferred to complain rather than produce useful legislation.[35]

The no-confidence motion was submitted on November 7, 1996, a move led by Marwan Barghuti, simultaneously one of Arafat's most constant PLC critics and head of Fatah on the West Bank. In effect, the government party's leading legislator was also one of the government's main enemies. The reason was that Barghuti represented cadres unhappy at being omitted from Arafat's ruling circle and to some extent the grievances of Fatah Insiders.[36] Nevertheless, the 1996 challenge soon dissipated, in part because Barghuti neither wanted nor dared to mount a full-scale confrontation with Arafat.[37]

A year later, the PLC again threatened a no-confidence vote unless Arafat changed his cabinet, signed bills passed by the PLC, and responded to its corruption charges. On December 28, 1997, Arafat met about fifty-five PLC members close to Fatah and promised to do better. Critics also demanded that he approve PLC resolutions—some listed thirty-seven while others demanded that he sign eighteen laws. In response, Arafat backers argued that the faltering peace process, his need to mobilize international support, and an Iraq crisis threatening to steal attention from the Palestinian issue required national unity. Two days later, the threat of a no-confidence vote was once more rescinded.[38]

When Arafat produced a new cabinet in August 1998, though, he demonstrated his power by keeping the same team, ignoring PLC demands that he fire four ministers it had accused of corruption or incompetence. Again, Arafat easily won the power struggle. Despite threats from the PLC, his choices were ratified by a wide margin, partly because he had brought even more PLC members in as ministers.[39]

The PLC had, however, begun that session on March 7, 1998, in an atmosphere of conciliation with Arafat. The speeches given that day by Khuri and Arafat illustrated their alternative perspectives on the executive-versus-parliament power struggle.

Arafat claimed great progress in "democratic dialogue and constructive discussions[,] . . . establishing the ground rules for our political system," helping "create a state of institutions and law," and building "the foundations . . . of democratic action and genuine parliamentary life." The Palestinian system, he said, "has won the admiration of the world" despite continued occupation and many difficulties. Arafat admitted that the executive had made mistakes but insisted that there had been steady improvement and even praised the work of Palestinian human rights groups that had frequently criticized his actions.[40]

His main themes were that building democracy would take time, that Israel was the main source of Palestinian problems, and that national loyalty and solidarity should constrain the legislature's behavior. "I would urge you," he told council members, "to be aware of the complex political situation surrounding us and to take these circumstances into consideration as you work to formulate this important set of basic laws . . . We are still on the road to mature democracy, which we have not yet reached."[41]

Instead of complaining about him and the PA, Arafat implied, the PLC should worry about Israel's alleged efforts to strangle the Palestinians economically by closing borders, blocking trade, and employing fewer Palestinian workers. These factors, he continued, led to high unemployment and dramatic declines in gross national product and living standards. On the political level, he said, the peace process has "almost taken its last breath."[42]

Arafat's message was that this crisis made divisions of power and internal conflicts a luxury Palestinians could not afford. The fact that this was a rationalization for Arafat's own interests did not mean that the assertion was necessarily untrue. But critics in the PLC were unimpressed. "Unfortunately, we heard the same talk that we heard in the past," said Ziyad Abu Amr, chair of the PLC's Political Committee. "We expected to hear a clear commitment to making the requested changes."[43]

In contrast, Khuri, who had just been reelected speaker by 55 votes against 15 for two other candidates, gave a speech focusing on the PLC's achievements.[44] Over three years, it had held 30 sessions and 260 committee meetings, producing 72 reports and 92 resolutions.[45] The PLC had debated and approved annual PA budgets and formed a special committee reporting on PA corruption.[46] During its second term, 183 questions were sent to ministers and officials, including some that urged them to improve the human rights situation.[47] Khuri's only reference to the conflicts with Arafat was a mention of "problems related to coordination and cooperation between the Legislative and Executive Authorities . . . which emerged mainly due to the newness of our experience, and . . . the complicated national transformation from the tactics of revolution and its liabilities to the tactics of a state and its requirements."[48]

The PLC was less reserved in complaining about Arafat on other occasions. A PLC report charged that by blocking Palestinian media coverage about the PLC, the PA "created an atmosphere of dissatisfaction and cynicism among the Council members[,] . . . lowered the Council's credibility, and negatively affected the Palestinian people's democratic experience," and that the lack of regulations governing relations between the PLC and the PA had hurt parliament's ability to "monitor, question and follow up on the Executive."[49] Critics claimed that the PA's treatment of the PLC weakened the Palestinian position against Israel and would destroy chances for democracy.

This was the consensus view within the PLC, but Khuri often tried to soften the institutional and personal rivalry. Like Arafat, he could suggest that all Palestinian economic and political problems would be solved only "when our land is returned," that is, not until after total independence. But he noted that while the PA had accepted PLC laws on social issues, it had ignored the security and economic resolutions, despite direct requests that Arafat endorse them.[50]

Some, like Kamal al-Sharafi, an independent from North Gaza who often criticized Arafat, acknowledged that PLC members' inexperience, despite their good intentions, was also a problem. Ziyad Abu Amr, while a strong critic of the PA, also charged that "many of the PLC members did not have the skills or expertise needed for parliamentary work." A Palestinian journalist wrote, "Council sessions are frequently characterized by disregard for rules and procedure."[51]

However the blame was distributed, there was undeniably a prevailing pessimistic mood in the PLC. Its members, said Azmi Shu'aybi (FIDA, Ramallah), "no longer hope [PLC] resolutions will be implemented. Now all we want is for the [PA] to deal with our resolutions. If the [PA] does not abide by the rulings of the Supreme Court, how can it be expected to respect [PLC] resolutions?" Ziyad Abu Amr summarized,

"Some members have resigned themselves to the [situation], while others can be said to have been coopted." Abd al-Shafi, complaining that the PLC had become a "joke," quit in 1997.[52]

The Basic Law, intended as an interim Palestinian constitution, was the PLC's most important single initiative. Both its content and its fate revealed the PLC's dilemma. Arafat's rejection of this proposed constitution was portrayed as a major subversion of democracy, but his opposition was also an understandable response to a program making the legislature master of the executive and limiting presidential powers. The Palestinian Society for the Protection of Human Rights and the Environment, which favored the PLC's Basic Law, stated this explicitly by declaring that "the Draft Basic Law assures the supremacy of the legislature over the executive."[53]

There were disputes on this issue from the start. Arafat wanted the PLO Legal Committee to pen the draft. Abu Midayn remarked that the PA did not yet need a constitution, pointing out that Israel had none and asking, "How can we talk about a Palestinian constitution when we only control 20 percent of the lands?"[54] At one point during the July 1996 PLC debate Arafat interrupted: "What constitution are you talking about? You didn't show this constitution to [me] or to the [PLO] Executive Committee. You can discuss a constitution but you cannot draft one." Arafat walked out and Khuri temporarily resigned. In the end, Arafat supporter Hasan Asfur brokered a compromise: the PLC would debate its version, but the document could be finalized only when Arafat's draft also was discussed. Some members, led by Ziyad Abu Amr, futilely demanded that Arafat set a date to produce his version.[55]

The Basic Law passed its first reading on August 15, 1996, and third reading on October 22, 1997. But Arafat never produced his own draft or approved the PLC version in order to ensure that no such constitution emerged. The "final" text of the Basic Law was a fascinating document, perhaps the most important summary of mainstream Palestinian political philosophy since the formation of the PLO and Fatah in the 1960s. It defined Palestinian identity and put forth the PLC's claim to be the determining force in establishing a very liberal democracy.[56]

It began significantly with the standard Islamic invocation, "In the name of God the Merciful and Benefactor." The document showed that the Palestinians were not establishing a secular state in the Western sense of that concept, though its orientation toward religion was relatively mainstream in the Arab context.

Article 4 proclaimed: "Islam is the official religion in Palestine while other divine religions have their respect and sanctity. Principles of the Islamic Doctrine [are] a basic source of legislation." While Article 11 promised equality to all religions, Islam was given primacy. The proposed constitution's wording on the role of "Islamic Doctrine" stems from a long debate in the Arab world. Islam was "a basic source" but not the only source for the country's laws, which might well contradict Islamic law (or, more accurately, the specific interpretations of it by "fundamentalists"). This phrasing discomfited some Muslim clerics and certainly did not please Hamas or Islamic Jihad. A few Islamic-oriented PLC members wanted, but failed, to have the Koran described as "the source of all legislation."[57]

More moderate Islamic forces were mollified by the Basic Law's Article 92: "Personal and individual issues are treated by Shari'a and religious courts according to law." This meant a leading role for different communities' religious laws—albeit subordinated to the state's laws—in marriage, divorce, and other personal status matters.

The Basic Law also defined Palestinians as thoroughly Arab. Article 1 of this document creating a new and separate Arab state expressed a deep-felt Pan-Arab sentiment, partly to provide cover for the separate nation-state nationalism that the Palestinians were promoting. "Palestine," it proclaimed, "is part of the great Arab homeland, and the Arab Palestinian people is part of the Arab nation; Arab unity is a goal which the Palestinian people work to achieve." Arabic was declared the official language.

The Basic Law's introduction praised the steadfast loyalty of "the Arab Palestinian people [to] the land of their . . . forefathers," and their long struggle to achieve "permanent national rights[,] . . . the right for return, self-determination and the establishment of the independent Palestinian state with Jerusalem as its capital under the leadership of the PLO, the sole legitimate representative of the Arab Palestinian people, wherever they exist." This formulation included many historic PLO slogans.[58]

In addition, the introduction presented the PLC view of the government as resting on "three basic pillars, the Legislative, Executive, and Judicial authorities," operating as equals. The Basic Law's purpose was to regulate the "balance" among these branches as well as their relationship with the people. Article 2 reiterated that the Palestinian people were the source of all authority, which should be exercised through three equal branches of government.

The Basic Law then set forth a long list of rights and democratic principles: parliamentary democracy and pluralism (Article 5), the rule of law (Article 6), the equality of all citizens without discrimination, plus personal liberty (Article 11) and freedom of thought and speech (Article 19). Private property and free economic activity were guaranteed (Article 21). Courts and judges "should be independent, answerable to the people, and free from any outside interference." In contrast to current PA practice, military courts would have jurisdiction only over those in uniform (Articles 88 and 89).

The people had rights to political participation (Article 26) and media freedom without censorship (Article 27), and recourse to courts (Article 30). The PA was to care for "families of martyrs, the injured and the handicapped" (Article 22), provide proper housing (Article 23), education (Article 24), and protection for children (Article 29). Security forces and police must obey the law and "respect citizen rights" (Article 75). An independent human rights commission was to be created, reporting both to Arafat and to the PLC (Article 31). Contradicting the Oslo agreement's provision on extradition, Article 28 insisted that no Palestinian must ever be "surrendered to any foreign authority."

In defining the ruling system, the Basic Law made the PLC coequal with Arafat: "The government will report to the president and the PLC" (Article 5). The president and cabinet were defined as the implementing "tool . . . to execute the program ratified by the" PLC (Article 50). Both the cabinet's membership and the government's policy statement must be approved by the PLC, which can remove any minister by a simple majority vote (Article 64). Perhaps most humiliating of all for Arafat, Article 72 limited the cabinet's mandate to fulfilling the "program approved" by the PLC, preparing the budget for presentation to the PLC, and implementing laws passed by the PLC.

The president would appoint diplomats, but Article 56 implied that the PLC, not the chief executive, issued their credentials. Arafat was not allowed to name his own successor; the speaker would fill a vacant presidency for up to sixty days until elections were held (Article 54). This would have made Khuri in constitutional terms the second most important Palestinian leader, and was also a way of asserting the PLC's institutional claims.

Offering more than the Standing Orders, the draft constitution at least gave Arafat a veto power, though the PLC could override him on any legislation, in a manner roughly equivalent to the American system. Article 57 asserted that "the President shall sign and promulgate the laws within 30 days after their approval by the Council." If he did not do so, they automatically would become law unless he returned them "to the Council attached with . . . reasons for his opposition." In that case, a two-thirds vote would enact them into law. Arafat knew that while he had a two-thirds majority within the PLC, the PLC could also sometimes mobilize a two-thirds majority against him.

Arafat, of course, still had much power. He would be the armed forces' commander in chief (Article 55), could propose laws to the PLC (Article 58), and must confirm any court's death penalty (Article 100). The president could declare a state of emergency for up to thirty days (extendable another thirty days if a two-thirds majority of the PLC approved) and rule by decrees, though these were annulled unless approved by the next PLC session (Article 101). But compared to Arafat's previous authority, or that of any other Arab chief executive, the Palestinian president's control would be quite limited.

This situation prompted Ziyad Abu Amr to write: "It is natural for competition [to exist] between the executive and legislative branches of government. In the Palestinian case, however, the [PA] is seeking to marginalize the legislature."[59] Yet while the PA was far more successful in this struggle, the PLC was also trying to marginalize the PA. As Rawiya Shawwa accurately explained the conflict's source: "There already exists a central executive authority and now there is a new elected legislative body that is trying to establish its role in formulating legislation that will monitor and possibly limit the Executive branch. But the Executive opposes this."[60]

A major aspect of this friction was the PLC's investigations concerning rampant corruption in the PA.[61] But the PLC had a difficult time gathering evidence since PA officials rarely cooperated with the inquiries. An exception was Agriculture Minister Abd al-Jawad Salah, who himself accused senior employees in his own ministry of relabeling Israeli fruit as Palestinian produce so it could be sold in Arab countries. He complained that the PA's attorney general had ignored his protests. In turn, Arafat supporters denied the charges and accused Salah of paralyzing the ministry's work.[62]

The main PLC investigation was aimed at companies holding PA-granted monopolies, whose profits Arafat controlled without full disclosure or bureaucratic supervision. Other privately owned businesses complained that they could not compete with rivals enjoying government favoritism and subsidies. These companies included the Palestinian National Company for Economic Development, the Petrol Board, the PA-owned Palestinian Company for Trade Services, and its powerful subsidiary the al-Bahr Company, which used the official PA letterhead on its stationery and had many government contracts for construction, public works, and importing goods.[63]

The PLC Economic Committee interviewed many ministers and officials in its investigation. But Hashim Abu al-Nada—who worked simultaneously as an Arafat aide, Ministry of Finance director general, and head of the al-Bahr Company's administrative council—refused to testify. So did Khalid Islam, Arafat's economic adviser, who was deeply involved in managing the monopolies.[64]

The Petrol Board made a great deal of money for the PA by raising prices higher in its territory than in Israel—a policy that contradicted economic logic—and becoming part owner of gas stations. The implication was that the board forced station owners to give it a share in their business in order to get licenses and access to fuel supplies. Israeli police would later arrest the officers of an Israeli gasoline company for paying large kickbacks to PA officials and reporting these as business expenses.

Questions were also raised about the Palestinian Company for Trade Services' highly profitable import, marketing, and taxation of cement. It was unclear who in the PA received this money or how it was used. All ministers denied any link or supervisory power over that company, though some high officials may have had a personal interest in it. There was also evidence that the company sabotaged private dealers' imports—with help from PA border police—in order to eliminate competition on cement imports from Jordan.[65]

After extensive hearings, the PLC issued a report criticizing six monopolies controlling such basic goods as flour, building supplies, cigarettes, meat, and fuel.[66] The PLC committee also concluded that the PA was riddled with conflicts of interest. Officials used powers such as the granting of licenses and government subsidies to profit their own businesses. Some of Arafat's advisers represented the PA in dealings with companies they partly owned. Security officers intervened in economic matters for their own benefit. All ministries suffered from inefficiency as well as poor planning and coordination. The PLC recommended laws to regulate companies having special privileges, including mandatory competitive bidding and strict oversight for PA purchases from abroad, and regulations restricting government employees' outside activities.[67]

At higher levels, officials did use money for questionable purposes, sold services, or siphoned money into business enterprises they owned. But not every accusation was necessarily accurate, and many involved petty graft.[68] Abu Mazin was criticized for building a "million-dollar" home in Gaza. The house, he responded, was an official residence owned by the PA, not himself. Moreover, one of Abu Mazin's neighbors in a similarly luxurious house was Khuri, head of the corruption-hunting PLC.[69]

The PLC focused especially on four ministers, though the charges involved small amounts of money and were not necessarily accurate. Information and Culture Minister Yasir Abd Rabbu allegedly used $7,500 from the ministry budget to install central heating in his home, while Sha'th was said to have taken PA funds for his wedding. Transport Minister Ali Qawasma was said to have accepted bribes to license cars that did not meet safety standards as well as kickbacks from bus and taxi companies. Civil Affairs Minister Jamal al-Tarifi was accused of giving exemptions from import taxes for many automobiles. The August 1996 report recommended dismissal and possible charges against Sha'th, Tarifi, Abd Rabbu, and Qawasma for alleged embezzlement, theft, and breach of trust.[70]

The PLC also declared that $150,000 had disappeared from the Ministry of Sports and Youth budget and went into a top official's account. The responsible minister, Tallal Sidar, ignored a subpoena to appear before the PLC committee. Accused officials called the PLC investigation a partisan effort. The Palestinian media ignored the PLC's report. Only when the foreign press picked up the story, leading to pressure from aid donors, did Arafat promise an investigation. But no PA report was ever issued, and no one ever lost his job or was arrested regarding the PLC's accusations.[71]

Yet despite these events the PA's reputation fared better than that of the PLC. An August 1996 Jerusalem Media Communications Center (JMCC) poll showed only 23.8 percent of the people believed that the PLC represented them satisfactorily, while 46.7 percent thought that the PLC was ineffective. Over 84 percent said that they knew little about the PLC's work. An April 1997 poll found that 48 percent rated PLC performance positively, 26.2 percent in neutral terms, and 16.8 percent thought it was bad or very bad.[72]

By 1998 the PLC had the lowest positive poll rating of any government institution at 45 percent. In comparison, Arafat received a 71 percent positive rating; the police and security services, 67 percent; the cabinet, 53 percent; and the courts, 49 percent. While 22 percent of those queried blamed the PA executive for the PLC's shortcomings, about 16 percent found the PLC alone culpable, and 48 percent blamed both branches of government. Moreover, the PLC was not well regarded by those it might have expected to be its most avid backers: city-dwellers, refugees, and the college-educated.[73]

There were a number of reasons for this public perception, noted Ghassan Khatib, who headed the JMCC. "Members do exert genuine efforts to perform their duties faithfully," he said, and "are courageous in addressing highly sensitive issues, such as questioning the [PA] on issues of corruption, management, peace negotiations, the absence of the rule of law, and human rights violations." But "Palestinians initially expected too much" from the PLC, and "the lack of coverage in the PA-controlled radio and television and the PA-influenced press minimized" popular understanding of the PLC's problems and achievements.[74]

The PA's blockage of Palestinian media reports on the PLC handicapped the legislature's ability to compete with Arafat's overwhelming popularity. As Khatib wrote, the PA made the PLC "appear before the public as a useless institution" because the people were not informed of the PLC's alternative vision or specific criticisms of the PA. While the PLC voted on April 21, 1996, to open meetings to the media, only those sessions attended by Arafat were fully covered. Ironically, the PA's Voice of Palestine radio—which knew exactly what the government would permit—provided better reportage on many issues than did the newspapers, which feared the consequences of mistakenly publishing something the PA did not like.[75]

When the PLC worked out an arrangement to transmit its sessions through a private television channel owned by al-Quds University, the PA jammed the transmissions, and on May 20, 1997, Daud Khutab, a respected journalist who was managing the program, was picked up by Palestinian police and held for several days.[76] PLC members often went to Israeli newspapers—whose West Bank and Gaza correspondents were quite sympathetic to Palestinian aspirations—to get their views into print. Details of the PLC's corruption report, for example, were available to Palestinians only through the Israeli media.

Yet there were also limits on the PLC's ability to claim positive achievements. Khatib put the resolutions passed by the PLC into three groups. Of these, he said, about one-third "cannot possibly be implemented, as they deal with issues outside the realm of the PA, according to the peace agreements with Israel." For example, Resolution 1–2–7 demanded that the PA "as soon as possible" stop "Israel's transgressions and violations" of the peace process and its "closure and starvation policies." Resolution 1–5–32 of May 15, 1996, demanded that the PA "intervene immediately" to stop house demolitions in the West Bank by the Israeli authorities.[77]

Another one-third of the resolutions were essentially "political communiqués," taking positions designed to win popularity. Resolution 1–14–76 of Juiy 23, 1996, denounces an alleged Israeli Supreme Court ruling giving an extremist Jewish group "permission to pray in the al-Aqsa Mosque." Resolution 1–4–19 of September 8, 1996, denounces "UNRWA's [United Nations Relief and Works Agency] decision to close the Teacher's College and the UNRWA services offices in the PA areas . . . and demands that the Education Ministry make UNRWA responsible for this before our students."[78]

The final one-third were constructive but "systematically ignored" by the media and PA. "The Council demands that the Executive Authority release students held by the security forces, in order to allow [them] to continue their education," read Resolution 1–4–25 of September 8, 1996. "Council sessions will be transmitted live by the Palestinian Radio and Television stations" (Resolution 1–4–21, May 8, 1996), and "The Council requests that the Cabinet stop monopolizing trade in basic goods" (Resolution 1–4–22, May 8, 1996).[79] In short, most of the PLC's efforts were either irrelevant or ineffective.

Equally, the PA did not keep the PLC fully informed of key developments, arguing that the PLC had no direct standing in the peace negotiations.[80] The PLC's Land and Settlement Committee, chaired by Ta'amri, protested that it had no access to PA negotiators and not even an advisory role in talks with Israel. The PA negotiated the Hebron protocol with no input whatsoever from the PLC, while, Abd al-Shafi noted, Israel's parliament debated ten hours before approving that agreement.[81] The PLC's Political Committee complained, "Most of the time, we were not able to view crucial official matters until they were published officially in the press or we overheard unofficial reports from [PLC] members who also serve in the Executive."[82]

The PLC did help lay a foundation for both a future state and a democratic system by constantly using its resolutions, debates, investigations, and questioning of ministers to raise the principle of executive responsibility to the legislative branch.[83] It could be argued, as Ziyad Abu Amr wrote, that the kind of open discussion and criticism of the national leadership taking place in the PLC was unmatched in any other Arab parliament.[84]

While the main fault in curbing any constructive role for the PLC lay with Arafat's tireless protection of his monopoly on power, the PLC also contributed to the confrontation by trying to take on executive responsibility. As a Center for Palestine Research and Studies (CPRS) report concluded, the PLC sought to exceed a legislature's usual role by setting policy through resolutions, then reacting angrily when the PA ignored them. By being forced to back down repeatedly—largely because the majority of members basically did support the government—the PLC lost credibility with Arafat and the public's respect.[85]

Moreover, as one sympathetic Palestinian writer noted, the PLC undercut its own popular support because "in practice, after the elections most [PLC members] tended to forget the voters and did not update them regarding the problems and issues they were dealing with." By not building alliances with civil society institutions, the PLC was further weakened and less able to compete with the executive branch of government.[86]

Given this situation, it was hard to dispute a Palestinian writer's conclusion that "the [PLC] has been relegated to dealing with matters more on the municipal level than a parliamentary level."[87]

3

DEMOCRACY, STABILITY, AND HUMAN RIGHTS

Few if any state-building efforts or emerging Third World societies have ever been under such intense scrutiny and held to such high standards as the Palestinian polity. Palestinians themselves were at the forefront of investigating the PA and demanding better performance. Despite the PA's abuses and errors, the especially difficult conditions of transition made it hardly surprising that establishing the rule of law and respect for human rights was no easy task.

Criticism often neglected this context. Glenn Robinson, a leading Western student of Palestinian politics, wrote: "The PA has become an authoritarian polity run by a despot. For those people who have followed Palestinian politics over the years, such a political outcome is both sad and surprising. After all, Palestinian politics were widely known as the most open in the Arab world."[1]

This was a strange conclusion on two counts. First, if the PA was so despotic, how could its internal opponents still speak so freely and criticize so openly on the floor of parliament and elsewhere? How could groups like Hamas, which openly urged the PA's future overthrow and tried to sabotage its policies, still function politically and run scores of institutions? Why were there not only serious abuses—including torture and killing of some prisoners—but also a willingness of many PA officials to correct those abuses? Even a comprehensive survey of the PA's actions against human rights and democracy showed a pattern of sporadic abuses and harassment rather than a systematic attempt to crush the opposition, unfettered speech, academic freedom, and other rights.

Arafat's propensities toward compromise and pluralism were reinforced by the PA's situation, which constantly forced it to maintain such
balances. The PA was restrained from authoritarianism more than other
Third World governments by its special incentive to heed foreign criticism, given its dependence on international aid and political support.
Similarly, Arafat's need to ensure the support of Palestinian public opinion had the same effect. Thus, Arafat certainly did not compel obedience from the violent groups among his Palestinian adversaries. The
failure to smash the opposition, silence critics, or even force conformity
within Fatah came about not because Arafat lacked the power to carry
out such a program but because he did not want to do so. Arafat did
seek to limit opposition and maintain control. But if he was willing to
give less latitude to civil society than in most democracies, he was also
ready to provide more than in most dictatorships.

On each issue there were forces constraining the PA from going too
far toward either passivity or severity. For example, Israel complained
that the PA failed to arrest those involved in attacks or quietly let them
go. Hamas complained when the PA did make arrests or issued sentences. Human rights groups added their criticisms about the conduct
of trials, or when people were held without trial. The PA did not want
to crack down on radical movements to the point where it would seem
an Israeli agent or might spark civil war. But it also did not want to
wreck the peace process or allow the opposition do so by giving it license
to commit violence. Consequently, some Hamas bomb makers and attackers were never detained while others were given long sentences;
some were allowed to "escape" or were released; others were held without charges and beaten up.

The principle of balance and inconsistency remained in effect. There
was no clear trend toward mounting authoritarianism. The opposition
sporadically claimed that the PA was about to impose a major crackdown, but each time this alleged threat quickly dissipated.[2] Similarly,
every temporary ban on demonstrations at tense moments in the peace
process led to accusations that the PA was going to stop all free speech.
Yet a few days later, things would return to normal. When a wave of
attacks against Israel led the PA to round up supporters of violent opposition groups, there were cries of imminent all-out repression. But the
PA offensive soon ended, and most prisoners were gradually released.
Thus, there was no inevitability to what Robinson called a "growing
authoritarianism."

On the contrary, the PA could easily have justified imposing more control than it did. The continuous peace process and ongoing violence embroiled its state-building effort in a series of crises requiring even more unity and discipline than would otherwise be needed by a newly independent state. The problem was intensified by the profoundly radical, antidemocratic nature of the strongest opposition groups, which used violence daily in an open effort to destroy the PA's policy and replace its leadership.

But Arafat knew that his survival required bridging gaps among Palestinians as much as possible through persuasion. He sought loyalists and partners from every direction, rejecting no one. He preferred to co-opt dissenters, including Hamas, rather than permanently alienate them. Consequently, the PA encouraged opponents to contest elections and offered compromises, including a share of power in exchange for restraint. Even convicted terrorists who agreed to support Arafat and join the PA's forces were released from prison.

Since the political and even social borders among Palestinians were still so much in flux, it is not surprising that each individual's stand was usually based more on personal perceptions, priorities, and connections rather than on broad categories of class or interest group. It was by no means clear that Insiders and intifada activists were generally critical of Arafat's policy while wealthy people and returning Outsiders usually favored him. Members of each group could be found in almost equal proportions on either side of the political divide.

Finally, incompetence, inefficiency, and institutional weakness within the PA was often an important factor in bringing about political abuses. For example, Arafat's failure to impose discipline over security services, partly in an effort to ensure their loyalty, was a bigger cause of human rights violations than any design to suppress dissent. The same factor applied to the corruption common in the PA bureaucracy. Journalists were made more insecure by the lack of clear guidelines as to what they were permitted to say than by any censorship system.

Clearly, there was a more complex explanation for the PA's behavior and the Palestinian style of state-building than a simple tale of a despot's triumph over the forces of freedom.

In addition, given the history of the PLO and Palestinian politics, no close observer should have found surprising the PA's problems regarding democracy. Several leading Palestinian figures had been murdered by PLO groups during past disputes, and many individuals had gained leadership positions because of their facility with violence. Moderates had been repeatedly intimidated into silence before 1993, paralyzing and postponing the Palestinians' ability to develop more realistic policies. For decades, too, the PLO had employed violent methods widely known as terrorism.

Only after an extremely long time and many political reverses was the movement able to work itself out of this dead-end system and situation. The political moderates who won foreign admiration had no organization or mass base of support of their own. They had lived in constant fear of saying or doing something that would subject them to punishment or even murder at the hands of the PLO or any radical group. But they were safe as long as they confined themselves to criticizing Israel and supporting the PLO.

The PA system could best be understood by comparison to its two Arab neighbors, Jordan and Egypt, and in sharp contrast to highly controlled dictatorships such as Syria and Iraq. Jordan and Egypt were certainly not fully Western-style democracies, especially given their rulers' refusal ever to yield power to the opposition. Yet each permitted a wide range of options for political and social pluralism and participation.[3]

There were also unique Palestinian aspects to this system. Ziyad Abu Amr defined that pluralism as "a measure of mutual tolerance and acceptance" that was "an extension of the variety that marks the world of tribal or familial relations"; he attributed it to "the participation of diverse groups" in the struggle against occupation, the fact that "no single group is strong enough to crush or dominate the others," and by default to the fact that "there is no strong central authority with the capacity to impose its will on all other groups."[4] Khalil Shiqaqi called this type of pluralism a "quota system" for member groups rather than democracy.[5]

Abu Amr made the most balanced analysis of the democratic element in Palestinian politics. "Palestinians do possess a modest 'democratic' tradition that reflects incomplete and fragmented patterns of democratic thought and practice," he explained. But the situation fell far short of "a full-fledged democratic tradition," lacking the necessary structures and ideological justification, "a long and profound experience with the rule of law, political participation and public accountability, respect for human rights, and most importantly alternation in power, typically through free and fair elections. On this last point, the Palestinian record is not impressive." The PLO and its constituent groups were never characterized by democracy or free elections, while dispersion outside and Israeli rule inside the homeland made such a system's emergence even more unlikely.[6]

Leadership had always been imposed from the top down and was not subject to replacement or accountability. As Abu Amr pointed out:

> Yasir Arafat has been the leader of the Fatah movement since its establishment in 1965; George Habash has been the leader of the PFLP since its foundation in 1967; Nayif Hawatma has remained head of the DFLP since its formation in 1969; Bashir al-Barghuti has been secretary general of the Palestine Communist Party (now the PPP) since its foundation in 1982; Shaykh Ahmad Yasin has been the leader of the Muslim Brotherhood Society in Gaza since the mid-1970s, and head of Hamas since it was formed in 1987 despite his imprisonment in Israeli jails since 1989; and Fathi al-Shiqaqi was the leader of the Islamic Jihad Movement in Palestine from its foundation in 1980 until his assassination in October 1995.[7]

It was hardly surprising, then, that the Palestinian political structure during the transitional phase was neither democratic nor tyrannical. Rather, Arafat's program was organized around three main strategies for building a pluralist but not fully democratic system.[8] First, he sought not to extirpate his opponents but rather to co-opt them as junior partners, trading some power and privileges in exchange for their cooperation, restraint, and acceptance of his overall leadership. This was the pattern he had followed in the PLO for thirty years, where he had never made a serious effort to centralize or discipline the movement.

Second, he needed to preserve his base of reliable supporters. This was why Arafat was more concerned with managing Fatah than with eliminating opposition or criticism from other groups. He also coddled the security services to guarantee their backing. Again, in each case conflict was cushioned by a consistent tolerance of differences and disputes.

Third, he put the main emphasis on preserving unity and obtaining the best possible deal with Israel so long as that eventually led to an independent Palestinian state. Arafat's internal problem in this regard was to achieve balance: between stopping Palestinian violence and avoiding domestic confrontation; between making demands on Israel and reaching agreements with it. This was a difficult task, and Arafat's effort to realize Palestinian aspirations often caused him to make so many demands on Israel or fulfill so few of his commitments as to stymie the peace process.

The January 20, 1996, Palestinian election was a good reflection of Palestinian democracy's positive as well as negative aspects. According to the Election Law, the purpose of the election was "to assert the unity of the Palestinian people in the West Bank and the Gaza Strip . . . and to establish a democratic parliamentary system based on free expression, the freedom to organize," minority acceptance of decisions supported by the majority, "the respect of the majority [for] minority views, human rights, social justice and equality among all citizens."[9]

One foreign election observer wrote, "It is doubtful if there was ever an election more closely observed and monitored."[10] While far from perfect, it was possibly the fairest balloting ever conducted in the Arab world. About 1 million voters—a vast majority of those eligible—participated. In contention were 670 candidates representing a wide variety of political philosophies and backgrounds.[11]

It was not the PA's fault that the main opposition group, Hamas, boycotted the election, as did the PFLP, DFLP, and Islamic Jihad.[12] On the contrary, Arafat had done everything possible to persuade them to run candidates. Their decision to stay away was due not to the PA's behavior but to their own rejection of the peace agreements with Israel, which defined the election, as well as to their knowing they could not win.[13] Hamas's dilemma, as Khalil Shiqaqi wrote, was that "taking part would mean losing the credibility already gained among opposition groups. Not taking part would mean losing a chance to be involved in political life and decision making that would influence the future of the Palestinian people."[14]

In the end, though, an estimated 60 percent of Hamas and Islamic Jihad and an even higher proportion of PFLP supporters voted.[15] Arafat was elected head of the PA with 85 percent of the vote, against 10 percent for his opponent, Ramallah activist Samiha Khalil, who ran as an independent though she was a veteran DFLP activist. Fatah also won 65 percent of the PLC seats. These results were clearly accurate reflections of public opinion, as shown by independent polls. The opposition parties that did run candidates—mainly the PPP and FIDA—had little support. Since Fatah candidates—and Fatah members running as independents—were of such diverse viewpoints, this was no case of a monolithic ruling party steamrollering its way into office.[16]

The irregularities that did occur affected the results for very few, if any, seats. The main problems included a very short campaign and pressure on several independent candidates from Fatah to withdraw so they would not take away votes from Arafat's own slate.[17] For example, Azzam al-Ahmad, a Fatah candidate in Jenin, warned independents of "serious consequences" if they did not pull out of the race. Others were offered jobs with the PA in exchange for dropping their candidacies.[18]

Palestinian television and radio provided only limited election coverage in general and none on the campaign of Arafat's opponent, Khalil. The France-based Reporters sans Frontières group claimed that Fatah candidates received far more airtime than their opponents and that journalists worked in "a climate of intimidation and fear."[19] Some PA ministers used official mobile phones and cars to help run their campaigns. There were allegations of ballot boxes disappearing in Ramallah (where there was a recount) and Hebron. In Salfit, where a Fatah candidate faced serious competition, the People's Party campaign manager was detained for several days, and opponents were allegedly prevented from voting.[20]

In practice, though, these factors had either no effect or only a marginal one on the outcome itself, which was inevitable once Hamas and smaller radical groups chose not to participate. Ziyad Abu Amr, one of the most outspoken democracy advocates, was correct in concluding that "despite minor and scattered mistakes or violations, the elections were conducted in a democratic fashion, as confirmed by teams of international observers."[21]

Arafat and his allies needed none of these manipulations to win an overwhelming majority. But he still wanted to gain the biggest possible landslide to provide an impressive mandate that would strengthen his hand at home, internationally, and in talks with the Israelis. Equally important, he was determined to guarantee success for those followers he deemed most loyal as well as to ensure that all sectors of the population were represented by his supporters.[22]

Still, the despair of many Palestinians over the nature of the emerging system of PA governance was completely understandable. Reality was bound to be disappointing, but for them the PA system was especially depressing. Over the long term, most of them had imagined that they would achieve a total victory over Israel, which would be followed by the emergence of an ideal state and near-utopian society. After 1993, many at least expected more democracy, rapidly improving living standards, relatively little corruption, and swifter progress toward statehood. Such high, unfulfilled hopes were something they had in common with many state-building movements, including the Zionist one in neighboring Israel. Palestinians certainly expected something better than what existed elsewhere in the Arab world.

The first, most common justification given for the PA's behavior was that this was a necessity during the transition period. Even such critics as Barghuti, Khuri, and others accepted this assumption even as they tried to counter it. They did not doubt that excessive divisions among

Palestinians could bring a costly civil war (as had happened in the 1930s), a weakened position relative to Israel, manipulation by Arab states, and an end to their dreams of achieving statehood.

An article in the newspaper *al-Sharq al-Awsat* admirably summarized the debate:

> Some think that intensifying pressure on the Palestinian leadership at this time will weaken its negotiating ability, particularly as it is exposed to formidable pressures from Arab and international parties that . . . are exploiting the reformers' demands and the embarrassed position of the Palestinian leadership in order to demand concessions from it. Others think that this is the very time to build strong foundations for the coming national entity. They believe that by acceding to demands for reform, the leadership will strengthen its negotiating position and increase its immunity to Arab and international pressures. They say that the question of timing—that others might take advantage of public criticism leveled at misguided policies—has remained a sword waved over our heads for nearly a quarter of a century; yet our enemies hang out their laundry, talk to each other bluntly, make the necessary revisions, and emerge stronger.[23]

Yet the argument against the reformers was more appealing for many Palestinians. The existence of a future Palestinian state or even a stable polity was far from secure. The PA was still in the midst of a struggle with Israel whose final outcome remained unknown. A serious miscalculation could produce a devastating internal explosion or war with Israel. Moreover, those in Fatah who were critical of Arafat or independents who advocate more democracy and human rights did not want to see a weak PA let Hamas have a free hand or even take over. This would mean not only the collapse of the peace process but also even less democracy and human rights for Palestinians. Explained Ziyad Abu Amr: "Palestinian Islamist groups . . . are indifferent at best toward democracy, and often dismiss it as a secular, Western concept predicated on legislation by man . . . The rise of Islamism in Palestinian society is likely to retard the advent of democracy."[24]

In addition to unity, the PA urged patience, suggesting that problems sprang from a temporary situation caused by the lack of a full-fledged state and continuing Israeli occupation. By threatening the struggle, dissent was unpatriotic at best and treasonous at worst. This legacy shaped and limited civil society's development. As *al-Sharq al-Awsat* put the dilemma, "What is the real problem of the Palestinian people: the absence of democracy or the need for freedom and independence?"[25]

Many believed that the two would go hand in hand, but the majority often concluded that they might be in contradiction and usually preferred to put the priority on the latter goal.[26] Even some oppositionists accepted this argument. George Giacaman, a leftist critic and Bir Zayt University philosophy professor, suggested that the PA system and its "one-man rule" was a temporary but "necessary stage for the transition" toward democracy, which would eventually be brought about by popular demand.[27]

The opposition tried to respond by claiming that the lack of democracy and human rights under the PA might so weaken the Palestinian people as to prevent them from establishing a state. In the words of Raji Surani, director of the Palestinian Center for Human Rights: "Palestinian human rights activists believe that the Palestinians' case would be much stronger if the PA acted according to the rule of law. When the human rights and governance situation is bad, people lose faith in the PA, which weakens its ability to move towards peace."[28]

Similarly, Ghassan Khatib remarked that the PA's "poor performance . . . leaves the Palestinian position vulnerable[,] . . . particularly the case when the criticism concerns issues on which Israel was formerly criticized, i.e., human rights, development, etc., because it then eases some of the continuing pressure on Israel for its practices against the Palestinians."[29]

Equally, the PA's critics insisted that if such features were not built into the political structure from the start, they would never be able to emerge once the system solidified. Khadir Shkirat, the general director of the Palestinian Society for the Protection of Human Rights and the Environment (LAW), complained: "It is indeed lamentable that the [PA] dedicates its efforts, like so many other Arab governments[,] to the subjugation of its people. It is also sad and extremely distressing to reflect that the Palestinian individual's main task has now become how to express his or her point of view, how to attain his or her rights, and how to best handle the PA."[30]

The second rationale for the PA's system and performance, and one that appealed to many Palestinians, was to blame all shortcomings on Israel. On this point even Arafat's critics were ready to defend his record. The Palestinian human rights group LAW noted in its 1997 report: "The Israeli occupation continues both in law and in fact and this affects every aspect of Palestinian life . . . Although the [PA] could explain its actions against Palestinians as being in response to pressure from Israel, it nonetheless carries responsibility for complying with these demands."[31]

Yet this argument also allowed the PA to charge that internal critics were unpatriotic in highlighting human rights issues. A top-level PA investigating committee into rights abuses suggested that such problems were merely "residues of the Israeli occupation."[32] If this questionable thesis were so, not only would the PA itself be innocent of any blame, but also the problems could be expected to disappear automatically once Israel withdrew and a state was established. Other state-building movements had used parallel arguments that, colonialism or capitalism being the cause of their social and structural problems, their removal would bring quick and easy solutions.

Blaming the lack of Palestinian democracy on Israel was a popular argument for both the PA and its critics in the Palestinian debate. Surani noted, "Despite the fact that nearly all Palestinians live under the jurisdiction of the PA, most place blame for human rights abuses on Israel," since the PA did not have "full jurisdiction" over all the territory and was "under great pressure by Israel on many issues, including counterterrorism, which has the effect of pushing the PA to ignore human rights violations."[33]

Yet all that Israel demanded of the PA in this context was to stop Hamas and others from waging war against its own citizens by arresting those who were planning or had carried out attacks. This did not require the PA to torture people, imprison them without trial, or arrest those who had committed no crime. Even more clearly, Israel had absolutely no interest in seeing peaceful oppositionists arrested or intimidated, nor did it oppose other aspects of human rights and democratic institutionalization. Still, attributing the problem to Israel provided an ironclad excuse for the PA leadership, unchallengeable for Arafat's critics, who were not ready to say anything which could be made to seem favorable or even exculpatory toward Israel.

Very few Palestinians were prepared to discuss their own society's defects, or at least its stage of development, as a factor in these problems. Ziyad Abu Amr came as close as anyone to this level of self-criticism: "It seems that the new Palestinian order . . . is incapable of effecting a smooth and incremental process of transition from the logic of the 'revolution' and exile to the logic of 'state' and civil society. Although the blame primarily falls on the incumbent regime, it also is true that the social, economic, and political forces in Palestinian society are weak or absent. Making such a transition in an interim period is inevitably difficult and complicated. Nevertheless, the PA has failed to do what . . . is objectively possible."[34]

Despite any longer-term hopes, then, Palestinian morale was low because of both problems in the peace process and discontent with the PA's performance. While elections had given Palestinians "an opportunity to lay the foundations for a democratic political system and society," Abu Amr wrote, they were "no closer to democracy . . . Democracy requires more than elections. It should ensure meaningful rotation of power, including the highest office in the land; oversight; separation of powers; the rule of law; respect for human rights; and freedom of assembly, expression, and the press."[35]

An interesting example of how civil society issues were handled was a 1994 controversy involving the Palestinian Women's Federation, an umbrella group whose members came from all PLO factions but mostly from Fatah. In 1994 the Fatah caucus and its allies in the organization invited Social Affairs Minister Intisar al-Wazir to open the federation's annual conference. PFLP and DFLP members led by Maha Nasr, a physics teacher heading the PFLP women's faction and also the federation's secretary, opposed the idea, calling it a symbolic attempt to subordinate the federation to the PA. Soon Nasr was receiving anonymous threatening telephone calls demanding that she change her mind. A bloodsoaked rag was left at her door, an intifada-era warning to suspected collaborators and adulteresses. Protests by human rights groups led the PA to denounce such behavior.[36]

While the PA explored the possibility of seizing control of mass organizations and public interest groups, it did not do so. At the same time, Wazir's own response to the 1994 controversy showed the PA hierarchy's prevalent attitude toward democracy. She argued, not inaccurately, that the federation had never been a purely independent organization but was part of the PLO. Inasmuch as the PA was heir to PLO assets, these groups were already, and should remain, quasi-state institutions.[37]

Wazir might also have pointed out that such groups were characterized not by democracy, in the sense of individuals making choices, but by a pluralism of factions each having its own political line. Equally, it was neither unreasonable nor antidemocratic to invite Wazir—who was arguably the highest-ranking, most influential woman in Palestinian history—as guest of honor on such an occasion. Wazir pointed out that a minority should not be allowed to "impose its opinion on the majority" which wanted her to open the meeting.[38] Since supporters of the PA and Fatah members were a majority in most public organizations, they thus had the right to set policy.

Certainly, the use of intimidation revealed a bullying approach, an unwillingness to accept an opposition that resisted the majority's effort. Wazir showed the underlying rationale for such methods when she noted: "This organization is an official organization. Throughout the world, women's organizations are an official arm of the government, in Damascus, in Cairo, in Amman, all over the world."[39] A vision of political models limited only to the Arab world, assuming that polities were all-encompassing and organized from the top down, did not bode well for democracy.

Of course, although the freedom to organize and run non-government organizations is an important earmark of democracy, the PA could also be cynical in knowing that few were neutral and in the end most would be controlled either by itself or by the opposition. While Wazir wanted the Women's Federation to be an arm of the government, her rivals wanted it to be a tool for the opposition. One Palestinian writer even made the intriguing suggestion that since anti-PA groups either refused to participate in the system (like Hamas) or were part of the establishment (like the internal Fatah critics), non-government organizations were actually the real opposition in Palestinian society.[40]

At any rate, if the PA did not always heed women's groups, it also did not stifle them. They became one of the best-organized lobbies, persuading the PA to withdraw a government regulation that "every woman learning to drive must have a family member with her, according to our people's ethics and values." Women's organizations claimed that the law violated personal freedom, was discriminatory, "and contradicts . . . the nature of the Palestinian society we are trying to build." The lobby also ensured a woman's right to obtain a passport without her husband's permission.[41] In 1998 a Palestinian Model Parliament on Women urged such reforms as classifying rape under "crimes conducted against persons" rather than "crimes violating morals and public manners"; harsh punishment for rapists and murderers of women in family honor killings; and a family protection law making punishment of incest or sexual abuse a public responsibility.[42]

When the PA did want to suppress critics, it turned to the security services. Generally, they acted at Arafat's instruction and in the system's interest. Yet many of the problems involving them arose not so much from a deliberate, systematic effort to subordinate society but rather as expressions of their own corruption, incompetence, ambitions, and conflicts. Here, too, history, context, and objective obstacles must be taken into account.

The 1997 report of the Palestinian Independent Commission for Citizens' Rights (PICCR) criticized the security services for "meddling in each other's affairs; political detentions; torture; and bad conditions in the prisons and detention centers."[43] While first and foremost intended to impose Arafat's and the PA's authority, these actions had other causes as well. The security services were also essentially new institutions whose limited resources and training reduced their efficiency and professionalism. They had been shaped not only by Palestinian political culture but also by individuals' training, ideology, and years spent in Arab police states.

Alongside arrogance, incompetence combined with difficult working conditions caused many problems. In 1996 alone, a policeman committed suicide because he could not support his family on his $233-a-month salary;[44] an eleven-year-old Gazan girl was killed when a Palestinian security man pulled a gun during a quarrel with a colleague;[45] Palestinian security forces sometimes carelessly opened fire on passing cars;[46] and one Palestinian was killed and two injured when police opened fire at a football match in Nablus to stop a riot among fans.[47]

The security forces' view of themselves as more society's master than its servant arose from their self-perception as being a vanguard fighting a hard struggle in which neither civilians nor legal technicalities should be allowed to interfere. The PA police saw themselves equally as a law enforcement force among Palestinians and as the Palestinians' armed defenders against Israel.[48] In the former role, the police arrested and tortured hundreds of people. But the latter role as symbol and protector of their sovereignty still made the police popular among Palestinians. This was especially clear in July 1994[49] and September 1996, when PA policemen exchanged fire with Israeli forces during violent demonstrations.

Many of the worst abuses seem to have sprung from local commanders' personal ambitions and arrogance. Newspapers were often closed or individuals detained because they had criticized or offended a top officer in one of the security services. Civilian officials sometimes stepped in to remedy injustices, even if only to respond to criticism from the PLC or foreign donors. The PA brought in Palestinian human rights groups to give police courses on legal procedure and dealing with the public. There was as much logic as wishful thinking to the remark of one officer in such a class: "These things are new, people are new in their jobs. Slowly, slowly, things will get better."[50] Still, Arafat always put a higher priority on pampering security forces as his main institutional support for retaining power, and patterns were being set which might shape the long-term future of the Palestinian polity.

The most difficult security issue was how to handle those directly engaged in violence against Israel intended to wreck the peace process. According to all the agreements, the PA was obligated to stop attacks against Israel. From Israel's standpoint this was by far the most important Palestinian commitment, and the one on which further Israeli concessions would be based. Israel at times complained that the PA deployed more police than permitted under their agreements, though it also wanted PA forces sufficient to be able to prevent terrorist attacks and cross-border criminal activity.[51]

Between September 1993 and March 1996, about 213 people were killed in Israel by Palestinian attacks. This assault's intensity helped bring the Netanyahu government to power, prompting a major shift in Israeli policy and a slowing of the peace process to the PA's disadvantage. Many Israelis argued that a PA that failed to prevent attacks on Israel could hardly be trusted with additional territory or full sovereignty. About seventy-five more Israelis were killed by Palestinian terrorism between March 1996 and March 1999 at a steadily declining rate.[52]

The PA did make serious efforts to block attacks, but evaluating this effort in terms of the Palestinian leadership's willpower and effectiveness in doing so was extraordinarily controversial. In general, Arafat tried to live up to his commitments but pulled back from the kind of all-out pressure on Hamas that might have ended its challenge. Between January and March 1996, PA ineptitude and laxity failed to stop a major radical bombing campaign. Arafat sought to compensate afterwards with massive arrests of extremists. For several months in mid-1997 the PA was relatively permissive toward attacks in order to pressure the Netanyahu government. After this tactic backfired and severely damaged the PA's international standing, Arafat returned to his usual policy. In late 1998, after the Wye agreement, the PA cracked down to show that it was implementing its renewed commitment to stop attacks.

In their public statements, though, PA and other Palestinian leaders usually did not connect Israeli measures such as closures or delays in negotiations as reactions to attacks.[53] A common response by the PA and Palestinian politicians was to claim that Israel was using attacks as a rationale to escape its commitments or even to destroy the PA altogether. One exception was when Arafat, speaking at a Gaza rally, condemned a February 1995 attack on an Israeli fuel truck which led to a closure: "Who is the genius who set out to close off the [Gaza] Strip and deprive its residents of basic staples? Who is the man organizing these conspiracies against Palestinian children, hospitals, and the Gaza Strip industry?"[54]

Nabil Sha'th, like other PA leaders, suggested that faster progress in negotiations, rather than punitive measures, would stop the violence. Ordering closures would only hurt the innocent without being effective, he argued. Hamas and Islamic Jihad "have set themselves up to destroy this Palestinian national authority and they are doing it by killing Israelis." The PA could not go too far to suppress the violence, however, because "once you really start to resist them on the streets, they are willing to kill us, too." The best approach, he suggested was better cooperation between the two sides and advancing the peace process.[55]

There were many examples of such cooperation, as well as other cases where it failed. The PA did occasionally hand over Palestinian criminals to Israel, such as a man selling counterfeit Israeli identification cards whom Israeli police suspected was also supplying them to terrorists.[56] On many occasions the PA announced it had stopped planned attacks, sometimes by deprogramming young would-be suicide bombers. For example, in 1996 it arrested a sixteen-year-old boy whom Islamic Jihad was preparing for such a mission. Arafat said that the group had promised his large needy family $50,000 if he succeeded. Instead, his mother informed the police. Arafat gave the family $5,000 and found the father a job with the PA, but he branded these as stopgap measures in the face of an economic crisis that allegedly drove people to such desperate acts.[57]

The PA sometimes but not always arrested specific individuals identified by Israel as leaders in planning and carrying out attacks.[58] A key institution in this process was the Higher State Security Court, established by Arafat in February 1995 to rule on "security crimes." The judges were police officers, sometimes with no legal experience, and appointed for a single case. This let Arafat take over jurisdiction and essentially dictate verdicts on key cases.[59]

On Arafat's orders, Palestinians arrested for attacking Israelis were quickly tried by these courts. Palestinian sources say that between their creation in April 1995 and the end of 1997, they sentenced forty-six Palestinians for involvement in anti-Israel terror. Israel charged that while the sentences seemed severe, at least eleven of those convicted were soon released. For example, Sa'id Salam Abu Musama of Hamas, sentenced to three years' imprisonment in May 1995 for inciting violence against Israel and the PA, was released after only seven months.

The PA security agencies also hired some who agreed to leave their old groups and pledge allegiance to Fatah. For instance, two Hamas activists accused of killing an Israeli soldier and wounding two others were sentenced in April 1995 to two years in prison but were released after only eight months after agreeing to defect to the PA.[60]

These courts, however, did put many suspected perpetrators in prison, albeit through methods contrary to generally accepted legal procedure. For example, in a closed thirty-minute trial in which they were not permitted their own lawyer, a State Security Court sentenced Nasir Abu Arrous and Jasir Salama to fifteen years' hard labor under the PLO's 1979 Revolutionary Punishment Law, for committing terrorist acts and damaging national unity. They had prepared the bombs used for 1997 suicide attacks in Jerusalem.[61] Two murderers of Jerusalem taxi driver Shmuel Ben Baruch were sentenced to life and a third participant received fifteen years' imprisonment after a half-hour trial.[62]

Such procedures were much criticized by Israel as a way to avoid extradition requests and by Palestinians as a human rights violation. The PA's own prosecutor general, Fayiz Abu Rahma, former chairman of the Gaza Bar Association, said: "As a Palestinian jurist, I am ashamed . . . I do not understand how trials of this kind can take place, without my knowledge . . . How is it possible to sentence three men so harshly in less than half an hour?"[63]

The PA's response, given by Military Attorney General Mahmud Bishtawi, was that the defendants had already admitted their guilt in most of these cases.[64] The PA was also avoiding protracted trials in which admitted terrorists might appeal to the public by justifying their deeds on political grounds and denouncing the PA. It also worried that if courts freed defendants on technical or political grounds, the PA would look complicit in the attacks and the peace process would be subverted.

For Hamas, whether the defendants were guilty of the charges was irrelevant, since it asserted their right to kill Israelis. In Hamas's view, the PA had no authority to punish anyone for carrying out such attacks. In the words of Abd al-Aziz al-Rantisi, a Hamas leader, "It is a shame that the PA buckles under Israel's pressure especially when . . . Netanyahu refuses to implement Israel's obligations." Rantisi warned that such trials could harm relations between the PA and Hamas.[65]

Nevertheless, the PA was ready to punish many Palestinians for terror attacks on Israelis. In 1995, for example, a military court sentenced Muhammad Qumayl to life plus ten years for aiding an April 1994 bombing in Afula that killed eight people,[66] arrested dozens of radicals suspected of planning attacks on Israel,[67] and sentenced two Hamas members to three years in prison for murdering an accused collaborator.[68] Abd al-

Majid Dudin was given twelve years' imprisonment for participating in bombings,[69] two men were sentenced to twelve years' imprisonment for murdering two teenage Israeli girls,[70] and a fifteen-year sentence was given to an Islamic Jihad member for training suicide bombers.[71]

The PA preferred, however, to co-opt other Hamas cadres who had been involved in attacks on Israel. By bringing such experts on Hamas's structure and operations into their ranks, the PA security forces argued that they might be better able to prevent future attacks. Yet when several of those who had been released broke their pledge and returned to violent activity, this seriously damaged PA credibility with Israel. Further, this policy violated two of the PA's commitments in the peace process: to extradite suspects sought by Israel and to obtain Israeli approval for anyone enlisted in the police.

In 1998 Israel published detailed lists of thirty major Hamas and Islamic Jihad activists involved in terrorism, of whom twelve had allegedly been enlisted in the PA police. Six of them had played central roles in February–March 1996 suicide bombings that killed sixty people. They included Adnan al-Gol, a senior Hamas officer who was number two on Israel's most wanted list, and Kamal Khalifa, who had planned attacks in Jerusalem and Ashkelon before being recruited into the PA's Preventive Security force.[72] Bassam Isa, a Hamas activist suspected of involvement in a 1994 attack that killed two Israelis in Jerusalem, became an officer in Preventive Security, as did Mahmud Sanwar, who had been involved in preparing the 1996 suicide attacks.[73]

Ironically, and symbolic of the situation's complexity, the most senior Palestinian official on Israel's wanted list was Ghazi Jabali, who as police commissioner for Gaza and the West Bank commanded twelve thousand men. Israel claimed that he had organized policemen into terror cells and ordered them to attack Israelis.[74] Yet this same individual had also incurred the Palestinian opposition's wrath for his efforts to preserve the peace. He had issued orders to block provocative anti-Israel demonstrations in September 1994; in December 1996 when Israeli flags were burned at a PFLP rally at al-Najah University just after that group had killed Israelis, and in January 1998 when marchers protesting U.S. policy on Iraq clashed with Israeli soldiers.[75]

Any domestic political gains for the PA from being lax in stopping attacks or from releasing convicted terrorists from prison and recruiting them into security forces were outweighed by the cost paid in relations with Israel. Undermining Israeli confidence reduced Israel's willingness to make concessions, pushed public opinion toward a harder line, and brought countermeasures—such as border closures and slowdowns in talks—which hurt Palestinians and the PA.

In several cases, Palestinian police themselves became involved in attacks on Israel. For example, one of the leaders of a Hamas cell that organized 1997 suicide bombings that killed twenty-one people was Abd al-Rahman Zabin, a Palestinian policeman in Nablus. Yet, in an illustration of the complexity of such situations, Zabin and his associates were caught with the help of the PA's Preventive Intelligence.[76]

In addition to those directly involved in attacks against Israel, there were three other classes of prisoners held by the PA. Each group was treated distinctly, since the PA's goal was different for each category. It aimed to make oppositionists belonging to violent groups more passive, to kill those who were collaborating with Israel, and to intimidate moderate critics.

First, members of radical opposition groups—mostly Hamas and Islamic Jihad, and some from the PFLP and DFLP—were arrested in large numbers after armed attacks on Israelis, more for their membership than for any active participation in these operations. Some were generally involved in supporting violent activities; others engaged only in verbal support. They were held for months, often without charge or trial, sometimes tortured, then gradually released. In the round of arrests after the January–March 1996 attacks, up to one thousand were detained.[77] A few Hamas detainees were killed in prison.[78] Leaders were arrested at tense moments and then let go when PA-Hamas dialogue was renewed. The PA's goal was to deter these individuals and their groups from launching more attacks.

Second, the prisoners who received the worst treatment were those accused of collaborating with Israel by providing it with information. Despite a PA pledge of amnesty for collaborators in the agreements with Israel, they were kidnapped or brought in for interrogation by security forces, then murdered. Between 1994 and 1998, sixty-seven Palestinians were killed by vigilante groups or PA security forces (including nine held in prisons) and ninety-six injured. At least five of those killed were real estate dealers accused of selling land to Israelis, an activity PA officials had proclaimed punishable by death.[79] Among those accused of collaboration or land sales who were killed in custody were Salman Quraysh (January 1995),[80] Khalid Habbal (August 1996),[81] Rashid Fityani (December 1996),[82] and Yusuf Isma'il Baba (February 1997). In Baba's case, three police interrogators were later arrested and charged with torturing him to death.[83]

An example of the treatment suffered by those accused of collaboration by PA security forces was the case of Iman Shihah, who had worked as a civil servant in the Israeli civil administration. She was seized at gunpoint, forced into a car, and held for three days in abandoned houses and fields before being released. Interrogators sprayed her with tear gas, melted candles over her body, and pulled her nipples with pincers. Other methods included sleep deprivation, beating, lack of medical attention, tying up, and blindfolding.[84]

A third group were human rights activists, journalists, and other democratic critics. They might be harassed, taken in for questioning, and held by police for several days.[85] But they were tortured far less often than radicals or collaborators, perhaps because bad publicity and international protests pressured the PA to let them go, though they also may have suffered less because the police thought them more easily intimidated than their radical counterparts. Thus, they were rarely sentenced by courts or imprisoned, except when an individual official sought revenge for some criticism or exposure of his activities. The worst-treated person in this category was Fathi Subuh, professor of education at Gaza City's al-Azhar University. Arrested on July 2, 1996, he was held almost five months without bail, despite a serious health condition, and threatened with a long sentence before finally being released. Apparently, Subuh's sole crime was assigning students to write an essay about PA corruption.[86]

The two main human rights groups—LAW and PICCR, established in 1993, with Arafat's endorsement, to "contribute to the development of democracy in Palestine"—usually operated freely but also suffered periodic harassment. Especially singled out for mistreatment was Iyad Sarraj, PICCR's commissioner general, a courageous human rights advocate and director of the Gaza Community Mental Health Program. He was arrested briefly in December 1995, then again in May 1996 for eight days after he gave an interview to the *New York Times* in which he criticized the PA as corrupt.[87] In June he was arrested for thirteen days and beaten. PA Attorney General Khalid al-Qidra claimed that the detention "was not related to his human rights activities," and rumors were spread that he was involved with drugs.[88] Next, Sarraj was charged with assaulting his interrogator and brought before a military court, but was released after his lawyers appealed to the Palestinian High Court, demanding a reason for his detention.[89]

Shortly after Arafat praised LAW in a meeting with its leaders and in his speech opening the 1998 PLC session, PA police detained LAW's executive director Shawqi Isa and Samih Muhsin, editor of its *People's Rights* magazine, for several hours. They were interrogated about articles criticizing the human rights record of the police and accused of slandering PA police chief Ghazi Jabali.[90]

While human rights activists were handled relatively mildly during the PA's first five years, twenty other prisoners died in custody, of whom at least thirteen may have perished as a result of torture or murder.[91] While many of these were alleged collaborators, other cases were more obscure. Sulayman Musa Ata Jalayitah died in January 1995 while being interrogated in a preventive security center in Jericho. Jibril al-Rajjub, head of Preventive Security there, claimed that he was a PFLP activist involved in murder and sabotage activities against the PA, who had died as the result of low blood pressure in a hospital.[92] In September, Azzam Muslih, a U.S. citizen, died while in Palestinian police custody, the PA claimed, owing to a heart attack.[93] In August, Nahid Dahlan was found dead in front of his Gaza home after reporting to the police for interrogation. Attorney General Qidra claimed that he had been released and subsequently committed suicide. A few days later the PA police arrested Muhammad Dahman, director of a group that helped political prisoners, and charged him with publishing false and provocative information claiming that Dahlan had died in custody. Dahman was imprisoned for four days.[94]

The best-known and most controversial such case was the July 31, 1996, death of Mahmud Jumayyil, a popular leader of the Fatah Hawks in Nablus during the intifada. His arrest may have been an attempt to prevent him from running in the PLC election as an independent. Jumayyil's body reportedly bore skull fractures and burn marks.[95] A few days after his death, a PA military court sentenced three police officers to long prison terms for torturing Jumayyil to death. But there was no investigation of whether high officials had ordered his arrest or murder.[96]

This incident set off a major crisis. Participants in the funeral chanted slogans against Nablus mayor Ghassan Shaq'a, who, Jumayyil's family claimed, had ordered Jumayyil's arrest and torture. When demonstrators gathered outside the prison and some threw rocks, police fired into the crowd, killing Ibrahim Hadaya, a Hamas member who had previously served eight years in Israeli prisons and had just been released from five months in a PA jail.[97]

Instead of dealing with the issue, the PA lied about what had happened, with Arafat telling reporters that armed Hamas men had tried to free prisoners and killed Hadaya by mistake.[98] A PA military court sentenced five demonstrators to prison. In compensation, Arafat made Hadaya a "Martyr of the Revolution," gave his family a pension, and ordered his brother Jamal released from prison. He also assigned a high-level "investigation committee" to look into the event.[99]

There was outrage even within Fatah. PLC member Husam Khadir, one of Arafat's toughest critics, claimed that there was more torture in PA prisons than in Israeli prisons. The Higher Fatah Committee of the West Bank issued a leaflet condemning "the ugly crime" and demanded that "the PA stop all acts of torture, and take all measures necessary to ensure the rule of law, and control the actions of all security personnel."[100]

Hamas was split on how to react. Jamal Hadaya, a Hamas leader and the deceased's brother, took a more moderate line, stating: "Hamas believes in unity, and paid a high price for it. Hundreds of its members were imprisoned without it firing one bullet in retaliation." Some Hamas officials—especially those abroad—disagreed and urged a struggle against the PA in an August 3 leaflet. It called the incident "merely a natural extension of the practices of the [PA]," simply one more in a series of many attacks "by the [PA] gangs against our people and its national institutions." Yet the leaflet's conclusion was contradictory, reflecting Hamas's ambiguity as to how to respond to treatment of its members. On the one hand, it said, "Hamas . . . refuses to be dragged into an internal conflict that will end the Palestinian people's unity—despite the continuous provocative practices by the [PA]." Yet on the other hand, it proclaimed that the latest incidents were "the beginning of a popular intifada against a [PA] that has sold itself to the occupier." It called the PA leadership "collaborators . . . [who] try to shackle us in the name of national slogans and the building of an independent state."[101] Nevertheless, Hamas continued to follow the line laid out by Jamal Hadaya.[102]

The PA investigating committee recommended releasing prisoners not charged with a crime, devising better ways to investigate complaints, and improving coordination of various security forces. Arafat and the PA cabinet promised to restrict the security forces' authority and investigate officers "accused of involvement in immoral acts and financial corruption," as well as those whose "loyalty to the nation is suspect."[103]

To quiet complaints, the PA attorney general's office even warned some victims' families that other relatives might be arrested if they continued to protest.[104] Arafat repeatedly promised full investigations of deaths, but though the security officials directly involved were sometimes punished severely, no detailed findings were ever made public.[105]

The Palestinian media almost always ignored these stories, or at least put the best pro-PA spin on them. When the PICCR released its 1997 human rights report, the Voice of Palestine radio highlighted one of its conclusions—that the PA's performance had improved significantly—while ignoring all the continued deficiencies it described. These included eighty-five documented cases of torture and six deaths in detention during the year.[106] The courts, as the PICCR report noted, still had to cope with uncooperative security services and a sometimes defiant PA, both of which believed themselves above the law. Despite these obstacles, the courts remained freer than in dictatorships, and the judges won more than a few battles.[107]

In one notorious case, for example, military intelligence arrested nine people from a village near Bethlehem in March 1996 on charges of killing seven Palestinians during the intifada years. They were tortured, refused legal counsel, and forced to sign confessions. Even when the district attorney, attorney general, and justice minister ordered their transfer to police custody, it took two months to force military intelligence to comply. Finally, on March 25, 1998, the District Court ruled that confessions acquired through torture were inadmissible in court, acquitted all nine, and ordered their immediate release. "This case will set a precedent, making the security services more careful and limiting torture in prisons," concluded the defendants' attorney, Shawqi Isa.[108] Isa proved over-optimistic. But at least in this situation, and despite the delay, PA officials and the courts did intervene to achieve justice.

The single case most threatening to judicial independence concerned ten Bir Zayt student supporters of Hamas arrested in March 1996 and jailed without charge or trial. On August 18, 1996, the Palestinian Supreme Court ordered their immediate release, but Attorney General Qidra declared that the students would remain in prison until Arafat said otherwise. This was an open declaration that Arafat's will was above even that of the highest court.[109] The students were finally sent home, but only after several PLC members, led by Barghuti and Ta'amri, linked their release with support for a no-confidence motion.[110]

Yet the PA still wanted to ensure that the courts were usually—though not necessarily always—pliable. Nine days after the ruling, Chief Justice Amin Abd al-Sala'am of the Ramallah Appellate Court was forced to retire. In January 1998 the same fate befell Chief Justice and president of the Palestinian Supreme Court Qusay al-Abadla, who had been appointed by Arafat but had led the court ordering the release of the Bir Zayt students.[111] The immediate cause of his forced retirement was an interview published two days earlier in which he had complained about Justice Minister Abu Midayn's interference with the courts, which, he said, was destroying an independent Palestinian judiciary.[112]

On this issue as on many judicial matters, the PA was not monolithic. A long feud between Attorney General Fayiz Abu Rahma, who had succeeded Qidra,[113] and Justice Minister Abu Midayn meant that the two men were usually on opposite sides of any issue. Abu Rahma criticized Abadla's removal and himself resigned after criticizing Abu Midayn. Abu Midayn had temporarily quit in July 1997 to protest Abu Rahma's appointment without his knowledge.[114]

As in other aspects of Palestinian society and state-building, the objective problems being faced were bad enough without these added clashes and improprieties. The court system was extremely overloaded, and there were not enough judges. Abadla had noted in his controversial press interview that court employees had not been paid for six months. There was a huge amount of work to be done to create a whole body of Palestinian law and to synchronize the different systems prevailing in the West Bank and Gaza.[115]

While many Palestinians were affected by the police and court system, the single biggest popular complaint about the PA was its corruption. Polls showed that 50–60 percent of Palestinians thought that PA institutions were riddled with corruption, with 40 percent expecting that it would gradually decrease and 50 percent believing that it would remain the same or even increase.[116] One Palestinian told *al-Bilad* that "the same people [in the PA] are running our life" who had stolen money from the families of the dead and injured during the intifada.[117]

But Nidal Isma'il, a writer who was certainly not a PA apologist, presented an impressive critique of specific charges. The PLC's investigations of corruption, he wrote, focused on alleged misspending of only $250,000.[118] Isma'il argued that the investigations were more a sign of democracy than the corruption uncovered was a proof of dictatorship. "This was the first event of its kind in the Arab world," he wrote, "truly an example of democracy in action: a democratically elected institution holding accountable other public institutions, and calling ministers before it to answer charges of corruption and mismanagement. But the media [were] interested primarily in scandal. And their emphasis on wrongdoing created a backlash against Palestinian democratic institutions from donor nations, threatening the very democracy they wish to develop."[119]

In responding to a May 1997 report by the PA's General Monitoring Commission claiming that $326 million, a large portion of the PA's total budget, had been misused or wasted, Isma'il argued that this analysis was wildly inaccurate.[120] The high figure resulted, for example, from including all the tax remissions given "every single returnee, immigrant, [and] investor [to] purchase a vehicle and all household furnishings without taxes." It "also concluded that all of the land 'donated' to special projects, like the Gaza industrial park at Karneh[,] meant lost tax revenues, but the committee never once considered the costs of the alternative: no investment."[121]

In addition, corruption charges might be based on partisanship or personal antagonism. For example, when the PA Finance Ministry withheld a subsidy from the East Jerusalem Palestinian magazine *al-Awda*, the magazine, edited by Raymonda Tawil, Arafat's mother-in-law, editorialized, "Why does [Finance Minister Muhammad] Nashashibi, who returned to Palestine five years ago, stay with his family at the five-star Palestine Hotel at the Gaza beach and build a grand palace in Amman?"[122] But this did not prove that Nashashibi was embezzling PA funds. He was a leading member of one of the largest, richest Palestinian families, with many relatives in Amman who had a claim on his hospitality. Of course the alternative to living in a Gaza hotel would be building a "grand palace" for himself in Gaza.

This is not to say that corruption was not a huge problem for Palestinian society, leading to waste and anti-democratic practices. The issue was manifested in three especially important ways. First, pervasive low-level corruption took money directly out of most Palestinians' pockets and eroded popular support for the PA. Government employees who were willing to steal from their own people rejected the role of "civil servant" on which democracy rests. People reported paying police kickbacks to avoid traffic tickets and extra bribes to obtain needed permits or other routine government services. Businesspeople claimed that security services demanded contributions from them.[123]

Venal officials' indifference to their own people's health and well-being was shocking. The PA imported flour to end profiteering, but when the improperly stored grain spoiled, it was sold to merchants at low prices, mixed with good flour, and resold to the public at a huge profit.[124] PA officials reportedly took bribes to facilitate the work of Is-raeli-Palestinian gangs smuggling meat, vegetables, and fruit in both directions, circumventing health laws, import regulations, and taxes.[125] Arafat ordered seven colonels in the PA security services arrested on charges of involvement in a smuggling ring that brought in spoiled food from Israel.[126]

Second, corruption undermined Palestinian-Israeli relations and mu-tual confidence, thus subverting the peace process. Israeli police arrested dozens of their Palestinian counterparts for car thefts and factory break-ins. Musa Abu Sabha, a PLC member and Justice Ministry employee, was caught by Israeli police in October 1997 driving a Mercedes stolen a few hours earlier from a Jerusalem dealership. Zakariyya Balusha, a general in the Gaza security services, was found driving a stolen BMW. Preventive Security chief Jibril al-Rajjub knew of "at least three cases where senior Palestinian officials ordered from the thieves a specific model of luxury car" to be custom-stolen.[127] Ironically, some of the sto-len cars still carried right-wing Israeli bumper stickers.

Third, Arafat found ways to siphon off large amounts of money for his own uses. Profits earned by PA-approved monopolies were put into special budget accounts under Arafat's control with no public account-ing.[128] This was not a matter of direct corruption—although Arafat's lieutenants on these projects reportedly took a percentage for personal commissions—but it did increase the PA's control over society. In part, such funds could be put to good state-building purposes. The PA solid-ified its base of support through patronage, subsidized Palestinian com-munities abroad, and provided political favors. For example, money given by the European Union to build apartments for poor Gazans was instead used to construct luxury apartments for high-level Outsider of-ficials. By strengthening the PA, such patronage even further increased the executive's margin of power over the PLC and made it more inde-pendent of judicial and legal regulation.

"A Palestinian should be able to feel safe in the hands of the Palestin-ian security forces, especially when he or she has not been officially charged or brought before a court," wrote a Palestinian journalist. "With each prison death, 'those responsible' are put on trial and sen-tenced to long prison terms, but the bloody deaths continue."[129] The number of people killed declined over time and the level of repres-sion eased. The decline in major terrorist bombing campaigns after 1996, along with the disposal of cases of pre-1993 collaborators and the consolidation of PA control, lowered the level of conflict. Still, the system's arbitrariness and the lack of institutional or legal controls over the security services remained.[130]

In the final analysis, the most important thing was that the struggle over a democratic society and polity was continuing. The PA was both flexible and inconsistent, neither foreclosing the debate nor seeking to impose a monolithic dictatorship. The PA had to take into account the Palestinian situation as well as the violent opposition seeking to drag it into the abyss of full-scale war. Arafat sought to safeguard not only his own tenure in power but also the Palestinian polity's survival and its progress toward becoming a state. Many of the PA's measures were necessary, though which ones and to what extent is a matter of opinion, debate, and political philosophy.

The Jordanian journalist Rami Khuri saw the situation in optimistic terms. "Something qualitatively and historically significant is taking place [among the Palestinians] with possible wider political implications for the Arab world," he wrote. Political forces were "challenging the rule of the state and government." Their coalition included non-government organizations, "elected legislators, Islamists, human rights activists, and other pro-democracy ordinary citizens—that are working together to pull Palestine back from the brink of the abyss of authoritarianism into which it risks falling."[131]

Perhaps the greatest irony was that the PA gained an international reputation as a dictatorship when it was unwilling or unable to act as a normal state structure by imposing its will on the violent opposition. Similarly, despite police harassment, open peaceful dissent continued from non-governmental organizations. And even within Fatah itself, Arafat did not try very hard to impose a single political line.

4

THE POLITY AND
THE PEOPLE

To construct an independent state while consolidating its own power, the PA needed to secure popular support. Nationalist legitimacy was a powerful factor, but this had to be supplemented by a proven ability to meet citizens' material needs, bridge gaps among Palestinians, and improve living standards. A wide range of institutions had to be constructed, too, including the banking, educational, and media systems.

The PA, however, not only had to build these institutions but also had to define their structure and purpose. Even the most basic questions, such as who constituted the PA's population and what was included in its territory, were open to interpretation and debate. The PA defined citizens as those Arab Palestinians currently living legally in the West Bank or Gaza Strip or children born abroad to a father meeting those conditions. Those authorized to come back by Arafat and approved by Israel for entry into the territories also received Palestinian citizenship. But Palestinian refugees living abroad were not PA citizens. Although the PA accepted the idea of dual nationality, it did not press the issue, given Israeli, Jordanian, and Lebanese opposition to it.[1] "No one can say so far with finality just which rights Palestinian citizens do possess," wrote a Palestinian scholar, "and there exists no official document to provide a guide."[2]

As for the PA's economic situation, it was no asset in trying to mobilize popular support and build a state. "We drink polluted water," Arafat complained, "the electricity grid is inefficient, and the schools operate in three daily shifts with more than 65 pupils in each class."[3] The PA ruled only part of a tiny land—totaling six thousand square kilometers—with no heavy industry and no valuable resources. The gross national product was barely $2.9 billion. Palestinians could not move easily among the PA's cities and often faced Israeli restrictions on visiting East Jerusalem, where another 250,000 Palestinians lived.[4]

The PA's population, around 2.5 million, was too small to make it an important state but close to the existing infrastructure's maximum capacity. The high birthrate—nearly 38.1 per thousand people in Gaza—brought a 3.7 percent annual demographic growth rate between 1995 and 1997, strained resources, and produced a large number of dependents outside the work force. On the positive side, fertility rates and infant mortality were steadily declining and life expectancy was rising.[5]

Being so comparatively late in state-building, Palestinians found many economic niches already filled, and the Middle East oil boom was long over. Other external factors were also inimical. Prospective investors saw instability, an uncertain future, and no reliable legal system to protect them. The UN Relief and Works Agency (UNRWA), which saved the PA money by employing many Palestinians to provide educational and welfare services, made cutbacks because of declining international contributions to its budget.[6] Arab financial support was almost totally lacking.[7] Arafat exclaimed in frustration that the shortage and slowness of development aid could "endanger the entire peace process."[8]

But as former Minister of Economics and Trade Ahmad Khuri recognized, "We are fed up [with] saying that the flow of assistance is so inadequate," since the people's expectations exceeded any possible level of aid.[9] Moreover, the PA had received far more foreign assistance proportionately than other Third World states, and it could be argued that much of the money had been wasted, stolen, or used ineffectively. In 1993, international donors granted the PA a total of $2.3 billion, almost all of it distributed by late 1998. The donors met again in November 1998 and pledged another $3.3 billion for the next five years. Of this amount, $2 billion was given by European countries and $900 million by the United States. Less than $200 million came from Arab states, mostly Saudi Arabia and Kuwait, equivalent to Norway's contribution.

As a result of all these elements, the PA economy continued to be reliant on Israel, which remained its main market, source of imports, and export route. Israel also reimbursed the PA for taxes, health insurance, and social security payments taken from its citizens working in Israel.[10] Yet this dependency clashed with the PA's goal of ensuring its independence and gave Israel potential political leverage. As a Palestinian businessman put it, "Israel can basically halt Palestinian exports to other countries at any time."[11] Still, if economic agreements with Israel were sometimes unfavorable for the PA, the economist Adil Samara pointed out, "the PA tends to forget that it negotiated them itself."[12]

Many of the economy's problems had political roots. Violence and the resulting delays in negotiations in 1995 and 1996 damaged the image of stability so necessary to gain investors' confidence. The PA's inability to stop attacks against Israelis led to closures which paralyzed commerce and kept Palestinians from working in Israel. According to UN estimates, the Palestinian economy lost $2.4 million a day as a result, while the PA claimed the cost was as high as $6 million a day from lost trade and workers' income in Israel. The PA also had to divert scarce development funds for emergency welfare and alternative employment programs.[13]

In addition, Israeli employers responded to security worries and closure-related absences by reducing their Palestinian work force from 120,000 in 1993—when it included 33 percent of the West Bank/Gaza labor force to only 30,000 in 1995. The number of Palestinians working in Israel climbed back to 49,000 by 1999. Still, this overall decline was especially costly since the average Palestinian worker earned twice as much in Israel as in the West Bank or Gaza.[14]

During the 1996 closure, the unemployment rate ran as high as 39.2 percent in Gaza and 24.3 percent in the West Bank. Real wages and consumption levels fell, though there was no shortage of food. More women and children went to work, and families borrowed money, used savings, or stopped paying bills in order to maintain consumption levels. Real per capita GNP declined 38.8 percent between 1992 and 1996, also reduced by high population growth rates. Average per capita income dropped from $2,425 in 1992 to $1,480 in 1996, though it climbed back slightly to $1,630 in 1998.[15] The PA could only respond with relatively small-scale public works projects offering temporary unskilled employment. At one point the PA education ministry received 19,000 applications for 650 job openings.[16]

Between 1992 and 1996, the PA's real GNP declined 22.7 percent, mainly as a result of lost employment in Israel and border closures. Average unemployment rose from below 10 percent to 30 percent. In the shorter-lived 1997 closure, Gaza unemployment was at 31.6 percent while the West Bank's rate was 18.2 percent.[17] The economy improved from 1997 on, however, when a decline in attacks drastically reduced the number of closures.

Deficiencies in financing, protective laws, and infrastructure were additional sources of economic difficulties. Nasir Abd al-Hadi, general manager of the Arab Hotels Company, cited lack of financing as a big obstacle for investors: "Banks are very careful in conceding loans and the required standards to get international funds are hard to reach for a developing country." On the domestic scene, only about 26 percent of bank deposits in the PA were used for loans, a Palestinian businessman noted, compared to 65 percent in Jordan and 80 percent in Israel. Abd al-Hadi added that unclear laws created a "chaotic situation [that] still confuses and worries investors, especially foreign ones, who do not feel adequately protected." Another obstacle was lack of infrastructure, including roads, electricity, communications, water, and sewage systems.[18]

Consequently, remarked Raji Surani, director of the Palestinian Center for Human Rights, in June 1998, "Today, the living conditions for ordinary Palestinian citizens are no better than they were before the signing of the Oslo Accords."[19] In a December 1996 poll, only 9 percent of Palestinians said that their economic conditions and living standards had improved during the peace process, while almost 48 percent (59 percent in the Gaza Strip) thought they had worsened and 40 percent (only 29 percent of Gazans) believed they were the same.[20] The following year, when asked about the peace process's impact on the economy, 42.7 percent responded that it had been negative and 27.4 percent "very negative."[21]

In 1997 and 1998, despite the deadlocked peace process, the PA economy improved to some extent. As terror attacks declined, so did closures. There were no closures in the first half of 1998 and very few in late 1998; by comparison, 14 percent of working days had been lost during the first half of 1997. As the number of Palestinian workers in Israel climbed, the unemployment rate declined from 20 to 15.6 percent. Given its lack of resources and without large-scale Arab economic aid, the Palestinian economy faced severe limits on its growth potential.[22]

The PA was more successful in beginning the transformation of local Palestinian institutions—albeit sometimes with a degree of control undermining democracy and free enterprise—and in winning broad support among its citizens. One of the most important institutions the PA took over was an educational system that included 2,400 schools and almost 29,000 teachers. After the many disruptions of the intifada years, schools returned to more normal conditions but were plagued by insufficient funds, underpaid teachers, poor facilities, and overcrowding. In the 1998–99 school year, there were 840,000 Palestinians enrolled, a rapid increase due to a high birthrate and a steep decline in the number of dropouts, from a range of 15–18 percent before 1994 to only 2.2 percent under the PA.[23]

Universities also continued to grow, incorporating over 45,000 students, of whom 43.3 percent were women.[24] But Palestinian universities faced an especially serious financial crisis. As European and Arab donors cut back funding, the PA reduced subsidies and raised tuition fees. Students complained by striking and protesting. Teachers went unpaid for months at a time. With UNRWA's income declining, its schools were also hit hard. These tribulations did not make the PA more popular among students, who already supported the opposition in greater proportions than did any other sector of Palestinian society.[25]

Students faced other stresses, too, as the PA struggled to reorganize the system. One PA high school graduation exam in mathematics was full of errors, causing students to fear that they would fail.[26] A few students committed suicide from despair at low grades, though involvement in anti-Israel attacks was always a way out of personal or family problems, instantly changing one's status from failure to hero. Years of anarchy and violence could also be reflected in youths' behavior, as when students at Khalil al-Wazir Secondary School in Gaza organized themselves into a militia and threatened teachers with guns and insults.[27] Still, despite the considerable problems, the PA was able to take over the educational system fairly easily and turn it into a tool for state-building.[28]

The PA's effort to make the media into its own instrument for consolidating power was more controversial but equally successful. Arafat's priority on the media was symbolized by the fact that his own Gaza office was located not in the PA government compound but in the same small building as the Palestine Broadcasting Corporation (PBC).[29] But while the PA ran its own television and radio stations, it also gave out licenses for competitors and left almost all the print media in private hands.

The PA did have legitimate concerns that the Palestinian media should not be instruments of foreign governments or of highly partisan opposition propaganda aiming to provoke violence. But its view of the media was also a distinctly statist, paternalistic one. As Hatim Abd al-Qadir, head of the publications department of the PA Information Ministry, said, "Total freedom means chaos." The PA's radio director, Ali

Khayan, remarked, "The opposition can express its own opinions, but some things are not allowed because we need time to explain what it means to be democratic." The PA's 1995 press law guaranteed freedom of opinion and a free press, barring only revealing secret material on security forces, inciting violence, promoting racism and sectarianism, harming "national unity," and taking money or direction from a foreign government. Penalties included a three-month publication ban, six months' imprisonment, and fines. Journalists had a right to protect a source's identity, but judges could require them to disclose this information in court.[30]

Yet the PA was quite eager to eliminate legitimate criticism as well and did not even abide by its own press law. Especially effective for persuading journalists to be supportive of the PA was the argument, common in Third World state-building situations, that the media must always support the nation's leaders in order to promote independence, social peace, national unity, and economic development. Anything that exposed abuses or undermined Palestinian claims—no matter how truthful—could be deemed as being close to treason. Many or most Palestinian writers and editors essentially shared this view.

The basis for that supportive attitude, Palestinian journalist Ruba Hussari explained, was the fact that the Palestinian press had begun as "a political tool dedicated to communicating information from the exiled PLO leadership and to promoting the struggle against Israeli occupation." It provided jobs for PLO activists whose articles were "political tracts" with no regard for journalistic standards.[31] This tradition continued after the PA's establishment. Of about four hundred Palestinian journalists, wrote an observer, "only about 20 have the skills to produce newspapers, radio and television news with fairness and balance . . . Professional journalism is a relative novelty in the . . . West Bank and Gaza Strip."[32]

When appeals to patriotism did not work—either because editors and journalists put professional standards first or because they were themselves opposed to the PA—economic subsidies and repressive pressure were used to limit press freedom. On the one hand, the PA was constrained by a desire to project a democratic image and avoid foreign criticism. Yet on the other hand, its model was a pluralist system like that in Jordan or Egypt, not a total dictatorship as in Iraq or Syria.[33] Since the PA was establishing patterns rather than reinforcing longstanding practices, however, this required more dynamic, visible action to tame the media.

In addition to appealing to patriotism, the PA's other methods included a blend of subsidies, closures, and arrests. The East Jerusalem magazine *al-Awda*, for example, received $10,000 a month until this stipend was ended in September 1998, after which it retaliated by accusing the PA finance minister of corruption.[34] Newspapers were punished by temporary, but expensive, shutdowns—ranging from a few days to several months—for running articles Arafat or lower-ranking officials disliked.

Editors of publications located in East Jerusalem, under Israeli rule, could still be intimidated by the PA's barring their issues from entering the West Bank and Gaza, or by undercover PA policemen kidnapping employees and taking them to PA-ruled territory for questioning and detention. After *al-Umma* in Jerusalem published an unflattering cartoon of Arafat in 1995, Preventive Security men raided the print shop, and the offices were later burned, driving the publication out of business.[35]

In earlier years, newspapers were subsidized by either Jordan (*al-Quds* and *al-Nahar*) or the PLO (*al-Fajr* and *al-Sha'b*). But the PLO had to close its own two newspapers when it lost Saudi and Kuwaiti aid money. After the PA's establishment, it set up only one daily newspaper, the sensationalist Gaza-based *al-Hayat al-Jadida*, which enjoyed the confidence of only 7 percent of Palestinian readers.[36] Instead, the PA tamed the higher-quality pro-Jordan newspapers. Since Palestinians trusted *al-Quds* by a large margin over other newspapers, the PA very much wanted to ensure that it was not too critical.[37]

In November 1994, after PA forces killed thirteen pro-Hamas worshippers during a confrontation outside a Gaza mosque, PA police estimated that only 5,000 people had attended a Hamas protest demonstration. *Al-Quds* and *al-Nahar* used a foreign press agency estimate of 12,500, and *al-Quds* also interviewed Zahar, a Hamas leader who blamed the PA for the clash.[38] The PA police blocked delivery of both newspapers into Gaza for several days. *Al-Quds* retaliated by publishing caricatures ridiculing PA police chief Jabali.[39] *Al-Quds* was also closed for one day in August 1995 after PA officials threatened editors.[40] In December 1995, Preventive Security held *al-Quds* editor Mahir al-Alami for six days after he ran an item on Palestinian Christian praise for Arafat on page 8 rather than page 1.[41] Alami complained, "None of my colleagues reported the fact that I was arrested."[42] Arafat, playing the role of benefactor, ordered him released and urged him to be more cooperative in the future. Despite such efforts, *al-Quds* still ran some critical articles about the PA, albeit with great caution. There were many stories it did not report at all.

As for *al-Nahar*, PA security officers barred its sale for one month during the summer of 1994, partly because they deemed that its coverage of the Jordan-Israel peace treaty was too pro-Jordanian and ignored Arafat's criticisms.[43] The Palestinian press took no notice of the punishment, and only eight journalists attended a demonstration protesting the banning order.[44] *Al-Nahar*, switching to a more pro-PA line, was allowed to resume publication in November.[45]

The third relatively respected newspaper, the smaller *al-Ayyam*, also reached an accommodation with the PA. Thus, of the four main newspapers, the three aimed at a more educated audience (*al-Quds, al-Nahar,* and *al-Ayyam*) remained independent but were slow to criticize or publish negative material about the PA, while the PLO used the fourth—and worst in terms of quality (*al-Hayat al-Jadida*)—as a demagogic vehicle.

In contrast, the treatment of radical opposition newspapers was based on the state of the PA's relations with its political sponsor. *Al-Watan*, belonging to Hamas, and *al-Istiqlal*, backed by Islamic Jihad, were temporarily closed in August 1995. *Al-Watan* was permitted to reopen only in October, when its editor Imad al-Faluji signed a pledge to respect the PA press law.[46] But *al-Watan* was again closed for a while in January 1996. In addition, the PA sometimes banned Israel-based Islamic newspapers from circulating in the West Bank and Gaza, though it had given them licenses to do so. Many other small independent or partisan publications were also closed.[47]

"The problem," said a Palestinian journalist, "is not that Arafat doesn't want this or that item to be published. The problem is, journalists are afraid that maybe he won't like it—so they just stay quiet." "Frankly," said another, "we wish the [PA] would tell us exactly what we can and cannot publish. That would be easier. It seems that it is impossible to talk about the security apparatus or violations relating to trials, prisons, and torture"—or about Arafat, who personally remained above criticism.[48] Ironically, the official Voice of Palestine radio, which did know precisely what the PA would tolerate, might provide more balanced coverage than the independent newspapers. Palestinian news sources also often went to the Israeli or sometimes the Jordanian media to get more accurate or complete coverage of their stories.

But Arafat knew well how to employ the media effectively in mobilizing popular support for the PA's line. This situation was illustrated by the contrast in treatment of human rights. Publishing news about PA violations was discouraged, while any criticism of Israel was welcomed and highlighted. At a press conference about PA torture, human rights activist Bassam Id asked a reporter from *al-Quds* why he was there, since he could not write about this issue. The reporter answered that he was hoping Id's report would mention Israeli abuses so he could do an article.[49]

During the September 1996 rioting, Khatib explained, Arafat orchestrated the media, first to ensure that the PA was seen as leading in the clashes with Israel, then to calm the people in order to ease tensions and reach a peaceful solution with Israel. Some private television stations were closed down so they could not show PA police quelling street protests. During the crisis, the Voice of Palestine's approval rating in polls rose from 49 to 62 percent. Similarly, the PA temporarily closed down nine television and radio stations in February 1998 on the grounds that they did not have the proper permits, but actually because it was trying to cool passions when demonstrations against U.S. pressure on Iraq threatened to get out of control.[50]

In comparison to print reporters, who might be independent-minded Insiders, many of those working for PA radio, television, and *al-Hayat al-Jadida* were veteran PLO propagandists. Their model was the state-controlled media in Arab states ruled by dictatorships, where they had lived for so long and received their training. They saw themselves as fighters leading the masses against the enemy. This is how the Voice of Palestine reported on a relatively routine occurrence of Palestinian stone-throwers being met with Israeli tear gas in Hebron: "Occupation forces, in great numbers, burst through the separation line in the city center and began to commit provocations against the citizenry, who responded to the provocations of the occupying soldiers and the attacks by the terrorist-settlers with stones and empty bottles. Occupation forces and gangs began to shoot directly at children and the elderly from very short range . . . [in] an attempt to injure the largest possible number of residents and strike at the Palestinian economy." Actually, Israeli forces had not even crossed the line, an act that would have provoked a bloody battle with Palestinian police.[51]

The press also publicized bizarre conspiracy theories about Israel which provoked mistrust and undermined support for the peace process.[52] For instance, quoting officials in the PA's Supply Ministry, *al-Quds* and other newspapers reported that Israel was selling spoiled foods in order to poison Palestinians. What they did not publicize, however, were detailed PLC reports that accused senior PA officials, including Minister of Supply Abd al-Aziz Shahin, of themselves distributing such food items for their own profit.[53]

The PA's own newspaper, *al-Hayat al-Jadida,* and its editor Hafiz al-Barghuti seemed to delight in provocative slurs, often citing the czarist forgery *The Protocols of the Elders of Zion.* "The conflict between the Jews and the Muslims is an eternal and ongoing conflict, even if it stops for short intervals," an article asserted. "The fate of the Palestinian people is to struggle against the Jews on behalf of the Arab peoples, the Islamic peoples and the peoples of the entire world."[54] The PA must, it told readers, "protect its people and itself from an enemy which bares its Jewish fangs from the four corners of the earth."[55] Israel was a "Shylock" which seized land and built settlements, Hafiz al-Barghuti wrote.[56] It planned to destroy the most holy Muslim shrine in Jerusalem, the al-Aqsa mosque, "starting with arson attempts . . . and the digging of tunnels and ending with the creation of artificial earthquakes that can be triggered from afar."[57]

While other editors were harassed for publishing a single article that displeased the PA, Barghuti was not reined in at all. In contrast, *al-Bilad* was banned after it inaccurately accused the PA of involvement in the slaying of Islamic Jihad leader Fathi Shiqaqi. A Gaza journalist who wrote an article in that magazine claiming that some Preventive Security agents were accepting $300 bribes to arrange permits for truck drivers to enter Israel, was arrested and held until he gave Preventive Security his sources' names.[58] Khalid al-Amayra, a journalist and member of the Board of Trustees of the Palestinian Human Rights Monitoring Group (PHRMG), was arrested and warned not to publish an article he had written about the PA police's torture of Hamas activists.[59]

This did not mean that the Palestinian media lacked credibility with readers and viewers. On the contrary, they steadily gained popularity and popular confidence. According to polls, 50.5 percent of the PA's citizens believed that Palestinian television was balanced, and another 10.2 percent said that it reflected the Palestinian people's mood. Only 23.8 percent thought that it represented just the PA's views. Palestinians were, however, ready to seek other viewpoints. While 25.8 percent of them preferred Palestinian television, 36.5 percent favored Jordanian television (easily seen only in the West Bank), 14.7 percent liked Israeli television, and 10 percent chose Egyptian television (available mainly in Gaza).[60]

By August 1996, a little more than two years after its establishment, 52 percent of Gazans preferred Palestinian television, and residents of the West Bank increasingly agreed after the PA took over there. Among television stations, Jordan's was most trusted by almost 31 percent in the West Bank, and Egypt's by 10 percent in Gaza, while over 7 percent preferred Israeli television's Arabic service. Confidence in the Voice of Palestine radio also grew between August and December 1996 from 33.4 to 44.5 percent. The Arabic-language services of Israel Radio and Radio Monte Carlo were second at 10.2 percent each, followed by Jordan's at 8 percent. Later surveys showed similar results.[61]

To win and hold popular confidence, the PA also had to handle a number of potential rifts within the population—between Muslims and Christians, Insiders and Outsiders, among towns or regions, and between refugees and the indigenous population. In general, it achieved better results than might have been expected, though a continuing focus on struggle with Israel was still a great force for preserving unity.

The PA worked especially hard to keep Islamic institutions out of Hamas's hands. The PA's Ministry of Waqf and Religious Affairs, as in Arab states, subsidized and controlled clerics and mosques, giving benefits to those deemed sufficiently supportive of the government. The PA thus had its own corps of Islamic officials more numerous than supporters of the radical Islamic opposition. But even those loyal to Arafat often held theological and political views close to those of Hamas—a group to which a number of them formerly belonged.

During the Muslim holy month of Ramadan, the PA published announcements in newspapers warning that anyone seen violating the fast (i.e., eating, drinking, or smoking in public) would be punished with a minimum of one day in jail.[62] This was certainly restrictive for Christians, yet it was also one of many ways in which the PA's integration of Islam into state and regime was intended to undercut Hamas's appeal.

This religious establishment was particularly important in advancing the PA's claim to East Jerusalem. The PA appointed clerics to replace Jordan's men managing Islamic holy sites there. Its own mufti, Ikrama Sabri, issued religious edicts prohibiting land sales to Jews and forbidding East Jerusalem Palestinians to apply for Israeli citizenship. In weekly sermons at al-Aqsa mosque, he urged violence against Israel and the United States. Sabri declared, "I am the mufti, appointed by the [PA], of all the Palestinian people, in Jerusalem, in the West Bank, Gaza, and in Israel."[63]

Some Christian Palestinians were nervous over their future, given an uncertain political climate and radical Islamic movements, prompting them to emigrate in disproportionately large numbers. But they often saw the PA as their protector from Hamas, and there was no significant discrimination against the Christian minority. On the contrary, Arafat worked to reassure them, frequently speaking about the unity of Palestinians, making himself patron of the Christmas celebrations in Bethlehem, and reserving six seats for Christians in the PLC. PA-backed priests continued the previous nationalist trend, popular among Palestinian Christians, of trying to take control of some denominations (and their substantial real estate holdings) from the foreign European clerics who had long had authority over them.

Palestinian society under the PA had become a mixing bowl in other respects as well. As tens of thousands of Palestinians returned from exile, the resulting friction was less than might have been expected. Some Insiders complained that the returnees were getting the best jobs and other privileges. Most upset were young Fatah men who had fought and been imprisoned, and who expected high posts for which they might not have been qualified. Some sources recounted that even Palestinian schoolchildren divided into separate Outsider and Insider cliques. If this Outsider-Insider gap were to widen and become bitter, the PA could face considerable problems.[64]

Born and raised in Kuwait, Abd al-Hakim Zurayqi returned in 1996, and a year later he finally a good job in the Department of Refugee Affairs in Ramallah, though half his salary still went to rent. He found "a huge cultural gap" between himself and relatives in a small village "that I simply don't know how to bridge." He added, "I've come to realize that . . . the beautiful images we had about the nature of people here are contradictory to what we found." Still, despite all the challenges, Zurayqi asserted: "The moment I set foot in Palestine, I felt as if a far away thing, with roots inside me, has come back. It was my soul."[65]

For twenty-five-year-old Rana Lahham, returning with her parents, "it is hard to adjust to life here. There is nothing to do and no place to go." Born in Beirut and raised in Lebanon and Jordan, Lahham complained that her village relatives "think I'm too open and too direct and I always feel as if I'm under their scrutiny. It is as if being a returnee makes you different from everyone else when you really aren't."[66]

These frictions seemed manageable, though, and likely to be gradually resolved over time. The PA's problem in this respect lay far more in the difficulty of attracting back talented or wealthy Palestinians who had been residing or studying in the West. Political and living conditions in the PA lands and criticism of Arafat often seemed to furnish a good excuse for those abroad not to come back and to refrain from doing more to help build their country.

Rivalries between towns and regions were another potential issue the PA had to watch carefully. Arafat tried to appoint people from all parts of the country and launched a campaign to strengthen the PA's hold on Israeli-ruled East Jerusalem. The PA had twenty unofficial offices and even its own governor in East Jerusalem, which Israel argued were violations of bilateral agreements.[67] It took over or founded schools, hospitals, and youth clubs. Plainclothes PA security officers patrolled streets, gathered intelligence, and tried to enforce PA directives there.[68] But any official or effective PA role in ruling part of the city could result only from an agreement reached after very difficult negotiations with Israel.

In the absence of East Jerusalem, Ramallah became the West Bank's new economic center and even the PA's virtual capital. It contained the main offices of several ministries, the central bureau of statistics and television studios, as well as many factories and offices. Wealthy Palestinians were investing in new construction, property and businesses there.[69]

This provoked some jealousy from other towns. Said Kan'an, a PNC member from Nablus, the second-largest city, complained bitterly, "There exists a clear policy to isolate Nablus," since no ministry headquarters had been located there. "Nablus and the rest of the north constitute over half of the population of the West Bank. And there are only two ministers to represent them."[70]

More important was the potential for rifts between the refugees, living in twenty-one camps now under the PA's jurisdiction, and indigenous citizens. The refugees tended to be poorer and were not ready to give up their personal property claims from 1948, which made them generally less willing to give up the idea of trying to incorporate all of Israel into a Palestinian Arab state.[71] "The refugees were harmed the most" by Israel's creation, insisted on a right of return, "and will not settle for anything less," said Ahmad Hanun, projects' director at the PLO's Department of Refugee Affairs. Despite having made the most sacrifices during the intifada, refugees usually benefited less from the new situation, Hanun asserted. They were "very depressed and they have legitimate concerns about their future. Many people in Balata refugee camp are still holding onto the keys of the homes they lost in 1948."[72] Historically, there had been a stigma among Palestinians about moving out of refugee camps, since staying there was seen as a symbol that they would accept nothing less than resettlement in their pre-1948 homes, now inside Israel. In the new situation there were some signs of change, but the official PA line was still—in the words of Asad Abd al-Rahman, head of the PLO's refugee committee—that there would be no resettlement of people from camps in PA territory before a full peace agreement. "Refugee camps were and remain the temporary home for our people, on the road of return to our homeland," he told a cheering crowd.[73] Yet this also meant that the PA did not wage a serious campaign to move refugees into better and less crowded housing.

Both the PLO and PA donated money to improve conditions in the camps.[74] But the PA also tried to charge people there rent and taxes in some cases, creating resentment.[75] So long as the PA could still maintain that it championed a right of return, the camps would remain supportive. Indeed, Fatah's long organizational efforts and leadership during the intifada made it stronger in the camps than in other sectors of society. Yet giving up the demand and hope for a return, an inescapable step if there were to be any peace treaty with Israel, could create internal problems for the PA from this sector.

The PA itself enjoyed overwhelming, if not always enthusiastic, support from its citizens. At the same time, though, Palestinian public opinion, which had remained roughly constant for a long time, now changed with events. In general terms, the people increasingly backed the peace process and gradually shifted away from supporting armed attacks against Israelis, though backing for violence against Israel was still high and increased temporarily at moments of crisis. Support for Arafat and Fatah remained strong, though variable, and backing for the opposition declined.[76] Surprisingly, these trends were strongest in Gaza, historically a more radical and pro-Hamas area, presumably because that territory was about 85 percent in PA hands and already functioning more like a state.[77]

Trends in Palestinian thinking toward more support for a negotiated, compromise peace and rejection of violence were already clear in the 1993–1996 period as, despite delays, hope for progress was periodically fulfilled. In January 1994, 51 percent of Palestinians supported the negotiations, albeit far more "cautiously" than "strongly," rising to over 65 percent in the first half of 1995. In an August–September 1995 poll, as the PA moved toward taking over West Bank towns, support for the peace process reached 71 percent. While the Palestinian-Israeli confrontation of autumn 1996 temporarily radicalized Palestinian thinking against the peace process, this was soon reversed, and support reached a record 79.3 percent by year's end. By 1998, Palestinian backing for peacemaking efforts with Israel had fallen back but remained relatively stable at 68 percent, compared to 59 percent among Israelis who supported the existing peace process.[78]

Even students, the most hard-line Palestinian sector, gave increasing approval for negotiations, growing from 44 percent in January 1994 to 62 percent in August–September 1995, with opposition dropping from 47 percent to 24 percent over the same period. In October 1995, after the signing of the Oslo II agreement, support for Hamas leader Ahmad Yasin declined from 20 percent to 14 percent, and for PFLP head George Habash from 7 percent to 3 percent.[79]

Popular support for Arafat was variable but generally strong, rising from 44 percent in November 1994 to 58 percent in October 1995.[80] By August 1996 Arafat's standing had improved further, with 72.3 percent of those polled in Gaza (though only 47.1 percent of West Bankers) saying he was doing a good job as the PA's head. Arafat was always the overwhelming choice when Palestinians were asked whom they most trusted. In December 1997, for example, he was the number-one pick of 46.4 percent of those polled.[81]

While remaining relatively high, Palestinian support for armed attacks against Israeli targets did decline—as long as the peace process progressed—from 57 percent in November 1994 to 46 percent in February 1995, and down to 33 percent in March after several major suicide attacks by Hamas and Islamic Jihad. In August–September 1995, only 18 percent of Palestinians supported attacks on Israeli civilian targets. Even among students, support for anti-civilian attacks dropped from 72 percent in November 1994 to 30 percent in August–September 1995.[82]

With Netanyahu in office, the process slowed, and after the September 1996 clashes, support for violence shifted sharply upward, with almost 53 percent of Palestinians approving attacks against Israel while 37.4 percent objected.[83] This dropped to 35.5 percent approval of attacks—as against 40 percent opposition—at the end of 1996, and rose slightly to about 44 percent approval by the summer of 1998. By April 1999, Palestinians approved armed struggle by 56 to 36 percent, but were against suicide bombings by 66 to 26 percent.[84]

While this bellicosity did not necessarily equal direct support for Hamas, it created the environment in which the PA's anti-terrorist efforts were constrained. The popular endorsement for murdering Israelis had shifted from a strategy for destroying Israel to a tactic for intensifying pressure to end the occupation. Killing Jewish settlers was always especially approved. These attitudes placed a severe strain on the peace process and limited the PA's maneuvering room.

Yet there also remained more basic hope of finding a resolution than many outsiders appreciated. By August 1996, 79.6 percent of Gazans felt optimistic or somewhat optimistic, while 68.7 percent of West Bankers felt the same way.[85] Even in December 1997, when the peace process was basically frozen, 59 percent of Palestinians and 62.5 percent of Israelis pronounced themselves generally optimistic that a peace settlement would eventually be reached.[86] Perhaps that was because they understood, far better than many foreign observers, how far the two sides had come despite the tremendous continuing difficulties.

But this did not negate deep Palestinian skepticism about the process. In September 1993, just 45 percent believed that the Oslo agreement would produce a Palestinian state. This figure hit 55 percent in February 1994 but fell to 51 percent by the end of 1996. By mid-1998, with negotiations at a standstill, only 37 percent of Palestinians believed that the process would lead to establishment of an independent state.[87] More immediately, though, 64.2 percent of Palestinians (almost 77 percent of Gazans and over 50 percent of West Bankers) said that they felt more secure with the PA ruling them. This contrasted sharply with the fact that only 9 percent of Israelis felt personally more secure since the peace process began.[88]

How can these diverse results be comprehended? Palestinians wanted to believe that the peace process would produce a state but often doubted it, mistrusting Israel's willingness to withdraw. Hence, while some saw violence as counterproductive, Hamas supporters considered killings an alternative to talks, while many PA supporters mistakenly thought that terrorism gave their side more leverage to force Israel out of the territories. Certainly, Palestinians did not feel that they derived any economic benefits from the peace process. But they had received important dividends in terms of national morale, social gains, feelings of personal security, and political changes.

Most intriguing was a Palestinian reinterpretation of the peace process itself. While originally many saw Israel as the advocate of the accords against Palestinian interests, now the PA was seen as the defender against Netanyahu's attempt to alter or abandon them. Palestinians who endorsed the peace process did so because they believed it would produce a Palestinian state in the West Bank and Gaza. There were two arguments among Palestinians who opposed the peace process. The radical approach of Hamas and other violent opposition groups (along with some radical Fatah Outsiders) was to continue trying to destroy Israel and replace it with a Palestinian state on all the land between the Jordan River and the Mediterranean Sea. The alternative militant view of many in Fatah including Insider critics of Arafat, was that the agreements were acceptable but Israel would only implement them under pressure.

Ironically, the Netanyahu government's policy convinced more Palestinians that the agreements were in their own interests, even while frustrating them over implementation. As Israeli leaders argued that the accords favored the Palestinians and demanded too many Israeli concessions, this idea became easier for Palestinians to accept. After 1996, the radical argument became weaker even as the militant one became reinforced.[89]

Consequently, mass support for Arafat, the PA, Fatah, and the security services remained strong despite opposition groups' efforts and regardless of corruption, economic problems, and lack of democratic and human rights. These were their leaders, and there seemed no viable alternative. Fear of punishment, hope for favors, patriotism, and traditional respect for hierarchy combined to promote popular support for the PA.

5

THE NEW PALESTINIAN
POLITICAL ELITE

The creation of the PA began a new era for the Palestinian people's leadership. Many of the PLO hierarchy's main figures were pushed aside, while others from the West Bank and Gaza joined the elite for the first time. New loyalties, tactics, issues, and conflicts replaced those which had driven PLO members and groups between the 1960s and early 1990s.

The new PA political elite, like its predecessor, was overwhelmingly male, Muslim, and Fatah, made up of people who had proved their dedication to the movement. Reaching the top level required enjoying Arafat's favor. But Arafat was willing to work with almost everyone, including critics. From his experience in the PLO era, he understood the need to build a broad front. Now, however, instead of diverse groups engaged in armed struggle, his coalition was based on a balance between Insiders and Outsiders, towns and regions, as well as a range of social backgrounds and political views. Except for mayoral posts, wealth and a large supportive clan were not prerequisites for participation.

There were three main routes to joining the leadership. First, there were those who had played important roles in the PLO or Fatah in exile and worked closely with Arafat. If proportionately more Outsiders than Insiders were pro-Arafat, this was because many leading Outsiders who opposed Arafat's policy refused to return. Outsiders came back to work for the PA itself or to help build a state within the framework established by the new regime. These people, in Khalil Shiqaqi's words, "owed their positions to Arafat rather than to their own power within the community." Their ideology and experience put the priority on national over democratic agendas.[1] Yet they had also served the movement for decades, making sacrifices and taking risks.

Second, there were senior Insider Fatah activists who had organized an underground movement, fought Israel, and often served several prison sentences. While few intifada street activists gained top or even mid-level posts, this was largely a function of their youth rather than willful discrimination. After all, when the PA was first established, most of them were still under twenty-five years old. They lacked the administrative and other skills needed in higher PA positions. But some of them would inevitably rise as generational change took place.

Third, there were Insider businesspeople and professionals who had long supported the nationalist movement and Fatah while pursuing their careers. Many of them were from wealthy, prominent families, but this did not dictate their political views. For example, professionals from powerful, or at least well-off, backgrounds had long provided the Palestinian left's leadership and now supplied the pro-democracy and human rights activists too. Even if they wore suits and ties, they had broken with the conservatism of the traditionalist notables to espouse a revolutionary cause. Some had become well known as PLO-approved mayors or negotiators with Israel during the 1980s and the pre-Oslo talks.

A popular but simplistic analysis suggested that the PA's main political divide was between older, Outsider PLO or Fatah bureaucrats allied with wealthy Palestinians and democracy-oriented young Insiders who had fought the intifada. While there was some basis for this view, it was very misleading about the nature of Palestinian politics and the PA's composition.

For example, while some Insider fighters became prominent critics of the PA (Khadir, Barghuti), others with equally good records in the struggle, including poor family backgrounds and years spent in Israeli prisons, became the PA's most dedicated protectors (such as the heads of the Preventive Security police units, Jibril Rajjub and Muhammad Dahlan) as well as its political supporters.

These dissidents were also far more numerous on the West Bank than they were in Gaza, where Fatah was more solidly behind Arafat. Hamas's past strength in Gaza persuaded Fatah members there of the need to stand solidly united behind Arafat.[2] The Palestinian political situation was better in Gaza because the paucity of Jewish settlements and the PA's control of the vast majority of territory made Palestinian progress there seem more extensive. In contrast to the fiercely independent Marwan al-Barghuti, Fatah's West Bank chief, Arafat appointed Zakariyya al-Agha as Gaza's Fatah leader. Agha was a perfect stand-in for Arafat. Coming from a wealthy family, he was a veteran activist but with neither a strong base of support nor a forceful personality. He had not been an open Fatah member but rather functioned publicly as one of the independents involved in negotiating with Israel. Several Gaza Fatah and PLO leaders resigned to protest Arafat's choice but could not overturn it.[3] Continued Fatah infighting there sometimes led to shoot-outs but caused Arafat few political problems.[4]

Just as the Insider revolutionaries were not united against Arafat, not all Outsiders or wealthy Insiders favored him. There were many critics of Arafat among the Outsiders (Khuri, Ta'amri, Hani al-Hasan) and also among wealthy or professional Insiders (Ashrawi, Abd al-Shafi, Abd al-Salah). The traditional elite played a much smaller political role in Palestinian politics than it ever had before, and wealthy or professional people—like Khuri and Husayni—needed good movement credentials to gain any real political power. Businesspeople as a group were less openly critical of the PA because they needed good relations with the rulers to survive economically, while privately grumbling about competition from PA-owned or favored companies. In contrast, professionals—teachers, doctors, pharmacists, lawyers, and engineers—were more likely to be outspoken.

In general, though, Arafat did not hold grudges against individuals or discriminate against any sector. The door remained open to everyone. While keeping some young rebels off Fatah's parliamentary election list, Arafat was happy to reconcile with most of those who won seats as independents. He was quite ready to accept anyone who was willing to cooperate with him, even if such people continued to be critical or held some different views. Critics who accepted cabinet posts (Khuri, Salah, Ashrawi) might conclude that they could not effectively change the PA and resign, but they were never fired.

To a large extent, one's place on the Palestinian political spectrum was determined by individual choice and institutional base. In choosing sides, each Palestinian—and especially every Fatah member—had to make a personal judgment. For those who accepted the peace process at all, being a PA supporter or critic depended on whether one put the priority on taking a nationalist patriotic stand behind Arafat's leadership or on battling for democracy and human rights. Were the latter goals an obstacle or necessary precondition to achieving a state? Would democracy's absence at the start inevitably doom a future Palestine to dictatorship? Or was the current phase a special situation, requiring absolute unity and Arafat's primacy, that would not necessarily continue after independence?

There were no simple answers, and many individuals held conflicting views on these issues. Some Arafat loyalists heatedly criticized him in private conversation, while even angry critics such as Khuri and Barghuti rallied behind leader and "party" when necessary. For those not part of the Fatah movement, it was easier to criticize the PA and demand more democracy or human rights. Those who rejected the peace process also used the demand for democracy and human rights—at times quite cynically—to undermine a regime whose legitimacy and policy they would have opposed regardless of its behavior on those specific issues.

As happens elsewhere, individuals' political stance was also linked to their institutional situation. Those in PA, national Fatah posts, or the police had a vested interest in maintaining the executive's power. Those whose main power base was in the PLC or local Fatah movement sought to promote their role and resented Arafat's ignoring them. Even some strong Arafat loyalists in the PLC voted to pass laws aimed at strengthening the legislature at the chief executive's expense.

One of the PA's and Fatah's most urgent and most delicate tasks was to combine former Outsiders and the Insiders into a single leadership group. Arafat optimistically assessed the situation: "We have merged Palestinian establishments based abroad with those based on Palestinian land and transferred their cadres in order to contribute to building the homeland. Everybody is building the homeland, hand by hand, because it is the homeland of all Palestinians."[5] If this picture was excessively rosy, he did solve this problem more completely than might have been expected.

The thinking and interests of indigenous Palestinians in the West Bank and Gaza as a group diverged somewhat from those of the exiled 1948 refugees. Outsider PLO leaders never met Israelis and could more easily misperceive their views, strength, and policies. Living relatively comfortably in exile, they could afford to dream of a revolution lasting additional decades to regain their original homes that were now inside Israel. Indigenous West Bankers or Gazans in Fatah had a more realistic perception of Israel's strength and a greater incentive to end the occupation sooner rather than later. Their own homes would be within the projected state. Thus, Insider pro-PLO and Fatah activists had generally urged more speed and moderation to find a solution, ultimately helping to push the PLO toward the Oslo agreement.

Palestinians from the West Bank and Gaza had always been underrepresented in the top PLO and Fatah leadership.[6] Of fifteen Executive Committee members serving between 1988 and 1991, only one—Muhammad Milhim, a West Bank mayor deported by Israel in 1980—lived for any length of time in the occupied territories. And even he was dropped from the Executive Committee in 1991.[7] The Fatah Central Committee had a similar composition. It was most revealing that when the Central Committee decided in 1989 to add some members to represent those who were struggling in the territories, the two men chosen to fill these slots had not even been there for two decades.[8]

After Oslo, both leading bodies dropped members who opposed the peace process and added Insider leaders. Of the PLO Executive Committee's eighteen members in 1991, only three obtained major PA posts (Arafat, Abd Rabbu, and Minister of Finance Muhammad Nashashibi). Two others also held important jobs (Abdallah Hurani and chief negotiator Mahmud Abbas).[9] Except for Abd Rabbu, the leaders of smaller PLO groups, who had once played a pivotal role on the Executive Committee, were deprived of their former veto power and ceased to matter very much. Of the Fatah Central Committee's eighteen members in 1989, only nine became leading figures in the PA (Arafat, Abu Mazin, Intisar Abu Wazir, Ahmad Khuri, Hakam Bal'awi, Abbas Zaki, Tayyib Abd al-Rahim, Nasir Yusuf, and Sakhr Abu Nasir).[10] Most of the others had resigned or become inactive.[11]

That meant that just one-third of those at the top level of Fatah or the PLO had been able to transfer that status to the PA's structure. Similarly, among the PLC's eighty-eight members, only nine had been significant figures in the exiled PLO, and four of them had only held diplomatic posts in the organization, while three others were technocrats. The only two figures with independent political standing among them were Wazir (who did not reach the top level until after her husband's death in 1988) and Abbas Zaki.[12] The same picture of new people being promoted into the leadership emerges with regard to Arafat's cabinets.[13]

The PLO's structure as a loose united front—leading a people divided by ideology, geography, and organizational loyalties—had been a central factor in shaping its destiny and leadership. Arafat proclaimed, "The PLO is not one of many Palestinian institutions, it is the all-embracing Palestinian institution that comprises all the institutions of the Palestinian people."[14] Yet this all-encompassing breadth, and the need to bridge so many different Palestinian views and interests, weakened the organization.

The PLO was the only movement, Arafat claimed in 1990, that "simultaneously performs the functions of a state and a revolution—a state which has yet to be established." It brought Palestinians pride and international recognition, transforming them "from a refugee people waiting in queues for charity and alms into a people fighting for freedom." But it was not, in fact, a state and that made for many institutional problems. After all, as Arafat added, half of its "people are under occupation and the other half in the Diaspora," with "each community living in different circumstances," and with a "difficult Arab [political] environment."[15]

As a result of this situation and its requirements, Arafat and the PLO obsessively sought to have as close as possible to 100 percent support from Palestinians. Unable to impose unanimity, Arafat often bowed to hard-line demands in order to preserve unity, adopting the lowest common denominator as his strategy. His minimal control over PLO member groups, their dispersion in multiple states, the interference of Arab regimes, and rampant decentralization made Arafat more coordinator than dictator.

Despite a cult of personal adulation surrounding him, Arafat's hesitant, compromising approach was quite different from the dominating, centralizing style typical of many Third World revolutionary leaders. Arafat's indecisiveness and refusal to impose his power on the PLO's many groups and factions may have originally sprung from his personality, but it was also necessary for him to preserve a loose but overriding sense of unity while ensuring his own popularity and legitimacy. With Palestinians so divided, Arafat became the only universally accepted symbol of nation and movement despite—or perhaps even more because of—his personal diffidence.

But in the new era of the PA and state-building, a very different situation and institutional framework prevailed. Arafat was now chief executive of a government, a single institution with a chain of command and day-to-day administrative responsibilities. With the PA in power, noted Ziyad Abu Amr, "PLO institutions such as the Executive Committee and the PNC are slipping into oblivion."[16]

Many Palestinians, however, still believed the PLO to be extremely important.[17] A typical poll showed great ambiguity on this point among residents of the West Bank and Gaza Strip. Asked who was the Palestinian people's legitimate representative, 18 percent replied the PA, over 25 percent thought it was the PLO, and over 38 percent said it was both of them.[18] Even Arafat gave lip service to the PLO's continuing importance as an institution and source of legitimacy which "has established the PA and legalized its program and positions."[19] The PLO Executive Committee continued to meet periodically to endorse Arafat's policies.[20]

Still, in practice, power had clearly shifted, and while being on the Executive Committee was an important credential, this applied only to those who continued to work with Arafat and live in the PA's territory.[21] Many PLO institutions were transferred to the PA, physically moved from the PLO's Tunis headquarters to its West Bank or Gaza. Other PLO agencies were shut down or faced budget reductions, while diplomatic offices abroad were increasingly controlled directly by the PA.[22]

The power balance between the PLO, PNC, and PA continued to be hotly debated. Those who criticized or opposed Arafat's policies thought they could use the PLO and PNC as platforms for gaining leverage against the PA. Another factor was concern over the representation and views of Palestinians outside the PA territories, who had no direct relationship with the PA.[23] A third issue was that those whose power came from the PLO and PNC feared that their own role would disappear as those organizations declined.

Jamal Hilal, a PNC member, complained: "The role of the PNC and the [PLO] . . . is limited lately only to providing legitimacy for the [PA's] agreements. Actually the current leadership is so dominant that it makes daily decisions without consulting the institutions mentioned above as it used to be. For example, the only decision the PNC is involved with is changing the Palestinian National Charter and nothing more." This problem was accentuated, he added, by the fact that the PLO was itself at a relatively weak point when the PA was formed. One danger was that there would be no national institutions to represent all the Palestinian people. At the same time, the centralization of power and finances in the PA also weakened those opposition groups that had formerly played a coequal role in the PLO structure.[24]

The one PLO exile figure retaining any major significance at all was Faruq Qaddumi, a founder of Fatah, head of the PLO political department, member of the PLO Executive Committee and Fatah Central Committee. Qaddumi had been so popular that he was the only one other than Arafat elected unanimously to the Central Committee in 1989.[25]

Born in Nablus in 1930, Qaddumi grew up in Jaffa, but his family returned as refugees to his hometown in 1948. Qaddumi met Arafat when they were Cairo University students, then worked for Kuwait's health ministry and the ARAMCO oil company in Saudi Arabia in the 1950s before joining the PLO, where he rose to head its political department in 1973. Qaddumi favored a close alliance with Syria, no compromise on the PLO's traditional goals, and opposition to the Oslo agreement. "In my opinion," Qaddumi declared, "the Arab land wherever it may be is my land and I do not differentiate between Syrian land or Palestinian land irrespective of whether it belonged to this state or that. I am a Pan-Arab man."[26]

Although Qaddumi was often called the PLO's foreign minister, their policy differences had made Arafat increasingly bypass him during the 1980s. Qaddumi continued to represent the PLO in the Organization for African Unity and the Arab League and in talks with Syria. But the PA's own international activity further reduced his role.[27] "I am opposed to the Oslo Accord, and anything that stems from [it] is not acceptable to me," Qaddumi said.[28] By staying abroad, Qaddumi further isolated himself and became largely irrelevant. Arafat and the PA "stopped listening to me," he admitted.[29]

He demanded that Israel withdraw unconditionally and immediately from the West Bank and interpreted every event, such as Rabin's temporary closure of the territories after terrorist attacks, as "conclusive evidence" that Israel was not interested in peace. "Half of the Palestinian people have been abandoned" without an end to the occupation, he complained, referring to those still outside the country.[30] While avoiding direct personal attacks on Arafat, Qaddumi insisted that the PA's policy would "prejudice the inalienable rights of the Palestinian people." Only "the continuation of Palestinian struggle . . . no matter how long this will take" would bring success.[31]

Qaddumi even launched a short-lived, ineffective campaign to undermine Arafat and reverse his course by building an alliance between hard-line PLO and PNC officials, Hamas and other opposition groups, and Syria. In 1995 Qaddumi went to Damascus for three days of meetings with all these forces.[32] The effort culminated in an October 4, 1995, statement signed by nine Executive Committee members (among them Qaddumi himself, Mahmud Darwish, Abdallah Hurani, Shafiq al-Hut, Mahmud Isma'il, and Taysir Khalid) and endorsed by two others (Samir Ghawsha and Jamal al-Surani) rejecting the Oslo II agreement. This revolt threatened to leave Arafat with a minority on the Executive Committee, and he was saved only by the resignations of several of these dissidents.[33]

After failing to take over the PLO, Qaddumi continued to insist, "I will not return to the homeland as long as that return entails the permission of the Israeli occupier." By the time he hinted at a change of mind in 1998, it was too late. Israel refused to let him come back.[34]

Meanwhile, Arafat was consolidating his control over both the PLO and Fatah, outmaneuvering the anti-Oslo dissidents. In addition to ensuring his control over the PLO's executive branch, Arafat also maintained leadership of the PNC, its parliament. Arafat had always controlled the PNC, which had about 450 active members, through a coalition of PLO officials, Fatah activists, and pro-Arafat independents—middle-class technocrats, bureaucrats, and businessmen—who far outnumbered other PLO groups' supporters. More seats were held secretly by West Bank and Gaza residents whom Israel blocked from active participation. Now Arafat expanded the PNC further by adding all 88 PLC members and about 100 more Insiders. The new, expanded PNC had 730 members.[35]

One of the PLO's commitments under the agreements with Israel was to abrogate its thirty-year-old Charter calling for Israel's destruction through armed struggle. While the Charter no longer set the PLO's program, changing it had enormous symbolic importance for both sides as an irreversible step toward a new, peace-oriented Palestinian worldview. This action could be taken only by a two-thirds vote of PNC members. Israel agreed to admit all PNC delegates, including those still engaged in violence, to facilitate a session on the PA's territory. Arafat rejected efforts by some hard-line members to postpone the session. Qaddumi and some others refused to attend at all.[36] Setting the tone for the session, Fatah organized large rallies in March 1996 in Gaza under the slogans "Yes to peace, No to violence" and "Terrorism is our enemy," to protest recent bombings.[37]

The PNC met in Gaza, April 22–24, 1996, and after a heated debate, decided—reportedly by a 504–54 vote (with 14 abstaining and 97 absent) to remove the Charter's passages that were contrary to its new commitments and to have the PNC legal committee look into composing a new Charter.[38] The Israeli and U.S. governments hailed this action as an important step toward peace. On three different occasions thereafter, Arafat wrote formal letters certifying abrogation of specific articles of the Charter.[39]

The PNC's other main task was electing a new eighteen-member Executive Committee far more favorable to Arafat's policy.[40] It added six new members, including—for the first time—resident Insiders, who now numbered five of the eighteen members. The new additions were Zakariyya al-Agha; Faysal al-Husayni; Ghassan Shaq'a; Emile Jarjou'i, a PLC member from Jerusalem who held the Christian seat; Riyad al-Khudri, the head of al-Azhar University, who was close to Fatah; and Asad Abd al-Rahman, the PA cabinet secretary and a veteran PLO official. All but Abd al-Rahman were Insiders.[41]

Many anti-Oslo dissidents were not reelected at the PNC meeting, though there were still five members who opposed the Oslo agreements: Qaddumi and the representatives of the small Arab Liberation Front, PFLP, DFLP, and Palestine Liberation Front. Only Qaddumi remained really active among the hard-liners.[42] The next month Arafat held the first Executive Committee meeting ever on PA soil, with the rebels deciding to stay away. He appointed Mahmud Abbas to replace Jamal al-Surani, an outspoken critic of the peace process, as the committee's secretary.[43]

As he secured control over the PLO, Arafat was also engaged in the ultimately more complex task of restructuring Fatah. Although he had an overwhelming majority on the Fatah Central Committee, there were also many problems of adjustment within his own organization.[44]

Next to Arafat and Qaddumi, the most important Fatah leader was Mahmud Abbas, the group's third official representative on the Executive Committee[45] and former PLO ambassador to Moscow. Abbas had helped negotiate the Oslo agreements and had even replaced the hardline Qaddumi as PLO "foreign minister" for the October 1993 signing ceremony on the White House lawn. Afterward, however, Abbas was also critical of Arafat's handling of the peace process and the lack of democracy. In his case, though, the problem was less one of ideology than of anger that Arafat had not given him an important enough role in the PA.[46]

When Arafat satisfied Abbas's personal demands by making him the Executive Committee's secretary and head of the Palestinian negotiating team, Abbas went to live in the PA territories, saying in 1995 that he had been fearful "for the experiment because there are many obstacles" but now felt more reassured because the PA "has passed the more difficult test of controlling security in its areas."[47] Upon his return, he began cultivating politicians and security officials, building a claim to succeed Arafat but never acting so boldly as to incur criticism or Arafat's wrath. Abbas was not charismatic, but perhaps this made him seem less threatening to Arafat. He was a moderate who wanted to make the peace process work, so long as it led to a Palestinian state. If those diplomatic efforts failed, he warned, "we may be the last generation of Palestinians that believes in peace . . . The word 'peace' may become a bad word."[48]

Arafat also asserted his control over Fatah. He had convened a Fatah congress in Gaza, attended by 469 delegates, in October 1995, which endorsed his policies and added two Insider members to the Central Committee: Husayni and Agha. In November the Central Committee established councils to organize Fatah's campaign for the upcoming parliamentary elections. West Bank Fatah members had held primaries in 1995 to choose leaders to run for the PLC elections. Arafat rejected the outcome and assembled his own slate, and Fatah threatened any members who ran independently with expulsion, a threat that went unfulfilled after several dozen activists ignored that warning.[49]

While this was universally seen as undemocratic, Arafat had reasonable cause for doing so. The primaries had selected younger activists who had come to the fore as grassroots leaders during the intifada. Arafat, though, wanted a broader representation, including non-Fatah people and returning Outsiders. A number of those he did not choose ran as independents despite being discouraged from doing so, and a dozen of them won. About two-thirds of these victors became Arafat supporters in the PLC, but the rest became his most severe and energetic critics.[50]

Ibrahim Kar'in, a Fatah activist, pointed out how the group's structure gave Arafat much leverage: "Fatah isn't an organized party [with] a hierarchy that makes decisions. With the Palestinians it's more elastic . . . We all go to [Arafat] and want him to solve our problems. Even if I fight with my wife—I go to Arafat. That's why everyone wants his blessing" for their candidacy and career ambitions.[51]

Nabil Amr, a Fatah member since its inception, suggested that Fatah's not being a party promoted a more stable, pluralist system. Since Fatah dominated all PA institutions, a higher profile and more disciplined structure would raise the specter of a Fatah dictatorship. At any rate, making Fatah a coherent, effective body would not be easy, given years of internal chaos and the fact that "the decisions . . . taken are usually forgotten the next day."[52]

Still, there were limits to Fatah's flexibility. When ten PLC members from Fatah voted against Arafat's government in a June 1996 vote of confidence, the organization's leading body decided to take disciplinary measures against them.[53] The Central Committee formed a twelve-member "emergency council" to revitalize Fatah activities in the West Bank and Gaza, providing a way to bypass the local West Bank leadership that had been a key center of anti-Arafat agitation.[54]

While Fatah, especially its highest circles, supported Arafat's political line, the organization also remained more radical than did the PA. Fatah bodies constantly urged Arafat to free all the Hamas and Islamic Jihad prisoners or to take a harder line toward Israel in negotiations.[55] Some Fatah leaders claimed in the organization's internal bulletin that since the PA was a united front government for all Palestinians, Fatah had a right to criticize it and pursue contradictory policies. This challenge was extremely serious in theory but was not implemented in practice.[56]

Fatah's internal debates and its criticisms of Arafat sprang from four intertwined issues. One was the personal ambition and disaffection of those left off Fatah's election list or excluded from positions of power or influence. A second set of arguments emerged from some Fatah members' call for more democracy, especially a balance between the executive branch and PLC. Third, a number of Fatah cadres either completely opposed the Oslo agreements or at least proposed adopting a far more militant strategy toward the peace process. Finally, there was an institutional interest. Fatah's expertise was in struggle, mobilization, and violence, so naturally promoting such tactics would seem to return Fatah and those specialists back to the forefront of leadership.

At the same time, though, even most of the minority of hard-line PLO veterans, intifada activists, and unreconstructed propagandists who criticized Arafat or called for radical deeds knew that there was no easy alternative. It was obvious that frustration frequently promoted tough rhetoric, yet the militant words were rarely reflected in action.

At least six Fatah Central Committee members, of whom three held important positions in the PA, continued to oppose the Oslo agreement. All of them were Outsiders and veteran PLO officials: Abbas Zaki,[57] head of Fatah's operations; Sakr Habash (Abu Nizar), chief of the Revolutionary Committee (the body below the Central Committee) and Fatah's ideological mobilization department; Salim al-Za'nun, the PNC's head; Muhammad Jihad, a Palestine Liberation Army (PLA) officer who had rebelled against Arafat in the 1980s; Rafiq al-Natsha, a former Central Committee member elected to the PLC; and Hani al-Hasan.[58] Zaki, Habash, and Za'nun still enjoyed Arafat's favor. Habash, from a 1948 refugee family that had fled to Nablus, had been one of the first to join Arafat's forces in Jordan after the 1967 war. Za'nun represented the 1948 refugees within the PNC's framework.

These men found it hard to adjust to the wrenching changes Arafat and the Oslo process had introduced. In contrast to the dissatisfactions of other Fatah cadres angry about events, their main complaint was not that Netanyahu was breaking agreements or that the process was advancing too slowly. They simply did not want to accept a two-state solution at all, voicing views little different from those of Hamas. As Muhammad Jihad put it, "Has there been a leadership in history which ceded four-fifths of its homeland's territory [the 1948 territory] in addition to abandoning two-thirds of its people, and is now bargaining over the remaining fifth of its homeland [the West Bank and Gaza]?"[59]

In a June 1994 article Habash also argued for continued revolutionary struggle: "The future role of Fatah should be a natural continuation of its previous role of resistance, armed struggle and safeguarding the Intifada . . . seeking to create a democratic Palestinian State on all Palestinian land, where Moslems, Christians and Jews live side by side without racial or religious discrimination." Even Israeli withdrawal from the West Bank, Gaza Strip, and East Jerusalem would merely constitute "a first step in the struggle that should be resumed by different methods in order to achieve all strategic goals."[60]

In February 1995, with the Rabin government still in power, Habash was urging all Palestinian forces to unite in finding an alternative to the Oslo accord. "Fatah has not laid down arms," he told an interviewer. "Our options are still open. And we will continue to work against the Israeli occupation by all means, first and foremost the intifada, armed struggle, and working to reduce the Palestinian areas directly controlled by the occupation army."[61]

Habash and his colleagues did not fit the conventional view that Outsiders were betraying Insider revolutionaries in order to obtain power. On the contrary, the radical Outsiders charged the Insiders with opportunism, saying that they were so eager to end the occupation that they were ready to surrender their larger claim on all of Israel in order to obtain their local West Bank and Gaza areas. The Outsiders, claimed Habash, had no such illusions. They recognized that "the shortcomings in the accord, the unfair terms stipulated in it, Israeli evasions, and the donors' procrastination are all aimed at thwarting the [PA's] task—which has prompted many people to believe that what started as Gaza and Jericho First could end up as Gaza and Jericho First and Last."[62]

Arafat did not fire these people but let Habash, Zaki, Za'nun, and others who agreed with them continue to hold key positions. This did not mean that he accepted their ideas. Yet they had been loyal colleagues for decades and had stuck with him despite these views, even when his policy directly contradicted them. Arafat wanted no more Fatah rebels sitting in Damascus and plotting against him.

The long revolution and intifada had sometimes brought violence and anarchy threatening the PA's stability. While the PA and Fatah gave considerable license to Hamas and other opposition groups and accepted debates among members, they would not tolerate actively disruptive behavior in their own ranks. In Nablus, the West Bank's second-largest city, where factionalism was rife, a Fatah Hawks militant group led by Ahmad Tabuk formed during the intifada had continued acting as vigilantes after the PA took over. Shots were even fired at the home of Mayor Ghassan Shaq'a.[63] In December 1995 PA police rounded up several dozen Hawks, some of whom tried to shoot it out.[64]

Even young Fatah leaders who supported Arafat could fall victim to factional struggles there. The popular Mahmud Jumayyil was killed in prison, while his friend and cellmate Nasir Jum'a, a Fatah member since age fourteen, was jailed for several years and reportedly tortured. Friends and relatives charged that they had been persecuted by Shaq'a, who saw them as potential challengers to his control over the city. Yet Shaq'a was no conservative traditionalist but a man who had also long struggled against the Israeli presence.[65]

If Arafat gave Shaq'a free rein it was because the PA leader had less of a personal commitment to the Insider dissenters opposing the mayor. Outsiders who had struggled for thirty years did not feel inferior to younger Insiders who had much shorter records. Nor had Arafat battled for a quarter-century in order to turn over power to others who had long been his minor subordinates the moment he finally arrived back home. Indeed, ceding a superior legitimacy to Insiders also created an existential problem, contradicting the idea that the PA was to be the government of all Palestinians and not just of those in the West Bank and Gaza.

Equally, as in many Third World state-building efforts, there was much postrevolutionary letdown and demobilization. Now there was a government whose job was to wage the struggle. The public's role was often reduced to applauding its leaders.[66] People were no longer commanded to go out in the streets or organize an underground movement. As Abd Rabbu explained: "During the past the public knew exactly what the national leadership want[ed] from them. [Now] the public isn't sure what is the main goal or the general plan the PA wishes to achieve." People felt "that the battle is not theirs" but was being fought by the government alone.[67]

For some Insiders in Fatah, this routinization and institutionalization of politics provoked nostalgia for the years of struggle. Many individuals who had been heroes could not easily find a place in the new framework. In addition to a natural disappointment at the slow pace of change and limited improvements to their lives, there was also inevitable disillusionment with the difference between reality and the utopian change they had expected.

During the intifada, Nidal Abu Akar went from being a high school student to spending three years in Israeli jails. His story, so vivid and typical, is worth quoting at length:

> I can't leave . . . Bethlehem for fear of arrest by the Israelis and I lost my job at a Bethlehem gas station following my arrest by the [PA]. Nowadays, I sit around and recall the beauty of the intifada . . . when we were wanted by the Israelis and how we fought together against a common enemy. We felt that we were making a step forward, no matter how small, toward a greater goal.
>
> The intifada made us feel so equal to the Israelis. The mood of the people was so elated. [But today they] feel that the sacrifices we made were all for nothing. The problem is that the intifada took all the energy of so many people and left them exhausted. And now the political situation . . . requires more—or different qualifications . . . Now, it seems to be institutions and not people who are involved. The parties are ordinary political parties and not fighting parties—not revolutionary parties.[68]

This feeling of frustrated militancy and unease with routinization was best represented by the Insider rebels in Fatah. Marwan al-Barghuti was the best-known figure of this group of Insiders demanding a bigger share of power. Barghuti had been one of the leaders of the intifada as a Bir Zayt University student, was deported by Israel, and worked several years at PLO offices in Amman before returning to become head of the Fatah Higher Council on the West Bank. Despite their differences, Arafat included him on the official Fatah list for the PLC elections.

Barghuti and some of the other Insiders felt that they had fought Israel, organized the intifada, spent years in jail, and risked their lives only to be pushed aside by an older, exiled leadership that had not participated directly in these battles.[69] Barghuti and his allies demanded more power for the PLC; criticized the PA on corruption, democracy, and human rights; charged that Arafat had made too many concessions to Israel; and urged that negotiations be suspended and the intifada reignited if Palestinian goals were not realized.[70] At a Bir Zayt University rally, for example, he told the crowd that Palestinians would remain in a state of war against Israeli occupation and recalled that "many martyrs were from the university, especially the [Hamas bomb maker] Yahya Ayyash."[71]

The main stronghold of Barghuti and his friends was the Tanzim, the local Fatah branches. One example of the friction between Outsiders and Insiders occurred in October 1998. After PA military intelligence, headed by Musa Arafat (a relative of Yasir Arafat), raided a Tanzim office in Ramallah for hidden weapons, Barghuti led a protest demonstration at Musa Arafat's Ramallah office. The security forces opened fire, killing a young man named Wasim al-Tarifi, a relative of Minister of Civil Affairs Jamal al-Tarifi. Musa Arafat blamed the demonstrators for the young man's death.[72]

In response, Fatah's Ramallah branch issued an angry leaflet proclaiming: "Musa Arafat and his dogs suck Palestinian blood by dealing with stolen cars, whorehouses, and selling weapons. They prefer to be Israeli prostitutes, working here as the Israeli intelligence arm to separate the Palestinian leadership and the Palestinian people." With Jamal al-Tarifi's influence, a military trial was held in which four of the security officers who had ordered the raid on the Fatah office were given prison sentences of three to four years. Another clash took place in December 1998. When PA police dispersed marchers demanding that Israel release Palestinian prisoners, to prevent them from clashing with Israeli troops, about two hundred Fatah supporters attacked the Nablus police station.[73]

Even more of a firebrand than Barghuti was Husam Khadir, from the Balata refugee camp near Nablus. He was the archetypal Fatah intifada fighter turned critic of the PA. Khadir, born in 1962, described the intifada as "the greatest phenomenon the political arena has ever witnessed" and obviously preferred that time to the more bureaucratic, less heroic PA era.[74]

Khadir attended his first demonstration at age ten and claimed to have been arrested by Israel twenty-three times since the age of fourteen. He helped lead the intifada in Balata until he was wounded, arrested, and deported. On his return, Khadir was elected as a Fatah representative in Balata with support from young activists, though Arafat replaced him and tried unsuccessfully to keep him out of the PLC. Khadir's response was to indict the Fatah movement as mere "archaeological remains," complaining, "The traditional leadership has put it in a freezer and prevented renewal through democratic elections for party leadership." During his PLC campaign, he told voters that they had a choice between creating a Palestinian state and supporting "the generation that views Oslo as the peak of the peace process and thinks it does its duty by wearing ties . . . and spreading the Israeli economic plan in the world." This came quite close to calling Arafat a traitor.[75]

Many of Fatah's intifada heroes and refugee camp activists did not feel this way. While the intifada itself was largely spontaneous, the leadership cadre was the product of Fatah's intensive youth organizing efforts in the 1970s and 1980s. Intifada activists recruited and trained by Fatah knew the importance of organizational unity and loyalty. The militancy of some and their antagonism toward PA policies were seen as more a matter of rhetoric than action. As one activist explained: "There's a contradiction in the activity of Palestinian leaders and key figures. On the one hand, they criticize the PA and its behavior. On the other hand, they do not implement this criticism or act to change the present situation. They remain loyal to the PA under all conditions."[76]

Fatah's discipline held better than it appeared. For example, there were few cases of Fatah members being involved in armed attacks on Israel. And the gap between intifada street activist and PLO official returning from Tunis was also not necessarily so wide as some observers claimed. The intifada had been directed from Tunis, and local activists had always obeyed the guidelines from headquarters. They were, after all, loyal soldiers of Fatah and the PLO and could not easily break such links and loyalties. Nor could they ignore accusations and guilt feelings that denouncing national unity would only help the Palestinians' enemies and might destroy any chance of achieving a state. Finally, supporting Arafat was the clearest route to personal advancement. Consequently, Fatah Insider activists who criticized the PA remained a minority.

For example, Dallal Salama was a member of the West Bank Fatah committee and, like Khadir, a Balata camp resident who had been elected to the PLC as an independent after Arafat rejected her. But Salama described herself as "mainstream" Fatah and strongly backed the leadership.[77] Ala' al-Din Yaghi, from Jabalya refugee camp in Gaza, had joined Fatah in 1982 at the age of eighteen. He became an important North Gaza Fatah leader, helping to establish the camp's rehabilitation center and family care association, run the youth club, and organize Fatah events in his area. People in Jabalya "are disappointed," he noted in 1997. "Most . . . say that the PA did not get the best out of the ne-gotiations." But Yaghi was also a strong PA supporter and an employee of its housing council, with four brothers in the PA police.[78]

Since no one single intifada leader or hero had emerged in the West Bank or Gaza, there was no single rival to Arafat behind whom local activists could rally.[79] If there was any Insider who could stand against Arafat it was Faysal al-Husayni, but he did not challenge the leader de-spite Arafat's punishing him as a potential competitor. For example, Arafat cut funding for Orient House, which Husayni headed, forcing drastic reductions in its employees' salaries.

Husayni was heir to the most prominent Palestinian family: son of the leading military commander in the 1948 war, nephew of the Pal-estinian political leader from the 1920s to the 1950s, and brother of a top Fatah military commander. After training by the Syrian army and a brief involvement in Fatah's violent activities during the 1970s, he was captured and imprisoned by Israel. But Israeli officials, aware of his in-fluence, visited his cell to talk politics. Husayni uniquely combined high social prestige, excellent PLO and intifada connections, and an under-standing of the need to build trust with Israelis. His very charisma made PLO headquarters nervous lest he threaten its monopoly on leadership.

Indeed, Husayni had understood better than Arafat where the intifada was leading and had played a major role in changing the PLO's policy. "The intifada is not a military operation," he said in 1989, but a political campaign concurrently mobilizing Palestinians for struggle while teach-ing them the need to compromise, since the "absolute justice" of their "legitimate dream" to regain all Palestine was unrealistic. More mod-eration and less violence would also be needed to win over Israeli public opinion.[80]

Despite Arafat's harassment, Husayni remained loyal to him. And even the more rebellious Barghuti and Khadir had mixed feelings about opposing his leadership. The Outsider hard-liners felt that no change in the PLO's traditional line was necessary, mistrusted the Insiders, and had little interest in democracy. In contrast, the Insider rebels—pre-cisely because of their Insider experiences and perspective—wanted the peace process to succeed in creating a democratic West Bank/Gaza state. Their problem was that they had doubts that this would happen—a reflection of mistrust toward both Israel and their own Palestinian leaders.

The new era of negotiations with Israel, according to Khadir, required "a change in our minds and in the means we are using . . . The PLO's political system, which fit in the intifada period, is no longer suitable to these new circumstances." At the same time, though, "we have been given the opportunity to start a new country, but we haven't done it well. Some people misinterpreted the power they were given; they have forgotten the honesty and loyalty of the years of the struggle for independence, so the battle now is also to stop corruption."[81]

Barghuti, too, was nostalgic for the heady days of battle and felt the strain of transformation from professional revolutionary to politician so common in state-building processes: "It was easy to have unconditional respect from people when I was a freedom fighter, but now it is much more difficult. At that time, we were only focused on the war against the occupiers. I didn't pay too much attention to the needs of the people, to the disastrous situation of electricity, sewage system, roads. But as a politician, I need to be aware of the people's priorities, of their needs. And sometimes it's hard to meet all their expectations, to earn their full trust and understanding."[82]

Many of these ideas were expressed with equal clarity by Hisham Abd al-Raziq, a Fatah man close to Barghuti and Khadir but much friendlier in his view of the PA. Raziq was first arrested by Israeli authorities at age sixteen. A second arrest, when he was caught carrying a bomb, earned him a twenty-year sentence. Now, he said, the peace talks had shifted the struggle "from weapons to a democratic parliament," "from the battleground to the table," and "from stones and violence to peaceful rallies."[83]

Raziq found it hard to criticize the PA's leaders, to "confront people you shared important resistance moments with." Opposition was a legitimate part of democracy, but also carried with it two obligations: to be peaceful and to join with the majority "in a common effort to establish a Palestinian state and a lasting and fair peace." He viewed this course as the only way to achieve a state and to ensure that it would become capable of political stability and economic progress.[84]

These men claimed to view democracy, media freedom, and a more representative government as appropriate for a postrevolutionary period and as the foundation for building a state. After all, though few Palestinians ever said so directly, the Arab world was full of examples they did not want to emulate. They had observed Israel's internal political system with a private admiration rarely expressed in their public rhetoric. At the same time, despite his militant anti-Israel position, Khadir's frankness made him willing to cross the red line of comparing the PA's treatment of Palestinian prisoners with that of Israel.[85]

Yet the militant Insider critique of PA policies did not derive solely from ideology or idealism. Supporting a more democratic system also coincided with the personal interests of these young Insiders. They would do very well in internal Fatah elections, where the overwhelming majority of voters would support them. PLC members hoped to promote that institution's strength to give themselves more power.

For the PA leadership, much of Fatah, and many non-Fatah Palestinians in the West Bank and Gaza as well, there was a powerful pragmatism behind the heated rhetoric of day-to-day politics. Despite skepticism about the peace process itself—certainly understandable for the 1996–1999 period—and glorification of the intifada, many understood that flexibility had achieved quickly what decades of violence had failed to bring.

In Abd al-Raziq's words: "Palestinians have been living with slogans for 100 years. But with peace the time came to put them aside, because we realized that peace would be the only solution to getting some of our rights back and to be able to start living like any other nation." And practicing democratic values is the only way "a truly independent country can blossom."[86]

Among the strongest advocates of such values were the scions of wealthy and middle-class West Bank and Gaza families. They were not traditionalist reactionaries accommodating themselves to foreign rule but political activists who had supported the PLO during the 1970s and 1980s.[87] Under the PA, members of this group became mayors—such as Awni and Mansur al-Shawwa in Gaza City[88]—PA officials, PLC members, and leaders of non-governmental organizations. Their lack of national ambition or appeal meant that they would not threaten Arafat's rule. But these people's main asset was their local bases of support, administrative skills, and expertise in health, economics, foreign relations, education, and other fields which the PA badly needed and professional revolutionaries were unable to provide.

Hashim Daraghma Salah, an independent PLC member and former mayor of Tubas, was probably representative of this group that wanted progress toward an independent state, stability, and a relatively open society. Both the PA's human rights violations and the violence of an opposition trying "to take the law into their own hands" were wrong. "We must take into account that we are living under exceptional conditions," he said, "and we don't want to show the world that we are an undemocratic society."[89]

At the social hierarchy's other end, the intifada had made it possible for new leaders to emerge from even the poorest segments of Palestinian society. Refugee camp residents constituted roughly 20 percent of the West Bank's and 65 percent of Gaza's population. Previously excluded from political power, they had become the new vanguard in those years, a position that provided them with an alternative hierarchy and a path for advancement through the Fatah movement. Although many living in the camps had complaints about unimproved living standards and slow political progress under the PA, they still remained an important element in the regime's base of support.

Security forces were another foundation for the PA's power and the state-building process.[90] They saw themselves as a revolutionary vanguard serving Arafat, the PLO, and the PA but certainly not as subordinate to courts, the PLC, or any system of laws. Arafat incorporated some officers into the political leadership—notably Nasir Yusuf, Muhammad Dahlan, and Jibril Rajjub—while restricting others to purely professional duties.

The police had a dual, potentially contradictory function. On the one hand, they were supposed to deter the violent opposition from challenging the PA's authority or launching violent attacks against Israelis. On the other hand, they stood ready to fight Israel if the peace process broke down completely. The participation of some police officers in the September 1996 rioting was an example of this mission.[91] The widespread perception of their patriotic role made the police quite popular despite their repressive function and the reality that local commanders sometimes used their forces to settle personal scores with critics.

The fact that the PA spent $500 million annually on the police, a large proportion of its foreign aid, showed the priority of those services.[92] But individual earnings were not lavish—unmarried privates got $450 a month, with $50 more for married men and an extra $25 per child—even if at times supplemented by graft. According to agreements with Israel, the PA was entitled to 24,000 police and roughly observed that limit. Israeli sources claimed that it in fact had many more personnel, perhaps because the numbers were raised by PA padding of employment rolls for patronage purposes. But the PA only partly kept a pledge to clear all members with Israel to ensure that they were not terrorists, precisely because some of them—mainly Hamas men recruited from prison in the hope that they would become genuine defectors—were in fact convicted terrorists.[93]

Asked why he needed so many security units, Arafat replied: "The Syrians have 14, the Egyptians have 12. I only have 6 to protect me."[94]

Ziyad Abu Amr complained that PA security service units, which he more accurately numbered at eight, "act independently . . . and sometimes in competition."[95] Yet while Arafat created different units in order to undermine any officer who might challenge his rule, each group also had its own distinct purposes, variously handling the tasks of police, national security, military, and intelligence agencies.[96]

In many but by no means all cases, commanders were career military men from Palestine Liberation Army units abroad who were fairly interchangeable and totally dependent on Arafat's patronage. At the top stood Major General Nasir Yusuf, a tough law-and-order man who commanded four units: national security, intelligence, civil defense, and civil police. Though a member of the Fatah Central Committee, Yusuf did not have political ambitions and thus was both a good and a safe choice from Arafat's perspective.

Yusuf was determined to maintain order and ensure the PA's hegemony, but for political reasons there were limits beyond which he could not go. He ensured the PA's authority but not Hamas's obedience. When Yusuf and the PA arrived in Gaza in April 1994, they tried a conciliatory line. "Hamas serves the people," he declared. "There are no problems between us." He obtained a one-month agreement that Hamas would stop killing alleged collaborators and leave such matters to the police, obviously hoping that this would become a permanent arrangement.[97]

Soon, however, Hamas returned to its old ways, killing two alleged collaborators. "This," said Yusuf, "is the continuation of a phenomenon which our people have suffered for too long . . . Those who attack our people are attacking our rights as a national authority." He called such vigilantes "killers" and "gangs," demanded Hamas surrender those responsible, and pledged to catch and punish them even if it cost a hundred police officers' lives. Hamas responded by calling Yusuf "a protector of collaborators" and insisted it would never give up its arms or freedom of action. Yusuf then issued an order, soon rescinded, banning the reading of political statements in public places, including mosques, without a police permit. He also tried to persuade Gaza's Arafat-appointed mayor, Mansur al-Shawwa, not to include Hamas leaders in his city council. After Shawwa refused, he was soon replaced by one of his relatives who abandoned the idea of such a coalition.[98]

Yusuf resented Hamas's defiance partly because he knew how costly its attacks were for the Palestinians. After all, the security forces had to deal with the results of this violence by arresting oppositionists, coping with the consequences of low living standards, and being prepared for a crisis that might require a confrontation with Israel. He told a meeting in Qalqilya when PA forces first entered that town, "We will control the security situation because it has a positive impact" on the ability of Palestinians to continue working inside Israel.[99]

At times Arafat had to enforce discipline when the security forces went too far. Occasionally but periodically, high-ranking officers responsible for beating or killing prisoners, especially in cases generating bad publicity, were tried and themselves imprisoned. He also wanted no defectors to the violent opposition. In February 1996 Arafat convened a military court to try the heads of the Preventive Security Service and police in Qalqilya who attended a Hamas memorial rally for Yahya Ayyash.[100]

The high-handed behavior of security forces, especially the elite units, disturbed many Palestinians. When two brothers belonging to the PA police murdered two other brothers, one a high-ranking Fatah official, during a Gaza family feud in 1998, the PA implemented death sentences for the first time. The step was popular among Fatah officials for avenging one of their colleagues, and among citizens as a way of curbing security officials' abuse of power. PLC member Hatim Abd al-Qadir, a frequent critic of Arafat, welcomed this decision: "It means there is a rule of law . . . Whoever attacks citizens, their lives and their property, will be punished as the law stipulates."[101] Arafat also issued regulations limiting police in carrying weapons off-duty.

Reporting directly to Arafat were Force-17 (his personal bodyguard) and the counterterrorist Preventive Security Service. There were also two proto-army units: military intelligence and the naval police. The largest unit by far was the civil police, which dealt with minor and criminal matters. Locally recruited, its members had low levels of training and equipment and were commanded by General Ghazi Jabali, who was widely seen as very obedient to Arafat.[102]

Far more elite was the Preventive Security Service, led by Colonel Muhammad Dahlan in Gaza and Colonel Jibril Rajjub in the West Bank. Both men were veteran Insider Fatah cadres who had been in Israeli jails: four years for Dahlan followed by deportation; seventeen years for Rajjub. They had a good understanding of both local conditions and of Israel. Dahlan and Rajjub were far more ready to use initiative than the PLA officers, since they had their own base of support and came from an unhierarchical grassroots revolutionary movement.

Both men were smart, articulate, and proud of their tough, highly motivated force. They were eager to obtain the best sources of foreign training and equipment, whether it be from the United States, Europe, or Russia.[103] Indeed, these top PA military figures were among those most in favor of a reasonable compromise solution. The intifada, said Dahlan in an interview with Israeli television, "was a time of war. I was on the Palestinian side whose interests [were] to fight Israel and this was my interest. But when the time came for us to sit together to talk together I saw that it is better than when it was war, but harder."[104]

Dahlan and Rajjub had learned some Hebrew while in jail, closely followed Israel's politics, and kept good contacts there. But they were also prepared to take militant action to ensure the birth of a Palestinian state. Rajjub threatened to shoot any Jews who came into the Palestinian part of Hebron with ill intent, warning, "Our people have the right to resist occupation."[105] In 1995, at a moment when tensions were high, Rajjub himself was detained by Israeli border police, who confiscated his identity card and ordered him back to PA territory.[106] PA forces also tried to smuggle in weapons or filch arms from Israel's army—including small antiaircraft missiles—to prepare for a possible future confrontation, at one point giving a $3,000 bribe to an Arab who had been a soldier in Israel's army to steal equipment.[107]

Their extremely delicate task was to stop Hamas and other radical groups from attacking Israel without triggering a Palestinian civil war. This required friendly persuasion—including meetings with Hamas military leaders—as well as threats or force. Otherwise, though, Dahlan and Rajjub had totally different personal strategies. Dahlan was a thoroughgoing loyalist who carefully maintained close links to Arafat. Deported by Israel when he was twenty-five years old. Dahlan had been introduced to Arafat by his favorite lieutenant, Abu Jihad, and stayed close to the leader thereafter, helped by the fact that Arafat was usually resident in Gaza. Through this connection, Dahlan was also involved in the negotiations with Israel.

In contrast, Rajjub was combative and outspoken, showing an ambition to succeed Arafat and making enemies as a result. Rajjub said, "I didn't fight for 18 years to see [Hamas spiritual leader] Shaykh Yasin lead the Palestinian people. I don't believe Palestinians want to live in an Islamic state." At the same time, he could accuse Netanyahu of being "a racist and a liar" whose behavior was leading toward war.[108]

Rajjub had a harder job than Dahlan, having to deal with territory over which he had less control, as well as trying to build a clandestine

Palestinian security presence to subvert Israeli control in East Jerusalem. His men kidnapped from that city people they wanted to question or intimidate. In contrast to the cautious and more diplomatic Dahlan, Rajjub criticized Arafat for being too soft on the violent opposition. A rumor campaign was started against Rajjub, accusing him of taking money from the Americans, of bragging that he would be Arafat's successor, and of handing over to Israel two Hamas men accused of terrorism. Rajjub strongly denied these claims.[109]

Rajjub's biggest clash began with a small incident that fed a feud with hard-line Fatah Central Committee member Sakr Habash. During a committee meeting, Habash threw out and insulted a woman who worked for Rajjub. Rajjub sent a protest letter to Arafat, leaked to the press, denouncing Habash and several others. Some Fatah leaders demanded Rajjub be fired. Arafat did not want to punish Rajjub—whom he valued highly—and instead created a Fatah investigating committee. During his own testimony there, Rajjub tried to restrain himself but got into another argument by insisting that his department deserved a portion of the budget for student movements since it employed so many students as informers. Seeing this as more evidence of his excessive ambition, the Committee voted to suspend Rajjub for six months from his membership in the PLO Central Council.[110]

The fact that both Habash and Rajjub remained key members of the PA power elite despite their diverse views, criticisms of Arafat, and personal maneuverings showed the PA's pluralist style. Arafat even continued to use a critic like Khuri as a negotiator with Israel and invited him to the PA's leadership meetings. Two other potential rivals—Husayni and Abbas—were given areas of authority but kept out of the chain of command. Specific cabinet members (Arikat, Sha'th, and Nashashibi), advisers to Arafat (Hurani, Nabil Amr, Abd al-Rahim), top security officers (Yusuf, Rajjub, Dahlan), and Fatah officials (Agha, Zaki, Habash) also played important roles.

Institutional roles divided these leaders more than did any issues of ideology, class, or political background. Those who were most active in the PLC wanted it to be more powerful. Fatah officials preferred their group to be more of an independent actor. Those who were mainly involved in the PA's executive branch supported Arafat's primacy. PLO officials and PNC members also wanted their historic organizations to remain significant.

Nevertheless, as nationalists, PLO veterans, and Fatah members, the leading figures formed a more or less cohesive new elite. Regional, class, and generational distinctions, programmatic disagreements, and differences between Insiders and Outsiders were generally subordinated. Whether this unity could survive, and how it would be adjusted after Arafat's departure from the scene, would be basic factors in determining the success and direction of Palestinian state-building.

6

THE PALESTINIAN
OPPOSITION

The radical opposition groups did not accept the PA's authority to rule but still wanted to avoid a confrontation.[1] Instead, they challenged that regime's monopoly on violence, rejected its key policy, and tried to sabotage its strategy through terrorism, which led to border closures, slowed negotiations, and victory for a right-wing government in Israel far more opposed than its predecessor to compromise with the PA. In short, they contributed toward creating a self-fulfilling prophecy in an unyielding Israeli government, an unworkable PA strategy, and a doomed peace process.

Support for the opposition declined sharply after 1993 and especially in 1995. Opposition factions had previously held about 34 percent of popular support, but public opinion polls showed the PFLP and DFLP losing about 60 percent of their backers, while support for Hamas and Islamic Jihad movements declined by about 40 percent.[2]

Only among college students did the opposition continue to pose a serious popular challenge to the PA. At most universities, Hamas and Fatah had roughly equal support, with secular leftist opposition groups often holding the balance.[3] At al-Najah, the largest university, the Hamas group came in first place during elections but could form a student government only in coalition with the secular leftist PFLP.[4] Similarly, at Bir Zayt in 1998, the Islamic bloc got almost 40 percent, Fatah almost 38 percent, and the left about 19 percent.[5] The pro-Fatah slate regularly won at Bethlehem University, with its many Christian students. In Hebron, however, Hamas did especially well. At the Polytechnic College there, the Islamic bloc won fifteen of the thirty-one seats on the student council, while Fatah won thirteen and the Islamic Group three.[6] In April 1997, at the Islamic University of Hebron, Hamas and Islamic Jihad won nineteen seats, Fatah fifteen, and the PFLP one.[7] At Hebron University in April 1998, Hamas took first place with twenty-one seats, Fatah won seventeen, the Communist Party gained two, and Islamic Jihad obtained one seat. After hearing the result, one thousand students demonstrated waving Hamas flags and chanting "God is great," and "We will strike at Tel Aviv." In April 1999, Hamas took twenty-two seats at Hebron University, while an alliance of PLO groups led by Fatah took nineteen.[8]

Yet apart from student elections, the opposition remained divided and politically weak. Separate efforts by Abd al-Shafi and former Nablus mayor Bassam al-Shaq'a to build a broad united front—including the PFLP, DFLP, Ba'th Party factions, Hamas, Islamic Jihad, and independents—brought people to meetings but not to any agreement. Abd al-Shafi's personal popularity rating in public opinion polls ranged between 4 and almost 7 percent, comparable to that of Ahmad Yasin, Hamas's leader, but he was unable to translate this into an organized movement.[9]

Nevertheless, the PA still had to cope with two alleged alternatives promoted by the opposition, supported by some within Fatah itself. The first was that the Palestinians could defeat Israel militarily, despite thirty years of PLO and fifty years of Arab experience proving otherwise. The second was that the Palestinians could succeed in negotiations to end the occupation and establish a Palestinian state while simultaneously attacking Israelis with guns and bombs to force such concessions. The PA was not averse to pressuring Israel, even with some acts of violence, but also understood that overusing this strategy was likely to wreck the peace process, extend the occupation, damage the Palestinian economy, and block achievement of a state.

Hamas and Islamic Jihad asserted a right to wage war and attack Israel, and denied that the PA had any right to stop them.[10] Rather than punishing it for attacking Israel, Hamas said, the PA should leave it alone and acknowledge its right to do so.[11] Yasin admitted that there was no distinction between the Hamas political and military sections, the Izz al-Din al-Qassam brigades: "We cannot separate the wing from the body. If we do so, the body will not be able to fly. Hamas is one body."[12] Similarly, Muhammad Nazzal, the organization's leading figure in Jordan, admitted that Hamas made "political decisions" whether to conduct a military operation against Israel, and the Qassam units simply handled the timing and implementation.[13]

The PA at times took tough action against these forces, but was often restrained from interfering by its own desire to avoid igniting civil war and alienating Palestinian public opinion. As PFLP spokesperson Abd al-Latif Ghayth pointed out: "The Palestinian street also puts pressure on the PA . . . [It] can't just wage war on the entire opposition. There are certain limits the Authority is constrained by."[14] When Arafat did not prevent or punish terrorism, Israel responded by pressuring the PA to do so through costly closures and slowed negotiations. But if Arafat were to close down opposition groups and arrest all those responsible for planning or making attacks, his domestic popularity could decline and internal Palestinian tensions intensify, with opposition to such steps coming even from within Fatah itself.

Hamas knew that this domestic leverage was one of its best weapons, but it strengthened its position further by a determination to avoid excessively provoking the PA. Hamas's Gaza spokesman Mahmud al-Zahar insisted: "The [PA] is our political opponent but not an enemy. Those in the [PA] are our brothers, our neighbors, our cousins."[15] Nafidh Azzam, a cleric close to Islamic Jihad, noted: "In the same home, we may find a member who belongs to [Islamic] Jihad, another to Hamas, a third to Fatah. This greatly reduces the chance [for] civil war."[16] That was literally true in some cases. The brothers of Zahar and of Musa Abu Marzuk, a leading member of Hamas's political bureau, worked in the Gaza police. Badr Yasin, Ahmad Yasin's brother, managed the PA's transportation office. Jibril Rajjub's brother was a radical pro-Hamas cleric.[17]

The violent opposition's behavior was also shaped by both a refusal to accept and an inability to comprehend the basic requirements of state-building. By ignoring the PA's claim to rule, they undermined Arafat's ability to achieve independence. Nabil Sha'th insisted, "We absolutely refuse to have two authorities on the Palestinian soil."[18] But to some extent this was precisely what happened. As revolutionaries rejecting concessions, Hamas and Islamic Jihad preferred to continue struggling for all of Palestine for generations rather than to build a state on part of it right away.

These contradictions were visible in the debate over the opposition's refusal to give up its arms. Weapons in the hands of such factions, PA Justice Minister Abu Midayn worried, could "promote the law of the jungle . . . There cannot be a dual authority in which everybody has his own rifle with him, as if we were living in the American West 200 years ago." Without a patriotic commitment to preserve unity and peace, Palestinians could face chaos, anarchy, and endless war like Afghanistan or Somalia.[19]

Even Islamic Jihad's publication *al-Istiqlal* admitted that the vast number of weapons in private hands could "lead to the militarization and destruction of the Palestinian society."[20] But Hamas leader Zahar avowed indignantly that his organization had "not fired on any decent or untainted Muslim or Palestinian." A wide spectrum of oppositionists asserted that it was perfectly all right for anyone wishing to do so to shoot Israelis or kill Palestinians identified as social deviants.[21]

Hamas's spokesperson in Gaza, Abd al-Aziz al-Rantisi, declared, "It is a crime to take away the weapon of any person in order to serve the interest of Israel." The Oslo agreement, he said, "does not obligate us . . . to stop jihad operations against the occupation . . . It is being alleged that Hamas's operations are causing embarrassment to the [PA]; however, the [PA] embarrassed itself when it signed this agreement."[22] Like many Hamas leaders, Rantisi came from a 1948 refugee family, studied in Egypt, and joined the Muslim Brotherhood there. One of Hamas's seven founders in 1987, he was imprisoned by Israel between 1988 and 1990 and expelled to Lebanon in 1992, where he became spokesperson for several hundred Hamas leaders briefly deported there.[23]

But even a far more moderate oppositionist like Abd al-Shafi, speaking in 1995 when talks were still advancing, could insist: "The peace process has been buried . . . As long as we are under occupation and confronted with a peace process that is not advancing, then every person has the right to engage in all forms of struggle." The PA, he added, should not see the opposition's being heavily armed as a challenge to itself.[24]

If Abd al-Shafi voiced such views, it was not surprising that Azzam insisted, "The opposition has the absolute right to use the appropriate method and course to alleviate the Palestinian people's pain and to defend their right . . . The PA cannot impose the peace process on the opposition."[25]

Although Arafat periodically demanded that the opposition give up unlicensed weapons and explosives or be imprisoned, the PA never really implemented this threat. Indeed, Hamas leaders were often granted permits for their own firearms.[26] Occasionally these guns were used to kill PA policemen, sometimes in attempts to steal weapons, though direct violence between the two Palestinian groups always remained limited.[27]

Arafat complained that the PA had explained to Hamas leaders "how detrimental such operations were to our economy and our nascent entity . . . [but] they continued to pursue their old policy" of attacking Israel, which discredited the PA.[28] But if the PA could not even stop the opposition's militia from trying to murder Israelis whenever it wanted, how could Arafat possibly live up to its other commitments? And if he could not meet these commitments, how could he possibly expect to persuade Israel to make concessions, and especially to accept a Palestinian state with sovereignty in East Jerusalem? This problem did not bother Hamas and Islamic Jihad, which hoped the PA would fail, but it was a dilemma of huge proportions for Arafat.

The PA's response to Hamas was well represented by Arafat's spokesperson Marwan Kanafani. He said that the PLO and PA were entitled to make deals with Israel since they were the Palestinian people's recognized leaders. Efforts to kill Israelis blocked "progress in the peace process, as well as progress of the Palestinian people toward establishing their state." The PLO had already tried armed struggle and paid in "many martyrs and much blood in order to accomplish what they have accomplished. Therefore, we should now do something useful to attain the state we want."[29]

This did not mean that the PA was itself satisfied with the peace process. Even in 1995, with Rabin still prime minister, Kanafani characterized it as "very slow . . . a source of agony," which required rethinking because Israel was so "intransigent." But Kanafani also understood that part of the problem was that Israel "believes that we are not partners in the peace process and that we are still treating each other as enemies observing a cease-fire."[30]

Anything seeming to prove this view made things even worse. While the PA claimed that attacks gave "the Israelis the pretext of so-called security" for refusing to advance the peace process, as Sha'th once put it, this was merely another way of saying that terrorism damaged the Palestinians. "If some people do not yet think that the PLO is the sole legitimate representative of the Palestinian people," Sha'th continued in a firm tone, "our Palestinian people know how to teach them manners and subject them to accountability."[31] Yet despite all the PA's roundups, trials, intimidation, and even physical abuse of prisoners, it was never fully able to impress that lesson on the violent opposition.

The militant opposition was primarily Islamic radicals. In comparison, the leftist opposition was small and divided. For example, in a 1998 public opinion poll, the leftist parties had 3 percent support while all Islamist groups held 17 percent.[32] Further, ideological and organizational conflicts prevented the left from agreeing on unity or a strategy. The PPP and FIDA parties, with about 1 percent each of popular support in public opinion polls, gave the PA critical support.[33]

The DFLP and PFLP did kill Israeli civilians in several attacks, and the PA periodically arrested their activists, sending some to prison. The PFLP's leader, George Habash, called for Arafat's "removal" as PLO leader.[34] But both groups were of little importance compared to their Islamic rivals. The PFLP held roughly 3 percent support among Palestinians in public opinion polls, while the DFLP never mustered more than 1 percent of popular backing. Habash was the leader preferred by less than 2 percent of PA citizens, while Arafat always scored higher than 40 percent.[35] These groups were also weakened by the fact that they had lost their Soviet patron, and their top leaders and most activists remained abroad, though they still enjoyed Syrian support. The PFLP experienced a serious split and financial trouble, which forced it to lay off full-time activists.[36]

In Islamic Jihad's case, though, the fact that its popular base of support was so small—ranging from less than 1 up to 2.5 percent in polls—made it focus almost entirely on violent activities.[37] Its first leader was Fathi al-Shiqaqi, born in Gaza in 1951 to a refugee family. As a medical student and doctor in Egypt during the 1980s, he became a member of the Muslim Brotherhood, then returned to start his own group. In 1986 he was sent to prison by Israeli authorities, then deported to Lebanon. Shiqaqi visited Tehran, where he met Ayatollah Ruhollah Khomayni, and returned there several times. His main office was in Damascus.[38] Shiqaqi was assassinated on October 26, 1995, in Malta by Israeli agents.[39]

Islamic Jihad choose as his replacement Ramadan Abdallah Shallah, born in 1956, who had also studied in Egypt, though at the time he was a teacher at the University of South Florida in Tampa.[40] The PA was less inhibited about cracking down on Islamic Jihad, which, while enjoying Iranian and Syrian support, remained small and did not build social institutions or a base of supporters.[41]

Hamas, then, was by far the main opposition group and perpetrator of attacks on Israelis. Hamas's main leader and the single most popular opposition figure, was Ahmad Yasin. Born in a village near Ashkelon in 1936, he fled with his family to Gaza in 1948. As a child he was paralyzed in an accident, but nevertheless persevered to become a teacher. In 1964, he went to Cairo as a graduate student in English and joined the Muslim Brotherhood. Back in Gaza, he was sentenced by Israel to twelve years' imprisonment for possession of weapons and explosives but was released in a 1985 prisoner exchange. On December 14, 1987, five days after the intifada began, Yasin announced the founding of Hamas. He was again arrested by Israel in 1989 and sentenced to life imprisonment. Arafat constantly urged his release.

After a botched Israeli assassination attempt against the Amman-based Khalid Mish'al, head of Hamas's political bureau, Israel freed Yasin from prison in October 1997. PA Justice Minister Abu Midayn had said two years earlier, "I hope that Shaykh Ahmad Yasin will be released, so we can see the real face of Hamas."[42] Now, though, Sufyan Abu Zayda, Arafat's adviser on Israeli affairs, lamented that if Israel had released Yasin earlier at Arafat's request, the PA would have had leverage to push Hamas toward moderation. It should have been clear all along that Yasin represented a hard-line stance even in the context of Hamas's politics. At any rate, Yasin's release strengthened Hamas's radical stand and weakened Arafat. For his part, Arafat sought conciliation. He hurried to meet Yasin, kissed him several times, and gave him a Land Rover and a PA diplomatic passport. In his first speech on returning to Gaza, Yasin urged Palestinian unity and praised Arafat. This attitude did not last long, however, and soon Yasin was fiercely attacking Arafat at home and abroad.[43]

Despite Abu Midayn's hopes, Hamas's ideology was not easily prone to moderation or compromise. It viewed the battle with Israel as a struggle between God and Satan which only violence could resolve. "So-called peaceful solutions are all contrary to the beliefs of [Hamas]," declared the group's Charter. "There is no solution to the Palestinian problem except by Jihad." Everything else was "a waste of time."[44] Hamas spokesman Ibrahim Ghawsha explained: "Hamas knows very well that the world respects nothing other than force. The Jews themselves only bow to force."[45]

According to Hamas's Charter, the Zionists sought to rule not only Palestine but the entire Middle East and the whole globe as well. They owned "the world media" and directed "the French and the Communist Revolutions." Their front groups created "to destroy societies and carry out Zionist interests [included] the Freemasons, Rotary Clubs, Lions' Clubs, [and] B'nai Brith." They ruled "imperialist states and made them colonize many countries" in order to exploit and corrupt them. They concocted World War I and World War II for profit and as an excuse to create Israel. "They inspired the establishment of the United Nations . . . to rule the world by their intermediary. There was no war that broke out anywhere without their fingerprints on it."[46]

Within the region, the Hamas Charter warned, "Zionist scheming has no end, and after Palestine they will covet expansion from the Nile to the Euphrates . . . Their scheme has been laid out in the *Protocols of the Elders of Zion,* and their present [conduct] is the best proof of what is said there." Withdrawing from "conflict with Israel is a major act of treason and it will bring [a] curse on its perpetrators."[47] All of Palestine must remain Muslim land "until the Day of Resurrection, no one can renounce it or part of it, or abandon it or part of it."[48]

Hamas leaders continued to accept the goals and strategy set forth by their Charter. For example, Rantisi pledged that even an unconditional Israeli withdrawal from all the West Bank and Gaza would bring only a temporary truce. Hamas would never end the war or recognize the "Zionist entity. For if I cannot liberate [Palestine] then future generations will inevitably do so." No matter how bad the situation, it did not "justify giving up Palestine." Some weak Arabs, he argued, cared only "for their personal life and wealth," but there were "thousands who feel their souls are a cheap price to pay for their country." Arafat's crime was that "he gave up Palestine and abandoned the . . . Charter." The PLO was thus not "the sole legitimate representative of the Palestinian people" since it did not represent Hamas supporters.[49] Zahar complained, "One faction acted alone in the Oslo agreement without consulting the other factions."[50]

No matter what the current conditions or balance of forces, Hamas and Islamic Jihad were certain that victory was inevitable. Asked, "But hasn't the peace process become a reality which cannot be bypassed?" Islamic Jihad leader Ramadan Shallah responded:

> I hear this question every day . . . The devil is a reality: Shall we . . . give in to his temptation or shall we counter him, in order to lead a clean and honorable life? We have been told that we must give in to the status quo and reality since the 1920s [and] following each one of our people's uprisings . . . It is not a question of fighting over a few meters or a few kilometers; it is a long and bitter struggle which generation after generation inherits . . . Peace is not a reality now; what is reality is the systematic destruction of our people's cause and goals through a process dubbed a peace process.[51]

Khalid Mish'al, chief of the Hamas political bureau, justified the use of violence and the rejection of negotiation in pragmatic terms: "The option of resistance is a legitimate right, and it is the only effective, useful route to achieving the objective, even if the path to victory takes a long time." It was untrue "to say that the choice of resistance hinders a just settlement currently available because there is no just settlement put forward at this time. Nor do I believe that there is another solution that can be attained without resistance."[52]

In short, endless violent struggle to destroy Israel was inescapably necessary and required for all Muslims. There could be no accommodation, save perhaps the most transient of truces. This view seemed to set Hamas on a collision course with the PA's most basic strategy, policy, and legitimacy.

Yet Hamas, in its ideology and goals, just as strenuously sought to avoid any such confrontation. Hamas knew that Arafat could crush it if a civil war ensued. Equally or more important, Hamas's leaders understood that provoking a civil war with the PA or being held responsible for the destruction of Palestinian dreams would destroy its base of support.

Thus, no matter how many Hamas members the PA arrested, how long it held them, or how badly it treated them, Hamas insisted that the PA was not an enemy. This, too, was justified by its Charter: "Hamas regards nationalism as part and parcel of the religious faith. Nothing is loftier or deeper in nationalism than waging Jihad against the enemy and confronting him when he sets foot on the land of the Muslims."[53]

Hamas made clear its often unrequited love for the PLO. Article 27 of the Charter states: "The PLO is among the closest to the Hamas. Our homeland is one, our calamity is one, our destiny is one and our enemy is common to both of us." Unfortunately, owing to Western and Christian influence, the PLO "has adopted the idea of a secular state. Therefore, in spite of our appreciation for the PLO and its possible transformation in the future, and despite the fact that we do not denigrate its role in the Arab-Israeli conflict," Hamas was confident that some day the PLO would adopt "Islam as the guideline for life." Until then, Hamas would view the PLO like "a son towards his father, a brother towards his brother . . . who supports the other in the confrontation with the enemies and who wishes him divine guidance and integrity of conduct."[54]

Hamas generally hewed to this line. Ghawsha said that Hamas cadres were hawks in terms of resisting occupation and careful in preventing intra-Palestinian fighting.[55] Even when most critical of the PA, Yasin promised not to "allow under any circumstances inter-Palestinian fighting to take place . . . We have to take the lesser of the two evils in this case."[56] At his most conciliatory, Yasin could suggest that "we do not want to embarrass the [PA] and are trying to stay away from areas under its control . . . The [PA] has reached a dead end and it does not hold the right cards to pressure Israel. The [PA] must understand that Hamas is a card [which puts] pressure on Israel . . . Maybe Israel will give them something."[57]

When released from a PA prison, Zahar told reporters, "Fatah and Hamas are like the two wings of a bird, they must work together."[58] His tolerance toward the PA clearly emerged in another interview:

> "I have been arrested twice [by the PA]," Zahar recounted, "held for a total of 105 days . . . I have been beaten with electric wires, they broke four of my bones, and shaved off my beard, which is a symbol of Islam."
>
> "Isn't that much the same way you were treated by Israel when you were arrested during the Occupation?"
>
> "Yes."
>
> "Doesn't this make you bitter, or angry?"
>
> "I understand what it means, to implement this accord with Israel . . . These things are being done under pressure from America. It's not a lasting policy."

Yet even Zahar could not completely restrain his anger. After insisting that any problems between the PA and Hamas were temporary and imposed by outsiders, he continued: "That's their style; they're never going to change. Our people are being tortured, but we are not going to retaliate . . . because that would pave the way for Israel being able to destroy us both."[59]

Hamas at times threatened the PA, trying to frighten it into passivity, but was not necessarily ready to implement such warnings. After one big wave of arrests, Imad al-Faluji—before his own conciliation with Arafat—warned the PA of a "popular explosion" if crackdowns continued.[60] Yet Hamas always backed down. Even after PA police killed a dozen Hamas supporters and wounded many others by firing at worshippers leaving a Gaza mosque, an official Hamas communiqué stated: "Despite all the fabrications and lies" from PA leaders, "our movement has so far refrained from reciprocating . . . hoping that this would make those who are behind this . . . campaign against our movement relent and wake up. We hope that the rational elements within the Fatah movement will come to realize the extent of the plots that are being hatched to pit the sons of our people against each other and push them toward a fratricidal fight which would serve nobody other than the Zionist enemy." Hamas would not "break national unity" even when the

PA treated its newspapers "in a manner which is worse than that practiced by the occupation authorities."[61]

While Hamas's self-imposed restraint in avoiding conflict gave the PA an advantage—especially since the latter was stronger and had more popular support—the PA still had to calculate precisely the right mix of pressure and cooperation, between imposing itself as a government demanding obedience to its laws and a nationalist movement operating as a coalition.[62] It tried to find a balance between limiting Hamas's attacks enough to satisfy Israel and keep the peace process advancing, while at the same time avoiding internal strife or a loss of its own popularity. Although the PA came close to this goal in the years between 1993 and 1996, its tolerance of Hamas neither won over nor intimidated that group. Instead, the PA's tactic backfired, simultaneously damaging the peace process and weakening the PA's own ability to build a state. By late 1998, when the Wye agreement with Israel linked stopping attacks very closely to its implementation, Arafat took tougher action. Over time, the PA gained control and more effectively reduced Hamas's attacks and political leverage.

In addition to pressuring Hamas and other groups, Arafat also worked tirelessly to co-opt or divide the opposition. He had some success in splitting opposition groups to form pro-PA parties, which, while of more symbolic than practical importance, broadened his coalition. Among secular parties, FIDA had already attracted a large number of DFLP cadres to back Arafat's strategy. The Syrian-sponsored, anti-Oslo Popular Front for the Liberation of Palestine–General Command (PFLP-GC) split, with a group called the Supreme Command Council supporting Arafat. One of its defecting leaders, Salim Abd al-Saud, said that the PFLP-GC's belief "that the military option is the only way to solve the Palestinian cause . . . is a worthless conception . . . We consider the [PA's] course of action as a first step on the road towards building the Palestinian state."[63] Elements in the PFLP also left after the group's Central Committee, according to one source, voted against participating in elections by only a 35–25 margin. Abu Nidal Musallami, a former political bureau member, and Tallal Ahmad, former chief editor of the group's magazine, joined the PA.[64]

There were also pro-Arafat Islamic parties. Following an internal dispute, a group calling itself the al-Aqsa Battalions left Islamic Jihad to support the PA. Hamas defectors formed several small parties urging an end to attacks on Israel and support for Arafat.[65] Faluji, long a ferocious critic of the PA, created a National Dialogue Office to work with the PA on the "changed reality" after the Oslo agreements.[66] When Faluji announced that he was running in parliamentary elections on the Fatah ticket, Hamas declared that he was no longer a member. Faluji, along with Tallal Sidar, a former Hamas deportee and head of the Young Men's Muslim Association in Hebron, joined Arafat's cabinet, though without abandoning all their former views.[67] Scores of low-level Hamas operatives, especially those working in religious-sector jobs now controlled by the PA, also defected.[68]

The most important group of all was the National Islamic Salvation Party (NISP), formed in November 1995 by moderate Hamas leaders in Gaza who wanted an outlet for political activity. They considered armed activity to be counterproductive. Several top Hamas leaders even visited the still-imprisoned Yasin in September 1995, hoping, in vain, for his endorsement, a barrier that kept them from directly participating in the project.[69]

While the NISP opposed the Oslo agreement, its members saw that framework and the PA as realities which could not be ignored.[70] In March 1996, Hamas was at a political low point, set back by the PA's electoral mandate, shaken by the PA's largest roundups yet of Hamas activists, and frightened at the potential backlash to its biggest, bloodiest offensive ever against Israeli civilians. On March 22, 1996, NISP leaders met with Arafat to discuss cooperation, perhaps even joining the PNC and PLO if they could do so without accepting the Oslo agreement.[71]

One participant, Isma'il Abu Shanab, suggested that the NISP's success would bring over more Hamas members. The party was "the result of sincere efforts by Hamas members to cope with the developments towards freedom. And if the [PA] is a part of the Palestinian reality, then the [NISP] will be part of the Hamas project."[72] The NISP offered the alternative of a nonviolent Islamic opposition, exactly what Arafat wanted. But because of strong opposition within Hamas—especially from West Bank and Outsider leaders—it was neither able to reach a formal agreement with Arafat nor able to bring a large portion of Hamas to accept its ideas.

The group did, however, establish its own newspaper in 1997, al-Risala. Its chief editor, Salah al-Bardawil, was a professor at Gaza's Islamic University, and assistant editor Ghazi Hamad was a former al-Watan editor. The PA even contributed $31,000 to help start the paper. It continued to attack PA policy—the first issue blasted the recent agreement securing Israeli withdrawal from most of Hebron—but was also cautious. As Hamad explained, "Experience has shown that strong and direct confrontation [with the PA] is not fruitful in an undemocratic situation."[73] Al-Bardawil put it a different way: "*Al-Risala*'s policy is based on its recognition of the PA but not the [acceptance] of the Authority's bad performance."[74]

The PA also tried to weaken Hamas by widening differences between the group's exiled Outsiders and the Insider leadership. Insiders understood the limits imposed by the PA's power, an unfavorable strategic situation, and the potential cost of pushing Israel to the limit. As one Palestinian writer put it, the Insiders insisted "that the Palestinian people must not be pushed to the point of suicide and extinction" by civil war or all-out confrontation with Israel. In contrast, Outsider leaders of Hamas tended to be more optimistic about total victory, eager to attack Israel as frequently as possible, and more willing to risk a confrontation with Arafat. Hamas's political situation, reflecting the relationship between Insiders and Outsiders, recalled an Arab proverb, "He who receives the lashes is not like him who counts them."[75]

For example, Ghawsha, Hamas spokesman in Jordan, argued that revolutions in Middle East states would soon produce an all-out war against Israel: "If Rabin is incapable of coming to terms with small Palestinian groups such as Hamas or [Islamic] Jihad, what will he do if Islam takes over in Egypt, Algeria, Tunisia, or Morocco? Or in Turkey, after having established itself in Iran already?"[76] He also declared that while "civil war" would be "a tragedy for us Palestinians . . . for the sake of the cause, it cannot be ruled out."[77]

In contrast, Zahar, an Insider, claimed that Palestinian civil war was an Israeli plot which must be stifled and that Arab states were too weak to help. Therefore, Palestinians could not rely on external support.[78] "We will not give Israel this opportunity," he said, "and we will endure all kinds of suffering including arrest, imprisonment, trials, and even killing just as we endured in the past. We have our political differences with the [PA], but we are not its enemies. Accordingly, we will endure . . . until conditions change."[79] Zahar called on leaders abroad to be sensitive to conditions in the territories.[80]

Arafat repeatedly accused the Hamas Outsiders of stopping Insiders from cooperating with the PA and suggested that the group was rendered ineffective by internal divisions: "There are some in the Hamas leadership who understand our viewpoint and believe that the joint task should be that of building the state which the Palestinian people dream of . . . We hope that the view of these parties will be the [basis] of decisionmaking in Hamas."[81] It was true that the Hamas leaders living in the Palestinian territories were stronger supporters of dialogue with the PA, but they also shared the same basic strategic views as their colleagues in Amman and elsewhere.[82] The Insiders were ready to restrain themselves enough to lower the level of violence and to avoid civil war but not to obey the PA. Once Yasin was released and again functioning as leader, any hope of Hamas's moderation seemed doomed.

Another PA technique was to discredit Hamas and Islamic Jihad to the Palestinian public by portraying them as Israeli agents, either directly or as a result of their actions. Arafat claimed that Palestinian forces opposing the peace process were "sharing the same trench" with antagonistic Israeli forces.[83] He called this "a plot in which many parties take part" and claimed to have evidence "proving beyond any doubt" that Hamas was cooperating with extremist Israeli forces seeking "to prevent the extension of [PA rule] to the West Bank [and] to strike at the very heart of the Palestinian economy."[84]

In begging Hamas to stop attacks, pro-Arafat PLC member Hani al-Masri argued dubiously, "Netanyahu wants terrorist attacks and is trying to provoke them because this unites the [Israeli] population and keeps the government in power." But he more accurately warned, "Military attacks at this juncture will turn all powers inside Israel against our people, and will allow Israel to portray itself as the victim."[85] Masri also argued that attacks harmed Palestinian interests, resulting "in the most undesirable political outcomes," making Israel slow down the peace process, withhold concessions, and take punitive actions. More suicide attacks would mean more Palestinian land confiscated, more Islamic holy sites lost, and more people made homeless and hungry.[86]

Arafat complained in 1995, "These operations have led to a Palestinian economic catastrophe," including 186 days of closures by Israel, in one year costing hundreds of millions of dollars lost from wages for Palestinians working in Israel and blocked exports. He called the perpetrators "misled" and "children who are systematically and intensively brainwashed."[87] Sha'th warned: "Carrying out military operations against this agreement will lead to the cessation of the peace process and not taking the West Bank back. Such operations will lead to denying the Palestinian people their daily livelihoods, keeping the prisoners in prison, and to supporting those Israelis who reject the peace process and attempt to circumvent it." The Palestinians would suffer even more by appearing to be at fault.[88]

Similarly, Arafat's spokesperson Kanafani analyzed a 1995 attack by saying that Palestinians would suffer most from this "ugly attack on civilians, which is prohibited by all laws, morals, and religious values." Its intent was to "keep the Palestinians hostage to Israeli military occupation . . . It was not an act of resistance to remove occupation or liberate lands or achieve any other goal for the Palestinian people. It only sought to destroy the peace process by striking at ordinary Israeli citizens in Israeli streets." Speaking in terms similar to those used by Rabin and Shimon Peres with the Israeli public, he concluded, "Everyone must understand that the delay in implementing peace gives the enemies of peace on both sides—and I stress on both sides—the impression that they will be able to halt the peace process."[89]

The PA's best argument against Hamas and other opposition groups was that it was the only force able to lead toward ending the occupation and gaining independence. If the PA was a government holding the Palestinian people's mandate, everyone must unite behind it and obey its decisions. Otherwise there would be chaos, disaster, and defeat. Abu Midayn asserted: "All factions must realize that we are in the process of building a state. This state must be governed by the rule of law."[90] In Arafat's words, "There is no parallel authority to the [PA]."[91] Masri suggested: "It is not acceptable for the fate of our entire nation to be determined by the decisions of a small group of its people, regardless of how brave this group is, and how willing it is to sacrifice for the good of its country. It is also not possible to ignore the will of the majority of the Palestinian people, and that of their legitimately elected leadership."[92]

Such contentions could persuade Palestinian public opinion and make Hamas leaders worry that they—not Israel or the PA—would be held accountable for Palestinian losses and suffering. Certainly, this approach made Hamas more cautious at various times. But the violent opposition more often ignored the PA's demands. It did not regard the PA as ruling a country and did not want it to succeed within the framework of a peace process with Israel. Hamas's majority did want Israeli policy to become more intransigent as a way to block a successful peace process. It did not want an independent Palestinian state to emerge at the price of recognizing Israel and giving up territorial claims. Equally, since much of Hamas's popularity was due to its unbending militancy, becoming more moderate could also reduce its support.[93] Yet the PA did not force Hamas to change course but to be restrained, which was the ultimate test for proving its credentials as the ruler of a country.

The leaders of the PA were painfully aware of how far it fell short of being a real national government during its first years of existence. Sha'th pointed out that no Arab country would "allow anybody in the opposition to violate agreements and to cross the border to carry out war."[94] Arafat, too, invoked comparison to Arab states, demanding to be treated as equal in sovereignty, hinting that his opponents had foreign loyalties, and suggesting his readiness to use force to ensure obedience. He asked why the violent opposition groups did not stage their attacks from Syria and Jordan rather than from PA-ruled territory: "Why are they making us look . . . responsible for this? Is it because we are the most vulnerable party?" They ought to show as much "respect for the Palestinian position and Palestinian-Israeli agreements" as they did for foreign Arab regimes. "Otherwise, they would weaken our own, rather than the Israeli position."[95]

The PLO was more easily able to ridicule the strategy of Hamas and Islamic Jihad because it had tried similar methods for decades and found them futile. "Neither one, nor two or even ten operations, for that matter, could weaken the Israeli position," Arafat noted. He and other veteran PLO activists considered the radical Islamic groups to be latecomers who had never done much for the cause and had no claim on Palestinian leadership: "Where were these factions when the PLO was fighting? Why did they fail to act then?"[96]

The opposition was sabotaging the greatest chance for state-building Palestinians had ever had, Arafat insisted. "For the first time since the beginning of this century, there is a Palestinian national authority that is controlling Palestinian territories and a Palestinian people."[97] Asked if he was acting as Israel's policeman to restrain Hamas, Arafat replied that he was acting as a national leader. If Israel held him responsible for Palestinian violence it was "because of my position as the official who signed an agreement with them; the person responsible for all the Palestinian people."[98]

Since neither side wanted clashes, the PA and Hamas held almost continuous contacts and frequent negotiations.[99] Hamas encouraged activists to join PA institutions including the police, though mainly to recruit supporters and provide intelligence.[100] Sha'th suggested that Hamas make a commitment "to stop all their acts of violence, even for just one year, for us to truly discover whether there is any hope of developing this peace into an independent Palestinian state, or whether the Israelis want nothing but stalling and procrastination." In exchange for such a commitment, Hamas would be offered a share in decision-making.[101]

But while PA-Hamas dialogues defused tense moments between the two and sometimes persuaded Hamas to reduce attacks against Israel, there was no political breakthrough. Hamas did not agree to participate in elections, join the PA, stop armed assaults, or change its policy. Probably Hamas never intended to do so and simply was trying to mitigate PA pressure while waiting for the day when the PA would accept its worldview and strategy. At the same time, though, there were differences within the organization, with several key leaders favoring a deal with the PA and transition to peaceful opposition.

The main rounds of dialogue arose from the November 18, 1994, killing of thirteen Hamas supporters in Gaza by Palestinian police,[102] the PA's attempts to stop Hamas from sabotaging Israeli withdrawal from West Bank towns in 1995, the aftermath of the February–March 1996 wave of attacks against Israel, the August 1996 PA police shooting of Hamas demonstrators at Tulkarm jail, and September 1996 clashes between rioters and the Israeli army. Each cycle usually included Hamas attacks on Israeli civilians, followed by PA police raids and arrests of Hamas leaders, after which came rising tensions between the PA and Hamas that negotiators sought to defuse.

Throughout the second half of 1995, the PA worked hard to secure Hamas's participation in the Palestinian elections and to stop attacks which might interfere with Israel's turnover of West Bank towns to the PA.[103] Far from seeking to promote Palestinian civil war, the Rabin government tried to help the two sides reach agreement by letting Hamas Insider leaders travel abroad to consult with their Outsider colleagues.[104] In October, four Hamas leaders went to Sudan to consult with Outsider leaders to prepare for talks with the PA, then returned to meet with Arafat, who told them that Hamas did not have to agree with the PA's policy but should only oppose "these commitments through peaceful and democratic methods."[105]

Arafat met twice with the returning delegation and then with eight Hamas leaders from the West Bank. He made a strong appeal for Hamas to stop using violence and to back the PA. "We support pluralism but oppose the existence of more than one authority," said Arafat. "We are on the threshold of an historic stage that requires us to show solidarity. We have made our first step toward our objective of establishing an independent Palestinian state with Jerusalem as its capital." This goal was achievable, he believed. "The Israeli [conservative] opposition now understands the agreements we have signed. It is no longer impermissible for Israeli officials to use the term: Palestinian state." Abd-al-Rahim backed him up, speaking on behalf of Fatah and the PA's departments, including security services. "We have begun building the foundations of the Palestinian state. We cannot build a state while armed militias still operate. We want a model state, not a Somalia or Afghanistan."[106]

Jamal Hammami, a prominent Hamas leader in the West Bank, seemed to accept these arguments, pledging, "We in the Islamic movement will not strip the PA of its role." He added that Hamas would continue to have reservations about agreement with the Israelis, but did not want to be responsible for blocking an Israeli withdrawal from the West Bank. Hamas wanted dialogue, not a conflict with the PA. But, as Nasir Yusuf insisted, "any accord with Hamas which does not set [an] end to the attacks on Israel would be nonsense. Without this clause no accord can be valid."[107]

At first, reports were encouraging about a deal in which Hamas would stop attacks to avoid jeopardizing an Israeli withdrawal from West Bank towns, while the PA would release Hamas members held prisoner. A leader of the Islamic movement within Israel, Abdallah Nimr Darwish, helped mediate between the two sides. He declared that a Hamas-PA agreement "is ready and only the signing on paper remains," while Shaykh Ahmad Bahr, a Hamas leader, nodded in agreement. Bahr had just been released by Arafat after four months' imprisonment. He became the first Hamas leader to declare that "Hamas may stop its attacks on Israel if that is in the interests of the Palestinian people."[108]

Yet while a number of leading figures on both sides expressed optimism about an agreement, the dialogue quickly collapsed when Hamas hard-liners vetoed the deal.[109] Abd al-Rahim attributed the failure to the Outsiders' rejection, but even in the territories much of the organization opposed the proposal, and Hamas leaders denied that they were considering ending attacks.[110]

The dialogue's culmination and failure came at a December 18–21, 1995, PA-Hamas summit meeting in Cairo. Hamas refused to participate in elections or cease attacks on Israeli targets.[111] This was the closest the PA ever came to neutralizing Hamas's threat to the peace process.

More confrontations led to renewed dialogue in the fall of 1996. In August, four Hamas leaders traveled from Gaza to the West Bank—with Israel's permission—to defuse the situation after PA police shot at a Hamas demonstration outside Tulkarm jail.[112] Hamas had split over a leaflet urging an intifada against the PA. More moderate leaders succeeded in calming their colleagues.[113]

The September 1996 Palestinian-Israeli clashes gave the PA an incentive to restart talks with Hamas. Arafat created a national dialogue committee and chaired its first meeting, held on October 13. Hamas welcomed the move, urging national unity to face "the current challenges." The PA released Hamas members from jail as a goodwill gesture. Still, there was no real change in either side's positions. The same thing happened with the next round of dialogue in 1997.[114]

Again, this does not mean that dialogue did not serve an important purpose. It postponed any showdown between the PA and Hamas and reduced some of Hamas's efforts to attack Israel. But by the same token, the tacit agreements also ensured that Hamas could continue to flout the PA's interests and policies, rejecting the notion that it was subject to a PA-led state bound by those leaders' decisions.

In its arsenal of tools to handle the violent opposition's challenge, the PA had both carrots (dialogue, praise, letting Hamas's social institutions stay open, releasing prisoners) and sticks (threats, raids and weapons seizures, arrests, imprisonment, and torture). The PA used both methods to try to restrain Hamas and meet its commitments to Israel. The key question, though, was what risks and resources the PA would use to achieve this goal, as well as how much ability it had to implement that policy.

Certainly, there were many times when, as Islamic Jihad leader Ramadan Shallah put it, those who wanted to attack Israel had a "lack of opportunity because of tightened measures" by the PA.[115] Ghawsha complained that military operations against Israel had "become difficult" because of PA-Israel security cooperation.[116] PA officials, including Arafat, repeatedly condemned and argued against attacks on Israelis. PA forces often stopped demonstrators from clashing with Israeli troops, but sometimes—especially in Hebron in 1997 and 1998—watched rock-throwers or even mobilized them to gain political leverage. The PA police sometimes raided Hamas arms caches or arrested those who were planning attacks. More often they reacted after a bombing or shooting to round up individuals believed to be responsible for or knowledgeable about the attack. Hamas sympathizers were taken into custody to discourage support for that group. Most were released after a period ranging from days to months, while those believed to have been involved directly were tried and imprisoned. The PA was far more likely to act in response to information from Israel than to take the initiative.[117]

Hamas's violent response was an outcry against the very existence of the Israel-PLO agreements, not a demand that they advance faster and succeed. As early as October 4, 1993, a Hamas member drove a car bomb into an Israeli civilian bus.[118] In February 1994 a Hamas gunman shot to death a pregnant Israeli woman.[119] Two months later a suicide bomber killed five Israelis on a bus in Hadera.[120] In April an Islamic Jihad gunman killed an Israeli at a bus stop near Ashdod and wounded four others. Arafat offered condolences to the victims' families.[121] Islamic Jihad killed Israeli soldiers in September 1994, followed by PA arrests of those thought responsible.[122]

When the PA began governing in Gaza and Jericho, the most Hamas offered was a brief commitment to stop killing alleged Palestinian collaborators with Israel.[123] There was occasional violence between Hamas and the PA, as when a PA policemen died in a September 1994 shootout in Gaza. But Arafat met with Hamas leaders and ordered the release of three men accused of killing the policeman.[124] This set a good precedent for peacemaking but also put Hamas on an equal level with the PA and signaled that the regime would not crack down effectively.

Moreover, Hamas quickly made it clear that there would be no end to armed struggle, except perhaps after Israel withdrew unconditionally from all the West Bank and Gaza Strip.[125] This position implied that Hamas violence, not PA negotiation, would secure Israel's retreat. What followed was eighteen months of all-out warfare against Israel.

During ten days in October 1994 alone, there were five major incidents. Two Hamas gunmen killed two people and wounded thirteen in downtown Jerusalem.[126] Two days later, Hamas kidnapped an Israeli soldier, Nahshon Wachsman, and threatened to kill him unless Israel released Yasin and many other Hamas prisoners. Israel sealed off the Gaza Strip and stopped negotiations.[127] Palestinian police arrested over two hundred Hamas members trying to find Wachsman, and Arafat met with Hamas leaders to urge that they help resolve the crisis.[128] Wachsman was killed by his Hamas captors when Israeli forces stormed their hideout in the West Bank. Three of the kidnappers and one Israeli soldier were also killed.[129] In Gaza City five thousand Hamas supporters demonstrated against the police crackdown and demanded General Nasir Yusuf be fired.[130] On October 19, 1994, a Hamas bomb on a bus in downtown Tel Aviv killed twenty-two people and wounded forty-six others. Israel closed off the Gaza Strip and West Bank in retaliation.[131] In November a Hamas member killed an Israeli soldier with an ax in Afula, Israel,[132] and there was a suicide bomb attack on an Israeli checkpoint in Gaza. In response, PA police arrested more than 130 Islamic Jihad members.[133]

On December 24 a former PA policeman who was a Hamas supporter blew himself up at a Jerusalem bus stop, wounding thirteen people.[134] At Israel's Bayt Lid crossroads in February 1995, two Islamic Jihad bombs at a bus stop killed nineteen soldiers and wounded sixty-one. Israel closed its borders with Gaza and the West Bank indefinitely and suspended negotiations.[135] PA security forces arrested Hamas and Islamic Jihad activists, killing in a shootout two of the latter suspected of involvement in the Bayt Lid bombing.[136] A military court sentenced an Islamic Jihad leader, Umar Shallah, to life in prison on charges of inciting others to commit the bombing. The PA's reaction was so strong that Islamic Jihad's head, Fathi al-Shiqaqi, complained: "I am worried because Arafat has gone far in responding to Zionist orders. He has not just lost his free will; his latest actions indicate that he has taken leave of his senses."[137]

Suicide bombings near Jewish settlements in Gaza during April 1995 led to more arrests and raids, with Arafat ordering security forces to take "firm measures."[138] On April 2, 1995, a Hamas bomb factory blew up in Gaza City killing seven people and leading to more arrests.[139] A June 25 suicide bombing and several planned attacks led to even more arrests, including that of Hamas leader Zahar, who was held until October 1995.[140]

Many suspects were also periodically released for several reasons: either there was insufficient evidence against them, the task of attempted intimidation had been fulfilled, or the PA wanted to ease tensions to avoid a clash with Hamas. Contrary to what many Palestinians thought, the Rabin government did not want to stop negotiations or institute closures. When the PA cracked down on terrorism, or during periods of relative quiet, Israel lifted punitive measures, especially when the PA showed its willingness to arrest suspects who had attacked Israel or were planning such deeds.[141]

Yet before the shock of one deadly attack faded, it was followed by another one. There was a July bus bombing by Hamas in Ramat Gan that killed six Israelis,[142] and on August 21, 1995, in Jerusalem a Hamas bus bomb killed five people and wounded sixty. Israel again suspended talks and closed borders.[143] One stern measure taken by the PA was the institution of security courts, which handed out heavy sentences.[144] Arafat also again stepped up arrests.[145] This wave of attacks came at a bad time for Arafat, as he was negotiating Israel's withdrawal from West Bank towns. The PA's crackdown on Hamas went in tandem with its arguments that attacks prolonged occupation and a dialogue attempting to gain Hamas's participation in elections. Knowing it was being blamed for the slowdown of Israeli withdrawal and postponement of elections, Hamas temporarily stopped its operations.

Given Hamas's ideology, some of its most important leaders were already dead—martyrs who provided an example to emulate. The most important was Yahya Ayyash, killed on January 5, 1996, by a booby-trapped mobile phone. The thirty-year-old bomb maker had been responsible for at least fifty-one Israeli deaths since 1992, including the October 1994 Tel Aviv bus bombing. In Gaza, Ayyash was hailed as a martyr by 100,000 who attended his funeral, some chanting, "Over a thousand Ayyashes will rise to fight the Zionists." Arafat paid a condolence call on Hamas leaders. In a speech soon after, he called Ayyash a martyr and held Israel responsible for his death.[146] But PA security forces had earlier tried—how hard was unclear—to catch him, and later bulldozed a monument to Ayyash in Khan Yunis.[147]

Some observers attributed the ensuing wave of attacks of February–March 1996, in which seventy-eight Israelis were killed, to Ayyash's death. But they would have happened anyway, given Hamas's strategy. Furthermore, since Israel had now withdrawn from West Bank towns, Hamas was no longer inhibited by a fear (and PA pressure) that its attacks would stop the redeployment. In fact, Hamas had to act quickly, since the PA's successes in liberating West Bank towns and winning the elections was reducing Hamas's popularity and even splitting the organization.

These assaults badly shook the peace process and arguably broke its spirit altogether. On February 25 a Hamas suicide bomber in Jerusalem blew up a bus, killing twenty-three people. Hamas called it revenge for Ayyash. Israel halted talks and instituted a closure.[148] The next day, in Ashkelon, Israel, a suicide bomber killed himself and an Israeli soldier at a bus stop.[149] On March 1 a Hamas attempt to invade a Gaza settlement was foiled, with two attackers captured by the PA police.[150] But two days later, on March 3, a Hamas bus bomb in Jerusalem killed nineteen people and wounded ten.[151] And the next day a Hamas suicide bomber killed twelve people and injured 126 more at a major Tel Aviv intersection. Again, Israel imposed a complete closure.[152]

Belatedly, the PA responded with its biggest crackdown ever, ending with almost two thousand Hamas and Islamic Jihad supporters in prison. At the same time, the PA worked with Israeli forces to stop the offensive, raiding safe houses, offices, and mosques. Those arrested by the PA included eight of thirteen Hamas leaders on Israel's most wanted list.[153] On March 6 a security court sentenced Hamas's Muhammad Abu

Wardah to life imprisonment for training suicide bombers and "harming the Palestinian people's interests."[154]

Large-scale attacks on Israelis by no means ended in March 1996. There were a number of shootings and bombings at settlements, on roads, and in Jerusalem and Tel Aviv in the following years. Suicide bombings in 1997 alone included attacks in a Tel Aviv café in March killing three Israelis, and in Jerusalem during July and September killing a total of nineteen more.[155] But the intensity did not equal that of the earlier era, since the peace process's slowdown made Hamas feel less desperate about any need for action to stop it. And while Hamas did try to continue attacks, countermeasures had also improved as PA security forces became established, organized their intelligence, and learned how to handle the problem better.

The strange case of Muhi al-Din al-Sharif, a thirty-one-year-old former electrical engineering student turned Hamas bomb maker, was a sign of either growing factionalism in Hamas or a tougher PA policy toward the violent opposition. Sharif was shot and his body dumped beside a car that was blown up in a Ramallah industrial era on March 29, 1998. Trained by Ayyash, he was behind major bus bombings in July and August 1995 as well as a 1998 Tel Aviv café attack that killed three women, one of them pregnant.[156]

At first the PA accused Israel, then reversed itself and attributed Sharif's killing to Hamas, and specifically to Hamas leader Amad Awadallah. Hamas denied any responsibility for the killing and alternated between blaming the murder on Israel and on PA security forces. After Rantisi, who had also blamed Israel, then claimed that the PA killed Sharif, security forces arrested him. PA Justice Minister Abu Midayn squared the circle by asserting that Israel was responsible even if a Palestinian had killed Sharif. But the death remained unsolved.

The story took an even more bizarre turn when Imad Awadallah—arguably the PA's most important prisoner—escaped from a PA jail in August, probably with help from a jailer. Awad's brother Adil Awadallah was head of the armed wing of Hamas on the West Bank and among Israel's most wanted men. Israel accused the Awadallah brothers of having organized a wave of suicide bombings in Jerusalem in 1997 that killed twenty-one. Israeli forces eventually killed the brothers in an attack on their hideout. The Awadallahs and Sharif had allegedly disagreed over both strategy and the use of funds.[157]

Whether or not Hamas leaders were arguing among themselves, the opposition was making no progress toward taking over the PA or changing its policies. Hamas and Islamic Jihad, however, had been able to challenge the PA's authority on a daily basis and survive. In doing so, they succeeded in striking heavy blows against the peace process. The opposition had no realistic alternative to the PA's policy, Khalil Shiqaqi wrote, but could only hope that failure of the peace process would bring it mass support and leadership.[158] Ziyad Abu Amr agreed, saying, "The opposition . . . didn't offer any actual alternatives . . . because it doesn't have any."[159]

Indeed, Arafat's alternative to the 1997–98 deadlock in the process was to negotiate the October 1998 Wye agreement, which for the first time directly based Israeli West Bank withdrawals on the PA's ability to constrain Hamas. A few days later, after a car bomb attack in Gaza narrowly missed blowing up a busload of Israeli children, Arafat cracked down on Hamas harder than he had done since early 1996, even putting Yasin under house arrest. Some Hamas leaders again threatened the PA but did not try to fight it.[160]

As happened repeatedly before, the violent opposition could try to ignore Arafat by attacking Israel, but they could not fight him directly. On a political level, however, these groups did more damage to the PA than to Israel. While failing to force Israeli concessions, their terrorism did severely disrupt the process, further hardened Israel's stand, and damaged the PA's economy and progress toward achieving a state. If Hamas had gained control, the losses would have been far higher, including the peace process's collapse, followed by a full-scale war and the probable destruction of the PA itself.

The opposition posed a paradox for the PA. Its inability to stop the violence had resulted from the PA's own lack of statelike power, yet this failure simultaneously inhibited the further development of such power. The PA gained increased control by the middle of 1996. But the violence had helped bring to power an Israeli government that embodied the PA's worst expectations. Still, as the PA took hold and violence declined, Israel turned back in a dovish direction at the 1999 election.

In terms of democracy, the PA faced the difficult reality that the great majority of the organized opposition did not accept its legitimacy, policy, method for gaining independence, or even democratic means. Under such conditions, the PA's effort to maintain pluralism and avoid civil war increased the already high barriers to the state-building process.

7

THE PALESTINIAN AUTHORITY AND THE MIDDLE EAST

A curious incongruity faced the PA in its relations with Arab states. These countries supposedly backed the Palestinian cause fully and passionately yet did surprisingly little to help the PA. They provided limited material support and did not use their full assets either to coerce Israel or to give it incentives to meet the PA's demands.

Arafat always insisted that the Palestinians had tremendous leverage among the Arab states. "If the [peace process] is frozen," he warned, "it will not only have repercussions in the Palestinian arena, but also at the Arab, Islamic, nonaligned, and international levels. The Palestine question is the core of the conflict in the Middle East."[1] Yet he certainly could neither orchestrate nor rely on these alleged allies.

More candidly assessing the problem, Nabil Sha'th mourned that no help could be expected from the Arabs, "whose terrible condition . . . drives one to tears."[2] No one would save the PA from civil war or conflict with Israel, said Justice Minister Abu Midayn, just as no one had come to the aid of besieged Muslim communities in Bosnia and Chechnya.[3]

Palestinians had hoped, PLC member Hanna Amira wrote, that the Arab world would unite and pressure Israel to attain Arab goals.[4] But instead, as Ala al-Din Yaghi, a Fatah activist, remarked, the Palestinians, "are weak. We don't have an army, or a lot of weapons. We don't have united Arab countries behind us." By contrast, the Palestinians saw Israel as strong and enjoying international backing.[5]

The PA badly needed to mobilize Arab state help since this backing was its only real international asset. Although its agreements with Israel forbade the PA to conduct foreign relations, this process went on, albeit within limits. A somewhat humorous example of such circumventions occurred when Arafat appointed Umar al-Khatib as the ambassador to Jordan from three different entities: "the State of Palestine, the PLO, and the [PA]."[6]

Specifically, the PA begged Arab states to send aid to promote development, provide jobs, and reduce dependence on Israel; to condition their own normalization of relations with Israel on its meeting PA demands; to promote PA demands in international institutions and with the West through rewards and punishments as well as words; and to stop supporting anti-Arafat Palestinians. The Arab states' indifference toward the PA, or sabotage of it, also hurt Israel by making the PA a weak partner in peacemaking and by helping radical groups that were killing Israelis.

Arafat did complain about the lack of Arab support, though he continued to flatter Arab leaders and express Palestinian loyalty to Arab causes. "Saudi Arabia is the only Arab country to have fulfilled its commitments in full," he stated. "We are proud of the ties binding us to King Fahd and the Saudi family. Likewise, we will not forget the special Egyptian role in this regard, and the support my brother President Mubarak has extended to the Palestinian position on all levels."[7]

Unlike the PA, Hamas still hoped that Islamic revolutions or policy changes in Arab states would lead them to fight with and destroy Israel. For Ghawsha, the only question was whether Hamas could delay the peace process until the Arabs and Muslims came to the rescue. "Or will the movement be destroyed before any Arab or Islamic nation rises in the region?"[8]

But Arab states lacked the willingness, even more than the ability, to assist the PA or make war on Hamas's behalf. Equally, while Arab nationalist and Islamic solidarity were still extremely important forces in the region, they did not always work on the PA's behalf. It was sadly ironic that after a half-century-long Arab and Muslim obsession with the issue, the Palestinians were largely abandoned when the real opportunity finally did come for them to build a state.

For the PLO, Arab states had been an indispensable base of support without which the movement would have collapsed or at least been ignored. In earlier decades, Arab states were sometimes willing to go to war, struggle diplomatically, and make economic sacrifices for the Palestinians. Yet the extent of this help never matched Palestinian expectations, and the gap widened over the years, sometimes owing to the PLO's own mistakes.

All Arab states rejected Israel's creation in 1948 and were continually hostile toward it during the next thirty years. Egypt made peace in 1978, but, despite secret contacts by Jordan, no country followed this example for another fifteen years. Instead, Egypt was isolated, boycotted, and ejected from the Arab League. Lebanon's 1983 agreement with Israel was killed by pressure from Arab states and domestic forces.

But these same forces often injured and tried to dominate the PLO, causing many of that group's casualties, setbacks, and internal divisions. "Virtually every Arab state has stabbed them in the back at one point or another," wrote a leading Arab scholar. A PLO intelligence chief estimated that Arab states were responsible for slaying three-quarters of the Palestinians who had been killed in the struggle.[9]

Arab states treated the PLO more as tool than partner, neither consulting it nor respecting its interests when setting their own policies. They saw the conflict with Israel largely as a way to mobilize domestic support or gain advantages over rival Arab states. Their rulers stood by, or even pushed, as the PLO was chased from Amman to Beirut, and from Beirut to Tunis. Voting on pro-PLO UN resolutions, donating money, or sponsoring terrorism were low-risk propositions. But a PLO trying to drag them into another losing war with Israel or endangering their links to the West was a nuisance. As Arab states themselves disengaged from conflict with Israel, they also felt less motivated to help the Palestinians.[10]

In a long-term cumulative process, the Arab states' inability to defeat a steadily stronger Israel, and the high cost of war and conflict, made them tire of the battle and seek ways to escape it.[11] Frustrated at their inability to destroy Israel, Arab states reduced their efforts. The high cost and negative outcomes of the 1967 and 1973 wars, inter-Arab disputes, and the Iran-Iraq war advanced this tendency. Arab states also became increasingly distinctive, gaining a deepening sense of individual interests. As many of the states concluded that only regional stability could preserve their independence and allow economic development, they needed to reduce regional conflict in order to retain power.

Once Egypt, exhausted from wasting limited resources for so long, broke the Arab consensus and made peace with Israel, Syria had more reason to avoid a conflict. Growing radical Islamic movements and also Iranian and Iraqi ambitions distracted and reoriented Arab regimes' policies. Arab states were largely passive during the 1982 Lebanon war and the post-1987 Palestinian intifada. Then came the Saudi-Kuwaiti aid ban to punish Arafat's support for Iraq's 1990 invasion of Kuwait.

By the late 1980s, these trends had accelerated owing to global and regional developments as well as to the evolution of the Arab-Israeli conflict itself. The cold war's end and the USSR's collapse left the United States the world's sole superpower, weakened radical Arab regimes, gave moderate ones an incentive to improve relations with Washington, and reduced U.S. constraints on the use of power. Arab states had to limit conflict and make peace with Israel if they wanted to improve relations with America.

Once the PLO unilaterally made an agreement with Israel in 1993, Arab leaders could say that the decision freed them to make their own deal, consider their obligation to the Palestinian struggle as ended, or condemn Arafat as a sellout. "For the long term," warned Abd Rabbu, "the Oslo and Washington agreements are a great danger to [our] relations with Arab countries. It weakens them and might even cause a break-up."[12]

Compared to the PLO, the PA was less reliant on Arab states while needing them more. Having its own territory and alternative funding sources made it less dependent. But it required massive material help to finance national development and provide leverage in talks with Israel.[13] Since Arab states' own interests and rivalries and the new shape of regional politics made them unwilling or unable to do much, the Palestinians remained—under the PA, as with the PLO—a minor player in Arab politics.

Moderate states were stingy with aid and eager to avoid confrontation. Some sought their own peace with Israel; others delighted in the PA's discomfiture. Radical states denounced Arafat, opposed the peace process, denied help to the PA, and funded its Palestinian rivals. Even when Arab states criticized Israel, such words were often a handy substitute for action and sometimes a subversive blow aimed against the PA. After all, to call Israel intransigent and the peace process doomed implied that Arafat had been wrong, his policy would fail, and the PA's very existence was either illegitimate or futile.

Most Arab states, however, did accept the PA's basic strategy and at least partly linked their attitude toward Israel with its treatment of the Palestinians. They were ready to make peace with Israel if it was able to make a peace agreement with the PA. A sign of this dramatic change was that the Arab League, which had once rejected negotiations and called for Israel's extinction, now insisted that Israel make peace. According to the June 1996 Arab summit resolution, peace "is a strategic decision."[14] For most Arab leaders the question was now price, not principle. "We call upon the new Israeli government," Egyptian president Hosni Mubarak told that meeting, "to cooperate with us so as to complete the peace process without slackness or hesitation." Jordan's King Husayn noted that the Arabs always knew that peacemaking would be hard, but the current process was "the only available option . . . [and] possible means to bring the conflict to a just and lasting solution that can endure."[15]

From 1993 onward, the peace process and the Arab states' behavior followed a consistent pattern. Some crisis would arise—delays in implementing Israeli withdrawals in 1995; Arab fears about the Netanyahu government's intentions in May–August 1996; the tunnel opening in Jerusalem in September 1996; the Hebron impasse of November 1996–February 1997; or the announcement of plans to build at Har Homa in East Jerusalem starting in March 1997—during which Arab states' criticisms of Israel increased and normalization slowed.[16]

The level of tension increased after the election of Netanyahu's government in May 1996. During the September 1996 riots, an Arab League meeting statement hailed "the intifada of the Palestinian people . . . in intrepidly confronting Israeli repressive practices" and said that it "considers what is happening [the tunnel opening in Jerusalem] to be part of an Israeli Zionist plot to destroy the al-Aqsa mosque, set up the Temple of Solomon, obliterate Islamic Arab landmarks and create more facts which harm the legal status of Jerusalem."[17] Arab states' refusal to participate in the November 1997 regional economic summit in Qatar was the beginning of a freeze on normalization with Israel mandated by the 1997 Arab summit.

But Arab countries took few or no concrete steps against Israel. Whenever Israel implemented an agreement, though its concessions fell short of earlier PA demands, moderate Arab states would take another step toward normalization. For example, after the Hebron agreement, Oman announced a thaw of economic relations with Israel. Abu Dhabi renewed contacts with Israel regarding cooperation in the exchange of tourism delegations. Projects with Dubai that had been suspended were revived. Qatar resumed contacts about sending a representative to Israel (an Israeli diplomat had already set up an office in Qatar). Relations with Morocco also improved. Dore Gold, then Netanyahu's foreign policy adviser, went to several Gulf states for meetings in late January 1997.

Shortly thereafter, Mubarak hosted a long, friendly visit from Israeli Defense Minister Yitzhak Mordechai and proclaimed a "new atmosphere" in the region. Officials discussed exchanging military delegations and other tension-easing methods. Egypt's president invited Netanyahu to Cairo, met with him and an Israeli business delegation, and promised that there would be no barriers to developing commercial links. Ibrahim Kamil, an Egyptian businessman close to Mubarak, visited Israel, bought a large amount of stock in its Koor Corporation, and proclaimed that the Egyptians had no hesitations about doing business with Israel.

Furthermore, Arab leaders and states repeatedly put their own image and interests ahead of helping the PA. For example, Mubarak ignored Arafat's pleas to attend a September 1996 Washington summit, thus bolstering the PA's position, because staying away made him seem tougher and reinforced his popularity at home. Despite the deadlock in the peace process and Arafat's appeals for action, the Arab response was governed by disputes, mistrust, and conflicting interests among Arab states on issues having nothing to do with the peace process.

Delays in organizing the 1998 Arab summit also illustrated these priorities. For example, several states—especially Kuwait—did not want Iraq invited to any meeting. There was also disagreement over placing other issues on the agenda: sanctions against Iraq, policy toward Iran, Algeria's civil war, and so on. Even the meeting's location was a source of dispute. Syria wanted the summit held in Damascus; Egypt preferred Cairo as the location. In the end, the session could agree only to reiterate past resolutions. A similar pattern occurred in 1999.

Differing interests among Arab states shaped their attitudes toward the peace process and even Israel itself. Syria even talked about peace. Aside from Iraq (still outside Arab councils) and a Libyan government many Arabs ridiculed, almost all Arab states now had a far different attitude toward the Arab-Israeli conflict than in the past. Even when in no hurry to make peace, they did not want to risk a crisis with Israel and problems in their relations with the United States.

Some had a real material interest in limiting confrontation. Egypt, Jordan, and several countries in North Africa and the Gulf were very much committed to a peaceful resolution of the dispute. Countries that had opened relations with Israel sought to save the peace process, while those opposing negotiations wanted Arab states to destroy the process and return to conflict with Israel.[18]

After the 1993 Israel-PLO agreement, about $2.3 billion was pledged to the PA in foreign aid for the next five years. According to the PA itself, as of 1998 almost all these funds had been disbursed. Of this amount, about 50 percent came from European countries, 13 percent from the United States, 13 percent from Japan, and about 5 percent from Western-controlled international lending institutions. Only 8.6 percent—$210 million—came from Arab states (and 60 percent of the Arab donation came from Saudi Arabia alone). Arab states actually sent less than 45 percent of their total commitment to the PA. In contrast, Norway alone sent more money than all the Arab states combined.[19]

But wealthy Gulf Arab states, whose income had been cut by a drop in oil prices, preferred to spend money at home or make profitable investments in the West. Real development—vital to promote stability and maintain the PA's base of support—required an infusion of capital that could ultimately come only from Saudi Arabia and Kuwait. Yet the Gulf Arabs donated far less money than they had before the 1990 Kuwait crisis, and only a tiny proportion of what they could easily have provided. Iraq, Syria, and Libya gave no funds at all to the PA but instead bankrolled its Palestinian rivals.

Sometimes moderate amounts were dispensed as a sort of alms. In 1996 the United Arab Emirates (UAE) offered a $164 million grant to build 3,800 housing units and support facilities in Gaza City.[20] Qatar's monarch gave $10 million to build low-income housing in Khan Yunis and Nablus.[21] Saudi Arabia invited Arafat to visit and gave more money than other states, though far less than it could easily have afforded.[22] Yet the Saudis also made clear their political distaste for Arafat, which was demonstrated in their lack of generosity, as reflected by newspapers close to the royal family. *Al-Riyad*, owned by a relative of King Fahd, published an editorial claiming, "The Palestinians are convinced [Arafat] is no longer up to the task [of leadership] because of his age, senility, and inability to take the initiative."[23]

To the extent that Arab states made their decisions on financing the PA based on profit-making opportunities, they chose not to invest very much. After all, the PA ruled an area that lacked resources and infrastructure, and its products often competed with those of Arab economies. Projects in other parts of the world were easily more attractive than the prospect of putting money into the West Bank and Gaza. Bureaucratic barriers and corruption, as well as fear of instability and an uncertain future, also discouraged investment.[24] With Arab states operating mainly on the basis of commercial considerations, the PA received little financing from them.

The 1996 Arab summit's final communiqué was both ironic and symbolic of these attitudes. It urged the European nations, Japan, and other countries "to continue providing political and economic support to the Palestinian people and their National Authority." But there was absolutely no pledge from the Arab states—not even a nonbinding recommendation—for their own aid program to the Palestinians.[25]

The PA wanted the Arab states to force Israel to meet its demands in negotiations. But while the Arab states could deny Israel regional benefits from the peace process, they could not so endanger Israel or raise the costs as to force it to change policy. The PA was certain to be disappointed, and Israel left unaffected, by Arab policy. Significantly, the line that Egypt, Syria, and Saudi Arabia tried to impose on other Arab states was that Syria, not the PA, should have veto power over normalization, which would occur only when Israel had also made full peace with Damascus, regardless of what happened on the Palestinian front.

Verbal complaints gained nothing, and efforts to persuade the United States and Europe to coerce Israel into making concessions did not work either. A freeze on normalization with Israel was rejected by the 1996 summit but adopted at the March 1997 summit. Contacts were to be cooled, multilateral talks discouraged, and economic projects curtailed. This did not affect countries having a peace treaty with Israel (Egypt and Jordan) and did not reverse earlier steps toward normalization taken by Morocco, Tunisia, Mauritania, Qatar, and Oman. But new deals and upgraded arrangements were discouraged, including plans by the UAE and Bahrain to open lines of communication with Israel. Despite providing moral support, however, this freeze did not do much for the PA.

In reality, Arab options were quite limited. The PA's radical enemies wanted a return to the no-war, no-peace era of 1974–1994. A resolution of the 1996 Arab summit warned Israel that breaking its commitments could bring "a resumption of tension in the region and compel all the Arab states to reconsider steps taken in the context of the peace process, vis-à-vis Israel."[26] Most Arab states, however, thought that such a step would endanger them, causing not only military defeat but also economic losses and gains for radical forces, and damaging relations with the United States. The collapsed economic boycott against Israel could not be reinstated without hurting the investment climate in the Arab world as well. Mubarak told the 1996 summit, "None of us wishes to return to war and destruction or seek to revert to the state of no-war, no-peace."[27]

Another important PA goal was to stop Iran, Libya, Sudan, and Syria from helping its Palestinian rivals. Islamic Jihad had backing from Libya, Syria, Sudan, and Iran. Radical nationalist groups receiving aid from Syria included the PFLP-GC, Abu Nidal's group, Fatah defectors, the PFLP, and the DFLP. Syria also had close links to some anti-Arafat PLO leaders, notably Faruq Qaddumi. Syria's Palestinian clients accused Arafat of treason, and some threatened to assassinate him.[28] At least one Fatah moderate, Asad Siftawi, was murdered in Gaza by a Syria-based group.[29]

For many years Hamas received aid from Islamic radical groups in Egypt, Jordan, and Lebanon, with very little help from Syria or Iran. During a triumphant regional tour in 1998, however, Yasin built far stronger links to Syria, Iran, Kuwait, and Saudi Arabia, as well as with governments or Palestinian communities in Qatar, the United Arab Emirates, Yemen, and Sudan.[30] Yasin praised Syrian President Hafiz al-Asad, saying that he had "extended all support for our struggle."[31]

In Iran, Yasin met with all the top leaders. Ayatollah Ali Khamena'i reportedly called Yasin "the real representative of the Palestinian people." Yasin claimed that all the countries he visited had "confirmed their support to all Hamas-sponsored jihad and resistance operations. This constitutes a change in the attitude of those countries towards the movement." Arafat, in contrast, was never invited to Iran, and made his first trip there in fifteen years only to attend the 1998 Islamic Conference Organization summit. "The Iranians," he complained, "support and pay anyone who seeks to undermine the peace process."[32] Nabil Amr, one of Arafat's closest advisers, complained that Yasin was weakening Arab and Muslim support for the PA.[33]

By strengthening violent groups, Arab states made it harder for Arafat to persuade or pressure radical Palestinian movements into becoming a legal, peaceful opposition. Arab state-sponsored terrorism strengthened his enemies, undermined his strategy, and led to costly Israeli border closures and to slowed negotiations. Inter-Arab professional groups often took hard-line anti-Israel stands that also in effect opposed the PA's strategy. The Arab Journalists' Union threat to blacklist any reporter who participated in conferences with Israelis, for example, forced the Palestinian Journalists' Union to threaten to punish members for non-compliance. Ironically, then, other Arabs were demanding that Palestinians obey their tougher guidelines on normalization rather than following the PA's lead on such matters.[34]

The PA was also disappointed in its hopes that Arab states would effectively pressure the United States to force Israeli concessions. It had to be cautious on this goal since, as a U.S. aid recipient, the PA had to avoid appearing to organize an anti-American campaign in the Arab world.[35] Again, though, moderate Arab states did not fulfill Arafat's hopes. They were also wary of jeopardizing relations with the United States. They needed U.S. protection, and their economies were intertwined with those of the West. Egypt did not want to risk the $2 billion it received annually in U.S. aid; Saudi Arabia and Kuwait would not jeopardize their investments and markets. Statements urging U.S. and European support for the Palestinians yielded no result. At any rate, the Arab states themselves now had far less leverage in Washington than during the cold war, when, despite threats to join the Soviet camp if dissatisfied, they had never persuaded the West to appease the PLO.

In relations with the PA, Middle East states fell into three categories: the Peace Camp, the Radicals, and the Dropouts (see Appendix 5). The Peace Camp consisted of Algeria, Morocco, and Tunisia,[36] as well as Bahrain, Djibouti, Egypt, Jordan, Mauritania, Oman, Qatar, non-Arab Turkey,[37] the UAE, and Yemen. These countries essentially wanted the Arab-Israeli conflict to go away so they would not be dragged into crises or forced to spend resources fighting it. They did not wish to return to the old era of all-out conflict and war. At the same time, though, these Arab states were also constrained by a wish to avoid attacks from radical forces or states accusing them of being Zionist or Western puppets and thus impious and unpatriotic.

These moderates restrained the Arab world as a whole from returning to the old high-priority, war-oriented approach to the Arab-Israeli conflict. They all supported an independent Palestinian state with its capital in East Jerusalem, but—except for Jordan—were indifferent about the details of any agreement. Whatever the Palestinians would accept was good enough for them. Breathing a sigh of relief, they could then get on with other concerns, problems, and interests.

What was especially interesting about the Peace Camp was that, except for Egypt, the Arab members were the region's weaker countries. Of course, Egypt, the most powerful Arab state, was the first to make peace with Israel, partly because any such pioneer had to be strong enough to defy and survive powerful pressures brought to bear against it. There was great sympathy in Arab countries for the Palestinians and real distrust of Israel. But the most important factor causing smaller states to slow normalization was concern over domestic—including Islamic—and inter-Arab reaction.

But the weakest countries were also readiest for peace with Israel. They had no ambitions for regional hegemony—unlike the radical states or Egypt—and felt more threatened by Arab neighbors and local problems than by Israel. On the contrary, they might find Israel a profitable trading partner and useful counterweight to stronger Arab or Islamic regimes menacing them. Having relations with Israel also strengthened links with their main defender, the United States.

Thus, half the Arab world's countries wanted more normal relations with Israel, and one-quarter of them had taken steps in that direction despite Syrian—and, at times, PA, Egyptian, and Saudi—pleas to wait until after a comprehensive peace agreement. The moderates were constrained mainly by fear of foreign Arab and domestic pressure, which they hoped progress in peacemaking would dissipate. They had no interest in fighting Israel and lacked the resources or unity to do so successfully. These smaller states found it relatively easy to abandon a conflict in which they had played only a marginal role.

Egypt was the single most influential Arab country. It was the PA's patron and the Arab state most willing and able to help it. Recognizing this role, Arafat met with Mubarak at least sixteen times between December 1994 and August 1997.[38] Arafat frequently appealed for Egyptian intervention in the process. For example, in August 1996 he asked Mubarak to mediate with Netanyahu to halt Jewish settlements. "I'm sure that Your Excellency will not spare any effort to get the peace process back to its correct track," he told him.[39] During tough negotiations over Hebron, Israel repeatedly charged that Egypt was telling the Palestinians to go slow and make more demands. But in June 1997 the United States and Israel accepted Egypt as intermediary in an effort to restart talks.

Still, Egypt's ability to help the PA was limited by several factors. It wanted to see the PA succeed and create a Palestinian state, but it did not have much money to give, would not jeopardize its Arab leadership role for the PA's sake, and did not pressure other Arab states to provide more aid.[40] As Syria's ally, Mubarak conditioned normalization with Israel on successful completion of a Syria-Israel agreement, not progress on the PA-Israel front. Similarly, Egypt would not endanger its good relations with the West or risk a major confrontation with Israel.[41] It also may have slowed efforts to advance the peace process out of a concern that Israel's integration into the region might create a strategic and economic rival to its own leadership.[42]

Jordan's standpoint also caused the PA problems. "The cause of Palestine is the cornerstone of Jordan's domestic, Arab and foreign policy," said King Husayn in 1967, "a matter of life and death."[43] The development of Jordanian-Israeli relations was partly based on the fact that Jordanian-Palestinian relations had often been competitive.[44] For many years Jordan tried to regain control of the West Bank. In May 1988 King Husayn renounced this claim, but he remained concerned about the fate of the lands west of the Jordan River. Consequently, much mistrust remained between King Husayn and Arafat.[45]

The 1993 Palestinian-Israeli agreement, wrote Khalil Shiqaqi in 1994, "had the effect of an earthquake . . . and caused [the Jordanians] great fear." He correctly predicted that this event would push the Jordanians into a treaty with Israel, which would not be to the Palestinians' liking.[46] Jordan signed a preliminary agreement with Israel in July 1994, followed by a full peace treaty in October.[47]

Jordan had a stronger national interest than any other Arab state in allying with Israel. By doing so it gained a counterweight to Iraq, Iran, and Syria, as well as some insurance on the Palestinian issue. An enhanced Jordan-Israel relationship also strengthened U.S.-Jordan links.[48] While public opinion in Jordan largely opposed a warm peace with Israel,[49] King Husayn was not deterred.

During early 1997, for example, Jordan invited Israel to attend a Mediterranean trade conference in Amman. Elscint became the first Israeli company to win a Jordanian government tender, a $1.5 million deal to supply the government hospital in Amman with CAT-scan equipment. In March 1997 the two countries agreed to build a jointly operated airport in Aqaba-Eilat. Israel and Jordan also signed accords on transport and on allocating water and making highway improvements.[50] King Husayn expressed his hope that peace would bring the "qualitative progress that we have always sought."[51]

Jordan knew that it must somehow ensure that any Palestinian state would not subvert its own citizens or someday fall into the hands of radical forces that could threaten Jordan's security. The presence of so many Palestinians within Jordan—whom the PA claimed to represent—created the basis for a potential struggle between them. Referring to a U.S. report which stated that there were about 1.2 million Palestinians in Jordan, Crown Prince Hasan commented, "From our perspective [these] Palestinians are Jordanian citizens."[52]

With the political relationship so sensitive, a 1994 Jordan-PLO agreement focused on economic rather than political cooperation. The following year detailed accords were signed on a range of economic and cultural issues, with PA dependence on Jordan symbolized by its decision to make the Jordanian dinar its official currency.[53]

Jordan's role as guardian of East Jerusalem's Muslim holy places was guaranteed in the Israel-Jordan peace treaty, conflicting with PA claims.[54] In January 1995, Jordan and the PLO made a deal in which Jordan promised to turn over control of the sites to the Palestinians whenever they gained authority over East Jerusalem.[55] Abd Rabbu wrote, "Relations with Jordan are extremely important . . . I'm against accelerating the struggle against Jordan in the question of Jerusalem. This issue is irrelevant as long as the city isn't free."[56]

Arafat did not agree with him. In October 1996 PA supporters were sent to seize the office administering the al-Aqsa mosque and Dome of the Rock. Jordan appealed for Israeli help to retain control, but the Netanyahu government instead dealt with the PA-approved group. The final humiliation for Jordan came when a plaque commemorating King Husayn's donation to refurbish the Dome of the Rock was destroyed, probably by PA supporters.[57] In December 1997, King Husayn struck back by suggesting a multinational Muslim, instead of an exclusively Palestinian, administration of the holy places, which, he said, should be "above the sovereign considerations of any state."[58]

For its part, the PA feared Jordan's ambitions over the West Bank and cooperation with Israel, and even Hamas. PA officials believed that Jordan secretly opposed a Palestinian state.[59] The PA had quickly intimidated pro-Jordanian newspapers into changing their political line. Arafat ordered all Palestinian professional unions to become independent from their Jordanian counterparts, with which they had been united, and to cease accepting Jordanian government subsidies.[60]

The PA also accused Jordan of giving Hamas too much freedom to operate in Jordan. In 1997 King Husayn passed on a Hamas cease-fire offer to Israel, circumventing the PA and seeming to open the door for an alternative Palestinian diplomatic partner.[61] Nevertheless, at Arafat's request, Jordan refused to let Yasin into the country and sometimes expelled Hamas activists involved in planning attacks.[62] There was occasionally even trilateral cooperation, as when Israel, Jordan, and the PA launched a joint international advertising campaign to attract tourists in 1997 with the slogan "Peace. It's a beautiful sight to see."

Despite these problems, the longtime official PLO position, taken over by the PA, was that it wanted a confederation between the future Palestinian state and Jordan. The Jordanians were reluctant, especially since a loose confederation would give them burdens without power, and insisted that any such plan could be discussed only after a Palestinian state was established.[63] Abu Amr predicted that Arafat also would not be so eager for such an arrangement, since he "regards himself as future head of a state and . . . will oppose a confederation with Jordan which might stop him from being that."[64]

While moderate states gave the PA insufficient help, the Radical Camp—Iran, Iraq, Libya, Sudan, and Syria—actively tried to subvert it. The radical states' regional and international isolation, lack of a superpower backer, unfavorable power balance, and shattered ideological taboos greatly reduced their influence. But they still rejected Israel's existence and saw Arafat's peacemaking as treasonous. A solution to the Palestinian problem, even one producing a Palestinian state, would strengthen moderation and deny the radicals an issue they could exploit to their own advantage. Only a revival of militancy and conflict could give them a chance to provide leadership and return to a more favorable situation.

If Israel were to be accepted as a normal part of the region, it would be better able to oppose their attempts to bully neighbors, promote revolutions, and become the dominant regional power. A Palestinian state that did not side with their ambitions, and whose existence might even reduce regional tensions, seemed a negative development from their standpoint. A successful peace process would also reinforce U.S. influence, further weakening radical forces.

Therefore, PA relations with the radical Arab states were paradoxical. Baghdad and Damascus claimed to champion the Palestinian cause but used that boast to justify criticizing and subverting the PA. Only by completely changing his strategy could Arafat win their approval. But even if he were to do so, they did not have the political or military power to solve his problems.

The radical states tried to humiliate the PA in many ways. One unfair punishment Syria and Iraq exacted was the refusal to admit students who held a PA-issued high school diploma into their universities.[65] Lebanon kept a Palestinian delegation from attending a 1998 Arab conference on population and development held in Beirut because it refused to recognize their PA passports. Indeed, until changing its policy in January 1999, Lebanon made it very difficult even for Palestinians holding Lebanese travel documents to reenter the country.[66]

Syria was especially hostile toward the PA, backing groups that were trying to subvert Arafat and the peace process.[67] Arafat was understandably suspicious about Syria's behavior but also repeatedly sought conciliation. Syria was uninterested. Instead of receiving Syrian help, the PA suffered from its sabotage.

From the 1960s on, Syria had repeatedly tried to seize control of the PLO through its own client groups, assassinations, and warfare, and by inciting splits. By letting pro-Syrian and pro-Iranian Palestinian groups operate freely in Lebanon while blocking pro-Arafat forces, Syria was helping to destroy any base of support for the PA among its exiled brethren there.[68] Periodically, Syrian leaders even argued that since Palestine (i.e., Israel, the West Bank, and the Gaza Strip) was actually "southern Syria," the PLO had no right to make any agreement over its future disposition.

A successful Palestinian-Israeli peace process would be disastrous for Syria on many levels. If Israel were allowed to become a normal regional power, even in exchange for accepting an independent Palestinian state, it could better oppose Syrian ambitions and interests in Lebanon and elsewhere. The emergence of a stable Palestinian state—especially one with good relations with the West and under Egypt's patronage—would deny Syria the chance to control the Palestinians or exploit the issue. Syrians and Palestinians were also competing over whose interests would take precedence in determining when the Arab world normalized relations with Israel. In short, making its own agreement with Israel would be of questionable value to Syria, while an Israeli-Palestinian peace treaty would be very negative.[69] Syria demanded that Israeli concessions to itself, rather than progress on the Israeli-Palestinian front, be the Arab states' criterion for normalizing relations with Israel.

The situation with Iraq was even stranger. Except for Syria, no other Arab country had done the Palestinians more damage. During the 1970s and 1980s, Iraq hired Abu Nidal to kill PLO officials. Baghdad also maintained its own client groups in the organization. Yet Palestinians never felt the antagonism toward Baghdad which many had for Jordan, Syria, or Saudi Arabia. Arafat supported Iraq against Iran in their 1980–1988 war, despite his own earlier good relations with Tehran's Islamic revolution. When Iraqi President Saddam Husayn began a bid for Arab leadership in 1988, Arafat again strongly backed him, and did so once more during his 1990 invasion of Kuwait and the subsequent crisis.

For its part, Iraq was hostile to the peace process but tried to avoid condemning Arafat. It even ordered client groups in the PLO to back him in voting to change the Palestinian Charter at the May 1996 PNC meeting.[70] To show its opposition to the peace process, however, Iraq withdrew three hundred scholarships previously granted university students from the West Bank and Gaza.[71]

To bridge these contradictions, Saddam Husayn reinterpreted Arafat to his own taste: "No matter how we Arab officials assess Yasir Arafat, he is now the man in command of his people . . . It is extremely important that we back him." But Arafat must be persuaded to return to revolution. "Until Palestine is liberated, the Palestinians must avoid building a material base for the state that could become a heavy burden when the Zionist entity threatens to destroy it or actually does destroy it. The so-called self-rule area must be more of a base for revolutionary struggle than of a state structure."[72]

In short, Saddam Husayn—like his Syrian counterpart Hafiz al-Asad—saw successful Palestinian state-building as threatening his interests. Arafat rejected the Iraqi leader's advice but still backed Iraq's reintegration into the Arab world, a policy that did not endear him to Saudi Arabia and Kuwait.

The 1998 crisis between the United States and Iraq showed both the Palestinians' continued sympathy for Baghdad and this sentiment's high cost to themselves. Iraq had stopped UN-mandated inspections of its arsenal, and the United States was considering military action. Many demonstrations throughout the West Bank expressed support for Iraq; some involved the burning of U.S. and Israeli flags and clashes with Israeli soldiers. Fatah's local West Bank leader Marwan al-Barghuti declared that "rejecting the U.S. attack is similar to rejecting Israeli policies, since there is a joint U.S.-Israeli position to attack our people, its achievements, and the general Arab will."[73] Hamas threatened to hit at Israel if the United States bombed Iraq.[74] High-level PA delegations visited Baghdad to convey their solidarity directly to Saddam Husayn.

In public opinion polls, Palestinians expressed sympathy with the Iraqi people (72 percent) and opposition to U.S. policies (63 percent); 29 percent indicated support for Saddam Husayn himself. About 77 percent wanted Iraq to attack Israel in retaliation for a U.S. strike, even though almost half of them feared that Palestinians would be injured in that event.[75] Israelis remembered how Palestinians had cheered Iraqi missile attacks on Israel in 1991 and wondered whether a future Palestinian state might become a base for Iraq's army. Cabinet secretary Danny Naveh accused Fatah of mobilizing Palestinians to ask Saddam Husayn to strike Israel. Most immediately, Israel worried that Palestinian demonstrations would escalate into violence. Israeli leaders warned that continuation of these marches could interfere with progress in negotiations.[76]

Arafat, whatever his feelings toward Iraq, was now leader of a government which had practical responsibilities. The PA responded quickly. Brigadier General Haj Isma'il Jabr, chief of Palestinian police in the West Bank, said, "We understand what is behind [Israel's warning], so we have to prevent those [pro-Iraq] demonstrations." He issued an order on February 10 prohibiting marches because violent confrontations might ensue. This was not a popular decision. Polls showed that Palestinians opposed the ban by a 58 to 33 percent margin. Nevertheless, on February 17 the PA cooled the situation by ordering thirty-four television and radio stations under its jurisdiction to shut down temporarily in order to curb the show of pro-Iraq sentiment.[77]

The irony of the situation was shown when PA Health Minister Riyad Za'nun asked the United States to provide Palestinians with gas masks and other equipment to protect them from any Iraqi attack.[78] The PA did not want a confrontation with Israel wrecking already troubled negotiations. To be seen again as Iraq's ally would ruin the PA's international image and lead to cuts in aid. Consequently, the PA complained that the crisis distracted attention from the peace process, expressed hope for a peaceful solution, and urged the United States to push Israel also to comply with its commitments.[79] When a UN-Iraq agreement ended the crisis, Arafat greeted that outcome with great relief.[80]

While the PA's link with Iraq remained its most dangerous political connection with an Arab state, its poor relations with the third category of states—the Dropouts, Saudi Arabia and Kuwait—were of tragic proportions for Palestinian state-building, denying it desperately needed financial resources. As moderate, wealthy states, these two countries seemed natural allies for the PA, able to ensure its success in raising Palestinian living standards and in developing a stable, growing economy. If they chose to use their riches on the PA's behalf, this would also give the PA far more leverage in persuading the West to press Israel for concessions and to offer Israel economic benefits in exchange for accepting a Palestinian state.

During the 1970s and 1980s, Saudi Arabia had been the PLO's most reliable financier. Aid dwindled as it spent more money at home and diverted funds to help Iraq in its war against Iran. Saudi investments in the West also discouraged its taking actions against Western interests in order to help the PLO. But the real crisis came when Arafat backed Iraq's

1990 seizure of Kuwait, provoking a strong, bitter Saudi response. Aid to the PLO and Palestinian institutions was cut off.[81]

Kuwait, whose many Palestinian residents had previously always made it sympathetic to the PLO, now totally reversed its attitude. After Iraqi forces retreated, Kuwait expelled most Palestinians from the country and boycotted the PLO. The PA's official Voice of Palestine radio characterized Kuwait's official treatment of the PA as a "campaign of hatred and hostility toward the Palestinian people and their leadership."[82]

Consequently, Saudi Arabia and Kuwait gave the PA little material aid or political support. The lack of Arab help made the PA both less stable and less able to fulfill commitments, reducing its success in negotiations as well as its ability to advance rapidly in the state-building process. The Arab states also interfered in the PA's effort to retain the loyalty of over 2.5 million Palestinians living in Arab countries.[83]

The PA wanted rich Palestinians abroad to invest in its territory, but they were reluctant to do so owing to the situation's uncertainty, doubtful prospects for profit, and their unhappiness with Arafat's policies. Arafat tried to put the best face on his disappointment at their poor response: "I am not satisfied but I say that they have made a start and I expect much more from the rich Palestinians who must contribute to the building of the homeland of their children and grandchildren . . . Capital is cautious by nature." Moreover, after Iraq's defeat in 1991 the wealthy Palestinian community in Kuwait had been expelled, and thus the community had become much poorer.[84]

In the new Palestinian politics there was theoretically a division of labor between the PA, the government of Palestinians living in the West Bank and Gaza, and the PLO, which would continue to lead Palestinians everywhere. A key PLO slogan for many years was that the organization represented "all our people in all places inside and outside their homeland."[85] The PLO, Arafat said at Fatah's thirtieth anniversary celebration in 1995, "will remain the symbol of Palestinian people at home and abroad."[86] A prominent PLO official remarked after the Oslo agreement, "We must not ignore our people's daily problems in all parts of the world."[87]

Successfully addressing the needs and views of these constituents was another matter.[88] Almost all the exiled PLO leaders themselves—like the refugees abroad—had originated from places now in Israel and hoped to go back one day to their pre-1948 homes once Israel had been eliminated.[89] For most Palestinians this was the struggle's whole purpose and essential outcome: the hope for a day when Palestinians would reclaim their homes and Israel would vanish as if it had never existed. To abandon one's vision of the Return, explained a Palestinian writer, "is to rip up the tree on which [one's] history and raison d'être grow [and] rush headlong on a trip to madness." How, asked Abu Iyad, one of the top PLO leaders, could he tell someone originally from Nablus that he can go home but not someone from Jaffa or Haifa?[90]

Many of the refugees abroad, especially those in Lebanon, had few direct ties to the West Bank and Gaza. The new developments posed a number of problems for them: Did they believe that the peace process would bring a Palestinian state at all? Would they be able someday to go and live in that country? Would they accept a Palestinian state there at the cost of giving up a claim to their pre-1948 homes, which were now in Israel, rather than continue to demand Israel's destruction and Palestinian rule over all the land?

The most encouraging sign was that the PA was able to bring back tens of thousands of Palestinians from exile. Yet for those still outside the West Bank and Gaza Strip, the peace agreements triggered more anxiety than celebration. Mamduh Nawfal, a member of the PLO Central Council, remarked: "Palestinians living abroad as immigrants or refugees have mixed feelings. They appreciate the right of compatriots at home to elect leaders but have concern about their personal and national future." They could find no one who could explain what would happen to them in that future.[91] Hani al-Hasan claimed that PA promises of a quick return had persuaded the refugees to support the Oslo agreements. But when this did not happen, many went back to their traditional hard-line position.[92]

One element of the Palestinian refugees' fear was knowing that Arab regimes wanted an excuse to displace them. This threat was most evident in Libya, whose leader, Muammar Qadhafi, expressed his opposition to the peace agreement by firing and expelling several thousand Palestinians. Hundreds of deportees could find no country to accept them and were temporarily stranded on boats or on the Libya-Egypt and Turkey-Syria frontiers without food or water.[93]

The PLO and PA opposed Palestinian refugees' being resettled or taking citizenship in other Arab countries. In Jordan, Palestinians already had that status. But even there, and certainly elsewhere, this official stance that they were awaiting a return to Palestine—shared by most of the refugees themselves—helped deny them a more secure status or better living conditions outside refugee camps. Of course, those who could afford to do so often did move into permanent housing, while many found roots in their country of residence.

Still, they all publicly embraced the promise of an eventual return to a Palestinian state. "Under Israeli law," an interviewer asked Arafat, "every Jew has the right to live in Israel. Can you obtain this same right for the Palestinians in the diaspora . . . a right to live in this Palestinian state?" Arafat replied, "This is the state of the Palestinians wherever they are, at home and abroad."[94] But implementing any such plan would have to await an Israel-PA final agreement that would determine these matters and, indeed, the existence of a Palestinian state.

Trying to keep up morale, Arafat opened a Palestinian refugee conference in September 1996 with the declaration, "Palestine is for the Palestinians and their right to return to it is sacred."[95] A week earlier, another such meeting had rejected the concept of compensation for their property lost in 1948 in exchange for giving up a claimed right of return to Israel.[96] The PA kept open its option of demanding a return for all Palestinian refugees to Israel. Yet since it knew that Israel would never accept such a solution, the PA would someday either have to let this issue wreck negotiations or make a devastating concession on that point.

Most of the refugees outside the PA-ruled areas lived in Jordan, Lebanon, and Syria. Additional Palestinians, who had never left their homes, resided in Israel. Each place presented a very different psychological and political situation.

The case of Palestinians in Syria was the clearest. When it came to any political expression, they were kept under tight government control by a dictatorship that favored anti-Arafat groups. Their potential problem was whether Syria's government would let them go to live under Arafat's rule in the PA or a future Palestinian state that Damascus rejected.

In Lebanon, Palestinian refugees were desperate, and the PA suffered serious political losses.[97] Aware of this problem, Arafat singled out for praise in his 1995 speech on Fatah's thirtieth anniversary "our masses in the steadfast [refugee] camps of exile in Lebanon where people have suffered and made great sacrifices."[98]

The government and many Lebanese wanted to be rid of them because of xenophobia, the PLO's past involvements in Lebanese politics, and fear among Christians of the Palestinian refugees' tipping the demographic balance even more in favor of Muslims. Few Palestinians there were ever granted citizenship. Soon after the Oslo agreement was signed, Lebanese Foreign Minister Faris Buwayz published a plan to send most refugees to the West Bank or Gaza, other Arab states, or the West. Not many of them would be permitted to remain in Lebanon.[99]

Some in Lebanon even accused the Palestinians of being under orders from Arafat to create settlements and take over part of the country. After Oslo, the Lebanese government made it harder even for Palestinians with residency certificates to enter the country. Palestinian sources accused Lebanon of conducting a "policy of hatred" against them and quoted the minister of tourism, who had called Palestinians "human trash."[100] UNRWA's cutbacks of social and educational services to the refugees, owing to its financial crisis, made their living situation even worse.[101]

Arafat did bring home hundreds of PLO soldiers and their families from Lebanon to join the PA police force.[102] But if this repatriation gave others a hope of returning, the removal of Arafat's most loyal supporters from Lebanon also further reduced his declining assets there. Sporadic armed clashes broke out between pro- and anti-Arafat forces. In Ayn al-Hilwa camp, Fatah leader Munit Makda defected to join the Islamist side and declared that Arafat should be assassinated.[103] On January 20, 1996, while Palestinians in the West Bank and Gaza were celebrating their election, all Palestinian refugee camps in southern Lebanon—except al-Rashidiyya, which remained pro-Arafat—called general strikes in protest.[104] "We are not part of the new Lebanon or the peace process in Palestine," said one Palestinian resident of Shatila refugee camp, injured in a Syrian-backed Amal militia attack in 1985. "It is as if there is a plan by all parties in the region, including the PLO, to bury us in the past."[105]

The loss of supporters in Lebanon was no mere spontaneous development. In 1983 a Syrian-backed split and revolt within the PLO had temporarily destroyed Arafat's forces in Lebanon. Fatah had rebuilt its infrastructure but never fully regained its previous strength there, given Syria's continued financial and logistical help for Arafat's adversaries.

Now a new challenge came from Iran and the Islamic groups it sponsored, especially the Lebanese Hizbullah. Yasin said that Hamas and Hizbullah "have a duty to cooperate and our cooperation, which is not a secret, will continue."[106] The Yasir Arafat Center for Social Activity in Ayn al-Hilwa camp turned into the Iran-financed al-Quds hospital, providing free care. Hizbullah paid pensions the PLO could no longer afford to families of martyrs and for the salaries of militias such as Makda's 1,500 men. While the PFLP and DFLP remained strong in the north

Lebanon camps, Islamist groups became hegemonic in the south.[107] Iranian instructors gave Palestinians military training. The Iranian-backed Shahid Filastin (Palestine Martyr) organization built new houses and mosques. More and more Palestinians turned to the style of Islam—and politics—advocated by Tehran and Hizbullah.[108] Short of achieving statehood and repatriating large numbers of Palestinians from Lebanon, the PA had no prospect of reversing this trend.

While several hundred thousand Palestinians in Lebanon faced the threat of having no home at all, Palestinians in Jordan—whose numbers exceeded those under Arafat's rule—faced the frightening prospect of having to choose between two homes. Since more than half of Jordan's citizens were of Palestinian origin, the Palestinian issue there was a domestic as well as a foreign policy question. The two peoples were close enough in every respect for King Husayn to call them "twins."[109] Palestinians often saw things in parallel terms. Ahmad Khuri remarked, "We are one people . . . It is a family, part of it here, part of it there."[110] While lots of Palestinians lived in poverty in refugee camps, many Palestinian families had become central to Jordan's economy, linked themselves to the monarchy, or attained comfortable lives.[111]

The PLO had usually—but not always—been cautious about appearing to foment an internal ethnic conflict in Jordan. Sometimes, though, the threat was unsheathed. A 1988 interview by PLO leader Salah Khalaf (Abu Iyad) must have chilled Jordan's king: "We refuse to accept [that Palestinians living in Jordan] should owe their principal loyalty to Jordan rather than Palestine . . . We have no objection that Palestinians in Jordan continue to live as Jordanian citizens until the establishment of the Palestinian state."[112]

This kind of attitude filtered down into daily behavior. At a 1990 dinner party, a Jordanian-Palestinian ambassador boasted that Palestinian loyalty to Jordan was beyond question. An official of East Bank origin asked, "Quick, who do you support more, King Husayn or Arafat?" There was silence. "That answers the question," said the East Banker.[113] But Palestinian-Jordanians knew that openly giving Arafat their prime allegiance could undermine their security. At the same time, Jordanian officials certainly did not want them to support Hamas, and the government tried to make sure that group did not recruit members within the country. Some Palestinians responded to the situation by flocking to other Islamic groups, led by East Bank Jordanians, which opposed the peace process but focused their main attention on conditions within Jordan.[114]

By reopening issues of loyalty, identity, and the future, the Oslo agreement raised tension between Palestinian and East Bank citizens.[115] Extremist East Bankers argued that all Palestinians should eventually be sent back. Others favored a "political return," forcing Palestinians in Jordan to take Palestinian citizenship, thus making them ineligible to vote or be involved in Jordan's politics.[116] Palestinians began to complain about discrimination in hiring and taunts from East Bankers asking why they didn't go home.[117]

Rejecting compulsory options, Jordan's official policy offered Palestinians there a choice between leaving and assimilating. As King Husayn put it in a September 18, 1993, speech: "Our [Palestinian] brethren here . . . are in their country and among their brothers and kinfolk. They have the same rights as we have and they have the same duties and responsibilities as we have until any of them decides on a different course or a new situation . . . Whoever opts to leave us and go to his original motherland, he is free to do so; whoever opts to stay here and to have all his rights, he is most welcome, and will stay with us as part and parcel of one nation."[118]

In other words, as a high-ranking Jordanian official explained, Palestinians in Jordan had three alternatives: they could retain Jordanian citizenship, return to Palestine, or stay in Jordan as Palestinian resident aliens.[119] The critical point was that each individual would have to decide someday to be either a Palestinian or a Jordanian, even if he could live on in Jordan as a foreigner. Jordan rejected the PA's call for dual nationality. In response, Khuri voiced the PA position: "We don't want to ask the people to choose between here or there."[120]

Given this uncertainty, the newspaper *al-Sharq al-Awsat* reported, "Palestinian refugee circles in Jordan are overwhelmed by anxiety and anticipation over their final status." One problem was that many could not admit that they wanted to stay in Jordan, since this was "politically incorrect" in Palestinian terms. According to a Palestinian political figure there, "Just as we refuse to have our problem solved as a problem of refugees in Jordan or in any other Arab or foreign country, we also refuse to cede our rights and refuse to have our issue resolved in the West Bank or Gaza because we have spent 45 years building in Jordan." If he could not return to his original home in Ramla, now part of Israel, he preferred staying in Amman to living in Jerusalem or Ramallah, even if they were in a Palestinian state.[121]

The PA's attitude toward the Palestinian minority in Israel was deliberately vague since this was an even more dangerous issue. While Arab citizens of Israel supported an independent Palestinian state in the West Bank and Gaza and expressed solidarity with the people there, any PA suggestion that Israeli-Palestinians should struggle against Israel could destroy the peace process. As the Palestinian writer Marwan Darwish noted, while the PA's emergence encouraged Arab citizens of Israel to increase their demands, both the PLO and PA found it hard to influence them politically. They remained independent in opinion and voted in Israeli elections as they had done before: about half for Zionist parties and a large proportion for the Communist Party. Support for an Islamic group also grew. One of its leaders, Shaykh Abdallah Nimr Darwish, had tried to help Arafat mediate a deal with Hamas to end attacks on Israelis. But there was no strong nationalist party allied to the PA.[122]

This situation was due in part to the fact that Israeli-Palestinians—who included almost 20 percent of the population—were partly integrated into Israel and did not want to endanger their status there, however little enthusiasm they might have for that country.[123] Few seemed inclined to move to PA lands or even to an independent Palestinian state. PA efforts to intervene in local politics fell afoul of factional conflicts among Israeli-Palestinians themselves. When Arafat's Israeli-Palestinian adviser Ahmad Tibi attempted to run in the 1996 Israeli parliamentary elections, he stirred so much partisan antagonism among Israeli-Palestinians that he had to withdraw. Thus, the PA remained cautious while still asserting that Arab citizens of Israel were part of the Palestinian people.[124]

The PA publicly insisted that the Arab world, Islamic movements, and the Palestinian diaspora gave it powerful support while knowing that this was by no means accurate. These forces often damaged the PA's interests. Certainly they provided far less help than it might have expected and often posed serious dilemmas for its peacemaking and state-building processes.

8

THINKING ABOUT ISRAEL
AND THE UNITED STATES

One of the PA's most difficult tasks was to reformulate the Palestinian view of Israel and the West. This was no mere theoretical problem. The PA's analysis of Israeli politics shaped its own policy, Israel's response, and the peace process's prospects. The basic position taken by particular Palestinian groups or individuals on this issue determined their entire political orientation.

For many decades, the PLO and the overwhelming majority of Palestinians had considered Israel's existence so illegitimate and contrary to their needs and rights as to make peace with it impossible. But while the basis of this idea lay in the material reality of Palestinian displacement, suffering, and anger, it was not the sole possible interpretation. Moreover, the predominant Palestinian concept of Israel's nature tried to reconcile two opposite notions. On the one hand, Israel was depicted as essentially weak, a front for the Western imperialist effort to control the region. On the other hand, Israel was portrayed as all-powerful, the core of a Jewish effort toward world conquest.[1]

Either way, the conclusion was that Israel was not a real, viable country and hence could be destroyed by military defeat, loss of external support, or collapse from within. Equally, if the United States was either Israel's master or slave, the Palestinian movement could not work with that government because its policy was unshakably hostile. The PLO's only path would have to be revolutionary armed struggle.

But over time it became harder to sustain that doctrine and strategy. The PLO faced many failures and setbacks from Israeli victories, Arab defeats, declining Arab state support for the Palestinians, and an inability to end occupation of the West Bank and Gaza Strip by any means except direct talks and a peace agreement with Israel. Consequently, the majority, perhaps 75 percent, of Palestinians living under the PA now favored negotiation and compromise. Radical opposition groups—Hamas, Islamic Jihad, the PFLP and DFLP—and a minority within Fatah did not change their thinking.

Among those ready for a negotiated solution, there were two variants on the proper strategy to follow. First, there were those who accepted in principle the possibility and preferability of negotiated peace but thought that they would have to force it on an intransigent Israel. Those who held this view—ranging from the PPP's and FIDA's critical support to often loyal Fatah critics of Arafat—participated in PA institutions but complained that Arafat made too many concessions and used too little pressure. Their differences with the PA, however, remained on a rhetorical level. They might cheer the radicals' violence but never engaged in it themselves.

Alternatively, the PA and its more consistent loyalists saw Israel as an adversary but believed they could successfully achieve a Palestinian state by negotiating with it. In this context the PA had many choices in setting its strategy, including mobilizing international backing, persuading the United States to favor its positions, making demands, wearing down Israel by delays, and offering concessions. It also sought to create facts by building a state's infrastructure and seeking to build momentum toward independence. A key element was the extent to which it would play on internal Israeli politics to achieve its goal.

This climate was influenced by the fact that numerous aspects of occupation still persisted, including an Israeli presence in most of the West Bank's territory and in some of Gaza. There were still periodic clashes between Palestinians and Israel's army, resulting in fatalities and recurrent killings of Palestinians by Jewish settlers (most notably the 1994 Hebron massacre); building continued in Jewish settlements, along with confiscations of land to construct bypass roads; and hundreds of Palestinian prisoners were still in jail for violent acts committed both before and after the 1993 agreement. Israeli politicians in power from 1996 to 1999 expressed distrust of the PA, opposed yielding land, and vowed that they would never accept a Palestinian state. There was a virtual Israeli consensus against concessions on East Jerusalem, and measures were taken to ensure that it would never be given up. The PA leaders also knew that Israel was the stronger party in the conflict. "Both sides felt that there were things which should have been amended" in the agreements, said Mahmud Abbas. "But the Palestinians do not have the power to make changes, while the Israelis do."[2]

Of course, as this statement and many others also showed, Arafat and his lieutenants doubted Israeli intentions to compromise. There were also real conflicts over both immediate issues and the proposed ultimate solution. In an August 1995 poll, when Rabin was still prime minister and shortly before Israel began turning over West Bank towns to the PA, just 7 percent of Palestinians said that they trusted Israel's intentions regarding the peace process, while 81 percent mistrusted them.[3] A year later, with Netanyahu in power, almost 91 percent said that they did not consider him to be a man of peace.[4]

The important political question, however, was how the PA would deal with these problems. The greater the PA's effectiveness in stopping violence and providing security, the more concessions Israel would make, and the faster the process would advance. Israel's motive for making peace was to gain security and a stable regional situation. Israel would give Palestinians what they wanted only if convinced that the PA had really changed its historic objectives and was a credible partner. Under these conditions the PA had a tremendous interest in positively affecting Israeli perceptions and dealing with Israeli domestic politics to strengthen conciliatory elements. In fact, the PA often failed, to its own detriment, to manage these issues to its best advantage.

The two sides' divergent perceptions were highlighted in a January 1995 interview with Sufyan Abu Zayida, a PA official who had spent twelve years in Israeli prisons, by Israeli journalist Nomi Levitzky of *Yediot Ahronot*.[5] This shows the atmosphere at a time when Rabin was still in power and the process was moving ahead, though prior to Israeli withdrawal from West Bank towns:

Levitzky: People here in Gaza were seen rejoicing after the terrorist attack [at Bayt Lid junction] . . .

Abu Zayida: . . . Let us say that some of the people here were not particularly upset. This is because the Palestinian people do not feel that the Israelis are giving them anything in return. Neither territory nor honor. The Palestinians are bitterly disappointed. There has been no improvement in their economic and social well-being . . . Except for the abolishment of the night curfew and your army's withdrawal from the refugee camps, nothing has changed . . .

Levitzky: . . . Even a moderate man like [Israeli President] Ezer Weizman, who supports reaching an arrangement, has called for a suspension of the process. This should be viewed as a serious warning.

Abu Zayida: Not only Ezer Weizman. I, too, sometimes have doubts about the process. [At first, there was] the impression that just by sitting down together, we had already made the required concessions, and now everything would work out. But this was followed by all the mistakes in the world.

Levitzky: How, then, can we totally eliminate this hatred?

Abu Zayida: . . . I believed that most of your public understood the situation. Apparently, I must have been wrong. Despite the Oslo agreement, most Israelis still think that the Palestinians as a people do not deserve the same rights as them . . . If you behave nicely, you will get half of the Gaza Strip. If you behave even better, we will let you have all of the Gaza Strip . . . Is it impossible for you to understand that the Palestinian people have a right to their own state, flag, and passport? . . . We are prepared to reach a compromise with you. Most of the Palestinian people are ready to accept a Palestinian state alongside with Israel. How much more blood must be spilled before Israel accepts such a compromise?

Levitzky: You Palestinians are shooting yourselves in the foot. Why not learn from Israel's history? Why does Arafat not follow Ben-Gurion's example? You were given a one-time opportunity, and you are wasting it. You cannot get everything at once.

Abu Zayida: We are not Israel, and Arafat is not Ben-Gurion. You were given a state; we were granted limited autonomy over part of the land. I agree that we had an opportunity to achieve something and that we have occasionally supplied you with excuses to delay the process and to avoid implementing subsequent stages of the agreement. We also tell Fatah members who have reservations about the process that violence will get us nowhere. We tell them that it only exacerbates hatred between our two peoples. We opted for the way of peace and must stick to it. There is no other choice. We constantly say the same thing to Hamas and the Islamic Jihad. We really want to stop the cycle of hatred and bloodshed. I agree with you that some of those who came from Tunis [PLO Outsiders] do not understand the Israelis. The gap is too wide; they do not understand the dynamics or what the Israelis are feeling. This poses a big problem for me and my friends from Fatah, who operate in the field. We keep on trying to persuade Arafat to speak to the Israeli public and build trust between the two peoples. So far, we have been unsuccessful.

Levitzky: But you, the field operatives, can do something. Where is the

Palestinian equivalent of Peace Now? Why did you not demonstrate in the street against the Bayt Lid murders? We demonstrated against Sabra and Shatila.

Abu Zayida: The entire Fatah organization is basically Peace Now. Our "Peace Now" is the governing authority. You do not understand what is holding the Palestinians back. The people still feel that you are stepping on their necks and trampling their honor. Although a lot of people told me they were shocked by the Bayt Lid murders, the day when we can stage such demonstrations is still a long way off. I wish we could, but this is the result of the harsh reality in which we live.

Levitzky: If Arafat would take the steps required of a leader, calm down the street, and talk to the Palestinian public about reconciliation, then maybe things would be different.

Abu Zayida: No soothing words will do the trick here. Even if Arafat spoke about reconciliation, his words would be meaningless. There are hundreds of Palestinians in prison. True, they are accused of killing Israelis. They have been imprisoned for 10 or 20 years. But Arafat dispatched them. They remain in prison today, although they support peace. They have thousands of relatives. Can you not understand how destructive this is? I recognize the fact that we Palestinians are not implementing any confidence-building measures. I would like us to do more, but you Israelis still behave like conquerors . . .

Levitzky: Israelis are very disappointed in Arafat . . . He does not talk to us, convince us, or take any steps to win the confidence of the Israeli public. What is the matter with him?[6]

The answer to Levitzky's question was not hard to discover. Arafat's decisions were based on a mixture of his own personal style, Palestinian domestic politics, the PA's limited options, and misperceptions of Israel. But the basic Palestinian view was that only by completing the peace process, achieving Israeli withdrawal, and creating a Palestinian state could an alternative reality be produced that would end the friction and allow the PA to control Hamas and stop the attacks. Palestinians wanted assurance that Israel was ready to accept that solution.

While Rabin and Peres understood and essentially accepted this approach, Israelis wanted to feel assured that territorial concessions would indeed bring them more security and real peace. Based on its experience with Lebanon and Jordan, Israel worried that a Palestinian state might become a base for launching terror attacks or even war, whether with that regime's approval or even against its will. To avoid this problem, it wanted to see that the PA was able to stop attacks and that the Palestinian leadership had truly abandoned its old ambition of eliminating Israel.

Although about half of all Israelis supported the Rabin-Peres approach, the other half doubted the PA's credibility and intentions. That opposition was also divided almost evenly between those wanting to keep the territory for religious and nationalist reasons and those open to persuasion that a compromise peace agreement might bring them a better situation. In practical terms, if Arafat wanted to obtain a state, he had to reinforce the peace advocates and persuade swing voters to agree with them.

These concerns were irrelevant, of course, for Hamas and Islamic Jihad, which wanted the conflict to continue. They doubted that even Rabin's government had any intention of handing over the West Bank to the Palestinians and, at any rate, considered Israel an illegitimate state and all of its parties identically criminal.[7] Rantisi said that Hamas had no interest in dialogue with anyone there: "I do not believe in the Peace Now movement. Whoever colonized my land and expelled me from it is an invader even if he is a leftist. If people occupy a country which is not theirs and found a peace movement, does this change the fact that they are occupiers?"[8]

Recognizing that Netanyahu's victory in the 1996 elections could intensify conflict, Hamas found this an attractive outcome.[9] Hamas spokesperson Ibrahim Ghawsha said that his group preferred Netanyahu in office as a way to destroy the peace process. He and other Hamas leaders criticized the more moderate Zahar, who suggested stopping attacks so as not to push Israelis into electing Netanyahu.[10]

At any rate, Hamas expressed confidence that no compromise was required since Israel would eventually collapse. Yasin predicted: "The first quarter of the next century will witness the elimination of the Zionist entity and the establishment of the Palestinian state over the whole of Palestine. The strong will not remain strong forever and the weak will not remain weak forever. Things change . . . There is now a growing resistance against Israel."[11]

The PA's leaders lacked such faith, since they, unlike Hamas, had already tested Yasin's theory for decades and found that it did not work. Sitting in his Gaza office, Arafat could hear Israeli fighter planes flying off the coast. His lights operated on Israeli-generated electricity, and he knew well how hard it was to cope with damage to the Palestinian economy and living standards caused by Israeli closures after Hamas's attacks.

Whatever the extent of justifiable complaint, misunderstanding, and continued hostility, PA leaders, and especially Insiders, had few illusions about their chances of destroying Israel or forcing it into concessions by violence. In fact, this imbalance of forces was the problem most bothering many Palestinians, who doubted that Israel would compromise precisely because of its relative power. PLC member Rawiya Shawwa, for example, wrote that Israelis "come from a more experienced and organized political and ideological background." The two sides were "unequal . . . an occupying force and an occupied people.[12]

However boldly they spoke in public, PA leaders knew that the power imbalance forced them to be cautious. A common pattern was for the PA to make concessions in negotiating agreements and then to claim that Israel was violating the accords by using those compromises to its advantage. Moreover, PA leaders were not above seeking private advantage through quiet cooperation with Israeli companies in business ventures. Members of the new Palestinian elite also put a value on knowing Hebrew and having personal connections with Israel. Palestinian workers wanted jobs in Israel, which paid double what they could earn at home, despite the long commuting time, interruptions by closures, and sometimes humiliating treatment they experienced.

Another sign of basic conciliation was that even militant Palestinians used Israel as their point of reference for democratic practices. "Although Palestinians are loath to admit it," noted Abu Amr, "the example of democratic politics in Israel has assuredly had an effect on their own political thinking and conduct." Thus, the hard-liner Abbas Zaki asked why the Fatah Central Committee, PLO Executive Committee, and PNC convened only rarely while Israel's parliament met regularly and continuously.[13]

A huge number of personal contacts, meetings, and conversations—often unpublicized—also showed a waning of Palestinian hostility toward Israel to an extent inconceivable before 1993. In November 1995, Arafat made his first official visit to Israel to offer condolences to Leah Rabin, widow of the murdered prime minister.[14] A delegation of PLC members, critics of PA policy among them, visited Israel's parliament in October 1996.[15]

Mahmud Abbas, the second most important Palestinian leader, gave what might be the clearest expression of a new Palestinian perspective:

Israel has been in existence since 1948, whether we like it or not. We have entered into numerous Palestinian and Arab wars with Israel, and at the end it was inevitable that we should stop and ask ourselves, "How do we deal with reality?" Whatever methods the two warring parties use against each other, at the end of the day it is necessary for the two sides to sit down together at the negotiations table . . . We must face reality and try as hard as we can to reclaim our rights . . . The peace process has begun, and no one, not the Arab Islamists nor the Jewish extremists, can turn back the hand of time.[16]

As true as Abbas's analysis was, the "methods" used by the parties could considerably delay a solution. During the 1993–1996 period, Arafat, Rabin, and their respective officials preached parallel themes: since extremists were using violence to wreck the process, the best response was to advance negotiations. Creating a new situation would force a change in opinions and behavior. As Arafat acknowledged: "We should know that in any negotiations, you cannot get everything. Likewise, the other party cannot get everything from you."[17]

Yusuf al-Qazzaz, a leading journalist, expressed similar ideas in a Voice of Palestine radio program following a major suicide bombing attack. "The planners and perpetrators . . . aimed at killing the peace process between the Israelis and Palestinians," he said. But slowing talks would damage the peace process and "strengthen the feeling of despair" among the Palestinians.

This only serves the enemies of peace among both the Palestinians and Israelis . . . We concur with . . . Rabin who said that complete separation between the Palestinians and Israelis is a practical step . . . Peace is a Palestinian strategic decision. The first step to activate the peace process is to achieve Israeli redeployment in the occupied Palestinian territory and Israeli withdrawal from these territories . . . Peace requires that both the Palestinians and Israelis should make sacrifices and show patience. Peace will place the region on the threshold of a new phase whose bases are stability, construction, and coexistence.[18]

This view was echoed by Abbas in suggesting that a negotiated peace would give Israel the most security: "All [Jewish] settlement in the West Bank and Jerusalem is a settlement of annexation not of security. If they want to solve the problem of security, we are willing to have that done through agreements . . . The Palestinians are the only party which can safeguard Israel's security borders. So let us agree on mutual measures to protect our interests and theirs, our borders and theirs, our security and theirs."[19]

Abbas best expressed how much Palestinian thinking had changed from the 1948–1993 period. "If Israel were to come tomorrow and say to the Palestinians that it wants to withdraw from all the territories of the West Bank, the Gaza Strip, and Jerusalem, to the 1967 borders so the Palestinian people can build their future on these territories," he suggested, "would any Palestinian in the world object and say that he is against that?"[20] This argument overstated his case, since Hamas, Islamic Jihad, and others opposed even this deal, requiring full recognition of Israel and an end to the conflict. Still, it reflected major changes.

At any rate, to get such an offer, the PA would first have to restrain those groups' violent opposition. Arafat sometimes expressed an understanding of this point. "I am well aware," he said, "of the Israelis' sensitivity to security. I appreciate this sensitivity. We have taken significant measures to avert such attacks."[21] Arafat knew "that as far as Israel is concerned, the security concern is a main concern. Nevertheless," he argued, "the implementation of the Oslo accords has transcended security matters and moved to the other main matters."[22] The implication was that attacks on Israel would end when Palestinians were satisfied with their improved situation and the PA had become strengthened enough by the process to persuade or force Hamas to change its behavior.

Asked whether he could meet Israeli and American demands to stop terrorism, Arafat responded: "No, I cannot stop that. But . . . I have to respect the agreement as much as I can. This is what I am doing now . . . The solution is not a security one. Rather, it is [a] political one that can be achieved through the accurate and faithful implementation of the agreement."[23] Abbas amplified this idea: "The traditional Israeli security concept as a whole collapsed and became outdated after the [1991] Gulf war. Geographical security is no longer comprehensible in the age of missiles." The most important point, he concluded, was that Israel would not enhance its security by holding on to the West Bank, nor could it keep the territories and have peace.[24]

The Rabin government accepted the idea that obsession with total security was more dangerous than compromise. But it would not acquiesce to a situation in which scores of Israelis were being killed in frequent attacks by groups operating openly from PA-ruled territory. Rabin's government pressured the PA to act more effectively through temporary closures and delayed negotiating sessions.

Jamal al-Tarifi, a key PA figure in talks with Israel, evinced the desperation of those who feared that peace might be slipping away in 1995 and 1996:

We, the Palestinians and the Israelis, understand that violent attacks are designed to halt the peace process and abort the existing agreements. We must pursue a strategy of pressing ahead with the negotiations in a real spirit of peace and hasten the talks . . . We must convince the Palestinian and Israeli people that something changed when the peace agreement was signed. The Israeli citizen feels that the security situation is more difficult now than before. The Palestinian public also feels that in numerous spheres things have become more difficult than before the establishment of the PA.[25]

Warning of the consequences if the PA did not succeed in stopping Hamas, the Israeli reporter Nomi Levitzky told Abu Zayida: "In the end, you will bring about the downfall of Rabin, the man who was willing to sit down and negotiate with you. You will get Benjamin Netanyahu instead. What will happen then?" Abu Zayida replied that it didn't matter:

> I am not so certain that it would really be so bad if Rabin were replaced by Netanyahu. What will Netanyahu do? Will he refuse to meet with Arafat? Will he revoke the agreement? Will he reenter the Gaza Strip? . . . If Rabin falls, it is because he did not know how to explain to the Israeli public that full peace demands concessions. Rabin and the Labor Party cannot go farther than they have come today. This is the most the Israeli public will allow them. When the Likud experiences a few bombings in central Israel, then the Israeli people will ask it what it is doing to guarantee security and why it is not stopping the attacks.[26]

He was partly right. Netanyahu did continue the process when he came to power, met with Arafat, and made additional agreements. But Abu Zayida was wrong in taking the view, typical of much Palestinian thinking and parallel to Hamas's perspective, that more attacks would bring additional Israeli concessions. In addition, Palestinians would find themselves far from happy with the change of government in Israel, since it brought an Israeli policy of both slowing negotiations and demanding more from the PA while offering less in exchange.

In contrast, Abd al-Rahim, secretary general of Arafat's office, had a very different view. He said that "of course" the Labor Party and the PLO were those most eager to implement the agreements.[27] Consequently, he suggested that the extremist Palestinian attacks sought to push Israel to the right politically so as to harden its policy and weaken the peace process. The intention was not only "to topple . . . the Labor Party but also to abort the . . . trend toward peace in Israel as demonstrated by the Labor Party, Meretz, Peace Now Movement, and other Arab parties calling for the creation of a Palestinian state."[28]

Like many of his colleagues, Rahim concluded that since "extremist forces in Israel" wanted to stop the PA from taking over more territory, and Palestinian opposition forces "seek to weaken the PLO," both these groups "hope the Likud will come to power once again." He warned the Israeli government that it should take a harder line against this "radical wing."[29] In similar terms, Abbas called on the Israelis to save the peace process by restraining "settlers and fanatics and halt[ing] . . . excessive settlement activities in the Palestinian territories." This was portrayed as parallel to the PA's effort to restrain those "seeking to sabotage the peace process" in its territory.[30]

One alternative for the PA during 1993–1996 was to see Israel's Labor Party government as a partner ready to reach a solution acceptable to Palestinians. In this context, problems arose not from the difference between Israeli and Palestinian goals so much as from the inevitable difficulties of remaking their relationship, their profound mutual mistrust, the complexity of interim arrangements, the efforts of extremists, and real remaining gaps—albeit narrower than ever before—between the two sides' proposed solutions. Consequently, the PA defined its enemy as Israeli rightists seeking excuses to sabotage the Rabin and Peres government and discredit the PA. In that case, the PA had to help its counterpart by showing moderation in words and by making a maximum effort to stop attacks.

Of course, meeting Israeli requirements was not the sole political task for the PA, which did not want to clash with the Palestinian radicals or alienate its own public opinion. The PA, Sha'th complained, was "caught between the hammer and the anvil," between Israel's demand to provide security and punishment for not doing so. It blamed both Israel's government and the violent Palestinian opposition for helping those Israelis "interested in obstructing this agreement."[31]

Despite his own complaints, Arafat often felt positive during the 1993–1996 era: "There are blatant Israeli violations of these accords," he claimed. "But on the whole, matters are moving forward. For our part, we knew from the beginning that we were not going to a wedding and that the process in which we are engaged was very difficult and involved major challenges." He pointed out that Israel-Egypt talks over a tiny border dispute "lasted for a long time," though that was far easier than the Palestinian issue.[32]

Yet equally or more often, Arafat portrayed the Rabin and Peres governments as the real problem, speaking of them in terms almost identical to those he would later use against Netanyahu. Like Abu Zayida, he said that there were no differences between the Israeli left and right, or at least that the incumbent regime either was appeasing the extremists or was severely infiltrated by them. Netanyahu might be preferable since he could make concessions beyond what domestic politics would let the left deliver.

Thus, Arafat suggested that "Israeli officers dissatisfied with the peace process were carry[ing] out some actions aimed at torpedoing [it] because they did not want to withdraw from the West Bank or stop expanding settlements." If an Israeli official predicted possible civil war among Palestinians, this proved that "he was and is working to foment sedition, thwart the Palestinian experiment, and destroy the peace agreement." Ironically, Arafat prophesied a military coup in 1996 in Israel, naming as its leader Chief of Staff Ehud Barak, who became Rabin's heir as head of the Labor Party and prime minister in 1999.[33]

At the same time, Arafat often accused Rabin and Peres of trying to cheat him on the agreements. In this context, Arafat complained in 1995 that Israel "took advantage" of attacks against itself to delay leaving West Bank towns and allowing Palestinian elections.[34] He insisted that the Israelis were withholding money owed the PA "for only one reason. They want to strangle us."[35] He complained that Israel "will delay . . . withdrawal until they establish new facts having to do with settlements."[36] Arafat asked: "Is this the peace we sought? Is this the peace of the brave?" No, he said, it was "the peace of the siege."[37]

Other PA elements articulated such ideas in more intemperate language. As an *al-Hayat al-Jadida* editorial put it: "The Israelis, in all their political tendencies, are promoting the policy of intensive settlement in the West Bank and Gaza Strip. This policy is being pursued provocatively and systematically" by government and settlers working together. Rabin's government was using settlements "to disconnect the occupied territories and turn the Palestinian geographic unit into isolated pockets so that the establishment of an integral Palestinian state will become impossible." If this policy continued, the Palestinians would have to return to warfare. "Our people . . . will not be losing anything since they are not gaining anything now."[38]

Building on this theme, Abbas said: "Terrorism is not confined to Arabs. All settlement activities on the Palestinian territories are acts of terrorism. Delaying the Israeli military withdrawal from the Palestinian territories gives a green light to the escalation of terrorism. The daily aggressions against al-Aqsa Mosque and Orient House in Jerusalem are an obvious act of terrorism."[39]

Leaving aside questions of proportion in Abbas's analysis, however, it was by no means clear that Palestinian frustration at Israeli policy was the cause of violence. Virtually every single attack, certainly the big ones, came from radical opposition groups who opposed the peace process and feared its success. They were more active in the 1993–1996 era, when talks were advancing and Israel was making concessions, than afterward, when the peace process was virtually paralyzed. Indeed, the worst wave of attacks came in early 1996, just after Israel's withdrawal from West Bank towns and the holding of Palestinian elections.

Still, Arafat and other leading PA officials lent their authority to claims that Israel itself was responsible for the Palestinian terrorism against it. "We have much evidence," Abd al-Rahim claimed, "proving the existence of coordination" between the Israeli right wing and Palestinians staging terrorist attacks.[40] Though no real evidence was ever presented, this claim proved a recurring theme.[41] A May 1997 PA press conference presented a Hamas prisoner who claimed that Israel had organized suicide attacks, an assertion Israel branded "a ridiculous lie."[42] Arafat asserted that Islamic Jihad suicide bombers who carried out the February 1995 Bayt Lid bombing had been trained by Israel.[43] Of course, if Israel was responsible for Palestinian terrorism, the PA itself would be blameless, thus neutralizing a major source of international sympathy for Israel.[44]

Claiming that Rabin was just using Palestinian violence as an excuse, Arafat underestimated this factor's importance. Putting less emphasis on stopping attacks, he predicted that Rabin would win the 1996 elections. At any rate, he added, there was no reason to fear Netanyahu's election, since "this agreement is binding on any Israeli government."[45] A Likud-led Israeli government could not be much worse for the Palestinian economy than the Labor-led government, according to the head of the Arab Economists' Association, Samir Abdallah, who said in 1996, "We don't expect more extreme measures" from Netanyahu.[46]

Back in January 1995, Arafat had pointed to "murder threats from extremist Israel forces" against Rabin. "I am certain that, if matters remain unsettled, these threats will find their way to implementation one day."[47] After the November 1995 assassination, the PA officially expressed sorrow over Rabin's death, calling him a "great leader and a man of peace." Arafat, Abbas, and Khuri visited Leah Rabin to offer personal condolences, and while Arafat did not attend Rabin's funeral owing to Israeli security concerns, a high-level PA delegation was present.[48]

Nevertheless, the PA was caught off guard by the February–March 1996 wave of terrorism which hardened Israeli public opinion and destroyed the successor government of Peres. The PA's inability to keep anti-Israeli violence at relatively low levels persuaded enough centrists to support Netanyahu so as to tip the balance to his favor in the May 1996 elections. It quickly became clear that Netanyahu and his supporters continued to believe that holding on to territory was the best way to preserve Israeli security against assaults by Arab states and an untrustworthy, irredentist Palestinian leadership. But Netanyahu also had to adjust to the new situation created by the Oslo accords and did not want the blame or crisis that would result from his walking away from the prior agreements.

For his part, Arafat reiterated his "commitment to peace" after Netanyahu's victory. One key reason for doing so was his own lack of alternatives, while another was concern over what Netanyahu might do if confronted by a rejectionist PA. "We have no choice," admitted Arafat, "but to adhere to reason, wisdom and courage as well as to the option of peace, based on comprehensiveness, durability and justice."[49] He could still hope that step-by-step progress, the momentum of events, evolution within Israel, and external pressure on it would eventually bring him to his goal.

Arafat also grasped that his best strategy after Netanyahu's victory was to show that the PA was adhering to agreements while claiming that Israel was breaking them. Israeli "unilateral measures . . . are liable to destroy the whole peace process," he stated. "Peace and terrorism cannot go hand in hand, [neither can] peace and settlements."[50] Implementing the PA's commitments, he claimed on another occasion, "secured for us the respect and trust of the world, in addition to the respect of half [of] Israeli society which voted [for the] Labor [Party]. The Netanyahu government, which does not implement agreements, does not enjoy such trust and respect. Thus, we place Israel before world opinion and the world conscience, so that it might feel compelled to implement its side of the agreement. The documents we signed with the Israeli government will prove to be worthless as a peace treaty unless every word in them is implemented."[51]

Ironically, the result was that with Netanyahu in office, Arafat tried harder than before to express the PA's moderation and willingness to compromise. Whether from fear of Netanyahu's reaction, lessons learned through earlier failures, improvements in the functioning of the PA police, or the hope of mobilizing international leverage, Arafat usually sought more energetically to prevent violence after 1996 than he had done before.

Indeed, he had ample incentive to do so. If the Palestinian leadership abandoned its post-1993 policy, it would lose not only any chance of achieving a solution with Israel, but also probably any Western assistance and possibly even the PA's very existence, without obtaining meaningful support from the Arab world or anyone else. Moreover, in those circumstances Israel would likely be even stronger and more hardline, and enjoy greater U.S. support.

Opening the PLC's third annual session in 1998, Arafat repeated support for the agreements with Israel based on "mutual recognition of the legitimate and political rights of both sides" to achieve both peoples' interests, including Palestinian national rights, "on the basis of equality, compatibility and mutual respect."[52] Mahmud Abbas agreed: "The Palestinians and the Israelis have opted for peace . . . The peace of the brave is a strategic Palestinian decision that seeks peace for all the Palestinian generations."[53]

But Arafat had many complaints about Netanyahu's policy, especially his slow pace and reports that he would build new settlements. Speaking of the months following the January 1997 Hebron agreement, for example, Arafat stated: "We believed the peace process was back on track and as we started to gain hope we were surprised by the decisions of the Israeli government to Judaize the city of Jerusalem, to build new settlements and to enlarge the existing ones in an attempt to pre-empt the final status talks . . . Those infringements are related to dozens of outstanding issues that are yet to be implemented."[54]

Only in 1998 did Palestinians begin to realize what had gone wrong with their analysis of Israel and their strategy toward it. Hasan Asfur, one of the Oslo accord's main architects, remarked on the fifth anniversary of its signing:

> The agreement could work with an Israeli partner [but] we lost the one partner who participated in setting up the accords . . . We did have problems with the Labor government in terms of implementation . . . but [these] were nonetheless still within the framework of the agreement. The real obstacle arose with the arrival of a government that from the very beginning did not believe in a peace agreement with the Palestinians. It does not believe that there is a Palestinian people and Palestinian land, or that this people has legitimate political rights. However, because it can't say this openly, it goes around the agreement by making verbal commitments all the while trying to kill it. This is the real political problem. It is not the text of the agreement itself that is the problem, but the lack of an Israeli partner willing to stick to the peace process and reach the political goal.[55]

To some extent, pro-PA Palestinians adopted this standpoint. According to a July 1998 poll, 62.2 percent of Palestinians now believed that a Labor Party government would strengthen the peace process, only 6.1 percent thought Likud would do better, and only 7.4 percent saw no difference between the parties on the peace process. About 48 percent thought that the Labor Party would win the next elections. Yet even in April 1999, just before new Israeli elections were held, half of all Palestinians did not think it mattered who won, while only one-quarter of them believed that a Labor Party victory would improve the situation.[56] Still, experience with Netanyahu sharpened the Palestinians' thinking on how important Israel's domestic debate was for themselves.

In Israel's May 1999 elections, Ehud Barak became prime minister. He advocated rapid progress toward an agreement based on compromises with the PA. While domestic factors played a major role in his victory, the peace process had made acceptable the idea of a Palestinian state. Declining terrorism showed the PA as a reliable partner. And the PA itself became sophisticated regarding Israeli politics. Arafat's willingness to postpone a unilateral declaration of independence on May 4 was partly based on his belief that such a confrontational step would help Netanyahu's candidacy.

Palestinians were entitled to their opinion if they wanted to consider Israel's creation as wrong and unjust. Now, however, the PA and its strategy were based on accepting that historic event. Its emphasis was supposed to be on building the future, not changing the past, on creating a Palestinian state rather than eliminating Israel, and on achieving the possible rather than seeking either revenge or total justice.

In his own rhetoric, Arafat understood this point. The content of his speeches changed dramatically after 1993, with much of the daily invective and the clear insistence that all of Israel should be subsumed in a Palestinian state having disappeared. He, and most other PA leaders, stuck to the new understanding that their maximum claim would be the West Bank, Gaza Strip, and East Jerusalem, to be incorporated in a Palestinian state.

A small but impressive symbol of Arafat's insensitivity was his naming as minister of Jewish affairs Rabbi Moshe Hirsch of the tiny anti-Zionist Neteuri Karta Jewish sect. While Hirsch never participated in PA activities, it was no public relations triumph to ally with a man whose greatest expressed regret was that "I still have not succeeded in destroying the Zionist state."[57] In contrast, though, Arafat went out of his way to give good treatment to the only non-settler Jews in his territory—the three hundred–member Samaritan sect living near Nablus.

Some leading PA and Fatah officials, however, consistently made antagonistic statements about Israel and Jews that damaged the peace process. One of the key issues shaping Israeli policy and politics regarding the PA was whether the Palestinian leadership seemed to be dropping its historic opposition to Israel's existence as a state, and whether the PA would end the conflict even if a compromise met its immediate demands. Historical circumstances made Jews highly sensitive to any rhetoric vilifying them. The fact that right-wing Israelis and, after 1996, the Netanyahu government were avidly seeking proof that the PA was a questionable partner should have been reason enough for Arafat to be careful in such matters. Yet he did not visibly discipline PA officials who engaged in that type of rhetoric or discourage them from doing so.

One implicit reason for this inflammatory talk was a misconceived attempt to counter certain perceived advantages Israel had in legitimizing its own claims and gaining international—or at least Western—support. Thus, Palestinians wanted to neutralize such Israeli "assets" as the biblical and historic Jewish connection with Jerusalem, international sympathy for Jews as a result of the Holocaust, Israel's positive media image, and its U.S. support.

Yet extremely provocative statements undermined Palestinian credibility with Israelis and seriously shook their support for a compromise peace. This problem also sabotaged the PA's own policy. For if Israel was an illegitimate, Nazi-like regime, why should the PA make peace with it? This was, after all, Hamas's argument.

More often, though, the use of extremist language was seen as a way of maintaining militancy. Within Fatah, propaganda and ideological sections were often controlled by relative hard-liners.[58] Arafat did not want to alienate supporters and drive them into the opposition camp even if they had some disagreements with him. Moreover, tough rhetoric from PA organs and officials also appealed to sectors of the Palestinian population who might otherwise back Hamas. Thus, the main sources for incitement came from the PA-appointed Islamic clerics, the Fatah hard-liners Abbas Zaki and Habash, and its demagogic newspaper *al-Hayat al-Jadida*.[59]

Not content to denounce Israeli oppression or repression, elements in the PA insisted that Israeli treatment of Palestinians was "equal with, if not more brutal" than Nazi behavior during World War II.[60] Zionism was labeled a "terrorist, racist" ideology close to Nazism. "While the Israeli government is speaking about the atrocities committed against the Jews at Auschwitz, Birkenau and Dachau concentration camps," claimed a PA Information Ministry press release, "our homeland was transformed into a big concentration camp."[61] If Netanyahu mentioned the high Arab birthrate, this recalled "Hitler's statements about the sterilization of undesired segments of the population."[62]

According to *al-Hayat al-Jadida:* "Since its establishment, the racist Zionist entity has been implementing various forms of terrorism on a daily basis which are a repetition of the Nazi terror . . . This also explains the cooperation between the Jews and the Nazis during World War II." Given this alliance, claims that Jews were slaughtered during the war were "forged."[63] "It is well known," said the host of a PA television program, "that every year the Jews exaggerate what the Nazis did to them. They claim there were 6 million killed, but precise scientific research demonstrates that there were no more than 400,000."[64]

The official PA Ministry of Information website carried an article voicing such views by Roger Garoudy, then on trial in France for denying that the Holocaust occurred.[65] Israel was portrayed as both anti-Christian and anti-Muslim, and even a relatively sophisticated politician such as Abd al-Jawad Salah could speak of "the Zionist-colonialist plot and its goals which destroy not only our people but the entire world."[66]

At a time when Palestinian violence was weakening the PA's position in the peace process, the respected newspaper *al-Quds* ran an article claiming that "the Jews succeeded, during their history, to turn the massacres they were subjected to into a "weapon of mass destruction . . . against their adversaries."[67] And when the PA was insisting that it was ready to accept Israel's existence, its undersecretary for culture Yahya Yakhlaf could intone: "Zionism remains . . . another face of racism. And if human history has swallowed all the dynasties of dinosaurian ideologies from Hulagu [the Mongolian conqueror] to Hitler, in addition to the racist ideology in South Africa, the survival of Zionist ideology on this piece of our planet is a deviant phenomenon and a historical lie."[68]

The most extreme among PA supporters were several Muslim clerics holding official positions, who fostered the same interpretations of Islam as those shaping Hamas ideology. The PA-appointed Mufti Ikrama Sabri denied any Jewish connection with Jerusalem holy sites and called Jews "the greatest enemies of us Muslims."[69] PA Waqf and Religious Affairs Minister Hasan Tahbub accused Israel of planning to destroy a Bethlehem mosque in order to build a synagogue there.[70] "Israel is not worthy of ruling since they know no religion and no God," declared

Shaykh Hamid al-Bitawi, head of the PA's Shari'a Court of Appeals in Nablus.[71] "The Jews always set a trap for the community of Muslims. The Koran repeatedly warns against [their] traps and plots," declared an al-Aqsa mosque sermon broadcast on the Voice of Palestine.[72]

Israel was also portrayed as engaging daily in the most horrible crimes against Palestinians. Mahir al-Dassuki, head of the Palestinian Consumer Protection Council, said that Jewish settlements distributed spoiled corn oil and milk tainted with mad cow disease. Abd al-Fatah Hamid, a top official in the PA Ministry of Supplies, called this part of a war against Palestinian society. Deputy Minister of Supplies Abd al-Hamid al-Qudsi added the accusation that Israel was trying to poison Palestinians with cancer-causing foods and "hormones that harm male virility" as part of "an organized plan and conspiracy which is under the auspices of the Israel Defense Forces."[73]

Chewing gum was also portrayed as an Israeli weapon, "smuggled into the West Bank and Gaza" to stimulate sexual desire and thus turn Palestinian women into prostitutes and informers, according to PA health officials.[74] According to PA police commanders, Israel was infiltrating "Jewish prostitutes with AIDS" into PA territories "to spread the disease among Palestinian youth."[75] At a UN Commission on Human Rights meeting in Switzerland, Nabil Ramlawi, the PA delegate, accused "Israeli authorities" of having "injected 300 Palestinian children with the HIV virus" during the intifada.[76] Israel was also allegedly conducting medical experiments on Palestinian prisoners.[77] One of Arafat's senior advisers, Abdallah al-Hurani, suggested that Israel might have carried out the terrorist attack in Egypt in which more than seventy foreign tourists were killed, to retaliate for Egypt's support of the Palestinians.[78]

At PA-run summer camps, children were taught that they should be martyrs in an armed struggle against Israel.[79] While the PA could legitimately, as PLC member Jamila Zidam put it, "mention the 'disaster' " of Israel's creation, claim a "right of return," and express determination "to continue in the paths of our fallen martyrs," this did not have positive implications for a lasting compromise peace.[80]

When children performing on the PA's television channel introduced themselves as coming from places now part of Israel, or a dance group sang, "My country, I love her / My home is Gaza / My roots are in Haifa," such statements in no way necessarily expressed hopes for a reconquest of Haifa.[81] But when General Abu Salam, the summer camps' supervisor, promised not only that "we will not forget the names of our cities and the villages that were destroyed by the occupation" but also that "we say to Netanyahu and his party that we will always work for [their] liberation," this had serious political implications.[82]

Arafat publicly repudiated these television programs and promised that such statements "will not recur," though it is not clear whether he actually took any action. He insisted that the PA's policy was one of "zero tolerance to terror and violence" and pledged to fight terrorism "irrespective of the status of negotiations."[83] By late 1998 he was taking his toughest stand against Hamas, making a greater effort than ever before to persuade Israelis of his serious intentions for peace. Despite continuing hostility, Palestinian attitudes had been transformed compared to the pre-1993 era.

For the PA, U.S. policy and public opinion were equally important or more important than their Israeli counterparts. Dealing with the United States required changes in Palestinian thinking as dramatic as those needed to negotiate with Israel. Arafat never lost sight of the international factor in the negotiations. He repeatedly insisted that the Israel-PLO deal was not just a bilateral agreement but an internationally sponsored one, hoping that western Europe—as well as his traditional Russian and Arab allies—would help him pressure Israel.[84]

But while important for Palestinian morale, passing pro-PA resolutions, or providing 38 percent of the PA's foreign aid, Europe was only of limited help on political matters.[85] Whether justified or not, Arafat repeatedly complained about the slow pace and low level of assistance.[86] Only France gave the PA enthusiastic diplomatic support as well. In October 1996, President Jacques Chirac became the first head of state to address the PLC, where he endorsed a Palestinian state that would include East Jerusalem. Chirac also laid the cornerstone for a planned Gaza seaport. During a visit to Jerusalem's Old City, Chirac complained loudly and bitterly about Israeli security arrangements and urged Israel to accept a Palestinian state.[87]

No country could come close, however, to matching the importance of the United States in ensuring the success or failure of PA efforts to negotiate successfully with Israel and achieve independence. Traditionally, the PLO had looked on the United States as an enemy, Israel's main backer, and an imperialist force blocking Arab unity and progress. The PLO's policy shift was based largely on a serious reevaluation of the U.S. role and intentions.

While understanding the strength of U.S. support for Israel, Arafat also needed to persuade the United States to take his side as often as possible in the negotiations. His clear strategy was to appear to be reasonable though firm, keeping his commitments and showing that Israel was not doing so. Yet many ideas and problems characterizing Palestinian attitudes toward the United States persisted from the previous era. And also, as with PA-Israel relations, propaganda themes directed at the masses often totally contradicted the PA's goals and actual behavior.[88]

Anti-Americanism reflected the thinking of individuals who still held radical views, as well as the Palestinians' frustration at a U.S. policy that they viewed as always favoring Israel. Some claimed U.S. leaders were pro-Israel because Zionists controlled them. Yet this was the same government that Arafat had accepted as the principal guarantor of all the peace agreements, his main source of aid, and a trainer for his security forces.[89] Moreover, Arafat tried far more often and harder than did Israel to persuade the United States to step in as the process's mediator and referee. These were the acts of a Palestinian leadership ready to risk its future on U.S. credibility, not one convinced that the United States was controlled by Israel.

In contrast, Hamas continued to be very hostile to the United States, though insisting it would not attack American targets. Hamas did, however, threaten retaliation against the United States when it was considering extraditing Musa Abu Marzuk, a key Hamas leader, to Israel.[90] Khalid Mish'al, chief of the Hamas political bureau, asserted. "Hamas is still adhering to its policy of restricting the conflict to occupied Palestine."[91] But it also argued that nothing good could come from the United States, which was essentially a Zionist puppet. Yasin saw the sexual liaison between President Clinton and White House intern Monica Lewinsky as a plot by "the Zionist lobby and world Zionism" to blackmail Clinton and stop him "from exerting pressure on Israel."[92]

Yet less radical, more sophisticated PA sources sometimes thought in similar conspiratorial terms. PA Justice Minister Frayh Abu Midayn could insist that "five Zionist Jews are running the policy of the United States in the Middle East."[93] Al-Hayat al-Jadida editor Hafiz al-Barghuti referred to the pro-Israel U.S. Congress as the "Council of the Elders of Zion," of which "the White House is a hostage."[94] According to Brigadier General Khalid al-Musmar, deputy head of the PA's Indoctrination Directorate, some American leaders were engaged in "blind submission to world Zionism," while Clinton and his administration were terrorized "through threats of sex and morals scandals which are disseminated by the obedient [American] media." The PA-appointed Mufti Ikrama Sabri called upon God, in a sermon broadcast by the Voice of Palestine, to "destroy America for it is controlled by Zionist Jews."[95]

In September 1997 there was a particularly revealing exchange between the PA's two views on America in the pages of *al-Hayat al-Jadida*. The newspaper reprinted an article from Fatah's newsletter urging the removal of Dennis Ross, a U.S. State Department official, as a mediator in the peace talks, calling him "part of the oppressive racist Zionist actions which are armed with immense imperialistic influence. Dennis Ross amuses himself on his visits like Shylock, deriving pleasure from imagining how he will slice three percent [of land the PA would receive in an Israeli redeployment] from the body of his victim."[96]

At that moment, however, Arafat was engaged in talks in which a sympathetic attitude by Ross and the U.S. government was urgently needed. Indeed, U.S.-Palestinian relations were reaching an all-time high point as the United States supported many of the PA's demands in negotiations leading to the October 1998 Wye agreement. To insult the key mediator—using an anti-Semitic slur against him, no less—was tremendously damaging. Pro-Arafat PLC member Nabil Amr wrote a response in the newspaper saying he agreed that U.S. policy was unfair and Ross was biased. Nevertheless, the insult to Ross "arouses disgust" and was wrong. "Describing Ross in this manner plays right into the hands of Israeli extremists, who can exploit this description in order to work against us at a time when we are in need of all parties to support our rights and our sincere peaceful approach."[97]

One of the newspaper's editors wrote a rebuttal defending the attack on Ross and saying that it was ridiculous to criticize words while the "gang" running Israel massacred babies and threatened to demolish holy sites. The article had merely quoted "international literature in describing our situation despite the fact that Shakespeare was never a member of Fatah."[98]

Yet despite the frequent expression of extreme views, PA leaders were usually far more sophisticated in evaluating U.S. behavior and in understanding that they must gain American help and support. In sharp contradiction to traditional PLO positions, the PA did not want to fight the United States or view it as an inevitable enemy, but wished to persuade the Americans to put pressure on Israel and back PA goals.

After one round of 1995 talks in Washington, Sha'th noted, "I do not believe I have witnessed [before] an international meeting where the U.S. president, vice president, the head of the National Security Council, [secretary of state] and the U.S. State Department team all at the same time were sending signals showing the utmost U.S. interest in pushing the peace process ahead." He explained Congress's tougher pro-Israel stance as a partisan Republican attempt to embarrass Clinton, and not as a Zionist conspiracy.[99]

Even when backing Arab governments at odds with the United States, the PA expressed its official positions in moderate terms.[100] Arafat frequently praised U.S. assistance in the negotiations and even Ross's performance: "The Americans have made and are making efforts they should be thanked for."[101] Arafat met with Clinton several times and with other U.S. officials including CIA director George Tenet. In the Wye agreement, the PA made the CIA the virtual arbiter of whether it was meeting its obligations in the agreements with Israel.[102]

U.S. support for the PA grew over time. Between 1993 and 1998 the United States gave $500 million to the PA, making it, after Israel, the largest recipient of U.S. aid per capita in the world. In late 1998, the United States established a joint commission with the PA similar to those usually set up with sovereign states.[103]

Clinton's visit to Gaza in December 1998 marked a new high in U.S. support for the PA, though not explicit backing for an independent state. After landing at Gaza airport, Clinton witnessed a show of hands by the PA elite, including PNC members, in once again repealing the PLO Charter.

In a very sympathetic speech Clinton told his audience, "I know that the Palestinian people stand at a crossroads; behind you a history of dispossession and dispersal, before you the opportunity to shape a new Palestinian future on your own land." He expressed understanding of the issues still left unresolved, but urged that determination and patience in making peace would bring progress. The fact that Palestinians now ruled their own territory "was made possible because . . . you made a choice for peace . . . I believe you have gained more in five years of peace than in 45 years of war."[104]

As Ghassan al-Khatib pointed out, Palestinians were still divided over their attitude toward the United States. Officials saw Clinton's visit as a great advance, embodying "indirect U.S. support for a Palestinian state." Much of the public, however, was less enthusiastic, continuing to be critical of the United States and its policies.[105] Indeed, a few days after Clinton's visit, some of the American flags that had been waved in his honor were burned during protests over the U.S. bombing of Iraq.

By the end of 1998 there were three basic stances among the PA and its supporters toward the peace process, Israel, and the West. First, there were remainders of the PLO's traditional standpoint that a compromise peace was undesirable. Only Israel's elimination and replacement by a Palestinian state would be an acceptable solution. This was the view in anti-Oslo groups such as Hamas, as well as in sectors of Fatah—especially among radical Outsiders whose lives had been based on this thesis, and refugees still outside the PA lands. Almost half the PLO Executive Committee had resigned or ceased activity because they could not accept the new line.[106] This represented Qaddumi's view and that of some veterans who continued working with Arafat, including Fatah Central Committee members such as Salim al-Za'nun, Abbas Zaki, and Sakr Abu Nizar.

Second, Fatah Insiders expressed harder-line views in a different way. While ready to make peace with Israel in exchange for an independent Palestinian state, they believed that Israel—even under Rabin and Peres—was not ready to accept such a deal, or would do so only under pressure, perhaps including violence. They were claiming not that Israel could be defeated but that raising the cost of maintaining the status quo would force Israel to make concessions it would not otherwise give. Unlike the Outsiders, they were less likely to underestimate Israel; unlike Hamas, they did not expect divine—or even Arab state—intervention on their side. And since Fatah's specialty was struggle, this analysis also gave their local organization—and hence themselves—an important independent role instead of just being the PA's appendage. Yet despite all the militant talk—and in sharp contrast to Hamas—Fatah activists almost never implemented their harsh words with action. In the end, they backed Arafat on all the important issues and decisions.

Finally, the solution offered by Arafat, as well as most of the PA and Fatah leaders, was not trust in Israel but belief that negotiations would succeed in finding compromises and that a Palestinian state would be built through step-by-step progress. Despite concessions made to domestic politics, the PA believed in a dialectic of benefits and persuasion that would unite Palestinians as they saw occupation end and statehood draw nearer. While ready to use pressure and militant rhetoric, the Palestinian leadership also knew that confrontation was counterproductive. Despite real shortcomings, then, the PA's leadership had achieved a more realistic sense of the situation, developing a strategy to outmaneuver limits imposed by Palestinian weakness and a desire to make progress rather than face additional decades of deadlock, stagnation, and occupation.

According to polls, large majorities of Palestinians (65 percent) and

Israelis (77 percent) believed that relations between the two peoples should be improved to strengthen support for peace.[107] The gigantic gap between beliefs and aspirations on the two sides which had existed before 1993 had been narrowed considerably to the point where it could be bridged. Differences, conflicts, and misperceptions were still considerable, but they no longer set policy.

9

RECOGNIZING FACTS, CREATING FACTS

Asked by an Israeli interviewer what he would tell a suicide bomber in order to dissuade him from carrying out a terrorist act, PA police chief Ghazi Jabali replied: "I would tell him to think of the hope. That very soon he will have a state of his own, and we will live in peace with Israel, and our economy will prosper. His life will be much improved if peace is made. I believe that. If I didn't, I wouldn't be here. I am not an assassin. I am not a hired gun. I'm a Palestinian patriot and I believe in peace. You didn't live in a refugee camp. I did. And I want a better future for my children."[1] This was both a moving statement and a superb summary of the PA's argument to the Palestinian people. Yet it also reflected the paradox of the transitional, state-building era, since Jabali was a man whom Israel accused of inciting terrorism and the Palestinian opposition blamed for antidemocratic excesses.[2]

Such were the complexities of the PA's simultaneous struggles to gain agreement from Israel to have a state while building one through its own daily activity. Both issues were far from resolved. Asked by an interviewer, "Has the revolutionary era ended? Has the state era begun?" Arafat answered passionately: "The revolution will go on until an independent Palestinian state is established with Jerusalem as its capital . . . We will struggle on all fronts to prove that this land is Arab, Arab, and Arab; we will defend every particle of Palestinian soil; and we will wage the battle of building a Palestinian state as we waged the liberation and peace battle."[3] Despite its militant tone, this statement reflected his drive for the minimal solution acceptable to Palestinians. After all, his critics in Hamas demanded this struggle be waged by violence, and defined "every particle of Palestinian soil" to include all of Israel.

Those advocating more emphasis on democracy and human rights gave Arafat critical support on the struggle with Israel, though many of them also wanted to make even more demands for Israeli concessions and to use harsher tactics. Most of all, though, they worried lest the character of the state be sacrificed in order to make it a reality.

"In the end," remarked PLC member and PA critic Salah Ta'amri, giving these issues a different emphasis from that of Arafat, "it doesn't matter what Israel does or how the world reacts. What is crucial is what we are doing internally to prepare for [independence], whether building our institutions, building our economy, achieving national unity, and so on."[4]

Ta'amri was right on the need to build the institutions of statehood to prepare for that next step and to make that outcome of the peace process seem inevitable. At the same time, though, there would be no Palestinian state in reality if there was no agreement with Israel. Even a consistent PA critic like Abd al-Shafi—who had advocated freezing negotiations as early as 1994—ridiculed the idea that the Palestinians could achieve anything without such a deal: "To declare a state without any jurisdiction over territory, without any sovereignty, with all the restrictions that we know that Israel imposes with regard to movement" made no sense.[5] The result would be to freeze a situation that was most unfavorable to Palestinian interests.

May 4, 1999, was the fifth anniversary of the detailed account which began implementation of the Oslo agreements. By this date, the signers had originally hoped, the two sides would have concluded a full peace treaty covering all the issues. In fact, owing to delays and disagreements, the final status talks had barely begun.

Months earlier Arafat had begun hinting that he would declare independence unilaterally on that date. At first this was intended as a way to mobilize Palestinian support for himself by showing that the PA leader was doing everything possible to make progress and succeeding in his effort. Many Palestinians questioned whether this step was a wise idea. They saw such a move as simultaneously meaningless and potentially counterproductive, triggering a confrontation which could be very costly to themselves. As a result, Arafat switched his emphasis, seeking to use his threat as leverage for gaining support from the United States, Europe, and the Arab world.

In the end, the May 4 deadline proved an anticlimax. Yet this in itself was an important outcome. There could be no instant solution, no victory by declaration, no total triumph of one side over another, or even an alternative to a difficult, unsatisfactory process of negotiation and compromise.

Peace talks with Israel were an inescapable precondition for creating a state; the state-building effort among Palestinians was essential for constructing a country. The peace process helped Arafat unite Palestinians, but he needed progress to show himself able to provide them with benefits or sovereignty. In order to get agreements he made promises to Israel—extraditing terrorists, disarming radicals, ending incitement—which he was not always ready to keep, given his domestic constraints. The state-building process strengthened Arafat's hand by showing that the Palestinians were on a road toward independence, but its incompleteness left him unable to control violent elements and hence reduced his chances for success.

In short, external peace and internal independence advanced both together and slowly. "We have glimpsed peace, and we have taken a few faltering steps toward it," said Abbas in 1996, "but we are far from reaching the final stage of peace."[6] Three years later that evaluation was still correct. Achieving an Israel-PA agreement was very difficult indeed, largely because of the Netanyahu government's policy, but also because of the PA's falling short—or at least its different interpretation—of what it was required to do under the agreements.

The peace process's most positive points were its strong foundation and basic direction. Based on a half-century's experience and events, the drive toward peace was much less fragile than it often appeared. Neither side could afford to walk away from the negotiations. Arab states were unwilling to return to an era of conflict; the Palestinian leadership did not want to be driven out of the territories; Israel had no desire to turn back the clock and reconquer those lands. A resolution to the dispute was no longer blocked by basic principles or a zero-sum approach. Instead, the struggle—bitter as it was—was about the price of a peace settlement rather than whether there would be one at all.

Further, while the peace process often advanced slowly, it always moved in the same direction, toward giving the PA more authority and placing more territory under its control. The alternation was between progress and delay, not between advance and retreat. From the very start of the process, though, many on both sides had been far too quick to pronounce it dead. Perhaps this was partly due to the difficulty Palestinians and Israelis had in believing that these amazing events were actually happening and that, after so long, they really could achieve peace.

Even Netanyahu's positions were evolving closer and closer to acceptance of a Palestinian state, as he made agreements which he could not have imagined accepting a few years earlier. By 1998 his official position favored a "state minus," with limits on its freedom of action in the military and foreign policy realms. He also wanted to restrict a Palestinian entity to a smaller area in the West Bank and to retain Israel's total control over East Jerusalem. In negotiations he moved as slowly as possible, owing partly to his own desire to avoid concessions, partly to the need to maintain support in his own party and governing coalition. Yet it was his willingness to negotiate the Wye agreement which led his coalition's right wing to bolt in December 1998, bringing down his government.

When the two sides engaged in hard bargaining, stalled, and threatened to walk out, this was often merely an element in their negotiating technique. The day-to-day discord obscured the far more significant fact that after fifty years of conflict they had decided to make a deal and were now bargaining over the details. Events followed a predictable cycle: each agreement led to predictions that it would be the last advance, months of bickering, and mutual accusations of bad faith, finally to be capped by another agreement.

But Abbas suggested that the Palestinians were also not in much of a hurry. In 1995 he said: "There is no harm in being a little late because we have no right, in the interest of time, to accept just any solution . . . We have time and there is no need to rush. We were late before, so let us be a little late again. What is the problem, if we want to achieve a solution to our advantage?"[7]

Abbas accurately noted that delays occurred because both sides preferred to wait longer if necessary in order to get agreements giving them more of what they wanted. Domestic politics was another factor in these delays, since "each side wanted to appear to its public as the side which made no concession," though PA and Israeli leaders were constantly making public declarations which they "would abandon inside the negotiating [room]."[8]

For his part, Khuri complained that disputes with Netanyahu had wasted two years in the peace process, lost "in putting on a show of negotiations for the television cameras." Yet he affirmed in September 1998 that "a lot has been accomplished." The PA "was established on Palestinian land" and was creating institutions as "a foundation for . . .

building towards the independent Palestinian state." In addition, "a kind of relationship with the Israelis has been established . . . a kind of understanding on the part of the Israelis of the rights of the Palestinian people . . . There is the beginning—and I stress the beginning—of the possibility for two neighbors to exist on one land and to think of a future of cooperation and coordination on various levels."[9]

From the PA's standpoint, the length and difficulty of the negotiations with Israel left it with four basic options.

First, it could, as the radical opposition proposed, scrap the Oslo agreements and return to armed struggle and maximalist demands, including a willingness to fight a war with Israel. Yet the entire experience which had brought the PA to the point it had reached was built on an understanding that this would be a disaster. The PA knew that it could expect very little help from abroad and that Israel was far stronger militarily. Indeed, Palestinian leaders had argued that Israel in general and Netanyahu in particular would welcome an excuse to crush them. This route would lead to defeat.

A milder variant on this strategy would be to ignore Israel and the negotiations altogether, unilaterally declaring independence and appealing for international support. While Arafat was certainly willing to use this as a tactic, he saw it as a way to improve his bargaining position, not as an alternative to negotiating altogether. As Arafat explained, "We reject any amendment to the Oslo agreement because we do not want to see it foiled." If the PA reopened these issues, Israel could do so, too.[10] It was equally true, as Hasan Asfur, one of the PLO's principal negotiators at Oslo, remarked: "We cannot give up on these accords because we paid a price . . . when we agreed to partition Palestine into two states. The Palestinians made historic concessions in order to achieve specific national goals." Even if the PA renounced the agreements, it would not actually retrieve those concessions.[11]

Arafat's third, equally unattractive alternative was to make major concessions in order to reach an agreement at any price. But he could barely manage the compromises already needed, and clearly preferred to wait longer to ensure attaining the goal of an independent Palestinian state with its capital in East Jerusalem. Abandoning these goals would lead to the PA's domestic downfall. Without the outcome the PA sought, Khuri asserted on the fifth anniversary of the Oslo agreement in 1998, there would be no real peace.[12] Even if the PA bargained over Palestine's precise territorial extent and the exact scope of its presence in Jerusalem, and accepted financial compensation in place of the 1948 refugees' return—though the PA never publicly or officially said that it would do any of these things—the gap with Netanyahu's views was still too wide. Consequently, Arafat lacked any incentive to make major concessions without knowing that he would get a state in return.

Finally, the only really effective alternative, as difficult as it seemed, was to continue on the same road the PA had followed since 1993: the peace process itself. Toward that end, Arafat continued to use his repertoire of negotiating firmly, trying to win U.S. support, periodically cracking down on the violent opposition, building internal support, and constructing a state in embryo ready for its day of birth.

An especially important element of the PA's strategy was to create a wide variety of state institutions as quickly and thoroughly as possible in order to ensure that Palestine would eventually come into being. The effort also included many symbolic gestures, meant to create the appropriate mindset among Palestinians and acceptance of their independence by others.

Thus, the PA often called itself the Palestinian National Authority, Arafat's title was given as president, and Palestine's existence as a country was stated as an accomplished fact. The PLC's Standing Orders set its oath of office as a pledge "to be faithful to the nation of Palestine."[13]

Palestine's independence day was also determined by such considerations. The celebration was set neither for May—when the PA first began governing in Jericho and Gaza and the five-year peace process was supposed to be successfully concluded—nor for July, when Arafat returned to Gaza and was sworn in as its leader. Instead, the holiday was set in November to coincide with the PNC's 1988 Declaration of Independence, thus disconnecting statehood from the Oslo process's jurisdiction or outcome.[14]

The PA continued the PLO's effort to construct a national identity and history which, apart from Pan-Arab ideology, would justify a separate Palestinian nationalism. In a typical statement of this doctrine, Arafat offered a view of the Palestinian past transcending the Arab past and incorporating Jewish history as well: "The Palestinian people have lived on their land throughout history. They helped to create civilization and raise the voice of peace, the voice of the only all-powerful God, the creator, the lord of the universe and of the three heavenly religions."[15]

In every area of life, the PA tried to imitate a state. It distributed identity cards, a policy which Deputy Interior Minister Ahmad Sa'id Tamimi explained would "reinforce Palestinian sovereignty." The PA's Interior

Ministry also issued Palestinian passports.[16] The al-Hakawati Theater in Jerusalem was designated the Palestinian National Theater, and a Palestinian team took part in the 1996 Olympics, marching behind the Palestinian flag, despite Israel's complaint.[17]

Similarly, the PA tried to circumvent provisions in its agreements prohibiting it from diplomatic activity regarding political matters. The PA pushed for fuller recognition as a country by the UN and other international organizations, while maintaining quasi-diplomatic missions in many places.[18] A majority in the UN General Assembly supported a nonbinding December 1997 resolution affirming the Palestinian people's right to self-determination, and also voted 124 to 4 to elevate the PA's status to the level of observer and to grant it added rights to participate in the organization's work.[19] But the PA was unsuccessful in its goal of obtaining full UN membership as a state.

The creation of Palestinian Airlines was a typical symbol of this campaign. It had its own planes, Dutch-trained pilots, and plans for the $106 million, 587-acre Gaza International Airport, to be built with German, Moroccan, and Egyptian funds. The Palestinian Civil Aviation Authority became a member of the International Federation of Airports and signed agreements to conduct flights from airports in Egypt, Morocco, Jordan, Tunisia, and Qatar.[20]

The first flight took place on January 10, 1997, taking pilgrims to Mecca. Pilot Jamal Hawwa called the trip a "great symbol for Palestinians in their struggle to found a Palestinian state." But still, as Deputy Waqf Minister Shaykh Yusuf Salama, who joined the send-off for the passengers in Gaza, pointed out, "airplanes without an airport are not enough." Indeed, the aviation situation had also symbolized the PA's continued limitations. The airline's passengers had to leave Gaza by bus, and the planes took off from an Egyptian runway. Without Israeli agreement, no airport could open in Gaza, and without Israeli agreement, there would be no Palestinian state on the ground either. As a result of the Wye accord, however, the airport was opened in December 1998, and Palestinian airlines began regular flights to several Arab countries.[21]

A wild card in this whole historic situation was the continued presence of Arafat himself as the PA's leader. Since so much of Palestinian politics and governance revolved around Arafat's person and personality, his death would unleash massive change on the PA's system. As many countries have discovered throughout history, replacing their founding father is the true test of their ability to survive. Born in 1929, Arafat had become the world's oldest revolutionary. He was badly injured in a 1992 plane crash, was chronically overweight, and showed symptoms of illness starting in April 1997, when he reportedly collapsed en route to Egypt and had to return to Gaza under a doctor's care.

Given Arafat's centrality to the system, his replacement would be a matter of the greatest urgency, especially given his refusal to name a successor or permit anyone to emerge as the number two Palestinian leader. A West Bank anecdote mocked his determination to have no understudy: Deciding to build himself a five-story house, he told his lieutenants they could have four-story homes. But each time someone reached the third floor, Arafat ordered him to stop.

"It is part of his strength and power to leave things unplanned and unprepared for a 'post-Arafat' period," wrote Ghasan Khatib. "This leaves everyone subject to fear of the chaos and problems to come after Arafat, which in turn causes them to make every possible effort to keep him in power in order to avoid the uncertainties, chaos and problems which will come in his absence." And if any were willing to present themselves as candidates before Arafat died or was ready to pick a successor, they would "stick out their political necks [only to find] they have put them on the chopping block."[22]

The effect of Arafat's departure from the scene would largely depend on when it happened. If he died as president of an independent Palestine, succession would be institutionalized. But if he passed away before the peace process was completed, the fallout could be more unpredictable and disruptive.

The three most serious candidates to replace him were Mahmud Abbas, Faruq Qaddumi, and Ahmad Khuri, each representing a specific stance and sector in Palestinian political life. Thus, while no one could guess who would succeed Arafat as Palestinian leader, each of these individuals and the forces they personify would continue to be important. Analyzing that issue also clarifies broader trends in Palestinian politics during the transition era and suggests key issues to be examined by analysts as well as to be addressed by Palestinians and their leaders.

Qaddumi led the Outsider hard-line faction which followed the traditional PLO line and rejected the Oslo agreement. Although much respected within the PLO and Fatah, he had far less support in the PA territories. Everyone knew that choosing him would bring the peace process's breakdown and a losing confrontation with Israel. The fact that he definitely did not enjoy Arafat's confidence also reduced Qaddumi's chances. And finally, since he was only one year younger than Arafat, Qaddumi was not a long-term contender to replace him.

Khuri represented a younger generation. He was a Fatah rebel but moderate enough to be on good terms with Arafat and a large majority of the PLC, an Outsider well regarded by many Insiders, and a PA official without losing his independence. Khuri wanted more democracy and a more expert approach to economic development. In contrast to Qaddumi, he was identified with the Oslo agreement. According to the PLC's Basic Law, which the PA had never accepted, Khuri as PLC speaker would hold power for sixty days after Arafat's demise until new elections were held. As leader, Khuri might be popular with the younger middle class, Fatah rebels, and human rights and democracy activists. Still, while his long-run prospects seemed better than Qaddumi's, he lacked the organizational base and leadership credentials to win power in the immediate future.

Abbas was, like Qaddumi, a prestigious veteran in the PLO leadership and a longtime member of both the PLO Executive Committee and the Fatah Central Committee. Like Khuri, Abbas had transferred his base of operations from the PLO to the PA. His Insider connections were far better than Qaddumi's, if not as good as Khuri's. Most important, Abbas stood in well with many of those PLO and Fatah cadres who supported Arafat. Abbas was smart and pragmatic, though not so colorful and charismatic. If Arafat made a choice, Palestinian leaders asserted—sometimes claiming to quote Arafat on this point—it would be Abbas.

Faysal al-Husayni was also a plausible long-term candidate for PA leadership. PA leaders respected him, and Husayni was the only Insider with a real chance of succeeding Arafat. But Arafat's determination to block Husayni's rise, and perhaps his own focus on the Jerusalem issue to the detriment of broader base-building, slowed his progress.

Neither opposition figures nor military officers are on this list. Both the violent and democratic oppositions had no control over any part of the government or military forces and were a minority in terms of mass support. Also, since the succession would take place within the Oslo framework, Hamas's rejection of that agreement would also be an insuperable obstacle, especially to participating in a presidential election.

Only by armed uprising could it hope to gain power, but Hamas had no intention of trying that route, largely because its leaders knew they would be ostracized for breaking Palestinian unity, could not win the struggle, and would be totally destroyed. PA police chief Jabali put it more colorfully, quoting an Arab saying that "a man who drinks cannot break the glass."[23] Instead, Hamas could continue to accept in principle a coexistence with the PA, remaining content to rely on divine intervention and the peace process's shortcomings to drop power into their hands.

It was equally easy to overrate the Palestinian military's political prospects. Unlike the situation in Arab countries, the police, like the PA itself, were still in a pre-state phase. They had not yet become integrated as a force, and officers' links to Arafat were more important than professional solidarity among themselves. Arafat created multiple military services and competing commanders precisely for this purpose. Not only did the soldiers, like the opposition, fear popular rejection for breaking national unity, but also they were unlikely to agree among themselves on either a bid for power or a consensus candidate. Police officers were not so politicized, and Preventive Security officers were nowhere near strong enough to seize power. Anyone putting his name forward for leader would find few reliable troops or cooperative commanders to follow him.

The key factor in picking Arafat's successor and setting the future course of PA policy would be the political interplay within and between the PLO and Fatah. As, in effect, the PA's ruling party—though not constituted as such—Fatah would have to select and unite behind a candidate to stay in power. Suha Arafat predicted that her husband's death would trigger "a destructive war" fomented by Israel.[24] Fear of an opposition takeover, worry over having to replace a seemingly indispensable leader, and suspicion of possible U.S., Israeli, or foreign Arab influence in the choice of a successor would be pressure enough to inspire harmony in Fatah.

Still, Suha Arafat's anxious feeling—common among Palestinians—did reflect a characteristic sense of weakness, fear of internal division, and difficulty in envisioning a post-Arafat era. In fact, though, outside powers would have little effect on who became the next Palestinian leader. None of Arafat's likely successors was anyone's puppet; each was determined to preserve Palestinian independence against any external forces. The merest hint that someone was the Israeli or American candidate would destroy his prospects of success.

The PA's future and a Palestinian state's prospects would be seriously jeopardized if Fatah could not agree on a new leadership. If, however, Fatah succeeded, the winning candidate would be more dependent on that organization than Arafat had ever been.

A bigger potential threat—signaling a more important potential role for Qaddumi—would be if there was a split between those living under PA rule and Palestinians living abroad. This division was institutionally embodied in the distinction between the PA and the PLO.[25] As he tried to do in 1995, Qaddumi might work to unite the smaller PLO member groups and dissident anti-Arafat exile organizations behind himself. Such an alliance could be fortified by Syrian sponsorship in a takeover bid and gain support from Palestinians in Syria, Lebanon, and elsewhere as an alternative leadership.

Palestinians abroad demoralized by slow progress toward a state, doubtful of their chance for repatriation, and depressed at losing the dream of a return to their pre-1948 homes might be willing to break with a PA no longer headed by Arafat. In Jordan, these problems had made local Palestinians more cautious, since they felt that their personal futures depended on good relations with the Jordanian government. In Lebanon, the same factors had a radicalizing effect on local Palestinians, making them rally behind anti-PA nationalist and Islamic movements.

Another issue was whether a less omnipotent successor to Arafat would have to accept a more democratic system. As Marwan Kanafani, a former Arafat adviser and a PLC member, noted, the transition issue proved that "we need a democratic apparatus in order to prevent problems arising in the days following Arafat's departure." Another PLC member often critical of Arafat's management, Hatim Abd al-Khadir, insisted, "Democracy must reign in the post-Arafat period."[26]

A key question in the state-building process was to what extent the pattern established on independence forms the basis for a country's future political structure. On the one hand, the existence of democratic structures on independence day did not save many Third World countries from becoming dictatorial regimes.[27] On the other hand, there were elements in the Palestinian situation that could promote democracy in a post-Arafat state. "The differing streams within Arafat's Fatah organization [showed] a lack of despotism," noted Abu Amr. "So was a broad acceptance—even by Hamas—that internal differences should be settled peacefully." Equally, "the challenge facing the Palestinians is whether they will be able to incorporate and indigenize ideas and concepts that have originated elsewhere but were universal, and to blend them in the authentic context of Palestinian society."[28]

PNC chairman Salim al-Za'nun, a Qaddumi supporter, suggested an alternative scenario that would promote organizational unity while undermining democracy. "The PLO's basic regulations are clear," he insisted. "The PNC elects the [PLO] Central Council and a chairman is elected out of its ranks. If a tragedy befalls [Arafat], the Executive Committee is empowered to elect [a new] chairman overnight. According to

[PLO] Central Council decisions from October 1993, the chairman of the Executive Committee [of the PLO] is the president of the [PA]."[29] Of course, as Za'nun knew, there were only four Insiders among the eighteen Executive Committee members, and that forum would offer Qaddumi a better hope of success than would general elections.

Other than Qaddumi, Arafat's likely successors would not change the PA's goals. The difference would more likely require a greater effort to secure personal and collective legitimacy as well as a shift in leadership style toward more power-sharing and consultation. A critical element would be whether the successor was more open toward the democratic opposition, more willing—or perhaps less able—to restrain Hamas, and better prepared temperamentally to build credibility with Israel.

In the long run, and especially if they succeeded in gaining a state, future Palestinian leaders would still face a monumental task of economic development, including repatriating and sustaining hundreds of thousands of Palestinian refugees returning from abroad. This would be a difficult and delicate undertaking even assuming continued international aid and additional compensation for pre-1948 property given up within Israel. Also important would be a need to avoid conflicts between Insiders and Outsiders, the West Bank and Gaza, refugees and indigenous residents, and rival towns each demanding its own share of resources and influence.[30]

A Palestinian state's prospective international situation would also involve a set of intriguing and complex issues. The overriding issue would be maintaining peace with Israel and blocking any efforts by radical groups to stage cross-border attacks. Also significant would be Palestine's alliances within the region, its role in the Arab political framework, and the part that state might play in future crises.

Just as Arab states had always competed for control over the PLO, they would try to put Palestine in their sphere of influence, including efforts to manipulate its internal politics. It should be clearly understood that even a fully independent Palestine would be one of the region's weaker states, in both economic and strategic terms.

The main radical regimes—Syria, Iraq, Libya, and Iran—might try to subvert a Palestinian regime by violence or by subsidizing the opposition. They would continue sponsoring Palestinian groups—both outside and inside Palestine—seeking to attack Israel in order to destroy the peace settlement. Finally, they could attempt to lure Palestine into foreign adventures or alignments destabilizing the region. The PA's leadership had some sympathy for Iraq but little (except for the pro-Qaddumi faction) for the other three radical states.[31]

For Palestine, a radical orientation would be very risky, jeopardizing any peace agreement with Israel, possibly bringing a confrontation with Jordan, and losing U.S. support. U.S. leverage on Palestine would be considerable. In a real sense the PA had become a U.S. client, and more than 90 percent of the Palestinians' aid came from the West and Japan, brokered through U.S. efforts. Despite their many differences in terms of interests, Egypt, Israel, and Jordan all wanted Palestine to be stable and moderate. They, too, might meddle in Palestinian politics, but such involvement would be on behalf of the PA's heir.

For example, Egypt's interests coincided with those of a moderate PA. Any Islamic radical takeover of Palestine would encourage similar revolutionary forces within Egypt, and any renewed Arab-Israeli conflict might drag in Egypt. If Iraq, Iran, or Syria were to turn Palestine into a satellite, Egypt's regional leadership would be seriously threatened. Thus, Egypt did not want an unstable or radical Palestinian government in power.

Jordan would pose a larger problem since its interests could continue to compete with those of the Palestinian leadership. While Jordan would accept Palestine's independence and control over East Jerusalem's Islamic sites, it would fear such a state's potential appeal to the loyalty of resident Palestinian citizens constituting over half the kingdom's population. Any confederation between the two countries would encourage constant maneuvering for influence. But whatever differences it had with a Palestinian government, Jordan would not want these issues to lead to a crisis or radicalization of Palestine either. The two states could easily live as peaceful neighbors, though there would always be an undercurrent of suspicion.

Another critical question would be whether Palestine could reconcile with Saudi Arabia and Kuwait to win them as major sources of aid. This task might well be easier for Arafat's successor, who would not be the object of those rulers' personal dislike or bear the sin in their eyes of having supported Iraq in the Kuwait crisis.

Despite Israel's serious reservations about creating a Palestinian state, its own security interests would dictate—once such an entity was established—that it be a stable, moderate, and prosperous country. From Israel's standpoint, the Palestinian government would have to be strong enough to block radical forces from attacking Israel and pragmatic enough not to foster irredentist programs.

Domestic or foreign Arab radical influences were extremely threatening in three ways. On an international level, if Palestine participated in a radical Arab alliance—especially if there was any chance of Syrian or Iraqi troops on Palestinian soil—war with Israel was likely. On a bi-lateral level, terrorist attacks across the Palestine-Israel border, with or without Palestinian government approval, might also bring military confrontation. In domestic Israeli terms, Palestine could try to subvert and encourage nationalist demands among the 18 percent of Israeli cit-izens who were Palestinian Arabs. Israel would have certain types of leverage—including military superiority and economic power—to avoid these outcomes and encourage Palestine to keep its commitments under any peace agreement.

An independent Palestinian state's interests would revolve around na-tional integration and economic development, avoiding steps that would make it any other state's satellite or cost it gains so painfully made after decades of struggle. A combination of efforts by the majority Pal-estinian leadership acting in its own interest, along with an Egyptian and U.S. role, and possibly reinforced by Jordanian or Israeli efforts, should suffice to ensure a successful two-state solution to the Israeli-Palestinian dispute. Given the workings of Middle East politics and the complexity of the Palestinian situation, however, a positive outcome could be ensured only through constant and energetic vigilance.

Of course, these problems still lay well in a future which would come about after many rounds of slow, detailed negotiations. Asfur remarked in 1998 that the Oslo agreement had met a real and agonizing Palestin-ian reassessment, "a huge turning point" after the Palestinians' "long journey of desolation and dispersion . . . The dynamics of the Oslo pro-cess served as the basic foundation for this new perspective on the Pal-estinian entity and nation." The agreement, he continued, "does not give us what we want but it also does not give them everything they want." It accomplished as much as was possible "to put the Palestinian people on the road to independence. But I always tell my brothers: We should not exaggerate what we achieved lest we lose it, and we should not underestimate what we achieved lest we waste it."[32]

Certainly, the PA had more than its share of incompetence and cor-ruption. The existence of political leaders who constantly speak of their love for the people while ignoring their needs or even robbing them was by no means restricted to Palestinian politics. Abbas's rationale for the PA's performance, however, did make sense in partly explaining this factor. "This experiment is new to us from beginning to end," he said. "We are ruling ourselves for the first time."[33]

In effect, though, the PLO's decision to recognize Israel and seek a solution to negotiations had totally altered the situation. He noted:

Over the past 50 years the clock was ticking but now, after Oslo, it is moving forward and the train is moving forward on its tracks. We may not reach the final station in one or several years but we will reach it eventually. For 50 years before Oslo the Palestinians used to leave the homeland. After Oslo their direction was reversed and they have begun returning to the homeland.

I am thus optimistic that the end of this century will see the completion of the peace process, and there will be peace, and security and stability in the Middle East, and this process will be crowned with the founding of a Palestinian state, with Jerusalem as its capital.[34]

While Abbas may have been overoptimistic, especially about the region's future, and not disregarding the fact that about 530 people had been killed during the first five years after the Oslo agreement, the overall political results had been mutually beneficial. The majority of people on both sides were adjusting to the new reality, so drastically different from what they had known before.

Despite many shortcomings, the Palestinians were consolidating stable postrevolutionary institutions and an elite capable of making the transition to statehood. That leadership preferred peace and economic development and would fight against either a militant Islamic takeover or any radical Arab regime's attempt to control Palestine. If the PA stayed the course and tried to meet its commitments, a Palestinian state was most likely. The only question was how long it would take to be realized.

PALESTINIAN AUTHORITY CABINETS, 1994–1999

May 28, 1994
Culture and Arts: Yasir Abd Rabbu
Economics and Trade: Ahmad Khuri (resigned September 1994)
Education: Yasir Amr
Finance: Muhammad Zudhi al-Nashashibi
Health: Riyad al-Za'nun
Housing: Zakariyya al-Agha
Interior: Yasir Arafat
Justice: Frayh Abu Midayn
Local Government: Sa'ib Arikat
Planning and Economic Cooperation: Nabil Sha'th
Social Affairs: Intisar al-Wazir
Telecommunications: Abd al-Hafiz al-Ash'ab
Tourism and Monuments: Ilyas Frayj
Youth and Sports: Azmi al-Shu'aybi

May 28, 1996
Agriculture: Abd al-Jawad Salah
Civil Affairs: Jamal al-Tarifi
Culture, Arts, and Information: Yasir Abd Rabbu
Economy and Trade: Mahir al-Masri
Education: Yasir Amr
Finance: Muhammad Zuhdi al-Nashashibi
Health: Riyad al-Za'nun
Higher Education: Hanan Ashrawi
Housing and Public Works: Azzam al-Ahmad

Industry: Bashir al-Barghuti
Interior: Yasir Arafat
Jewish Affairs: Moshe Hirsch
Justice: Frayh Abu Midayn
Labor: Samir Ghawsha (resigned January 26, 1998)
Local Government: Sa'ib Arikat
Planning and International Cooperation: Nabil Sha'th
Social Affairs: Intisar al-Wazir
Sports and Youth: Tallal Sadir
Supply: Abd al-Aziz Ali Shahin
Telecommunications and Post: Imad al-Faluji
Tourism and Archaeology: Elias Frayj (resigned for health reasons, May 1996; died March 1997)
Transportation: Ali Qawasma
Waqf and Religious Affairs: Hasan Tahbub
Without Portfolio (Jerusalem Affairs): Faysal al-Husayni

August 5, 1998

Agriculture: Hikmat Zaid
Civil Affairs: Jamal al-Tarifi
Economics and Trade: Mahir al-Masri
Education: Munther Salah
Environment: Yusuf Abu Safiyya
Finance: Muhammad Zuhdi al-Nashashibi
Health: Riyad al-Za'nun
Higher Education: Munther al-Salah
Housing: Abd al-Rahman Hamad
Information, Culture, and Arts: Yasir Abd Rabbu
Industry: Sa'adi al-Karnaz
Interior: Yasir Arafat
Jerusalem: Faysal al-Husayni
Justice: Frayh Abu Midayn
Labor: Rafiq al-Natsha
Local Government: Sa'ib Arikat
Parliamentary Affairs: Nabil Amr
Planning and International Cooperation: Nabil Sha'th
Prisoners' Affairs: Hisham Abd al-Raziq
Public Works: Azzam al-Ahmad
Social Affairs: Intisar al-Wazir
Supply: Abd al-Aziz Ali Shahin
Telecommunications and Post: Imad al-Faluji
Tourism and Archaeology: Hanan Ashrawi (rejected post)

Transport: Ali Qawasma
Waqf and Religious Affairs: Not filled
Without Portfolio: Salah al-Ta'amri, Ziyad Abu Ziyad, Bashir Barghuti, Yasir
    Amr, Hasan Asfur, Abd al-Jawad Salah (rejected post), Tallal Sadir
Youth and Sports: Not filled

MEMBERSHIP OF THE PALESTINIAN LEGISLATIVE COUNCIL (PLC)

Name	Area	Rank	Affil.	Biography

Group 1: Arafat/PA supporters
(Do not always vote for Arafat but can generally be relied on to support the PA and its policies)

Name	Area	Rank	Affil.	Biography
Azzam al-Ahmad	Jenin	3/5	F	M Public Works, O 1998; A Iraq
Mitri Abu Aitta In	Bethlehem	4/4	I	C; ex-H WB lawyers' union; pro-F; PLC 2nd Deputy PLC Speaker
Nabil Amr O +	Hebron	4/10	F	b1947; RC; A USSR; M Parliamentary Affairs, 1998
Sa'ib Arikat In +	Jericho	1/1	F	M local government; 1994 negotiator with Israel; close to Arafat
Abd Rabbu Abu Awn In	Rafah	1/5	F	b1953; teacher, UNRWA schools
Hasan Asfur O * +	KY	6/8	I(F)	F; PA negotiator participant in Oslo talks
Mahmud Mahmud d'As In	Qalqilya	1/1	F	
Hakim Bal'awi O +	Tulkarm	2/4	F	b1936; A Tunisia; CC close to Arafat

Name	Area	Rank	Affil.	Biography
Ahmad al-Batsh In	Jerusalem	3/7	I(F)	
Ahmad al-Diyak In	Salfit	1/1	F	
Uthman Ghashash O	Qalqilya	1/2	I(F)	Worked in PLO embassy in Jordan
Ibrahim al-Habash In	DB	5/5	I	b1951; pharmacist
Abd al-Rahman Hamad In	N Gaza	4/7	F	H PECDAR projects; Bir Zayt U lecturer
Abd al-Fatah Hamayal D	Ramallah	3/7	I(F)	b1950; Fatah since 1967; sentenced to life in 1969; released 1985; imprisoned 1990 and deported
Ghazi Hanania In	Ramallah	6/7	F	C; dentist; co-founder P. Red Crescent; president Ramallah-America Federation
Muhammad Hijazi O	Rafa	2/5	F	
Muhammad al-Hurani In	Hebron	5/10	F	b1961; imprisoned several times
Fu'ad Id In	N Gaza	2/7	F	Imam of mosque
Ahmad Irshid In	Jenin	4/5	F	b1937; secretary-general youth committee
Burhan Jarrar O	Jenin	1/5	F	
Emile Jarjou' In	Jerusalem	7/7	F	b1934; C; pediatrician; EC
Sa'di al-Kurunz In	DB	2/5	F	
Jalal al-Masdar In	DB	4/5	I	Wealthy landlord
Sharif Ali Mash'al (Abbas Zaki) O +	Hebron	1/10	F	b1942; RC; CC H mobilization and organization
Mahir al-Masri In +	Nablus	4/7	F	b1946; business; prominent family; M Economy and Trade 1994

Name	Area	Rank	Affil.	Biography
Frayh Abu Midayn In	DB	1/4	F	M Justice 1994
Abd al-Karim Musalam In	KY	8/8	I	
Ibrahim Musa Abu al-Naja In *	KY	5/8	F	PLC 1st Deputy Speaker
Ahmad Nasir In	KY	7/8	F	
Rafiq al-Natsha O	Hebron	6/10	F	b1934; A Saudi Arabia; dropped from CC for taking hard line 1988; M Labor 1998
Zahran Abu Qabita In	Hebron	7/10	I(F)	
Ali al-Qawasma In	Hebron	8/10	F	M Transport 1996
Tayyib Abd al-Rahim O +	Tulkarm	1/4	F	b1943; director-general Arafat office; ex-A, Japan, Jordan, Egypt, Yugoslavia
Mfid Abd Rabbu In	Tulkarm	3/4	I(F)	b1957; secretary-general youth M
Nahid al-Rayiss In	Gaza	3/12	F	Veteran nationalist
Ali Abu Rish In	Hebron	8/10	I(F)	
Musa Abu Sabha In	Hebron	2/10	F	
Yusuf Abu Safiya In	N Gaza	1/7	F	Environmentalist; energy research center; al-Azhar U lecturer
Hashim al-Salah In	Tubas	1/1	I	Tubas mayor; traditional leader
Dallal Salama In	Nablus	6/7	F	W Balata refugee camp; M WB Committee
Salum Imran al-Samirai In	Nablus	—	I	Reserved seat: Samaritans
Faraj al-Saraf In	Gaza	12/12	F	
Jamila Saydam O	DB	3/5	F	W

Name	Area	Rank	Affil.	Biography
Nabil Sha'th O +	KY	1/8	F	M International Cooperation and Planning 1994; F CC
Ahmad al-Abd al-Shu'aybi In	KY	4/8	F	M Youth & Sports 1994–1996
Abd al-Aziz Shahin O +	Rafah	5/5	F	b1946; F military leader; M Supply 1996
Ghassan al-Shaq'a In +	Nablus	3/7	F	Mayor of Nablus; EC
Fakhri Shaqura O * +	Gaza	2/11	F	H PA Mil. Intelligence Gaza; RC; F Higher Military Council; Founder PLA; H PLC Interior and Security Committee
Rawiya al-Shawwa In	Gaza	11/11	I	W journalist; member leading family; sometimes criticized Arafat
Jamal Salah al-Shubaki In	Hebron	3/10	F	
Sulayman Abu Snana In	Hebron	9/10	F	
Jamal al-Tarifi In	Ramallah	4/7	I	Businessman, M Civil Affairs 1996; negotiator with Israel
Jawad al-Tibi In	KY	2/8	F	
Intisar al-Wazir (Um Jihad) O +	Gaza	4/11	F	b1941; W; founder P Women's Union; M Social Affairs 1994; CC
Riyad al-Za'nun O *	Gaza	5/11	F	b1937; physician, M Health 1994
Fayiz Zaydan O +	Nablus	1/7	F	H PA Civil Aviation
Dawood al-Zayr O	Bethlehem	2/4	I(F)	b1939; businessman
Ahmad Hasim al-Zghayar In	Jerusalem	6/7	F	b1935; H agriculture marketing coop and Palestinian agric. union

Name	Area	Rank	Affil.	Biography
Group 2: Critical supporters				
Kamal al-Afghani In	Nablus	7/7	I(F)	
Marwan al-Barghuti D In *	Ramallah	6/7	F	b1959; 6 years in prison deported 1987–1994; RC Secretary WB Committee Chair, PLC Land & Settlement Committee
Qaddura Faris In	Ramallah	2/7	I(F)	Imprisoned 14 years
Rawhi Fatuh In	Rafah	4/5	F	RC
Hatim Abd al-Qadar Id In	Jerusalem	5/7	F	Spokesperson, Orient House
Marwan Kanafani O *	Gaza	9/11	I(F)	Former Arafat spokesperson
Husam Khadir In *	Nablus	5/7	I(F)	Balata refugee camp; intifada activist
Ahmad Khuri O (Abu Ala)	Jerusalem	1/7	F	PLC Speaker; CC; ex-M Economics; May–Sept 1994 chief negotiator at Oslo
Asad Abd al-Qadir O (Salah Ta'amri)*	Bethlehem	1/4	I(F)	b1942; veteran Fatah member
Hisham Abd al-Raziq In	N Gaza	3/7	F	Intifada activist; member prisoner release talks
Jamal Shati al-Hindi In	Jenin	2/5	F	
Azmi al-Shua'ybi D	Ramallah	5/7	FIDA	b1947; dentist; co-founder Palestine National Front; deportee 1985–1993; ex-deputy M Sports and Youth 1994–1996

Name	Area	Rank	Affil.	Biography

Group 3: Opposition, Oslo opponents

Name	Area	Rank	Affil.	Biography
Bishara Sulayman Daud	Bethlehem	3/4	I	Ex-Bayt Jala mayor; close to PFLP
Imad Faluji In	N Gaza	7/7	F	Former Hamas leader, mediated between PA and Hamas; M Telecommunications & Post 1996
Waji Haghi In	Gaza	7/11	I	Close to Hamas
Hasan Khraysha In	Tulkarm	4/4	F	Abu Nidal supporter who now claims allegiance to Fatah; views not clear
Mu'awiya al-Masri In	Nablus	2/7	I	Physician; Islamist
R'afat al-Najar In	KY	3/8	I	PFLP member
Sulayan al-Rumi In	Rafah	3/5	I	b1961; close to Hamas; Muslim preacher
Haydar Abd al-Shafi In *	Gaza	1/11	NDC	b1919; H P Red Crescent; H peace talk deleg. 1991–1993; chaired PLC Political Committee; resigned PLC 1997
Yusuf al-Shanti In	Gaza	10/11	I	Islamist
Kamal al-Sharafi In	N Gaza	6/7	I	Close to PFLP
Musa al-Za'but In	Gaza	8/11	I	b1949; pediatrician; Islamic U lecturer
Karam Zaranda In	N Gaza	5/7	I	Islamist

Name	Area	Rank	Affil.	Biography

Group 4: Opposition: Moderate Democrats

Name	Area	Rank	Affil.	Biography
Ziyad Abu Amr In	Gaza	6/11	I	b1950; Bir Zayt U lecturer
Hanan Ashrawi In	Jerusalem	2/7	I	W; C; univ. teacher; spokesperson P delegation 1991–1993
Abd al-Jawad Salah D	Ramallah	1/7	I	b1931; ex-mayor al-Bira. M Agriculture 1996–1998 resigned cabinet 1998; M PLO Executive Comm. 1974–1981
Fakhri Turkman In	Jenin	5/5	I	b1946
Ziyad Abu Zayad In	Jerusalem	4/7	I	H delegation to multilateral arms talks

Note: This chart is based on JMCC, "Final Results of the Elections," March 1, 1996, but has been completely altered with many changes and much additional material from author, including the classification of PLC members into groups, changes in spelling for transliteration, updating, and biographical details. In some cases, individuals are on the borderline between groups or are hard to classify, so the analysis is an approximation.

Abbreviations
A = former PLO ambassador
b = year of birth
C = reserved seat for Christians
CC = member of Fatah Central Committee
D = deportee
DB = Dayr al-Balah
EC = member of PLO Executive Committee
F = Fatah
H = head of
I = independent
In = Insider
I(F) = elected as an independent but a member of Fatah
KY = Khan Yunus
M = minister
O = Outsider
RC = member of Fatah Revolutionary Committee
W = woman
WB Committee = Fatah Higher Committee for the West Bank

* Leading figure in PLC
+ Leading figure in PA

THE FATAH CENTRAL COMMITTEE

This chart lists those members of the Central Committee (CC) elected at the August 1989 Fatah congress and those dropped or subsequently added. Prior to 1995, all members were Outsiders. Each person's main post or institution is given in the position column.

Name	Position	Biography
Involved in PA Leadership		
Yasir Arafat	Head of the PA	
Mahmud Abbas (Abu Mazin)		At first inactive, joined Arafat as head of Election Committee and of PA negotiating team with Israel. Secretary of PA EC from May 1996.
Hakam Bal'awi (Abu Marwan)	PLC	PLO ambassador to Tunis for many years; Arafat adviser.
Abdallah Franji	Diplomat	PLO ambassador in Germany for many years.
Sakr Habash* (Abu Nizar)	Fatah official	Fatah Revolutionary Committee; head, Ideological Mobilization department; hard-liner.

Name	Position	Biography
Ahmad Khuri (Abu Ala)	PLC speaker	Director-general of PLO economic department; negotiated Oslo accord; Minister of Economics and Trade 1994, but resigned. Elected PLC Speaker in 1996.
Sharif Ali Mash'al* (Abbas Zaki)	Fatah official	PLO director of Arab and foreign relations; head of the Higher Committee to Support the Intifada. In charge of mobilization and organization after returning in September 1995. Hard-liner.
Tayyib Abd al-Rahim	Arafat adviser	PLO envoy to Yugoslavia, Jordan, Japan, and Egypt; PA Secretary-General.
Nabil Sha'th	PLC, Cabinet	Chairman of PNC political committee from 1971; president, Arab world's largest consulting and training company. PA Minister of Planning and International Cooperation.
Nasir Yusuf	Security forces	Public Security Police commander.
Intissar al-Wazir (Um Jihad)	PLC, Cabinet	Minister of Social Welfare.

Not involved in PA (opposed to Oslo agreement)

Muhammad Ghana'im* (Abu Mahir)		Ex-Fatah representative in Kuwait. Bid to return in 1998 rejected by Israel.
Hani al-Hasan*		Veteran Fatah activist. Returned to West Bank.
Abd al-Hamid Ha'yil (Abu al-Hawl)		PLO security man and head of the Western Sector. Responsible for attacks on Israel. Not reelected in 1995.
Brig. Gen. Muhammad Jihad*		Former Palestine Liberation Army officer, briefly joined anti-Arafat, Syrian-sponsored revolt in 1983.

Name	Position	Biography
Subhi Abu Karsh* (Abu Munzir)		Former aide to Abu Jihad and deputy PLO representative in Saudi Arabia. Not reelected in 1995.
Faruq Qaddumi*	PLO	PLO "foreign minister" based in Tunis.
Salim al-Za'nun*	Chairs PNC	PLO representative in the Gulf; head of PNC.

Deceased

Khalid al-Hasan		Died of natural causes.
Salah Khalaf (Abu Iyad)		Assassinated by Abu Nidal group 1991.

Not reelected in 1990

Rafiq al-Natsha* (Abu Shaker)	PLC	PLO ex-ambassador in Saudi Arabia; opposed 1988 PNC political resolution and attacked Arafat's policy at 1990 Fatah meeting. Elected PLC in Hebron on Fatah ticket. Minister of Labor 1998.

Added to Fatah Central Committee in 1995

Zakariyya al-Agha		Head of Fatah in Gaza.
Faysal al-Husayni		Head of Fatah in East Jerusalem; cabinet and leading figure on West Bank. PA minister responsible for Jerusalem affairs.

* Very critical of peace process and Oslo accord framework

THE PLO EXECUTIVE
COMMITTEE (EC)

Name	Biography
Fatah representatives	
Yasir Arafat * + (Abu Ammar)	PLO: leader of PLO and Fatah. PA: head of the PA
Faruq Qaddumi + (Abu al-Lutuf)	Head of PLO political department. Signed October 1995 anti-Oslo II statement, opposed peace process. Bid to return in 1998 rejected by Israel.
Mahmud Abbas * + (Abu Mazin)	PA: dead of Electoral Commission. Head of negotiations with Israel. Secretary of EC from May 1996.
Smaller groups	
Muhammad al-Abbas (Abu al-Abbas) (Ali Ishaq + replaced him in 1991)	Palestine Liberation Front (PLF). Organized terror attacks, forced off of Executive Committee in 1991 owing to Western pressure. Returned to PA territories, but no public position.
Ahmad Abd al-Rahim (Abu Isma'il) (replaced by Mahmud Isma'il +)	Iraq-controlled Arab Liberation Front. Opposed Oslo agreement. Isma'il signed the note opposing Oslo II.

Name	Biography
Samir Ghawsha +	Palestine Struggle Front, endorsed October 1995 anti–Oslo II statement. PA Minister of Labor 1996; resigned 1998.
Taysir Khalid +	PFLP representative, resigned 1993 to protest Oslo agreement; signed 1995 anti–Oslo II statement.
Abd al-Rahman Mallul +	DFLP representative from 1991. Resigned to protest Oslo agreement 1993; reelected to EC in 1996.
Sulayman Najjab +	Palestine Communist Party leader.
Yasir Abd Rabbu * +	DFLP representative until his defection in 1991. Head of FIDA party. PA Minister of Information and Culture.

"Independents"

(Includes Fatah members not officially representing the organization)

Yasir Amr +	PLO: veteran Fatah activist. PA Minister of Education 1994–1998; Minister without Portfolio 1998.
Mahmud Darwish	Poet; ex-Israeli citizen; signed October 1995 anti–Oslo II statement; resigned from EC. Lives in France.
Jawad' Ghusayn	PLO: head of finance. PLO and PA: head of Palestine National Fund. Not reelected to EC in 1996
Abdallah Hurani *	PLO: in charge of information. Signed October 1995 anti–Oslo II statement, but won back by Arafat. PA: in charge of PA refugee affairs. Not reelected to EC in 1996.
Shafiq al-Hut	PLO official in Lebanon. Signed anti–Oslo II statement in 1995; resigned from EC.
Elias Khuri	Christian minister. Not reelected to EC in 1996.
Muhammad Milhim	Pro-Fatah West Bank mayor, elected 1976; expelled by Israel 1980; EC member 1988–1991. Headed PLO's Occupied Homeland Affairs Department. PA: adviser to Arafat.
Muhammad Zuhdi al-Nashashibi * +	PLO: Executive Committee secretary, member from 1993. PA Minister of Finance 1994.

Name	Biography
Jamal al-Surani	PLO negotiator and legal expert. Succeeded Nashashibi as EC secretary, but endorsed 1995 anti–Oslo II statement and Arafat removed him from that post May 1996. Not reelected to EC in 1996.
Gen. Abd al-Razaq Yahya *	PLO representative in Jordan. Elected to EC 1988, not reelected 1991. PA: head of PA Safe Passage Committee and Security Liaison Committee.

Added members in 1996

Zakariyya al-Agha * +	"Independent" activist. PA: head of Fatah in Gaza; failed candidate in PLC elections.
Faysal al-Husayni * +	PLO: leading Fatah figure in West Bank. PA Minister for Jerusalem Affairs, Fatah CC.
Emile Jarjou'I * +	Pediatrician; PLC; Christian.
Riyad al-Khudri +	Head of al-Azhar University; close to Fatah.
Asad Abd al-Rahman * +	PLO: Arafat's spokesman; involved in publications. PA: secretary of cabinet.
Ghassan Shaq'a * +	Fatah CC; mayor of Nablus; member of PLC.

Note: For PA cabinet ministers, date of first appointment is given.

*   Active in PA as of 1999
+ Member of PLO EC as of 1999

MIDDLE EAST STATES AND THE PALESTINIAN AUTHORITY

States friendly to the PA (Peace Camp): Algeria,* Bahrain,* Djibouti,* Egypt,†
Jordan,† Mauritania,† Morocco,† Oman,† Qatar,† Somalia, Tunisia,† Turkey,
UAE,* Yemen.

States hostile to PA; aided anti-Arafat Palestinians, oppose peace process (Radical
Camp): Iran, Iraq, Lebanon,‡ Libya, Sudan, Syria.

States cool to PA (Drop-outs): Kuwait, Saudi Arabia

* States open in principle to normalization of relations with Israel.
† States having some form of relations with Israel.
‡ Lebanon's presence in this category was involuntary, and it was not an active member of this
group.

NOTES

1. The Rulers, the Ruled, and the Rules

1. *Palestine Report* (hereafter *PR*), January 17, 1997. U.S. Department of Commerce, *Foreign Broadcast Information Service* (hereafter *FBIS*), January 30, 1995.
2. Quoted in *Yediot Ahronot,* January 27, 1995.
3. For Arafat's speech at the signing of the declaration of principles, September 13, 1993, see Walter Laqueur and Barry Rubin, *The Israel-Arab Reader,* 5th ed. (New York, 1995), pp. 613–615.
4. The story of Israeli-Palestinian negotiations was, of course, closely linked to the evolution of Palestinian politics. But this requires a book in its own right and is not this volume's subject. Consequently, the issues and complex sequence of events involved in Israeli-Palestinian negotiations will be discussed only minimally here.
5. Mohammed S. Dajani, "The Palestinian Authority and Citizenship in the Palestinian Territories," from Palestine National Authority (PNA) Official Website: <http://www.pna.net/reports/mcitizen.htm>.
6. Khalil al-Shikaki [Shiqaqi], "The Peace Process, National Reconstruction, and the Transition to Democracy in Palestine," *Journal of Palestine Studies,* Vol. 25, No. 2 (Winter 1996), p. 9.
7. There are a number of parallels here with Israel's creation. But some of the differences are even more important: that state's full independence was declared and largely established on a single day, May 15, 1948. Some new states faced serious internal conflicts, like post-Communist Yugoslavia; others had to deal with serious external threats. It is the multiplicity of problems converging simultaneously that is so striking in the Palestinian case.
8. *Palestine Times,* December 1997.
9. *PR,* January 17, 1997.

10. Ziad Abu-Am [Ziyad Abu Amr], "The Palestinian Legislative Council: A Critical Assessment," *Journal of Palestine Studies*, Vol. 26, No. 4 (Summer 1997), p. 94.
11. Quoted in *New York Times*, November 20, 1984.
12. *Al-Majalla*, November 21, 1989.
13. Arafat, *al-Qabas*, May 10, 1990 (*Mideast Mirror*, May 10, 1990, pp. 10–13).
14. Ibid.
15. Quoted in *New York Times*, November 20, 1984.
16. Abu-Amr [Abu Amr], "The Palestinian Legislative Council," p. 94.
17. *Yediot Ahronot*, January 27, 1995 (*FBIS*, January 30, 1995).
18. *Washington Post*, September 17, 1994. On PECDAR, see Samir Abdallah, *Palestinian Economic Council for Development and Construction (PECDAR)* [Arabic] (Nablus, 1994).
19. Nidal Ismail, "Is Corruption the Problem?" *PR*, November 28, 1997.
20. See Ahmad Harb, "Cultural Impact of the Declaration of Principles" [Arabic], *al-Siyasa al-Filastiniyya*, Vol. 1, No. 1–2 (Winter–Spring 1994); Manuel S. Hassassian, "The Transformation in the Political Attitudes in the National Movement" [Arabic], *al-Siyasa al-Filastiniyya*, Vol. 2, No. 7–8 (Summer–Fall 1995).
21. This story is told in Barry Rubin, *Revolution Until Victory?: The Politics and History of the PLO* (Cambridge, Mass., 1994). See also Yezid Sayigh, *Armed Struggle and the Search for State* (Oxford, 1997).
22. Speech to Royal Commonwealth Society, December 11, 1989 (text in *Mideast Mirror*, December 12, 1989).
23. The text of the agreement is in Laqueur and Rubin, *The Israel-Arab Reader*, pp. 599–612. For the speeches of President Bill Clinton, Rabin, and Arafat, see pp. 612–615.
24. Ibid., pp. 629–642.
25. Israel Foreign Ministry, *Israel-Palestinian Interim Agreement on the West Bank and Gaza Strip, September 28, 1995* (Jerusalem, 1995). The elections are discussed in Annex 2, "Protocol Concerning Elections."
26. U.S. Information Service, *Official Text of the Wye River Memorandum*, October 23, 1998. The complex arrangements included the transfer of 12 percent from Area C to Area B, 1 percent from Area C to Area A, and 14.2 percent from Area B to Area A. This was supposed to produce the following division of territory: Area A, 18.2 percent; Area B, 24.8 percent; and Area C, 57 percent.
27. Voice of Palestine, January 1, 1995 (*FBIS*, January 6, 1995).
28. The goal here is not to provide a comprehensive account of developments but to indicate the background of events in which Palestinian state-building developed. I have also made no attempt to give a picture of Israeli policy or debates or the details of bilateral negotiations. Such matters are very important but require dedicated books on those topics.
29. *Financial Times* and *Wall Street Journal*, May 25, 1994; *New York Times* and

Washington Post, July 3, 1994. For discussion of complaints about aid funds being misused, see *Arbeiderbladet* (Norway), August 29, 1995 (*FBIS,* August 30, 1995).

30. *New York Times* and *Washington Post,* May 21, 1994.

31. *New York Times,* July 6, 1994. On the cabinet, see discussion later in this chapter and Appendix 1.

32. *New York Times,* July 13, 1994.

33. *Wall Street Journal,* September 26, 1995; *New York Times,* November 19 and 20, December 24, 28, and 31, 1995; *Wall Street Journal,* September 26, 1995; and Voice of Palestine, December 27, 1995 (*FBIS,* December 28, 1995).

34. See Chapters 2 and 3.

35. These issues are discussed in much more depth in Chapter 6.

36. *PR,* January 3, 1997.

37. Transcript of press conference after Netanyahu-Arafat meeting, September 4, 1996.

38. Barry Rubin, *The Palestinian Charter: Prospects for Change* (Tel Aviv, 1996).

39. *PR,* October 4, 1996.

40. *PR,* October 18, 1996.

41. *New York Times,* January 15, 16, and 20, 1997; *al-Quds* and *Washington Post,* January 20, 1997.

42. Arafat's speech in Gaza, March 15, 1997, PNA Official Website, <http://www.pna.net/speeches/0397/1501e.html>.

43. Abu-Amr, "The Palestinian Legislative Council," p. 91. See also Salah Zafit, "The PLC" [Arabic], *al-Siyasa al-Filastiniyya,* Vol. 5, No. 17 (Winter 1998), pp. 94–99.

44. Reuters, August 5, 1998.

45. Three resigned in protest—Khuri, Ghawsha, and Abd al-Jawad Salah—and Yasir Amr, who served as education minister, was the only person dropped in 1998, for poor performance.

46. Voice of Palestine, May 9, 1996 (*FBIS,* May 10, 1996). The relative weight of the PLO Executive Committee, Fatah Central Committee, cabinet, and PLC are discussed in Chapter 5.

47. See Rubin, *Revolution Until Victory?* chap. 8.

48. This is an important point since some observers have depended solely on an analysis of the cabinet in defining the PA's leadership, thus mistakenly concluding that Arafat had excluded revolutionaries and promoted apolitical or tame notables to ensure his control.

49. It is amusing to note that Western reporters sometimes confused Abu Jihad's picture with a man he physically resembled, Iraqi President Saddam Husayn.

50. *Jerusalem Report,* August 3, 1998.

51. Abd Rabbu's portfolios had slightly varied names during different cabinets.

52. For his views, see *al-Akhbar,* July 26, 1996.

53. In each case, because some people held multiple portfolios, there were fewer ministers than ministries. Numbers can vary slightly, given resignations and other factors.

54. *PR*, January 17, 1997.

55. *Washington Post*, September 17, 1994.

56. *Ha'aretz*, January 28, 1998.

57. *PR*, January 17, 1997.

58. Reuters, August 5, 1998. New ministries included parliamentary affairs, environment, and Palestinian prisoners in Israeli jails. Only one member of the previous cabinet, Education Minister Yasir Amr, was dropped. See Appendix 1 for a complete list of cabinet members.

59. Indeed, this was such an effective tool for taming parliamentarians that Salah Ta'amri, a leading PA critic in the PLC, concluded that the legislature had been mistaken to insist that most of the cabinet be chosen from its members. *PR*, September 18, 1998.

60. Husayni was referred to as a minister without portfolio or the holder of the Jerusalem file (portfolio).

61. *Al-Bayadir al-Siyasi*, June 4, 1994, in *Joint Publications Research Service* (hereafter *JPRS*), August 9, 1994. In June 1995, the PA cabinet reportedly approved forming its own Jerusalem city council. *Financial Times*, June 13, 1995.

62. *Ha'aretz*, January 10, 1996; *al-Majalla*, January 20, 1996. On one occasion he supposedly suggested that Arab states send funds for Jerusalem directly through him, a deed which would have infuriated Arafat. *Al-Hayat*, January 12, 1995.

63. Off-the-record interviews.

64. Off-the-record interviews.

65. Other PA agencies include the Economic Policy Research Institute; Bureau of Statistics; the Red Crescent Society and Council of Health, both headed by Dr. Fathi Arafat; WAFA Palestinian News Agency; Council for Environment; Council for Medical Services; Health Services Council; Palestinian Housing Council; and Palestinian Oil Council. There were committees to aid those held prisoner by Israel, headed by Hisham Abd al-Raziq (elevated to ministerial rank in 1998), and a Released Prisoner Committee, headed by Abd al-Qadir Hamid.

66. These security services are discussed in Chapter 5.

67. See Appendixes 3 and 4 for a list of members.

68. The journalist Salah Qallab remarked that the category of "independents" was "an invention" of Arafat's and consisted of "Fatah supporters who were not among the movement's official members" and who were close to Arafat personally in many cases. *Al-Sharq al-Awsat*, April 16, 1994.

69. He was, however, a member of the second-highest group, Fatah's Revolutionary Committee.

70. Voice of Palestine, January 1, 1995 (*FBIS*, January 6, 1995).

71. See Barry Rubin, "External Influences on Israel's 1996 Election," in Dan Elazar and Shmuel Sandler, eds., *Israel's 1996 Election* (London, 1998).

2. The Palestinian Legislative Council

1. For the framework of elections, see the 1993 Oslo agreement, Annex 1 in Laqueur and Rubin, *The Israel-Arab Reader*, p. 605; the 1994 Cairo agreement, Article 7, ibid., pp. 634–635; and the 1995 Israeli-Palestinian Interim Agreement on the West Bank and Gaza, ibid., Annex 2, Protocol Concerning Elections. Israel made concessions in agreeing to a larger PLC than it had originally preferred and accepting the participation of East Jerusalem Palestinians in the voting.

2. Seats were distributed as follows: 11 for Gaza; 10 for Hebron; 9 for Nablus (including 1 reserved for the Samaritans); 8 for Khan Yunis; 7 each for North Gaza, Jerusalem, and Ramallah; 6 for Jenin; 5 each for Dayr al-Balah and Rafah; 4 for Tulkarm and Bethlehem; 2 for Qalqilya; and 1 each for Jericho, Salphit, and Tupas. Of these, 2 each of the Bethlehem and Jerusalem seats and 1 each in Gaza and Ramallah were set aside for Christians.

3. On the Palestinian election law, see *al-Quds*, December 9–12, 1995 (translation, *FBIS*, December 19, 1995, Supplement). On the Samaritans, see *Ha'aretz*, December 12, 1995.

4. Quoted in *Ha'aretz*, January 22, 1996.

5. Abu-Amr, "Pluralism and the Palestinians," *Journal of Democracy*, Vol. 7, No. 3 (1996), p. 83.

6. This group included Nabil Amr, Hasan Asfur, Hakim Bal'awi, Khuri, Sharif Ali Mash'al (Abbas Zaki), Rafiq Darwish al-Natsha, Nabil Sha'th, Fakhri Shaqura, and Intisar al-Wazir.

7. Each member received a monthly salary of $2,500, a car, driver, and mobile telephone. A list of those elected can be found in *Mideast Mirror*, January 22, 1996. For a full list and analysis, see Appendix 2. See also *PR*, January 17, 1997; *Ma'ariv*, May 12, 1996.

8. During 1994, Abd al-Shafi, who had led the "non-PLO" Palestinian delegation to the 1991 Madrid conference and ensuing talks with Israel, launched two petition drives against Arafat's "autocratic" policies among PLO members. *Washington Post*, January 3, 1994; *New York Times*, January 4 and April 26, 1994.

9. Palestinian Authority Website, <http://www.pna.net>, "The Palestinian Legislative Council (Parliament)." The First Deputy Speaker was Ibrahim Musa Abu al-Naja (Fatah-Gaza), general political commissioner for the Gaza Strip. Second Deputy Speaker Mitri Abu Aitta (Independent-Bethlehem) was a lawyer and former head of the West Bank Lawyer Committee. The secretary was Rawhi Fatuh, a Fatah member from Rafah, who headed the Palestinian Popular Organization and was a member of the Fatah Revolutionary Council.

10. Abu-Amr, "The Palestinian Legislative Council," p. 91.

11. Abu-Amr, "Pluralism and the Palestinians," p. 83.

12. *Al-Hayat al-Jadida,* March 13, 1998.

13. See the detailed analysis in Appendix 2.

14. *PR,* January 17, 1997.

15. Abd al-Shafi had been critical of Arafat's conduct of negotiations from the beginning. See, for example, *New York Times,* April 26, 1994.

16. Abu Amr suggested that Hamas, despite its official boycott, gave its supporters permission to vote in order to ensure that there would be some representatives of its viewpoint in the PLC. Abu-Amr, "Pluralism and the Palestinians," p. 88.

17. These two documents are discussed later in this chapter.

18. Abu-Amr, "The Palestinian Legislative Council," p. 95.

19. *PR,* January 17, 1997.

20. This and subsequent citations are taken from the translation in *PR,* August 9, 1996, "Standing Orders of the Palestinian Legislative Council."

21. Ibid. In April 1996, six Gaza members returning home from a session in Ramallah were detained by Israeli authorities and accused of transporting Palestinian students who had no travel permits from Gaza to the West Bank. In another case, twenty-two members traveling from Gaza to Nablus were detained for two hours until Israeli officers arrived to check their documents and search their briefcases. *PR,* January 17, 1997.

22. Ibid. Article 44 established eleven permanent committees: Jerusalem; Lands and Settlements; Refugees and Palestinians Abroad; Political (negotiations, international relations); Legal (including constitutional, judicial, and Standing Orders questions); Budget; Economy; Interior (including security and local government); Education and Social Affairs; Natural Resources and Energy Committee; and Human Rights, Public Freedoms, and General Purposes. Palestinian women attending a Gaza conference demanded establishment of a women's committee within the PLC. The committees tried to meet twice weekly,

23. Ibid.

24. Ibid. For a discussion of this issue, see CPRS Parliamentary Research Unit, *Comparative Analytical Study of Presidential Veto Power* (Nablus, 1997).

25. *PR,* June 28, 1996. Ta'amri, who had been captured by Israel during the 1982 fighting in Lebanon, was an early advocate of a compromise peace. He was one of the few PLC members who held regular meetings with constituents.

26. Arafat later raised the proportion in this cabinet to 67 percent.

27. *PR,* June 14, 1996.

28. *PR,* October 25, 1996.

29. *PR,* July 12, 1996.

30. Ibid.

31. *PR,* July 5, 1996. There were six abstentions and three blank ballots.

32. Ibid.
33. *PR*, November 7, 1997.
34. *PR*, November 22, 1996.
35. *PR*, August 23, 1996.
36. *PR*, November 15, 1996.
37. For an independent evaluation of this period, see CPRS Parliamentary Research Unit, *Evaluation of the Palestinian Legislative Council's First Year. 1996* (Nablus, 1997).
38. *Jerusalem Post,* December 31, 1997.
39. *Ha'aretz,* March 8, 1998.
40. Arafat's speech at PLC's Third Term Opening, March 7, 1998 (*PR*, March 13, 1998).
41. Ibid.
42. Ibid.
43. *Ha'aretz,* March 8, 1998.
44. *PR*, March 8, 1998. The other candidates were Kamal al-Sharafi (10 votes) and Shaykh Sulayman Rumi (5 votes). Sharafi, from the Jabalya refugee camp, chaired the Comptroller and Civil Rights Committee and had headed the key committee investigating corruption allegations against the PA. He represented a tougher critical line against Arafat. Rumi, from the Rafah refugee camp, represented an Islamic orientation.
45. See CPRS Parliamentary Research Unit, *Committees in the Palestinian Legislative Council: Proposals for Their Development and Restructuring* (Nablus, 1997).
46. The PA submitted the budgets late and reluctantly, but the PLC did review them.
47. In June 1998 the PLC draft law on charitable and nongovernmental groups required that they be registered by the Justice Ministry rather than, as the PA wanted, the Ministry of Interior, thus stressing a legal over a security framework.
48. Palestinian National Authority Official Website, <http://www.pna.net>, "Speech of Ahmad Khouri (Abu 'Ala), at the opening of the first session of the Third Term, March 13, 1998." For a complete list of the ninety-six resolutions passed by the PLC in 1997, see Palestinian Independent Commission for Citizen's Rights Newsletter, Third Annual Report, February 1998.
49. PLC Self-Evaluation Report, October 30–31, 1996, (cited in *PR*, November 8, 1996).
50. *PR*, October 25, 1996, and November 28, 1997.
51. *PR*, January 17 and 31, 1997; Abu-Amr, "The Palestinian Legislative Council," p. 95.
52. Ibid. See also Haydar Abd al-Shafi, "Excerpts from His Letter of Resignation" [Arabic], *al-Siyasa al-Filastiniyya*, Vol. 5, No. 17 (Winter 1998).
53. Text of PLC draft of the Basic Law as passed on the third reading, October

2, 1997. Unofficial translation by the Palestinian Society for the Protection of Human Rights and the Environment (LAW). Hereafter referred to as Basic Law text.

54. *Al-Quds,* February 24, 1998.

55. *PR,* January 17, 1997, and March 13, 1998.

56. All quotations that follow are taken from "Palestinian Legislative Council Basic Law Draft Resolution, Third Reading Passed October 2, 1997." Unofficial translation by LAW.

57. *PR,* September 13, 1996.

58. Of particular note is the claim to represent all Palestinians everywhere, a jurisdiction including Jordan and Israel. See Chapters 7 and 8 for a discussion of this concept's implications. Article 3 also defines Jerusalem as the capital of Palestine.

59. Abu-Amr, "The Palestinian Legislative Council," p. 91.

60. Cited in *PR,* January 17, 1997.

61. The corruption issue is discussed at greater length in Chapter 3.

62. *PR,* November 28, 1997.

63. Another company, Somod, had historically represented the economic enterprises of the PLO in exile. See *Globes,* January 14, 1997.

64. *PR,* June 20 and October 31, 1997.

65. Ibid. See also Basim Makhul, *Cement Trade in the West Bank: A Preliminary Evaluation* [Arabic with English summary] (Nablus, 1997).

66. *Ha'aretz,* February 5, 1997.

67. Ibid.

68. This, of course, does not excuse misuse of funds but does suggest that the PA was not so unusual and that this type of behavior was not incompatible with democratic government.

69. *Guardian,* July 14, 1997. This article claimed that the house cost $5 million.

70. Khaled Abu Toameh, *Jerusalem Report,* January 8, 1998, p. 26.

71. Ibid.

72. JMCC Public Opinion Poll No. 19 (Jerusalem), April 1997. CPRS Public Opinion Poll No. 27, conducted the same month, found that 33.8 percent considered the PLC's performance good, 27.7 percent believed it average, and 24.1 percent found it bad. See also JMCC poll, December 13–14, 1996 (*PR,* January 3, 1997).

73. CPRS Poll No. 33, June 3–6, 1998.

74. Ghassan Khatib, "Why the Legislative Council Has an Image Problem," *PR,* October 25, 1996.

75. *PR,* January 17, 1997.

76. *PR,* May 16, 1997; *Washington Post,* May 21, 1997; and *New York Times,* May 22, 1997.

77. *PR,* May 16, 1997.

78. Ibid.

79. For PLC and journalists' efforts to give the legislature more coverage, see Voice of Palestine, May 23, 1996 (*FBIS,* May 28, 1996); *PR,* May 3, 1996; and *al-Quds,* May 31, 1996.

80. Khalil al-Shiqaqi, "The Future of Democracy in Palestine" [Arabic], *al-Siyasa al-Filastiniyya,* Vol. 4, No. 15–16 (Summer–Autumn 1997), p. 59.

81. Quoted in Abu-Amr, "The Palestine Legislative Council," p. 94.

82. *PR,* January 17, 1997.

83. CPRS, *Evaluation of the Palestinian Legislative Council's First Year.*

84. Abu-Amr, "The Palestine Legislative Council," p. 95.

85. CPRS, *Evaluation of the Palestinian Legislative Council's First Year.*

86. Zuhira Kamal, "Relations between the Executive and Legislative Branches: Expectations and Realities" [Arabic], *al-Siyasa al-Filastiniyya,* Vol. 5, No. 17 (Winter 1998), p. 92. She was general manager in the Planning and International Cooperation Ministry.

87. *PR,* January 17, 1997.

3. Democracy, Stability, and Human Rights

1. Glenn E. Robinson, "The Growing Authoritarianism of the Arafat Regime," *Survival,* Vol. 39, No. 2 (Summer 1997), p. 42.

2. *PR,* January 10, 1997.

3. Denis J. Sullivan, *NGO's and Freedom of Association: Palestine and Egypt, a Comparative Analysis* (Jerusalem, 1995).

4. Abu-Amr, "Pluralism and the Palestinians," p. 88.

5. Shikaki, "The Peace Process, National Reconstruction, and the Transition to Democracy in Palestine," p. 15. Abu-Amr added: "The PNC, sometimes described as the Palestinian parliament in exile, allocated political representation through a quota system in which the constituent factions of the PLO were represented according to their size. Only trade unions, women's and students' groups, and professional associations elected their representatives to the PNC." Abu-Amr, "Pluralism and the Palestinians," p. 89.

6. Abu-Amr, "Pluralism and the Palestinians," p. 86. He adds: "Palestinian society's levels of economic, social, and human development (as indicated by per-capita income, rates of literacy, and so on) do not meet the minimal standards that much historical evidence has pointed to as necessary for the establishment of a democratic order. Palestinian political culture, moreover, is far from being 'civic.' Despite a significant and growing emphasis on the value of political participation, as well as the increasing exposure of elites and masses alike to universal ideals of human rights, self-government, and the rule of law, Palestinian political culture remains highly traditional, patriarchal, and parochial. Political loyalties to family, tribe, region, religion, and faction remain exceedingly strong." He cites elections for professional

groups in the West Bank and Gaza and the intifada's grassroots activities as forces promoting democratization.

7. Ibid., p. 88.

8. There were fifteen legally registered political parties in the West Bank and Gaza Strip. *PR,* November 28, 1997.

9. Dajani, "The Palestinian Authority and Citizenship."

10. Michael Foley, "Democracy Courtesy Thomas Cook," *Index on Censorship,* February 1996.

11. Al-Sharq al-Awsat, *Palestinian Elections* (Cairo, 1996). Some sources give slightly different numbers of candidates. *New York Times,* December 26, 1995.

12. For the PFLP and DFLP statement boycotting the elections, see *New York Times,* November 15, 1995. The Syrian-backed anti-Arafat Palestinian groups announced their boycott on al-Quds Palestinian radio, November 27, 1995 (*FBIS,* November 28, 1995). On the PA's negotiations with Hamas, see, for example, *Financial Times,* December 19, 1995. On the opposition and attitudes toward elections, see Ali Jarbawi et al., *Palestinian Opposition: Where To?* [Arabic], (Nablus, July 1994); Riyad al-Malki, *Palestinian Opposition: Analysis of Alternatives* [Arabic] (Nablus, August 1993); Jamal Hamami, *Islamists and the Next Phase* [Arabic] (Nablus, October 1994); and Ali Abu Hilal and Walid Salim, *National Opposition and National Elections* [Arabic] (Nablus, May 1995). For Hamas's announcement of its refusal to participate, see *al-Hayat,* October 13, 1995 (*FBIS,* October 16, 1995).

13. *Al-Nahar,* December 24, 1995 (*FBIS,* December 27, 1995); *Christian Science Monitor,* January 4 and 29, 1996; and Kol Israel, January 28, 1996 (*FBIS,* January 29, 1996). On these issues, see also Jamal Mansour and Jamal Salim, *Islamists and Elections* [Arabic] (Nablus, May 1995).

14. Khalil Shiqaqi, ed., *Palestinian Elections: Political Environment, Electoral Behavior, Results* [Arabic] (Nablus, 1997), p. 22.

15. CPRS poll, cited in *Ha'aretz,* January 19, 1996.

16. For information on public opinion, see Chapter 4.

17. Carl Lidbaum, head of the European Union observers' team, made several criticisms about Arafat's unilateral apportioning of seats, the short election campaign, and the Electoral Commission's independence. He suggested, however, that Gaza was given two seats more than it merited by population to encourage local Hamas leaders to run. *Ha'aretz,* January 2, 1996. Ramallah was favored because it was to be the PA's West Bank capital, and Hebron got additional seats to make up for the delay in Israeli withdrawal there. As a result, Ramallah, the larger city, was left somewhat underrepresented.

18. Peacewatch Elections Observer Team, Statements No. 1, January 4, 1996, and No. 3, January 11, 1996.

19. Foley, "Democracy Courtesy Thomas Cook."

20. LAW, Report of the Monitoring Unit on the Elections for the PLC, January 23, 1996; LAW press release, January 9, 1996.

21. Abu-Amr, "The Palestinian Legislative Council," p. 91.

22. For analyses of the election results, see Khalil Shiqaqi, *Transition to Liberal Democracy in Palestine: The Peace Process, the National Reconstruction, and Elections* (Nablus, 1996); Jamal Hilal, "The Elections of the Palestinian Legislative Council: A Preliminary Reading of the Results of the Election," and Islah Jad, "Palestinian Women's Movement and the Elections" [Arabic], *al-Siyasa al-Filastiniyya*, Vol. 3, No. 10 (Spring 1996); and Shiqaqi, *Palestinian Electionsl*; see pp. 12–15 for a discussion of the advantages provided by the elections.

23. *Al-Sharq al-Awsat*, April 16, 1994.

24. Abu-Amr, "Pluralism and the Palestinians," p. 88.

25. Al-Sharq al-Awsat, *Palestinian Elections*.

26. See Nazer Izat Said and Rima Hamami, *Research into the Political and Social Trends in Palestine* [Arabic] (Nablus, 1997). See esp. Jamal Hilal's argument in chap. 5 that creating democracy is essential for the struggle with Israel and the building of a proper society.

27. *PR*, November 14, 1997. Abu Amr, too, suggested that "sociopolitical pluralism might, if all goes well, pave the way for gradual democratization." Abu-Amr, "Pluralism and the Palestinians."

28. Abu-Amr, "Pluralism and the Palestinians."

29. *PR*, March 13, 1998.

30. LAW press release, May 22, 1996.

31. LAW, *Human Rights Annual Report, 1997*, March 29, 1998.

32. *PR*, August 19, 1996.

33. Raji Sourani [Surani], "Human Rights in the Palestinian Authority: A Status Report," Washington Institute for Near East Policy, Peacewatch No. 168, June 10, 1998. Government supporters on its board of directors fired Surani as head of the Gaza Center for Human Rights after he criticized Arafat for creating the State Security Courts. *Jerusalem Post*, April 5, 1995.

34. Abu-Amr, "The Palestinian Legislative Council," p. 93.

35. Ibid., p. 90.

36. *Ha'aretz*, August 26, 1994.

37. Ibid.

38. Ibid.

39. Ibid.

40. Rima Hamami, "Palestinian NGOs: Professionalization of Politics in the Absence of Opposition" [Arabic], *al-Siyasa al-Filastiniyya*, Vol. 3, No. 10 (Spring 1996). To cite one example of the overlap between political opponents and non-government groups, in 1998 Abd al-Shafi was elected as the head of the Palestinian Independent Commission for Citizens' Rights (PICCR). PICCR, press release, September 26, 1998.

41. *PR*, July 19, 1996.

42. On the women's movement, see also Majida Masri, "Palestinian Women's Movement" [Arabic], *al-Siyasa al-Filastiniyya*, Vol. 4, No. 14 (Spring 1997);

Ziyad Uthman, "The [Women's] Model Palestinian Parliament: Gender and Legislation between Renewal and Stereotyping" [Arabic], *al-Siyasa al-Filastiniyya*, Vol. 5, No. 19 (Summer 1998); Khalil Shikaki, "Palestinian Public Opinion, the Peace Process, and Political Violence," *Middle East Review of International Affairs Journal*, Vol. 2, No. 1 (March 1998); and *PR*, August 9, 1996. For examples of family honor killings, see *PR*, July 19 and August 23, 1996.

43. Palestinian Independent Commission for Citizens' Rights, *Third Annual Report, 1998*, <http://msanews.mynet.net/gateway/piccr/reports.html>. See also Bassam Id's report for the Palestinian Human Rights Monitoring Group, cited in *Washington Post*, May 27, 1997.

44. *PR*, August 16, 1996.

45. *PR*, August 30, 1996.

46. Palestine Independent Commission for Citizens' Rights, press release, April 1, 1996. For another such case, see *PR*, April 25, 1997, and *Jerusalem Post* May 17, 1997.

47. *PR*, October 4, 1996.

48. *Jerusalem Report*, December 25, 1997.

49. *New York Times*, July 18, 1994.

50. *PR*, June 28 and July 5, 1996; *New York Times*, March 5, 1998.

51. *Yediot Ahronot*, June 24, 1994; Prime Minister of Israel's Office, press release, October 24, 1996, and April 21, 1998. While the PA probably exceeded the agreed-upon force limits, Israeli official estimates also exaggerated the number of police by using PA projections as actual figures.

52. Peacewatch, "Number of Israelis Killed in Terror Attacks Has Doubled since Oslo Accord," March 11, 1996; *Ha'aretz*, September 13, 1998.

53. On the economic, educational, and medical impact of the closure and curfew imposed by Israel after the February–March 1996 attacks, see LAW press releases of March 11, 1996, "Statement on the Current Human Rights Situation in the West Bank," and March 13, 1996, "Update on the Human Rights Situation in the West Bank."

54. Kol Israel, February 6, 1995 (*FBIS*, February 7, 1995).

55. Voice of Palestine, January 24, 1994 (*FBIS*, January 24, 1994); *Jerusalem Post*, January 24, 1995.

56. *PR*, March 6, 1998.

57. *PR*, November 15, 1996. See also *al-Hayat al-Jadida*, February 6, 1995, and *PR*, November 7, 1997.

58. *Ha'aretz*, October 13, 1995; Peacewatch press release, March 7, 1996.

59. Text of the decree, Voice of Palestine, February 8, 1995 (*FBIS*, February 9, 1995). See also Kol Israel, February 8, 1995 (*FBIS*, February 9, 1995). For text of the order to establish the security courts, see *al-Siyasa al-Filastiniyya* [Arabic] (Winter 1995), Vol. 2, No. 5 pp. 183–186. For criticisms of the courts, see *Mideast Mirror*, February 13, April 5, and May 25, 1995. For PA defenses,

see *al-Sharq al-Awsat,* February 18, 1995; *al-Hayat al-Jadida,* February 20, 1995; and *al-Majalla,* November 11, 1995.
60. *Yediot Ahronot,* August 22, 1997.
61. LAW press release, January 19, 1998; *Jerusalem Post,* January 20, 1998.
62. Khaled Abu Toameh, "Letting His People Go," *Jerusalem Report,* March 5, 1998. For a detailed discussion of one such trial, see *Davar,* September 14, 1995 (*FBIS,* September 15, 1995). According to Peacewatch, between February and September 1995, forty-five defendants were tried by these courts: twenty-eight were from Hamas and Islamic Jihad, ten from the PFLP, and seven were arrested for criminal offenses such as selling guns or tainted food.
63. *Jerusalem Report,* March 5, 1998.
64. *Al-Quds,* February 15, 1998. It should be noted that this rationale is not so far-fetched. Hamas and Islamic Jihad members involved in attacks on Israeli civilians were proud of their deeds, which were fully justified by their ideology and organizations. Moreover, these groups maintained that those arrested should not be punished even if they were guilty. Hamas and Islamic Jihad did not use the argument that the PA had sentenced the wrong people in these cases.
65. *Jerusalem Post,* January 20, 1998.
66. Kol Israel, January 30, 1995 (*FBIS,* January 31, 1995).
67. Kol Israel, January 31, 1995 (*FBIS,* February 1, 1995); *New York Times,* August 30, 1995.
68. Kol Israel, April 24, 1995 (*FBIS,* April 25, 1995).
69. Voice of Palestine, August 26, 1995 (*FBIS,* August 28, 1995); *New York Times,* August 27, 1995.
70. *New York Times,* September 13, 1995.
71. *New York Times,* November 14, 1995.
72. *Ha'aretz,* July 3, 1998; Prime Minister Benjamin Netanyahu, *The Prime Minister's Report,* Vol. 2, No. 35, November 5, 1998. The July 1998 report gave twenty-one names, and there were both repetitions and differences between the two lists (*FBIS,* April 26, 1996).
73. *Ha'aretz,* July 3, 1998.
74. Abu Toameh, "Letting His People Go." Jabali denied the charge in an interview with *Ha'aretz,* November 6, 1998.
75. *PR,* March 30 and December 20, 1996; LAW press release, February 10, 1998.
76. *Yediot Ahronot,* March 6, 1998.
77. This group, and the political fallout from these arrests, is discussed in Chapter 6.
78. Kol Israel, August 30, 1995 (*FBIS,* August 30, 1995); *Mideast Mirror,* August 31, 1995; and Agence-France Presse, August 31, 1995 (*FBIS,* September 1, 1995).
79. *Ha'aretz,* April 7, 1998. The May 4, 1994 (Article 20, para. 4), and September 28, 1995 (Article 16, para. 2), Israeli-Palestinian agreements provided that

"Palestinians who have maintained contact with the Israeli authorities will not be subjected to acts of harassment, violence, retribution or prosecution."

80. *Washington Post,* January 19, 1995.
81. *PR,* August 16, 1996.
82. *New York Times,* December 6, 1996; *PR,* December 13, 1996.
83. *New York Times,* February 2 and 4, 1997; *Washington Post,* February 2 and 17; and *PR,* February 7 and 21, 1997.
84. Shiham Bahatia, "Arafat's Torturers Shock Palestinians," *Guardian Weekly,* September 24, 1995.
85. The treatment of journalists is discussed in Chapter 4.
86. *PR,* November 28, 1997. To avoid future problems, the president of al-Azhar University prohibited anyone working there from making any statement relating to the university without specific authorization. Cited in Palestinian Independent Commission for Citizens' Rights Newsletter, No. 1, January 1998.
87. *New York Times,* May 6, 22, 27, and 28, 1996. He was released shortly after his family wrote a note saying he had been misquoted. Later, though, Sarraj confirmed that the quotes were accurate.
88. *New York Times,* June 11, 1996.
89. *PR,* June 14 and 28, 1996; LAW press releases, June 12, 14, 16, 17, and 27, 1996; and *Washington Post,* June 27, 1996.
90. LAW press release, March 12, 1998. The Palestinian police also abducted and held for a day an Israeli citizen, Bassam Id of the B'tzelem human rights organization, on January 3, 1996, after he had helped write reports critical of the PA. *New York Times,* January 4 and 19, 1996. Preventive Security chief on the West Bank Jibril al-Rajjub responded to Id's human rights work by accusing him of being an "Israeli police agent." *Jerusalem Post,* August 27, 1995.
91. For an excellent detailed study of deaths in PA prisons, see Palestine Human Rights Monitor, No. 5, September–December 1997.
92. Voice of Palestine, January 18, 1995 (*FBIS,* January 19, 1995).
93. *Washington Post,* September 30, 1995.
94. *PR,* August 16, 1996; LAW press release, August 13, 1996.
95. *New York Times,* July 31, 1996; *Washington Post,* August 20, 1996.
96. *New York Times,* August 4 and 5, 1996; Human Rights Monitoring Group, "Deaths in Detention: A Pattern of Abuse, Illegality, and Impunity," cited in *Ha'aretz,* December 18, 1997; Voice of Palestine, August 1, 1996 (*FBIS,* August 2, 1996); *New York Times,* August 2, 1996; and *Washington Post,* August 20, 1996.
97. *Mideast Mirror,* August 15, 1996.
98. Amin Hindi, head of PA Intelligence Service, told reporters that the riot was organized by the Hamas political leadership in Jordan.
99. *PR,* August 9, 1996. Included on this committee were ministers Muhammad

Nashashibi, Frayh Abu Midayn, Jamal Tarifi, and Sa'ib Arikat, as well as PA Secretary General Tayyib Abd al-Rahim.
100. Ibid.
101. Ibid.
102. See Chapter 6 for a more detailed discussion of this debate.
103. *PR*, August 30, 1996; for a summary of the committee's recommendations, see *PR*, August 19, 1996.
104. This could also happen to citizens who complained. For example, a father who came to the police station to protest his son's beating reportedly was thrown into a cell for two hours. LAW press release, August 14, 1996; *PR*, August 23, 1996.
105. Bassam Id, "Death in a Palestinian Prison: A Report on Human Rights in Palestine," *PR*, December 19, 1997.
106. PICCR, *Third Annual Report; al-Hayat al-Jadida*, February 15, 1998.
107. For the legal system's background, see Raja Shehadeh, *The Declaration of Principles and the Legal System in the West Bank* (Jerusalem, 1994).
108. *PR*, April 3, 1998; LAW press release, March 26, 1998.
109. *PR*, July 5, 1996; LAW press releases, June 27, August 18 and 20, 1996.
110. *PR*, November 22, 1996.
111. Voice of Palestine, May 26, 1994 (*FBIS*, May 27, 1994).
112. *PR*, January 19, 1998.
113. It was rumored that Abu Qidra was dismissed for taking money from families in exchange for securing the release of relatives.
114. *Yediot Ahronot*, August 22, 1997.
115. *PR*, July 5, 1996; PICCR, *Third Annual Report.*
116. JMCC polls cited in *PR*, November 8, 1996, and January 3, 1997; CPRS poll reported in Reuters, August 5, 1998.
117. He was arrested the next day. *Ha'aretz*, June 1, 1997.
118. Nidal Ismail [Isma'il], "Is Corruption the Problem?" *PR*, November 28, 1997.
119. Ibid.
120. Ibid., Abu-Amr, "The Palestinian Legislative Council," p. 92; *Guardian*, July 14, 1997.
121. Ibid. See Chapter 2 for a discussion of the PLC's role in investigating corruption.
122. Cited in *Jerusalem Post*, September 27, 1998.
123. Off-the-record interviews.
124. *Al-Bilad*, reprinted in *PR*, February 7, 1997.
125. *Jerusalem Report*, December 25, 1997.
126. *PR*, September 20, 1996.
127. *PR*, November 7, 1997; *Jerusalem Report*, December 25, 1997. Some Palestinians, including senior officials, saw such actions as a legitimate weapon against the Israeli economy. As one put it, "The Jews stole all of our land, so why can't we steal back some of their property?"

128. During the revolutionary PLO days, virtually the entire organizational budget had been handled this way.
129. *Al-Sharq al-Awsat,* February 1, 1995; *Jerusalem Times,* November 24, 1995; and *Sunday Times,* November 29, 1998.
130. For an analysis of the police and security services, see Chapter 6.
131. Rami Khouri [Khuri], "A View from the Arab World," June 16, 1998, <http://msanews.mynet.net/Scholars/Khouri/>.

4. The Polity and the People

1. As in most Arab countries, Palestinian women took their husband's citizenship. Granting dual citizenship could have threatened the security of Palestinians living in Jordan and Lebanon, while Israel would have perceived it as a violation of the PA's undertaking to respect its sovereignty. See Chapters 7 and 8.
2. Dajani, "The Palestinian Authority and Citizenship."
3. Voice of Palestine, February 6, 1995 (*FBIS,* February 7, 1995).
4. Dajani, "The Palestinian Authority and Citizenship"; *PR,* November 15, 1996.
5. *PR,* February 18, 1998. For very detailed analyses of PA census figures, see <http:www.pcbs.org>.
6. *PR,* October 4, 1996.
7. *PR,* August 30, 1996. On economic issues, see also Palestinian Economic Research Institute, *Poverty in the West Bank and Gaza Strip* (Jerusalem, November, 1995); and Jamal Hilal, "Features of Poverty in Palestine" [Arabic], *al-Siyasa al-Filastiniyya,* Vol. 3, No. 12, (Fall 1996).
8. *Al-Wasat,* January 9-15, 1995 (*FBIS,* January 13, 1995).
9. *The Star* (Amman), January 26-February 1, 1995 (*FBIS,* January 26, 1995).
10. For PA complaints on this point, see, for example, *PR,* February 7, 1997.
11. Quoted in *PR,* October 18, 1996.
12. *PR,* January 3, 1997. See also *New York Times,* April 30, 1994; and Hisham Awartani et al., *Evaluation of Paris Agreement: Economic Relations between Israel and the PLO* [Arabic with English text of the Agreement] (Nablus, November 1994).
13. Dajani, "The Palestinian Authority and Citizenship"; *al-Quds,* November 15, 1996.
14. Ibid.; *PR,* September 25, 1998.
15. *PR,* November 8, 1996.
16. *PR,* August 23, 1996.
17. *PR,* July 5, 1996, and November 28, 1997.
18. Analysis of United Nations Special Coordinator's Office (UNSCO), *The West Bank and Gaza Strip Private Economy: Conditions and Prospects* (cited in *PR,* February 19, 1998).

19. Sourani [Surani], "Human Rights in the Palestinian Authority."
20. JMCC poll, December 13–14, 1996 (*PR*, January 3, 1997).
21. April 1997 poll, *PR*, December 15, 1997.
22. United Nations Special Coordinator in the Occupied Territories (UNSCO) report on economic and social conditions in the West Bank and Gaza, October 25, 1998, <http://www.arts.mcgill.ca/mepp/unsco/unfront.html>.
23. PA news agency WAFA (cited in *PR*, August 28, 1998); Palestinian Central Bureau of Statistics report (cited in *PR*, September 25, 1998).
24. *Al-Quds*, February 22, 1998.
25. *PR*, September 13, 1996, November 7 and 28, and December 5 and 15, 1997. *Al-Ayyam*, February 12, 1998. For a discussion of student politics, see Chapter 6.
26. *PR*, July 5, 1996.
27. *PR*, November 7, 1997.
28. But for issues involving academic freedom, see Chapter 3.
29. The PBC's Gaza office, with 120 workers, broadcast one channel of imported Arab programs and one featuring local entertainment, news, and shows. The Ramallah office had 180 workers and broadcast six hours a day. *Ha'aretz*, February 2, 1996.
30. For a summary of the law, see *Ha'aretz*, July 13, 1995 (*FBIS*, July 21, 1995). See also *Ha'aretz*, November 5, 1995.
31. Ruba Hussari, "Arafat's Law," *Index on Censorship*, March 21, 1996.
32. Foley, "Democracy Courtesy Thomas Cook."
33. "These new rulers have learned from the dictators of the Arab world how to govern. Their socialization has occurred in restrictive, military dictatorships, some of which have the facade of democracy, one or two of which actually have moved closer to such a liberal system." Sullivan, *NGO's and Freedom of Association*, p. 49.
34. *The Independent*, September 25, 1998.
35. *Mideast Mirror*, February 13, 1995; Israel Television, May 3, 1995 (*FBIS*, May 5, 1995).
36. December 1996 JMCC poll, *PR*, January 3, 1997.
37. It received 52.6 percent approval in a December 1996 JMCC poll, over six times more than its leading rival. *PR*, January 3, 1997
38. Associated Press, November 28, 1994.
39. *PR*, November 1, 1996.
40. *Washington Post*, November 30, 1994; *New York Times*, December 1, 1994. Kol Israel, August 19, 1995 (*FBIS*, August 22); Channel Two Television (Jerusalem), August 22, 1995 (*FBIS*, August 23, 1995); and *Mideast Monitor*, August 21, 1995. For *al-Quds* editorial protesting the closing, see *al-Quds*, August 20, 1995 (*FBIS*, August 25, 1995).
41. *New York Times*, December 28, 1995, and January 1, 1996; *Washington Post*, January 1, 1996.

42. Interview with Kol Israel, December 31, 1995 (*FBIS,* January 2, 1996).

43. Associated Press, November 28, 1994.

44. Roni Ben Efrat, "The Telltale Silence of the Post-Oslo Palestinian Press," paper delivered at the conference "A Twenty-first–Century Dialogue: Media's Dark Age?" Athens, May 24–28, 1998.

45. Ibid., *Washington Post,* July 29, 1994; *New York Times,* July 30 and September 6, 1994.

46. Agence-France Presse, August 5, 1995 (*FBIS,* August 7, 1995); *al-Nahar,* October 5, 1995 (*FBIS,* October 6, 1995).

47. Other small publications that were suspended included the PFLP's *Kan'an* (August 1994), *al-Bayan* (August 1994), and *al-Tali'ah* (*FBIS,* July 28, August 2 and 8, September 9, 1994). *Al-Rasid* was closed for an article allegedly damaging PA-Jordan relations (*FBIS,* February 27, 1995).

48. Efrat, "The Telltale Silence."

49. *PR,* October 25, 1996; *Washington Post,* May 27, 1997.

50. *PR,* October 25, 1996. On the media and the Iraq issue, see Chapter 7.

51. *Ma'ariv,* June 27, 1997.

52. See Chapter 8.

53. See Chapters 3 and 8 for the details of this affair.

54. *Al-Hayat al-Jadida,* September 1, 1997.

55. *Al-Hayat Al-Jadida,* August 6, 1997.

56. *Al-Hayat al-Jadida,* November 5, 1997.

57. *Al-Hayat al-Jadida,* October 26, 1997.

58. *PR,* July 5, 1996; Radio Monte Carlo, November 3, 1995 (*FBIS,* November 3, 1995); and *Ha'aretz,* November 5, 1995 (*FBIS,* November 7, 1995).

59. *PR,* November 14, 1997.

60. *PR,* January 3, 1997, from a JMCC poll conducted December 13–14, 1996. See also *PR,* August 30, 1996.

61. *PR,* January 3, 1997, from a JMCC poll conducted December 13–14, 1996. See also *PR,* August 30, 1996.

62. *PR,* January 17, 1997.

63. *Ha'aretz,* January 12 and 26, and February 12, 1997; *Jerusalem Post,* January 31, 1995.

64. *PR,* March 27, 1998.

65. Ibid.

66. Ibid.

67. *Al-Nahar,* January 18, 1996 (*FBIS,* January 19, 1996).

68. *Ha'aretz,* January 12 and 26, and February 12, 1997.

69. *PR,* August 23, 1996; *Ha'aretz,* October 27, 1995.

70. *PR* July 5, 1996. The ministers were Mahir al-Masri (Economics and Trade) of Nablus and Azzam al-Ahmad (Public Works), who was from Jenin.

71. See, for example, the story of the Balata camp near Nablus in *PR,* November 7, 1997.

NOTES TO PAGES 83–87

72. *PR*, November 7, 1997.
73. *PR*, September 20, 1996, and November 7, 1997. Ironically, this taboo did not apply to returning outsiders like Abd al-Rahman himself.
74. See, for example, *PR*, January 16, 1998.
75. *PR*, September 13, 1996.
76. Popular support for the opposition is discussed in more detail in Chapter 6.
77. See the discussion later in this chapter for evidence regarding this analysis. For background on this issue, see Faysal Awartani, "Determinants of Palestinian Public Opinion Regarding the Performance of the PNA and the Opposition" [Arabic], *al-Siyasa al-Filastiniyya*, Vol. 4, No. 13 (Winter 1997); JMCC and Arab Thought Forum, *Palestinian Public Opinion since the Peace Process* [Arabic] (Jerusalem, 1998); and Shikaki, "Palestinian Public Opinion."
78. Shikaki, "The Peace Process, National Reconstruction"; *PR*, November 8, 1996; JMCC poll, December 13–14, 1996, *PR*, January 3 and 17, 1997; CPRS poll reported in Reuters, August 5, 1998; and *PR*, January 16, 1998. Results of polls conducted by the JMCC and the Tami Steinmetz Center for Peace Research during late November and early December 1997.
79. Shikaki, "The Peace Process, National Reconstruction."
80. Ibid.
81. *PR*, August 30 and November 8, 1996, and December 15, 1997.
82. Shikaki, "The Peace Process, National Reconstruction."
83. Palestinian Center for Public Opinion poll, September 28–29, 1996, *PR*, October 4, 1996.
84. *PR*, January 17, 1997 and April 9, 1999, CPRS poll reported in Reuters, August 5, 1998.
85. *PR*, August 30, 1996. See also JMCC poll, December 13–14, 1996, *PR*, January 3, 1997.
86. *PR*, January 16, 1998. Results of polls conducted by the JMCC and the Tami Steinmetz Center for Peace Research during late November and early December 1997.
87. Shikaki, "The Peace Process, National Reconstruction": *PR*, November 8, 1996; and CPRS poll reported in Reuters, August 5, 1998. Of course, some of those who doubted the peace process's success were oppositionists who preferred it to fail.
88. *PR*, January 16, 1998. Results of polls conducted by the JMCC and the Tami Steinmetz Center for Peace Research during late November and early December 1997. See also *PR*, August 30, 1996.
89. On Palestinian public opinion, see Leila Darbub, "Palestinian Public Opinion Polls on the Peace Process," *Palestine-Israel Journal*, No. 5 (1995), pp. 60–63; Leila Darbub, "Palestinian Public Opinion and the Peace Process," *Palestine-Israel Journal*, Vol. 3, No. 3–4 (1996), pp. 109–117; Manuel S. Hassassian, "State, Territory, and Boundaries: Attitudes and Positions in the

Palestine National Movement," Israeli-Palestinian Peace Research Project, Working Paper series, Vol. 2, No. 12 (Jerusalem, 1991); Ali Jarbawi, "The Position of Palestine Islamists on the Palestine-Israel Accord," *The Muslim World*, Vol. 84, No. 1-2 (1994), pp. 127-154; Riad al-Malki, "The Palestinian Opposition and Final-Status Negotiations," *Palestine-Israel Journal*, Vol. 3, No. 3-4 (1996), pp. 95-99; Fouad Moughrabi and Elia Zurayiq, "Palestinians on the Peace Process," *Journal of Palestine Studies*, Vol. 21, No. 1 (1991), pp. 36-53; CPRS, "PA and PLC Performance, Democracy, Armed Attacks, Local Councils, and a Permanent Status Plan: Opinion Poll No. 27" (Nablus, April 10-12, 1997); Lauren G. Ross, "Palestinians: Yes to Negotiations, Yes to Violence," *Middle East Quarterly*, Vol. 2, No. 2 (1995), pp. 15-24. Data from public opinion polls was also frequently published in *Palestine Report*, the weekly publication of the JMCC. Articles dealing with both groups include Peacewatch, "The Standing of Israel and the Palestinians in Their Commitments in the Matter of Jerusalem" [Hebrew], *Yediot Ahronot*, August 3, 1994; and Majid Al-Hajj, "The Day after the Palestinian State: Arab and Jewish Attitudes in Israel," *Middle East Focus*, Vol. 13, No. 4 (1991), pp. 23-26. My thanks to Elisheva Brown for compiling this list.

5. The New Palestinian Political Elite

1. Shikaki, "The Peace Process, National Reconstruction," p. 15. One Palestinian political figure estimated that 60-70 percent of returning Outsiders were Fatah members. Jamila Saydam, interview in *al-Siyasa al-Filastiniyya*, Vol. 5, No. 19 (Summer 1998), p. 151.
2. While there were dissenters, too, in Gaza, they resigned and Arafat was able to impose his own nominees fairly easily. See discussion later in this chapter.
3. Kol Israel, December 27, 1993 (*FBIS*, December 27, 1993); *al-Nahar*, December 28, 1993 (*FBIS*, December 29, 1993). See interview with Agha in *al-Siyasa al-Filastiniyya*, Vol. 5, No. 19 (Summer 1998).
4. At least three leading Fatah activists were killed in late 1993 and another was shot to death in April 1996 in cases never solved but apparently involving internal disputes. *New York Times*, September 22, 1993; *Yediot Ahronot*, November 19, 1993 (*FBIS*, November 22, 1993); and JMCC Press Service, April 1, 1996 (*FBIS*, April 2, 1996).
5. *Al-Wasat*, January 9-15, 1995 (*FBIS*, January 13, 1995).
6. Though Arafat himself came from a Gaza family. He was born in Cairo.
7. Milhim headed the PLO's Occupied Homeland Affairs Department from Amman until he returned to the West Bank to become an adviser to Arafat.
8. They were Abdallah Franji, PLO envoy in West Germany, and Nabil Sha'th, a former professor who owned a successful business consulting firm.
9. Jawad al-Ghusayn, head of the Palestine National Fund, and Faruq al-

Qaddumi, head of the PLO political department, retained their old posts but played no role in the PA as a government.

10. Nabil Sha'th was added to the Central Committee later.

11. See *New York Times* and *Washington Post,* September 11, 1993, for the resignations of the DFLP and PFLP delegates. Palestine Liberation Front leader Muhammad Abu al-Abbas returned to the West Bank and at the 1996 PNC meeting apologized for the 1985 *Achille Lauro* hijacking and the killing of Leon Klinghoffer. Voice of Palestine, April 22, 1996 (*FBIS,* April 22, 1996); *New York Times* and *Washington Post,* April 23, 1996; and *PR,* April 26, 1996.

12. The nine who had been PLO leaders were Nabil Amr, Hasan Asfur, Hakam Bal'awi, Abbas Zaki, Rafiq al-Natsha, Sha'th, Shaqura, al-Wazir, and Khuri. Of these, Amr, Bal'awi, Natsha, and Abd al-Rahim had only held PLO diplomatic posts, while Asfur, Khuri, and Sha'th were technocrats.

13. See Chapter 1.

14. Interview, *Journal of Palestine Studies,* Vol. 11, No. 2 (Winter 1982), p. 10.

15. *Al-Qabas,* May 10, 1990 (cited in *Mideast Mirror,* May 10, 1990, pp. 10-13).

16. Abu-Amr, "Pluralism and the Palestinians," p. 91.

17. Shikaki, "The Future of Democracy in Palestine," p. 59, points out that the PLO had signed the original agreement with Israel, decided to create the PA, and even would be able to veto PA decisions. Therefore, "the PA doesn't inherit the PLO's authority but depended on its endorsement."

18. JMCC poll, December 13-14, 1996, *PR,* January 3, 1997.

19. *Al-Wasat,* January 9-15, 1995 (*FBIS,* January 13, 1995). "Most Palestinians," wrote Khalil Shiqaqi in 1997, "treat the PLO institutions as superior to the PA because they represent all the Palestinians and not just those in the territories." Shiqaqi, "The Future of Democracy in Palestine." But this balance could be expected to shift over time—at least among Palestinians in Gaza and the West Bank—in the PA's favor. For a discussion of PLO-PA relations, see Jamal Hilal, "The PLO and the PA: The Upside-Down Equation," Nufil Mamdu, "The Growth and Development of the Relations between the PLO and the PA," and Taysir Kuba'a, "The Relations between the PLO and PA," all in *al-Siyasa al Filastiniyya,* [Arabic], Vol. 4, No. 15-16 (Summer-Autumn 1997).

20. Middle East News Agency, February 22, 1995, *Financial Times,* August 17, 1995.

21. See Hani al-Hasan, *The Relationship between the PLO and PNA Institutions* [Arabic] (Nablus, 1996).

22. Samih Habib, "The PA and PLO: National and Administrative Relationships" [Arabic], *al-Siyasa al-Filastiniyya,* Vol. 4, No. 15-16 (Summer-Autumn 1997), pp. 54-55.

23. Ibid. This issue is discussed more fully in Chapter 7. Habib recommended developing the branches of Palestinian mass organizations outside the PA

territories, establishing a newspaper aimed at the diaspora, and strengthening some PLO agencies outside the homeland. See also *al-Sharq al-Awsat,* January 8 and 17, 1995.

24. Hilal, "The PLO and the PA." A similar analysis can be found in Mamdu, "Growth and Development of the Relations between the PLO and the PA." Mamdu was a member of the PLO Central Council.

25. Off-the-record interviews.

26. *Al-Hayat,* August 20, 1995 (*FBIS,* August 25, 1995).

27. See Chapter 8.

28. *Al-Hayat,* August 20, 1995 (*FBIS,* August 25, 1995). See also Danny Rubinstein, "Bio Sketch: Faruq Qaddumi, the PLO's #2," *Middle East Quarterly* (March 1996), pp. 29–32.

29. *Al-Hayat,* August 20, 1995 (*FBIS,* August 25, 1995).

30. *Al-Hayat,* August 15, 16, 17, and 27, 1995; *al-Sharq al-Awsat,* September 18, 1995.

31. Middle East News Agency, January 23, 1995; Radio Monte Carlo, July 10, 1995 (*FBIS,* July 11, 1995).

32. *Mideast Mirror,* August 18 and 22, 1995; *al-Hayat,* August 18, 20, 21, and 29, 1995 (*FBIS,* August 25, 1995).

33. Syrian Arab News Agency, October 4, 1995 (*FBIS,* October 5, 1995). Of these eleven men, Arafat won back only Hurani and, temporarily, Ghawsha. For Darwish's resignation from the Executive Committee, see Laqueur and Rubin, *The Israel-Arab Reader,* pp. 597–599.

34. Reuters, August 8, 1998. Also denied entry were DFLP leader Nayif Hawatma and Fatah Central Committee member Muhammad Ghana'im (Abu Mahir). Since the request was made by the PA, Qaddumi never went on record as asking for admission. See also Qaddumi's remarks cited in *Ha'aretz,* June 29, 1998. During earlier years, Israel had forbidden from returning only those directly involved in killing Israelis.

35. For a discussion of the role and composition of the PNC, see Rubin, *Revolution Until Victory?* chap. 8.

36. *New York Times,* April 16, 1996; *al-Dustur,* April 12, 1996 (*FBIS,* April 16, 1996). On the PLO Executive Committee's position, see *Washington Post,* February 7, 1996.

37. *Mideast Mirror,* March 4, 1996; Voice of Palestine, March 4, 1996 (*FBIS,* March 4, 1996); and *Washington Post,* March 5, 1996.

38. *New York Times,* April 23 and 25, 1996; *Mideast Mirror,* April 24, 25, and 26, 1996; Voice of Palestine, April 24, 1996 (*FBIS,* April 25, 1996); and *Washington Times,* April 25 and May 1, 1996. A baseless attempt was later made by Israeli rightists to deny that the Charter had been revoked. The claim rested on statements by a few hard-line Palestinians who had always opposed any change and insisted that nothing had been altered. For a discussion of issues around the Charter, see Rubin, *The Palestinian Charter.* See also

Filastin al-Muslima, May 5, 1996; *al-Hadath,* March 25, 1996 (*FBIS,* March 26, 1996); and *Ha'aretz,* April 11, 1996.

39. *PR,* February 6, 1998. In his letter to U.S. Secretary of State Madeleine Albright, he specified articles fully nullified as 6–10, 15, 19–23, and 30. The articles nullified in part were 1–5, 11–14, 16–18, 25–27, and 29. For the full text, see Laqueur and Rubin, *The Israel-Arab Reader,* pp. 218–223.

40. Voice of Palestine, April 25 and 26, 1996 (*FBIS,* April 26 and 29, 1996); *Mideast Mirror,* April 26, 1996.

41. See Appendix 4.

42. See Appendix 4.

43. Voice of Palestine, May 22, 1996 (*FBIS,* May 22, 1996). But the PFLP and DFLP did participate.

44. Although Arafat generally controlled the Central Committee, he had not always been able to prevent the election of a few people he did not want, such as Wazir, nor was he always able to name everyone he wanted to add, such as Abd al-Rahman. Off-the-record interviews.

45. With Qaddumi and Arafat himself.

46. *Financial Times,* December 6, 1993.

47. *Al-Hayat,* September 12, 1995 (*FBIS,* September 13, 1995).

48. *PR,* November 7, 1997.

49. Voice of Palestine, November 21, 1995 (*FBIS,* November 21, 1995); *al-Hayat,* November 22, 1995 (*FBIS,* November 30, 1995); *PR,* December 1, 1995; *al-Nahar,* December 24, 1995 (*FBIS,* December 27, 1995); *New York Times,* January 6, 1996; and *Washington Post,* January 16, 1996.

50. For Fatah's debates and politics, see *al-Sharq al-Awsat,* January 12, 1998.

51. *Ha'aretz,* December 9, 1995.

52. *Al-Hayat al-Jadida,* March 13, 1998. Sakr Habash discusses this issue at length in an interview in *al-Siyasa al-Filastiniyya,* Vol. 5, No. 19 (Summer 1998), pp. 164–165. He insists that Fatah should remain a revolutionary national movement until a state is established.

53. *PR,* July 2, 1996.

54. Voice of Palestine, June 11, 1996 (*FBIS,* June 11, 1996).

55. See, for example, *al-Hayat al-Jadida,* March 24, 1997.

56. *Al-Sharq al-Awsat,* January 17, 1995 (*FBIS,* January 19, 1995).

57. On Zaki's return, see Voice of Palestine, September 7, 1995 (*FBIS,* September 8, 1995). For his criticisms of Arafat and Khuri, see *Financial Times,* April 26, 1994. Like Qaddumi, Zaki was welcome in Damascus and among the anti-Arafat Palestinian groups there. See *al-Bilad,* July 12, 1995 (*FBIS,* July 12, 1995). On opponents of Oslo in Fatah, see also *Jerusalem Times,* February 3 and September 15, 1995; *al-Sharq al-Awsat,* March 5, July 23, and October 22, 1995; *Mideast Mirror,* March 23, 1995; and *al-Hayat,* March 23 and November 18, 1995.

58. See the interview with Natsha in *al-Siyasa al-Filastiniyya,* Vol. 5, No. 19 (Sum-

mer 1998), p. 153, in which he says that Fatah is not being run democratically and that the PLC should make more concessions to the opposition. That issue also contains an interview in which Habash expresses his perspective. For Hasan's criticism of Arafat and Khuri, see *Financial Times*, April 26, 1994, and also his interview in *Mideast Mirror*, October 9, 1993, in Laqueur and Rubin, *The Israel-Arab Reader*, pp. 622–623.

59. Interview in *al-Sharq al-Awsat*, July 23, 1995 (*FBIS*, July 28, 1995).

60. Sakher [Sakr] Abu Nizar, "The Role of Fatah Movement in Shaping the Palestinian Future," April 1994, from the Fatah homepage, <http://www.fateh.org>.

61. *Al-Sharq al-Awsat*, February 5, 1995.

62. Ibid. On Outsider-Insider tensions with Fatah, see also *Ha'aretz*, January 6 and August 3, 1995, and *al-Sharq al-Awsat*, October 19, 1995.

63. Kol Israel, August 24, 1995 (*FBIS*, August 24, 1995).

64. *New York Times*, December 18 and 21, 1995; *Jerusalem Post*, September 12, 1995; and *PR*, August 12, 1995.

65. *PR*, August 16, 1996.

66. Shiqaqi, *Palestinian Elections*, p. 20.

67. Yasir Abd Rabbu, *Analytical Review of the Reality and Nature of the Palestinian National Authority*, [Arabic] (Nablus, 1995), p. 15.

68. *PR*, November 7, 1997.

69. See Chapter 2.

70. See, for example, *Al-Manar*, January 2, 1995, and *Jerusalem Post*, December 9, 1997.

71. *PR*, December 20, 1996.

72. *Al-Ayyam*, October 30, 1998; *Ha'aretz*, December 22, 1998.

73. *Ha'aretz*, December 22, 1998; *al-Quds*, December 11, 1998.

74. *Al-Hayat al-Jadida*, December 7, 1997.

75. *Davar*, January 26, 1996.

76. Fadal Sliman, quoted in Hasan, *The Relationship between the PLO and PNA Institutions*.

77. *Davar*, January 26, 1996.

78. *PR*, November 7, 1997.

79. At the time, the PLO was determined not to allow any competing leadership to emerge in the territories.

80. Interview with Radio Monte Carlo, December 7, 1989 (*FBIS*, December 8, 1989).

81. *PR*, February 27, 1998.

82. Ibid.

83. Ibid.

84. Ibid.

85. Ibid.; off-the-record interviews; and *PR*, August 9, 1996.

86. *PR*, August 9, 1996.

87. On the West Bank elite's evolution, see Emile Sahliyeh, *In Search of Leadership: West Bank Politics since 1967* (Washington, D.C., 1988), and Moshe Maoz, *Palestinian Leadership on the West Bank: The Changing Role of the Mayors under Jordan and Israel* (London, 1984).

88. *Globes*, December 13, 1995; Kol Israel, July 26, 1994 (*FBIS*, July 27, 1994). When the PA took over West Bank towns in late 1996, it removed the incumbent mayors and replaced them with its own appointees.

89. *PR*, August 9, 1996.

90. In practice, these forces constitute the PA's military establishment. See Gal Luft, *The Palestinian Security Services: Between Police and Army* (Washington, D.C., 1998).

91. Palestinian Center for Public Opinion poll, September 28–29, 1996, in *PR*, October 4, 1996.

92. Sara Roy, "Report from Gaza: Alienation or Accommodation," *Journal of Palestine Studies*, Vol. 24, No. 4 (Summer 1995), pp. 73–82; Graham Usher, "The Politics of Internal Security: The PA's New Intelligence Services," *Journal of Palestine Studies*, Vol. 25, No. 2 (Winter 1996), pp. 21–34.

93. *Ha'aretz*, April 1, 1998.

94. Bahatia, "Arafat's Torturer's Shock Palestinians."

95. Abu-Amr, "The Palestinian Legislative Council," p. 92. See also *al-Dakhiliya*, October 1997.

96. One way to put it, in American terms, is that the civil police corresponded to a regular police department, Preventive Security to the Federal Bureau of Investigation, Force-17 to the Secret Service, military intelligence to army intelligence, and the naval police to the Coast Guard. This is not to say that these units were as democratic or effective as such counterparts, but merely that the existence of different forces in itself was not so absurd.

97. *Jerusalem Post*, June 7 and 10, 1994.

98. Ibid.

99. Voice of Palestine, July 17, 1995 (*FBIS*, July 21, 1995).

100. Voice of Palestine, February 28, 1996 (*FBIS*, February 29, 1996).

101. Reuters, August 30, 1998.

102. For an interesting discussion of the background and relations among Palestinian officers, see *Ma'ariv*, October 13, 1995 (*FBIS*, October 17, 1995). See also Jabali's interview in *Ha'aretz*, November 8, 1998.

103. On their visit to Russia, see *Yediot Ahronot*, April 9, 1998. On Palestinian police training in Germany, see *Ha'aretz*, April 4, 1998.

104. Channel Two television documentary, June 7, 1997, translated in *Mideast Dispatch*.

105. *Jerusalem Post*, March 17, 1998.

106. Kol Israel, October 19, 1995 (*FBIS*, October 20, 1995).

107. *Ma'ariv*, March 1, 1998, and *Yediot Ahronot*, March 25, 1998.

108. *Mideast Dispatch*, July 28, 1998.

109. *PR,* December 9, 1997, and June 30, 1998; *Globes,* December 9, 1997; and *Ha'aretz,* December 14, 1997.
110. *Ha'aretz,* December 14, 1997.

6. The Palestinian Opposition

1. On this issue, see Basma Qadamani-Darwish, "The Palestinian Authority and the Opposition" [Arabic], *al-Siyasa al-Filastiniyya,* Vol. 2., No. 6 (Spring 1995); Ribhi Qatamish, "The Crisis of the Palestinian Opposition," a panel discussion, "The Palestinian Opposition: Where To?" [Arabic], *al-Siyasa al-Filastiniyya,* Vol. 5, No. 19 (Summer 1998); and Muhammad Jadallah, *Opposition and the Palestinian National Authority* [Arabic] (Nablus, 1994).
2. *PR,* January 31, 1997.
3. See CPRS, "Voting Patterns to Student Unions in al-Najah and Bir Zayt Universities" [Arabic], *al-Siyasa al-Filastiniyya,* Vol. 2, No. 7–8 (Summer–Fall 1995); Majdi Malki, "Characteristics of the Palestinian Student Movement: Bir Zayt University Elections" [Arabic], *al-Siyasa al-Filastiniyya,* Vol. 3, No. 11 (Summer 1996); Umar Abd al-Raziq, "Analysis of the Results of Al-Najah University's Student Elections" [Arabic], *al-Siyasa al-Filastiniyya,* Vol. 4, No. 13 (Winter 1997); and Majdi Malki, "Student Elections at Bir Zayt University" [Arabic], *al-Siyasa al-Filastiniyya,* Vol. 4, No. 14 (Spring 1997).
4. See CPRS, "Special Poll: Voting Behavior of al-Najah University Students: Election Day Poll," Nablus, July 19, 1996.
5. In the March 1996 elections, a Hamas–Islamic Jihad slate won twenty-three seats and Fatah seventeen, with eleven going to other parties. The previous year Fatah won twenty-one and Hamas eighteen. *Mideast Mirror,* May 10, 1996.
6. *PR,* March 27, 1998.
7. *PR,* April 18, 1997.
8. On Bir Zayt election results, see <http://www.birzeit.edu/scouncil/>; *PR,* June 14 and December 20, 1996; and *Jerusalem Post,* July 12, 1995. Hamas supporters tended to dominate the voting at the College of Science and Technology at Jerusalem University, the Girls' College of Literature in Ramallah, and the College of Medical Professions. *Filastin al-Muslima,* July 1995 (*FBIS,* July 28, 1995). For the comparable 1999 student election results, see *PR,* April 9, 1999.
9. *PR,* June 14, 1996, and November 14, 1997; al-Sharq al-Awsat, *The Palestinian Elections.* The estimate comes from averaging a large number of CPRS public opinion polls from 1996 to 1998. For another attempt to coordinate violent opposition groups, see *New York Times,* February 28, 1997. On the efforts to build a united front, see *Filastin al-Muslima,* April 1995; *al-Hayat,* May 22 and 24, 1995; and *Jerusalem Times,* May 26, 1995. For Abd al-Shafi and other Insiders' criticism of Arafat's leadership and demands for more

consultation, see Laqueur and Rubin, "West Bank-Gaza Palestinian Leaders: Memorandum to Chairman Yasir Arafat, November 1993," in *The Israel-Arab Reader,* pp. 624–627.

10. See, for example, Azzam S. Tamimi, "The Legitimacy of Palestinian Resistance: An Islamist Perspective," paper presented to the Seventh Annual Conference of the Center for Policy Analysis on Palestine, Washington, D.C., September 11, 1998.

11. *Al-Watan,* October 19, 1995 (*FBIS,* October 24, 1995).

12. Reuters, May 27, 1998.

13. *PR,* August 23, 1996.

14. *PR,* December 20, 1996.

15. *PR,* June 28, 1996.

16. *Al-Istiqlal,* May 19, 1995 (*FBIS,* July 19, 1995).

17. *Ha'aretz,* December 15, 1995.

18. Radio Monte Carlo, April 13, 1995 (*FBIS,* April 18, 1995).

19. Interview with Radio Monte Carlo, April 14, 1995 (*FBIS,* April 18, 1995).

20. *Al-Istiqlal,* May 19, 1995 (*FBIS,* July 21, 1995).

21. *Al-Hayat al-Jadida,* January 2, 1995.

22. Ibid. See also Muhammad Abd al-Hamid, "Terrorism: Violence, and 'Suicide Operations' " [Arabic], *al-Siyasa al-Filastiniyya,* Vol. 5, No. 18 (Spring 1998).

23. *Kul al-Arab,* January 16, 1998; *Ha'aretz,* January 21, 1998. Rantisi gave the names of the other founders as Ahmad Yasin, Abd al-Fattah Dukhan, Mohammed Shama, Ibrahim al-Yazur, Isa al-Najjar, and Salah Shahada.

24. *Kul al-Arab,* January 16, 1998. Or consider a statement by the moderate Abu Amr which could be construed in similar terms: "Negotiation does not mean neglecting other goals. I recommend that the Palestinian leadership provide the opposition all means to deal with other goals, like the Vietnamese, Algerians, and people of South Yemen who went to negotiation and at the same time achieved other goals." Al-Malki, *Palestinian Opposition,* p. 24.

25. Al-Malki, *Palestinian Opposition,* p. 24.

26. Voice of Palestine, February 28, 1996 (*FBIS,* February 29, 1996); *Washington Post,* February 29, 1996; and Kol Israel, February 29, 1996 (*FBIS* February 29, 1996).

27. *PR,* December 20, 1996.

28. *Al-Sharq al-Awsat,* July 26, 1995 (*FBIS,* July 27, 1995).

29. Voice of Palestine, July 25, 1995 (*FBIS,* July 26, 1995).

30. Ibid.

31. Radio Monte Carlo, April 13, 1995 (*FBIS,* April 18, 1995).

32. CPRS Poll No. 33, June 3–6, 1998.

33. The estimates come from a large number of CPRS public opinion polls from 1996 to 1998. For a Communist perspective, see Bashir Barghuti, *The Development of the Palestinian National Movement* [Arabic] (Nablus, 1996).

34. *Al-Hayat,* September 14, 1995 (*FBIS,* September 15, 1995).

35. The estimate comes from averaging a large number of CPRS public opinion polls from 1996 to 1998.

36. See, for example, *al-Ra'y*, September 26, 1994 (*FBIS*, September 26, 1994); Kol Israel, August 18 and 22, 1995 (*FBIS*, August 18 and 22, 1995); and *Shihan*, January 21–27, 1995 (*FBIS*, January 24, 1995). On the DFLP, see Voice of Palestine, October 2, 1994 (*FBIS*, October 3, 1994). See also Radio Monte Carlo, February 7, 1995 (*FBIS*, February 8, 1995); and *Wall Street Journal*, February 8, 1995.

37. The estimates come from averaging a large number of CPRS public opinion polls from 1996 to 1998.

38. *The Independent*, January 30, 1995. See also "Islamic Jihad Movement in Palestine: Ideology and Structure," *al-Sharaa*, January 4, 1993. On Islamic Jihad, see also *al-Watan al-Arabi*, May 15, 1995, and November 27, 1995; *al-Wasat*, November 6, 1995; and *Ha'aretz*, November 1 and December 10, 1995.

39. Kol Israel, October 30, 1995 (*FBIS*, October 30, 1995); *Mideast Monitor*, October 30, 1995; and *Washington Post*, October 30 and November 1, 1995.

40. Kol Israel, October 29, 1995 (*FBIS*, October 30, 1995); *New York Times*, October 30 and November 1, 1995; *Mideast Monitor*, October 31, 1995.

41. *Mideast Mirror*, April 11, 1995.

42. Interview with Radio Monte Carlo, April 14, 1995 (*FBIS*, April 18, 1995).

43. *Jerusalem Report*, October 30, 1997.

44. Hamas Charter, Article 13, cited in Laqueur and Rubin, *The Israel-Arab Reader*, pp. 530–531.

45. *Al-Urdun*, October 9, 1995 (*FBIS*, October 10, 1995).

46. Article 22 of the Hamas Charter, in Laqueur and Rubin, *The Israel-Arab Reader*, p. 532.

47. Article 32, ibid., p. 536.

48. Article 11, ibid., p. 530.

49. *Kul al-Arab*, January 9, 1998.

50. Middle East News Agency, February 10, 1995 (*FBIS*, February 13, 1995).

51. *Al-Nahar*, October 16, 1996. Hamas spokesman Ibrahim Ghawsha concluded that the Arabs lost the 1948 war only because they had insufficient unity, ideology, and Islamic leadership. Ibrahim Ghosha [Ghawsha], "The 1948 Nakba: Facts and Lessons," *Palestine Times*, May 1998.

52. From an interview with *al-Quds al-Arabi*, September 10, 1998, reprinted in *Palestine Times*, October 1998.

53. Hamas Charter, Article 12, in Laqueur and Rubin, *The Israel-Arab Reader*, p. 530.

54. Article 27, ibid., pp. 533–534.

55. *Al-Urdun*, October 9, 1995 (*FBIS*, October 10, 1995).

56. *Palestine Times*, June 1998.

57. *Al-Bilad*, November 30, 1997.

58. *Ha'aretz*, October 10, 1995.

59. *PR,* June 28, 1996.
60. *Mideast Mirror,* April 11, 1995.
61. Text of Hamas Communiqué No. 118, December 5, 1994, *Filastin al-Muslima,* January 1995.
62. Al-Malki, *Palestinian Opposition,* p. 24.
63. *Al-Hayat al-Jadida,* August 20, 1995 (*FBIS,* August 23, 1995); *Al-Urdun,* October 2, 1995 (*FBIS,* October 2, 1995).
64. Al-Sharq al-Awsat, *The Palestinian Elections; FBIS,* December 4, 1995. See also *Mideast Mirror,* April 24, 1995; *al-Sharq al-Awsat,* October 3, 1995; *Hamshahri,* September 12, 1995 (*FBIS,* September 21, 1995); and Syrian Arab News Agency, October 4, 1995 (*FBIS,* October 5, 1995).
65. For one such group, the Palestinian Islamic Front, see Voice of Palestine, August 25, 1995 (*FBIS* August 28, 1995). See also "Presentation of Candidacy of Islamic Jihad—Al-Aqsa Battalions for the Elections to the PLC" [Arabic] (no publisher, 1996), which states: "We confirm that the PLO is the only and legal representative of the Palestinian people. The National Authority is a part of the PLO and our movement is a part of PLO. We forbid any kind of violence and extreme behavior no matter what its origin because Islam is a religion of justice, law, and forgiveness."
66. *Ha'aretz,* December 12, 1995 (*FBIS,* December 14, 1995).
67. *Jerusalem Post,* August 24, 1995 (*FBIS,* August 24, 1995); Voice of Palestine, November 26, 1995 (*FBIS,* November 27, 1995); and *Jerusalem Times,* December 29, 1995.
68. *Ha'aretz,* December 15, 1995.
69. *Al-Sharq al-Awsat,* September 11, 1995 (*FBIS,* September 12, 1995).
70. *Ha'aretz,* November 20, 1995; *al-Hayat,* November 27, 1995 (*FBIS,* November 28, 1995).
71. Kol Israel, March 23, 1996, and Agence France-Presse, March 24, 1996 (*FBIS,* March 25, 1996); *PR,* March 29, 1996. One source of problems was the PA's continued suspicion of the party. PA police grabbed an NISP leader, Fu'ad Nahal, on his way home from meeting Arafat and questioned him for twenty hours about Hamas fund-raising. *Mideast Mirror,* April 22, 1996; *al-Quds,* May 26, 1996 (*FBIS,* May 29, 1996).
72. *PR,* February 21, 1997.
73. *PR,* February 21, 1997. *Al Risala* printed six thousand copies of the first issue and had nine employees.
74. Ibid.
75. *Al-Manar,* April 11, 1994 (*FBIS,* April 13, 1994).
76. *Die Presse* (Vienna), February 6, 1995 (*FBIS,* February 7, 1995). In this, as on many other points, Hamas recapitulated ideas which had dominated the PLO's thinking in earlier decades.
77. Ibid.
78. Middle East News Agency, February 10, 1995 (*FBIS,* February 10, 1995).

79. Ibid. For a similar statement, see *PR*, July 5, 1996.
80. Voice of Palestine, May 17 and 18, 1996 (*FBIS*, May 20, 1996).
81. *Al-Sharq al-Awsat*, July 26, 1995 (*FBIS*, July 27, 1995). See also Agence France-Presse, October 14, 1995 (*FBIS*, October 16, 1995); and *Al-Sharq al-Awsat*, January 8, 1995 (*FBIS*, January 10, 1995).
82. *PR*, August 23, 1996.
83. *Al-Sharq al-Awsat*, January 8, 1995 (*FBIS*, January 10, 1995).
84. *Al-Sharq al-Awsat*, July 26, 1995 (*FBIS*, July 27, 1995).
85. *Al-Ayyam*, November 16, 1996.
86. Ibid.
87. *Al-Sharq al-Awsat*, July 26, 1995 (*FBIS*, July 27, 1995).
88. Radio Monte Carlo, April 13, 1995 (*FBIS*, April 18, 1995).
89. Voice of Palestine, August 21, 1995 (*FBIS*, August 21, 1995).
90. Interview with Radio Monte Carlo, April 14, 1995 (*FBIS*, April 18, 1995).
91. *Al-Sharq al-Awsat*, January 8, 1995 (*FBIS*, January 10, 1995).
92. Ibid.
93. See also Abd al-Sattar Qasim, *The Islamic Movement and the Future of the Opposition* [Arabic] (Nablus, 1996).
94. Radio Monte Carlo, April 13, 1995 (*FBIS*, April 18, 1995).
95. *Al-Hayat*, February 21, 1995 (*FBIS*, February 23, 1995).
96. Ibid.
97. Ibid.
98. Ibid.
99. For Nazzal's Outsider perspective on this process, see *PR*, August 23, 1996.
100. *Al-Hayat al-Jadida*, January 2, 1995.
101. Voice of the Arabs, April 15, 1995 (*FBIS*, April 18, 1995).
102. *Al-Hayat al-Jadida*, January 2, 1995.
103. *Washington Times*, August 25, 1995; Kol Israel, October 11, 1995 (*FBIS*, October 11, 1995); Voice of Palestine, December 7, 1995 (*FBIS*, December 7, 1995); and Voice of Palestine, December 12, 1995 (*FBIS*, December 12, 1995). What was described as a draft PA-Hamas agreement was published in the Egyptian press in September 1995, though it was perhaps more likely a PA-proposed version, providing for dialogue and Hamas participation in PA bodies. *Al-Ahram Weekly*, September 14–20, 1995 (*FBIS*, September 19, 1995).
104. *Mideast Monitor*, October 11 and December 13, 1995; Voice of Palestine, December 13, 1995 (*FBIS*, December 14, 1995).
105. Voice of Palestine, October 14, 1995 (*FBIS*, October 16, 1995).
106. *Al-Ahram*, October 16, 1995 (*FBIS*, October 20, 1995).
107. Ibid.
108. *New York Times*, October 17, 1995.
109. Agence-France Presse, October 17, 1995 (*FBIS*, October 18, 1995).
110. Middle East Broadcasting Corporation Television, October 8, 1995 (*FBIS*,

October 10, 1995); Agence-France Press, October 11, 1995 (*FBIS*, October 12, 14, and 16, 1995); *al-Hayat*, October 11, 1995 (*FBIS*, October 12, 1995); Middle East News Agency, October 15, 1995 (*FBIS*, October 15, 1995); Islamic Republic News Agency, October 13, 1995 (*FBIS*, October 13, 1995); and Voice of Palestine, October 13, 1995 (*FBIS*, October 16, 1995). On rejecting any deal, see, for example, Nazzal in *al-Sabil*, October 17–23, 1995 (*FBIS*, October 18, 1995); and Hamas statement quoted in *al-Nahar*, October 18, 1995 (*FBIS*, October 20, 1995).

111. *Mideast Monitor*, December 18 and 20, 1995; *New York Times*, December 22, 1995; Middle East News Agency and Voice of Palestine, December 18, 1995 (*FBIS*, December 19, 1995); Middle East News Agency and Voice of Palestine, December 19, 1995 (*FBIS*, December 20, 1995); Voice of Palestine, December 21, 1995 (*FBIS*, December 21, 1995); Middle East News Agency, Radio Monte Carlo, and Voice of Palestine, December 21, 1995 (*FBIS*, December 22, 1995); and *al-Quds*, December 22, 1995 (*FBIS*, December 26, 1995).

112. See Chapter 3.

113. *PR*, August 16, 1996.

114. *Mideast Monitor*, March 21 and 25, 1997; *Washington Post*, March 24, 1997; and *PR*, March 28, 1997. The members of PA dialogue committee included PNC Speaker Salim Za'nun, Orient House head Faysal al-Husayni, DFLP Politburo member Taysir Khalid, PFLP Politburo member Taysir Quba'a, PPP head and Industry Minister Bashir Barghuti, Information and Culture Minister Yasir Abd Rabbu, and Finance Minister Muhammad Zuhdi Nashashibi.

115. Quoted in *PR*, November 1, 1996.

116. *Washington Post*, September 30, 1998.

117. *Ha'aretz*, April 1, 1998.

118. *New York Times*, October 5, 1993.

119. *Washington Post*, February 20, 1994.

120. *New York Times*, April 14, 1994.

121. *Washington Post*, April 8, 1994.

122. *New York Times*, September 6, 1994, and Kol Israel, September 11, 1994 (*FBIS*, September 12, 1994).

123. *Financial Times*, April 24, 1994.

124. *New York Times*, September 19, 1994, and Agence-France Presse, September 22, 1994 (*FBIS*, September 23, 1994).

125. Voice of the Islamic Republic of Iran, May 19, 1994 (*FBIS*, May 20, 1994).

126. *New York Times*, October 10 and 11, 1994.

127. *New York Times*, October 12, 1994.

128. *Washington Post*. October 13, 1994. On their release, see Kol Israel, October ·17, 1994 (*FBIS*, October 18, 1994).

129. *New York Times*, October 14 and 15, 1994.

130. *Washington Post,* October 18 and 19, 1994.
131. *New York Times,* October 20 and 21, 1994; Agence-France Presse, October 20, 1994 (*FBIS,* October 21, 1994).
132. *New York Times* and *Washington Post,* December 1, 1994.
133. *New York Times,* November 12 and 14, 1994; *FBIS,* November 13 and 17, 1994.
134. *Washington Post,* December 25, 1994; *New York Times,* December 27, 1994.
135. *New York Times,* February 19, 1995.
136. *FBIS,* January 19, February 26 and 27, and March 18 and 20, 1995; Agence France-Presse and Kol Israel, February 3, 1996 (*FBIS* February 5, 1996).
137. *Mideast Mirror,* April 11, 1995.
138. *FBIS,* March 22, April 12, 17, 18, and 19, and May 16, 1995; *New York Times,* April 17 and May 15, 16, 17, and 30, 1995; *Washington Post,* April 17, 1995; and *New York Times,* May 15, 1995.
139. *New York Times* and *Washington Post,* April 3, 1995; *al-Hayat,* April 4 and 5, 1995. For another case of Hamas terrorists being killed by their own bombs, see *FBIS,* September 14, 1995.
140. *Financial Times,* June 27 and October 9, 1995; *New York Times,* October 17, 1995. See also *FBIS,* May 29, July 5, and August 10, 1995.
141. For example, IDF Radio, August 21, 1995 (*FBIS,* August 21, 1995); *Washington Post,* August 19 and 22, 1995; Kol Israel, August 16, 1995 (*FBIS,* August 17, 1995), and August 19, 1995 (*FBIS,* August 22, 1995); *Mideast Mirror,* August 21, 1995; and *New York Times,* August 22 and 25, 1995.
142. Voice of Palestine, July 25, 1995 (*FBIS,* July 26, 1995); *al-Sharq al-Awsat,* August 4, 1995; and *Filastin al-Muslima,* August and September 1995.
143. *Washington Post,* August 21, 1995; *New York Times,* August 23 and 31, 1995; and Kol Israel, August 24, 1995 (*FBIS,* August 25, 1995).
144. Voice of Palestine August 26, 1995 (*FBIS,* August 28, 1995); *New York Times,* August 27, 1995; and Voice of Palestine, September 14, 1995 (*FBIS,* September 15, 1995).
145. Kol Israel, August 29, 1995 (*FBIS* August 30, 1995); *New York Times,* August 30 and September 13, 1995; *al-Sharq al-Awsat,* October 16, 1995 (*FBIS* November 14, 1995); *Jerusalem Post,* October 6, 1995 (*FBIS,* October 6, 1995); Radio Monte Carlo, November 28, 1995 (*FBIS,* November 28, 1995); and Middle East News Agency, November 15, 1995 (*FBIS* November 16, 1995).
146. Voice of Palestine, January 6, 1996 (*FBIS,* January 7, 1996); *New York Times,* January 6 and 7, 1996; *Mideast Mirror,* January 8, 1996; *Filastin al-Muslima,* February 1996; and *al-Hayat al-Jadida,* July 21, 1996.
147. Kol Israel, September 3, 1995 (*FBIS,* September 5, 1995), and March 12, 1996 (*FBIS,* March 12, 1996); Voice of Palestine, August 27, 1995 (*FBIS,* August 28, 1995).
148. *Washington Post,* February 25, 1996; *New York Times,* February 26, 1996.

149. *New York Times,* February 26, 1996.
150. Kol Israel, March 2, 1996 (*FBIS,* March 4, 1996); *New York Times,* March 4, 1996.
151. *Washington Post,* March 3, 1996; *New York Times,* March 4, 1996.
152. *New York Times,* March 5, 1996.
153. *Financial Times,* March 7 and 12, 1996; Kol Israel, March 6, 12, and 22, 1996 (respectively, *FBIS,* March 6, 12, 15, and 22, 1996); *New York Times,* March 10 and 11, 1996; Jordanian television, March 16, 1996 (*FBIS,* March 18, 1996); Kol Israel, March 10, 1996 (*FBIS,* March 11, 1996); and *Washington Post,* March 11, 1996.
154. *Mideast Monitor,* March 6, 1996; Voice of Palestine, March 6, 1996 (*FBIS,* March 6, 1996). For example, see Kol Israel, May 14, 1996 (*FBIS,* May 15, 1996); and *New York Times,* March 23 and April 3 and 4, 1997.
156. Given heavy self-censorship in the Palestinian press, the best accounts are in *Ha'aretz,* April 2, 6, 7, 9, 10, 12, 13, 19, and 28, 1998.
157. See articles cited in note 156; *PR,* August 21, 1998; *Palestine Times,* May 1998; and Reuters, September 11, 1998.
158. Shiqaqi, *Palestinian Elections,* p. 16.
159. Al-Malki, *Palestinian Opposition,* p. 24.
160. Reuters, November 1, 1998.

7. The Palestinian Authority and the Middle East

1. *Al-Sharq al-Awsat,* January 8, 1995 (*FBIS,* January 10, 1995).
2. Radio Monte Carlo, April 13, 1995 (*FBIS,* April 18, 1995).
3. Interview with Radio Monte Carlo, April 14, 1995 (*FBIS,* April 18, 1995).
4. *Al-Quds,* August 5, 1996.
5. *PR,* November 7, 1997.
6. Voice of Palestine, August 22, 1995 (*FBIS,* August 25, 1995).
7. *Al-Hayat,* February 21, 1995 (*FBIS,* February 27, 1995).
8. *Al-Urdun,* October 9, 1995 (*FBIS,* October 10, 1995).
9. Yezid Sayigh, "Fatah: The First Twenty Years," *Journal of Palestine Studies,* Vol. 13, No. 4 (Summer 1984), p. 115. Walid Kazziha, *Palestine in the Arab Dilemma* (London, 1979), pp. 15–19.
10. The historical record on Arab state–Palestinian relations shows themes similar to those analyzed here. For my own discussion of the 1920–1956 situation, see Barry Rubin, *The Arab States and the Palestine Conflict* (Syracuse, Syracuse University Press, 1982). On the 1956–1993 history of Arab state–PLO relations, see my *Revolution Until Victory?* esp. chap. 6; "Is the Arab-Israeli Conflict Over?" *Middle East Quarterly,* Autumn 1996; and *Assessing the New Middle East: Opportunities and Risks* (Tel Aviv, 1995).

11. Abraham Sela, *The Decline of the Arab-Israeli Conflict: Middle East Politics and the Quest for Regional Order* (Albany, N.Y., 1997). Rubin, *The Arab States and the Palestine Conflict.*

12. Rabbu, *Analytical Review*, p. 12.

13. According to Hani al-Hasan, the PA needed support from all Arab states to create a "balance of power" with Israel and attain "economic stability." Hasan, *The Relationship between the PLO and PA Institutions*, pp. 15–18. Yasir Abd Rabbu noted: "The path to establishing a state depends also on strengthening relations with the Arab world. The Israeli plan is to separate the Palestinian entity from the Arab world. We are part of Arab and Muslim civilization and culture. The ties which bind us are not only national but also social, economic, and political. So that is why one of the ways to defend the Palestinian entity is good relations with the Arabs, including turning over a new leaf with countries and organizations with whom our relations had worsened for various reasons. We are an entity in transition that has many points of weakness. In order to be on the same level as our opponents, we must lean on the Arab world and develop improved contacts with it. I must say that we are not making enough effort toward this direction." Rabbu, *Analytical Review*, pp. 12–13.

14. Official text of the resolution obtained at the summit.

15. Egypt's Ministry of Information, State Information Service, text of June 22, 1996.

16. For Arafat's successful effort to get King Husayn to protest Israeli construction in East Jerusalem, see *Washington Post*, March 9, 1997, and *New York Times*, March 12, 1997.

17. *Washington Post*, September 27, 1996.

18. Zoe Danon Gedal, "The Doha Summit: A Virtual Conference," Peacewatch No. 147 (Washington, D.C., November 11, 1997).

19. Palestinian National Authority Official Website, Special Reports, Donor Assistance Report, June 30, 1998, <http://nmopic.pna.net/reports/aid _reports/150898/index.htm>.

20. *Ha'aretz*, November 19, 1996; *PR*, November 22, 1996.

21. Wafa report, cited in *PR*, February 13, 1998.

22. *Washington Post*, June 13, 1994; *al-Hayat*, February 21, 1995; *PR*, August 9 and 23, 1996; and Agence-France Presse, May 25, 1998.

23. Agence-France Presse, May 30, 1998.

24. Robinson, "The Growing Authoritarianism of the Arafat Regime," pp. 40–54.

25. Ibid.

26. Resolution obtained at the summit.

27. Text of June 22, 1996.

28. For example, Abu Musa of the Syrian-backed Fatah Uprising group which split from Fatah in 1983. *Washington Post*, October 9, 1993.

29. *New York Times,* September 17, 1993. For an example of Iran–Islamic Jihad cooperation, see Israel Defense Forces Radio, April 7, 1996 (*FBIS,* April 8, 1996). On Siftawi, see *Washington Post,* September 10 and October 22, 1993. His son was an Islamic Jihad leader.

30. Reuters, May 27, 1998; *al-Hayat,* April 19, 1998; and *Ha'aretz,* April 20 and 28 and May 3, 1998.

31. Reuters, May 27, 1998.

32. *Al-Wasat,* January 9–15, 1995 (*FBIS,* January 13, 1995).

33. *Dawn,* June 1, 1998; *Palestine Times,* June 1998.

34. *PR,* March 27, 1998.

35. See Chapter 8 and Rubin, *Revolution Until Victory?*

36. On Israel and the North African states, see Michael Laskier, "The Israel-Maghreb Connection: Past Contacts, Future Prospects," *Jerusalem Letter/Viewpoints,* No. 355, April 1, 1997.

37. Israel-Turkey cooperation was an important regional development, intimidating the radicals (especially Syria) while also discomfiting Egypt, which saw this alignment as challenging its own—and Arab—regional hegemony. Barry Rubin, "Notes on Turkey-Israel Relations," *Middle East Review of International Affairs (MERIA) News,* No. 1977/7 (July 1997).

38. Middle East News Agency, May 25, 1995 (*FBIS,* May 25; 1995), June 5, 1995 (*FBIS,* June 5, 1995), February 29, 1996 (*FBIS,* February 29, 1996), April 29, 1996 (*FBIS,* April 29, 1996), and May 12, 1996 (*FBIS,* May 13, 1996); Voice of Palestine, April 16, 1996 (*FBIS,* April 17, 1996); and Arab Republic of Egypt Radio Network, May 10, 1996. See also *FBIS,* December 16, 1994, May 5 and 6 and August 9, 1995, June 26, 1996, and March 11, 1997; *New York Times,* June 26, October 17, and December 30, 1996, and January 12 and March 21, 1997; and *al-Hayat al-Jadida,* August 12, 1997.

39. Reuters, August 20, 1996.

40. Rasim Khamaysa, Basim Makhul, and Adnan Awda, eds., *Conference on Palestinian-Egyptian Economic Relations* [Arabic] (Nablus, 1995).

41. Although some argued that Arab passivity might be more likely to produce confrontation by making Israel feel that it could increase its demands until the peace process was destroyed. As the Egyptian newspaper *al-Ahram* put it, "If Israel thinks Arabs will not act, then the region will return to what it was before negotiations." Quoted in *Washington Post,* September 27, 1996.

42. Fawaz A. Gerges, "Egyptian-Israeli Relations Turn Sour," *Foreign Affairs,* Vol. 74, No. 3 (May–June 1995); Mubarak interview, *Jerusalem Report,* March 19, 1997.

43. King Husayn's throne speech, November 1, 1967, *al-Dustur,* November 2, 1967; *International Documents on Palestine: 1967* (Beirut, 1967), p. 691.

44. Asad Abd al-Rahman, *Relations between Palestinians and Jordan after the Palestinian-Israeli Declaration of Principles Agreement* [Arabic] (Nablus, May 1994); Mustafa Hamarneh, Rosemary Hollis, and Khalil Shikaki, *Jordanian-*

Palestinian Relations: Where To? Four Strategies for the Future (London, 1997); Asad Abd al-Rahman, "The Evolution of Palestinian-Jordanian Relations" [Arabic], and Khalil al-Shiqaqi, "Jordanian-Palestinian Relations and the Process of National Reconstruction" [Arabic], *al-Siyasa al-Filastiniyya*, Vol. 3, No. 10 (Spring 1996); Tarik al-Tal, "Myth and Misunderstanding in Jordanian-Palestinian Relations" [Arabic], and Center for Strategic Studies, "Jordanian-Palestinian Relations: Domestic Dimension" [Arabic], *al-Siyasa al-Filastiniyya*, Vol. 3, No. 12 (Fall 1996); Adnan Abu Awda, "Jordanian-Palestinian Relations" [Arabic], *al-Siyasa al-Filastiniyya*, Vol. 4, No. 14 (Spring 1997); and Mahmud Ja'fari, *The Palestinian-Jordanian Trade Agreement* [Arabic] (Nablus, 1997).

45. Arafat met King Husayn fairly frequently to try to coordinate policies. For example, see *FBIS*, May 24, 1995, July 8 and December 24, 1996, and January 30, 1997; and *New York Times*, June 6, 1996.

46. Quoted in Rahman, *Relations between Palestinians and Jordan*, p. 27.

47. Texts in Laqueur and Rubin, *The Israel-Arab Reader*, pp. 655–674.

48. See Lori Plotkin, *Jordan-Israel Peace: Taking Stock, 1994–1997* (Washington, D.C., 1997).

49. To cite one example, Jordanian opposition lawyers rushed to defend a Jordanian soldier who murdered seven Israeli junior high school girls. *Jordan Times*, March 19, 1997.

50. Associated Press, June 24, 1997.

51. *Ma'ariv*, June 6, 1997.

52. Speech to Washington Institute for Near East Policy, September 12, 1989. On the issue of Palestinian citizens of Jordan, see the discussion later in this chapter.

53. Since the Palestinians were still unable to create their own stable currency, the only alternative would have been a politically unacceptable one: the Israeli shekel. "Agreement between the Hashemite Kingdom of Jordan and the Palestine Liberation Organization," January 7, 1994, text in *Palestine-Israel Journal*, Spring 1994; *Mideast Mirror*, May 25, 1995; and *al-Sharq al-Awsat*, January 14 and 25, 1995.

54. In October 1994, Fatah along with other groups called for protests against these provisions of the treaty. *Al-Quds*, October 26, 1994; *New York Times*, October 27, 1994.

55. *Financial Times*, January 27, 1995.

56. Rabbu, *Analytical Review*, p. 19.

57. *Al-Sharq al-Awsat*, January 8, 1995, p. 5, interview with Arafat in *FBIS*, January 10, 1995; and *PR*, November 15, 1996. According to PA Waqf Minister Hasan Tahbub, the agreement was that Jordan would supervise the sites in East Jerusalem until a Palestinian state was created.

58. Quoted in Rob Satloff, "The King Is Back and Final Status Talks May Be Just Around the Corner," Peacewatch No. 150, Washington, D.C., December 10, 1997.

59. *PR,* August 19, 1996. Jordan claimed that Hamas there was confined to propaganda and political activities. *Voice of Palestine,* March 6, 1996 (*FBIS,* March 7, 1996).

60. *PR,* July 26, 1996.

61. *Ha'aretz,* December 19, 1997.

62. Reuters, May 27, 1998; *al-Hayat,* April 19, 1998; *Ha'aretz,* April 20 and 28 and May 3, 1998; and Radio Monte Carlo, May 31, 1995 (*FBIS,* June 1, 1995).

63. Tal, "Myth and Misunderstanding."

64. Rahman, *Relations between Palestinians and Jordan,* p. 28.

65. Voice of Palestine, August 23, 1995 (*FBIS,* August 25, 1995).

66. Agence-France Presse, September 22, 1998.

67. For Asad's reaction to the 1993 Israel-PLO agreement, see Laqueur and Rubin, *The Israel-Arab Reader,* pp. 620–622. On Syria-PA relations, see *al-Hayat,* February 21, 1995.

68. See the discussion later in this chapter.

69. Syria would benefit little by making its own peace agreement with Israel since it could not expect much Western aid or investment, and there would be a risk of domestic rebellion. With the Israel-Palestinian issue defused, Syria would find it harder to obtain aid from rich Arab states or to mobilize its own population in support of the minority Alawite regime.

70. Interviews with PNC delegates. Iraq also recognized the PA-issued Palestinian passports. *PR,* November 28, 1997.

71. *Al-Nahar,* August 9, 1996 (*FBIS,* August 11, 1996).

72. Saddam Husayn, National Day speech, July 17, 1997 (*FBIS,* July 18, 1997); *Washington Post,* October 3, 1996.

73. *Al-Quds,* February 13, 15, and 22, 1998; *al-Hayat al-Jadida,* February 15, 1998.

74. For Yasin's view, see *al-Hayat al-Jadida,* February 20, 1998.

75. Results of February 14, 1998, poll, JMCC release, February 20, 1998.

76. *PR,* February 20, 1998.

77. *PR,* February 10, 1998; *al-Quds,* February 12 and 15, 1998; results of February 14, 1998, poll, JMCC release, February 20, 1998; and *New York Times,* December 21, 1998.

78. *Al-Quds,* February 15, 1998.

79. For example, Sha'th in *al-Quds,* February 15, 1998.

80. *Al-Quds,* February 14, 1998.

81. Saudi Arabia discouraged other Gulf Arab states from normalization to ensure its hegemony over the smaller monarchies. It also displayed a fear and demonization of Israel extreme even by general Arab standards and concern about domestic reaction to any steps toward normalization.

82. *Washington Post,* October 3, 1996; Voice of Palestine, July 18, 1995 (*FBIS,* July 20, 1995).

83. All figures for the total number of Palestinians or even those living in any given country are highly controversial and often vary enormously. On these issues, see Abbas Shiblak, "The Peace Process and Its Implications for the

Refugees" [Arabic], *al-Siyasa al-Filastiniyya*, Vol. 2., No. 6 (Spring 1995); Tawfiq Abu Bakr, "The Impact of Netanyahu's Victory on Diaspora Palestinians" [Arabic], *al-Siyasa al-Filastiniyya*, Vol. 3, No. 11 (Summer 1996); Norma Masria, "Reasons for the Failure of Plans to Resettle Refugees" [Arabic], and Najah Jarrar, "Palestinian Refugees and Civil Rights" [Arabic], *al-Siyasa al-Filastiniyya*, Vol. 4, No. 13 (Winter 1997); and Salim Ta'amri, *Political, Economic, and Social Dimensions of the Reintegration of Refugees* [Arabic] (Nablus, 1995).

84. *Al-Sharq al-Awsat*, January 8, 1995 (*FBIS*, January 10, 1995).
85. *The Middle East*, May 1983. This slogan was displayed prominently, for example, at the PNC's 1988 session in Tunis.
86. Voice of Palestine, January 1, 1995 (*FBIS*, January 6, 1995).
87. *Al-Sharq al-Awsat*, July 31, 1994 (*FBIS*, September 22, 1994).
88. There were smaller numbers of refugees from 1967 whose original homes were in the West Bank or (as in Arafat's own case) Gaza. The peace agreements provided for talks on their earlier repatriation, though little progress was made on this issue.
89. These included Abu Jihad (Ramle); Abu Iyad (Jaffa); the al-Hasan brothers (Haifa); Abu Mazin, Abu al-Hawl, and Nabil Sha'th (Safad); Shafiq al-Hut (Jaffa); George Habash (Lod); Abdallah Franji (Beersheva); and Qaddumi (born in Nablus but grew up in Jaffa.)
90. Fawaz Turki, "The Future of a Past: Fragments from the Palestinian Dream," *Journal of Palestine Studies* (Spring 1977), p. 68; Abu Iyad, interview with author in Tunis, August 1989.
91. Al-Sharq al-Awsat, *The Palestinian Elections*.
92. Hasan, *The Relationship between the PLO and PA Institutions*, p. 14.
93. *PR*, February 6, 1998; *Ha'aretz*, December 22, 1995; Middle East News Agency, August 10, 1995 (*FBIS*, August 11, 1995). See also *al-Hayat*, January 7, 1995; Agence-France Press, September 11, 1995 (*FBIS*, September 12, 1995); Libyan News Agency, October 9, 1995 (*FBIS*, October 11, 1995); Agence-France Presse, October 18, 1995 (*FBIS*, October 19, 1995); Cyprus Broadcasting Corporation Radio, October 18, 1995 (*FBIS*, October 19, 1995); and *New York Times*, October 19, 1995.
94. *Al-Wasat*, January 9–15, 1995 (*FBIS*, January 13, 1995).
95. *PR*, September 20, 1996.
96. *PR*, September 27, 1996.
97. Rosemary Sayigh, *Too Many Enemies: The Palestinian Experience in Lebanon* (London, 1994). Figures vary widely for the number of Palestinians in the diaspora as a whole and in specific countries. The most common number given for those in Lebanon is about 300,000.
98. Voice of Palestine, January 1, 1995 (*FBIS*, January 6, 1995).
99. *Ha'aretz*, August 26, 1994.
100. *Al-Nahar*, July 28, 1995 (*FBIS*, August 1, 1995); Abu Bakr, "The Impact of

Netanyahu's Victory," p. 78. The latter article also gives a general survey of attitudes among diaspora Palestinians.

101. *Al-Sha'ala,* November 19, 1993; Agence-France Presse, September 7, 1998.

102. *Al-Dustur,* January 12, 1995, *(FBIS,* January 13, 1995). Hamas tried to turn even this action against the PA. According to Hamas spokesman Ibrahim Ghawsha, "transferring some Palestinian fighters from southern Lebanon is a suspect and rejected move." Instead of these forces' being employed to fight in Lebanon, "they are being moved to the Gaza Strip and the Jericho region to protect this Zionist occupation and torture the Palestinian people." Voice of the Islamic Republic of Iran, January 7, 1995 *(FBIS,* January 11, 1995).

103. *The Guardian,* April 18, 1995.

104. Radio Lebanon, January 20, 1996 *(FBIS,* January 22, 1996); *Mideast Mirror,* January 22, 1996.

105. *PR,* September 18, 1998.

106. Reuters, May 27, 1998.

107. *Intelligence Newsletter,* July 26, 1994.

108. *Ha'aretz,* August 26, 1994.

109. *Mideast Mirror,* November 27, 1989.

110. *The Star* (Amman), January 26–February 1, 1995 *(FBIS,* January 26, 1995).

111. But there were also many refugees living in camps, and, as in Lebanon, UNRWA cutbacks of services and assistance added to their fear. *PR,* November 22, 1996, and January 31, 1997.

112. Interview, *al-Anba,* September 7, 1988 *(FBIS,* September 9, 1998).

113. Witnessed by the author.

114. Shmuel Bar, *The Muslim Brotherhood in Jordan* (Tel Aviv, 1998), pp. 41–50. The most important such group was the Islamic Action Front.

115. Tal, "Myth and Misunderstanding."

116. Ibid.

117. *Al-Hayat,* January 25, 1995; *Los Angeles Times,* February 1, 1995; and *Mideast Mirror,* April 5, 1995.

118. Dajani, "The Palestinian Authority and Citizenship."

119. Off-the-record interview.

120. *The Star* (Amman), January 26–February 1, 1995 *(FBIS,* January 26, 1995).

121. *Al-Sharq al-Awsat,* July 31, 1994 *(JPRS,* September 22, 1994).

122. Marwan Darwish, "The PLO Policy toward the Palestinians in Israel" [Arabic], *al-Siyasa al-Filastiniyya,* Vol. 3, No. 9 (Winter 1996). On Abdallah Nimr Darwish's role, see *New York Times,* April 18, 1995, and the section on PA-Hamas dialogue in Chapter 8. For Israeli writings on this topic, see Elie Rekhess, ed., *The Arabs in Israeli Politics: Dilemmas of Identity* (Tel Aviv, 1998), and *Arab Politics in Israel: At a Crossroads* (Tel Aviv, 1996); Jacob M. Landau, As'ad Ghanem, and Alouph Hareven, *The Arab Citizens of Israel towards the Twenty-first Century* (Tel Aviv, 1995); and Alouph Hareven,

Retrospect and Prospects: "Full and Equal Citizenship"? (Tel Aviv, 1998).
123. For a Palestinian nationalist assessment of this issue, see Nadim N. Rou-
hana, *Palestinian Citizens in an Ethnic Jewish State: Identities in Conflict* (New
Haven, 1997).
124. There were very few Palestinians from Israel in the PLO hierarchy. The most
senior of them, Muhammad Darwish, a PLO Executive Committee member, had resigned to protest the peace process. See Elie Rekhess, "Arabs in
a Jewish State: Images vs. Realities," *Middle East Insight*, January–February
1990; CPRS, *Palestinians inside Israel and the Peace Process* [Arabic] (Nablus,
1994); Ali Jarbawi, "Separation: Israel's Palestinian Ghettos" [Arabic], *al-
Siyasa al-Filastiniyya*, Vol. 2, No. 5 (Winter 1995); and Darwish, "PLO Policy
toward the Palestinians in Israel." After feuding with the PA, Tibi was
elected to Israel's parliament in 1999.

8. Thinking about Israel and the United States

1. While for many groups historically—even in such hotbeds of anti-Semitism
as medieval Europe and modern Germany or Russia—conflict with Jews was
largely imaginary, the Israeli-Palestinian conflict was real. While other groups
almost always dealt with Jews who were in a weak position, the Palestinians
had to cope with Jews victorious in war and even governing them.
2. *Al-Hayat*, September 12, 1995 (*FBIS*, September 13, 1995). The best analysis
of the prisoner issue is in *Ha'aretz*, December 29, 1998. There were 1,622
security prisoners held by Israel. Of this number, 630 were jailed for pre–Oslo
agreement offenses and 992 for actions taken after that date. Of the total, 670
had been convicted of involvement in murder or attempted murder.
3. Shikaki, "The Peace Process, National Reconstruction," p. 7. Of course, some
of those who doubted the peace process's success were oppositionists who
preferred it to fail.
4. Palestinian Center for Public Opinion poll, September 28–29, 1996, in *PR*,
October 4, 1996.
5. *Yediot Ahronot*, January 27, 1995 (*FBIS*, January 30, 1995).
6. Ibid.
7. See, for example, Islamic Jihad leader Fathi Shiqaqi, quoted in *Mideast Mirror*,
April 11, 1995.
8. *Kul al-Arab*, January 9, 1998.
9. Kol Israel and Radio Monte Carlo, May 30, 1996 (*FBIS*, May 31, 1996); Agence
France-Presse, June 2, 1996 (*FBIS*, June 3, 1996).
10. *Al-Ayyam*, November 16, 1996; *al-Hayat al-Jadida*, May 23, 1996; and *al-
Shira*, June 3, 1996.
11. Reuters, May 27, 1998. See also *New York Times*, October 22, 1997.

12. *PR,* February 21, 1997.
13. Abu-Amr, "Pluralism and the Palestinians," p. 90; *al-Sharq al-Awsat,* July 8, 1995 (*FBIS,* July 13, 1995). Many such examples could be offered. The PA's system for handling the state's relationship with religion paralleled that used in Israel. Faysal al-Husayni and others suggested an electoral system close to that employed by Israel.
14. *New York Times,* November 10, 1995.
15. *PR,* October 25, 1996. The Palestinian delegation included Jamal Salah al-Shubaki, Marwan al-Barghuti, Dallal Salama, Husam Khadir, Qaddura Faris, Abd al-Fatah Hamayal, Kamal al-Afghani, Mu'awiya Masri, and Musa Abu Sabha.
16. Interview in *PR,* September 13, 1996.
17. *Al-Sharq al-Awsat,* January 8, 1995 (*FBIS,* January 10, 1995).
18. Voice of Palestine, January 23, 1995 (*FBIS,* January 23, 1995).
19. *Al-Hayat,* September 12, 1995 (*FBIS,* September 13, 1995).
20. Voice of Palestine, August 22, 1995 (*FBIS,* August 23, 1995).
21. *Al-Hayat,* February 21, 1995 (*FBIS,* February 23, 1995).
22. *Al-Sharq al-Awsat,* January 8, 1995 (*FBIS,* January 10, 1995).
23. *Al-Hayat,* February 21, 1995 (*FBIS,* February 23, 1995).
24. Voice of Palestine, August 22, 1995 (*FBIS,* August 23 1995).
25. Voice of the Arabs (Cairo), February 9, 1995 (*FBIS,* February 9, 1995).
26. *Yediot Ahronot,* January 27, 1995 (*FBIS,* January 30, 1995).
27. Voice of Palestine, August 25, 1995 (*FBIS,* August 23, 1995).
28. Ibid.
29. Ibid.
30. Ibid.
31. Radio Monte Carlo, April 13, 1996 (*FBIS,* April 14, 1996). On the PA's critique of the Palestinian opposition's violence, see Chapter 6.
32. *Al-Sharq al-Awsat,* January 8, 1995 (*FBIS,* January 10, 1995).
33. Ibid.
34. Ibid.
35. Voice of Palestine, February 6, 1995 (*FBIS,* February 7, 1995).
36. Radio Monte Carlo, January 12, 1995 (*FBIS* January 13, 1995).
37. Voice of Palestine, February 6, 1995 (*FBIS,* February 7, 1995).
38. *Al Hayat al-Jadida,* January 16, 1995 (*FBIS* January 19, 1995).
39. Voice of Palestine, August 22, 1995 (*FBIS,* August 23 1995).
40. Voice of Palestine, August 22, 1995 (*FBIS,* August 23, 1995).
41. In at least one case, a right-wing Israeli group did falsely claim that it had made such contacts. See Yossi Klein Halevi, "The Lies and Times of Agent Champagne," *Jerusalem Report,* November 9, 1998, p. 22.
42. *New York Times,* November 23, 1995, and May 4, 1997.
43. Spanish News Agency, November 23, 1995 (*FBIS,* November 24, 1995); *Le*

Nouvel Observateur, November 23, 1995 (*FBIS,* November 27, 1995). He continued to make similar claims, for example, as cited in *Yediot Ahronot,* November 10, 1998.

44. In an effort to discredit Hamas, Palestinian nationalists, including PA leaders, frequently claimed that the group was Israel's creation. The truth was that Israel had not moved against the Muslim Brotherhood and other Islamic groups in Gaza until the 1980s since they had restricted themselves to nonviolent and even non-political activity. When Hamas was formed as a political organization and began launching attacks and leading the intifada, Israeli authorities took firm action against that group.

45. He added, "It is also binding on any PLO Executive Committee and any Palestinian National Authority." *Al-Sharq al-Awsat,* January 8, 1995 (*FBIS,* January 10, 1995). For another perspective on the election's effects, see Marwan Bishara, "The Defeat of Peres—A Defeat for Oslo" [Arabic], *al-Siyasa al-Filastiniyya,* Vol. 3, No. 11 (Summer 1996). Despite the title of his article, Bishara concludes that if Peres had won the election, Israeli policy would have been the same.

46. *PR,* June 14, 1997.

47. Ibid.

48. Israel Defense Forces Radio, November 4, 1996 (*FBIS,* November 6, 1996); Voice of Palestine, Middle East News Agency, Radio Monte Carlo, and France-Inter Radio Network, November 5, 1996 (all in *FBIS,* November 6, 1996); and *Ha'aretz,* November 6 and 7, 1996.

49. Text of Arafat speech, March 15, 1997, Palestinian National Authority Official Website, <http://www.pna.net/speeches/0397/1501e.html>. For the best detailed analysis of Netanyahu's policy, see David Makovsky, "The Winding Road to Wye," *Ha'aretz,* December 4, 1998.

50. Arafat speech, March 15, 1997.

51. *PR,* September 13, 1996.

52. Arafat's speech at the PLC's Third Term Opening, March 7, 1998, in *PR,* March 13, 1998.

53. Voice of Palestine, August 22, 1995 (*FBIS,* August 23, 1995).

54. Arafat speech, March 15, 1997.

55. *PR,* September 11, 1998.

56. JMCC poll, July 1998, in *PR,* August 21, 1998. See also Rubin, "External Influences on Israel's 1996 Election"; *PR,* April 9, 1999.

57. *Yediot Ahronot,* August 12, 1994 (*JPRS,* November 2, 1994).

58. See Chapter 5 for a detailed discussion of this group.

59. On the situation regarding the press, see Chapter 4; on Fatah hard-liners, see Chapter 5.

60. PA Information Ministry press release, December 10, 1997; *al-Quds,* November 17, 1997.

61. PA Information Ministry press release, April 22, 1997.

62. PLC member Nahid Munir al-Rayyis quoted in *al-Quds*, October 15, 1997.

63. *Al-Hayat al-Jadida*, September 3, 1997. In response to such material, Amnon Rubinstein, an Israeli dove and former minister of education, wrote: "Anyone who has taken part in Israeli-Palestinian dialogue knows full well just how much the hostility to Israel is intertwined with anti-Semitic propaganda. The well-known Arab claim is that the Palestinians had to pay for the Nazis' crimes. It is not difficult to understand this argument from their point of view. But to go so far as to ignore what happened to the Jews of Europe" was another matter. In contrast, regarding Israel's treatment of the Palestinians, "anyone familiar with Israeli literature, poetry, theater, and cinema knows that it is replete with awareness of this tragedy." The 1998 *Tekuma* television series on Israel's history, for example, had presented this issue sympathetically and in detail, including interviews with Palestinians. *Ha'aretz*, March 12, 1998.

64. PA television station, August 25, 1997.

65. Roger Garoudy, "Biblical and Historical Myths," October 1997, <http://www.pna.org/mininfo/>.

66. *Al-Hayat al-Jadida*, November 6, 1997. See also Hasan al-Kashif, director general of the PA Information Ministry, quoted in *al-Hayat al-Jadida*, July 7, 1997.

67. *Al-Quds*, November 11, 1997. See also *al-Quds*, November 1, 1997.

68. *Al-Ayyam*, August 7, 1997.

69. *Al-Ayyam*, November 22 1997; *al-Bilad*, July 31 1997; *New York Times*, May 18, 1997; and Voice of Palestine, July 11, 1997.

70. *PR*, September 20, 1996.

71. *Al-Hayat al Jadida*, July 27, 1997.

72. Weekly Friday prayer sermon at al-Aqsa mosque, broadcast on Voice of Palestine, October 24, 1997.

73. *Al-Hayat al-Jadida*, December 8, 1997; *al-Ayyam*, October 29, 1997; and *Yediot Ahronot*, June 25, 1997.

74. Quoted in *al-Hayat al-Jadida*, May 26 and June 12, 1997.

75. *Al-Hayat al-Jadida*, May 15, 1997.

76. *Jerusalem Post*, March 17, 1997.

77. *Al-Quds*, October 15, 1997.

78. *Al-Bilad*, November 30, 1997.

79. *PR*, August 16, 1996; Itamar Marcus, "Report on Palestine Authority Summer Camps," Palestinian Media Watch, July 12, 1998. Specific quotes have been checked for accuracy.

80. *Al-Hayat al-Jadida*, July 22, 1998.

81. Palestinian Authority Television, June 4, 19, 25, and 29, and July 2, 7, 10, 12, 20, 27, and 28, 1998; Palestinian Authority Television, July 7, 1998, cited in Marcus, "Report on Palestine Authority Summer Camps."

82. *Al-Hayat al-Jadida*, July 12, 1998.

83. *New York Times,* September 28, 1998.
84. Russia was of little significance despite the temporary role of Yevgeny Primakov, who advocated a strong pro-Arab position, to foreign minister and later prime minister. Robert O. Freedman, "Russia and the Middle East: The Primakov Era," *Middle East Review of International Affairs Journal,* Vol. 2, No. 2 (May 1998). Russia's provision of two armored personnel carriers to the PA was a relative high point of Moscow's material help. Voice of Palestine radio, October 18, 1995 *(FBIS,* October 19, 1995); *al-Sharq al-Awsat,* January 8, 1995 *(FBIS,* January 10, 1995).
85. See, for example, *PR,* August 16 and October 25, 1996, and Arjan al-Fassad, "European Involvement in Palestine: Political or Financial?" [Arabic], *al-Siyasa al-Filastiniyya,* Vol. 5, No. 17 (Winter 1998). On European aid, see Palestinian National Authority Official Website, Special Reports, Donor Assistance Report, June 30, 1998, <http://nmopic.pna.net/reports/aid_reports/150898/index.htm>.
86. See, for example, *al-Sharq al-Awsat,* January 8, 1995 *(FBIS,* January 10, 1995).
87. *New York Times,* October 24, 1996; *PR,* October 25, 1996.
88. For a discussion of historic PA attitudes, see Rubin, *Revolution Until Victory?* and "Misperceptions and Perfect Understanding: The US and the PLO," in Avram Sela and Moshe Ma'oz, eds., *The PLO and Israel: From Armed Struggle to Political Settlement* (New York, 1997).
89. On Palestinian reaction to the U.S. grant of free trade status to the PA territories, see *PR,* October 18, 1996.
90. He was deported to Jordan. Al-Quds radio, July 28, 1995 *(FBIS,* July 31, 1995); *al-Sharq al-Awsat,* July 30, 1995; and *Filastin al-Muslima,* September 1995.
91. Interview in *al-Quds al-Arabi,* September 10, 1998; *Palestine Times,* October 1998. But when the U.S. State Department put Hamas on its list of terrorist organizations, Rantisi warned, "Hamas will remain a thorn in America's throat and will continue its jihad process until the total liberation of Palestine's soil, from the sea to the river." Reuters, October 10, 1997.
92. Kol Israel, January 25, 1998. Actually, Israel was highly supportive of Clinton.
93. *Yediot Ahronot,* April 13, 1997. He was referring to Madeleine Albright, William Cohen, Dennis Ross, Aaron Miller, and Martin Indyk. Cohen was a convert to Christianity, as were Albright's parents.
94. *Al-Hayat al-Jadida,* October 14 and 30, 1997.
95. *Al-Ayyam,* November 22 1997; *al-Bilad,* July 31, 1997; *Filastin al-Yawm,* August 21, 1997; and *New York Times,* May 18, 1997.
96. *Al-Hayat al-Jadida,* September 17, 1998. The original article is available at <http://www.jmcc.org>.
97. Amr's article appeared in *al-Hayat al-Jadida* on September 20, 1998, and was reprinted in *PR,* September 25, 1998.

98. Fu'ad Abu Hijlih, "We Write While They Shoot," *al-Hayat al-Jadida,* September 21, 1998, reprinted in *PR,* September 25, 1998.
99. Voice of Palestine, February 13, 1995 (*FBIS,* February 14, 1995).
100. On the PA reaction to U.S. friction with Iraq, see Chapter 7. For the PA statement regarding U.S. bombings against targets in Sudan and Afghanistan following attacks on U.S. embassies in Kenya and Tanzania, see *PR,* August 21, 1998.
101. *Al-Sharq al-Awsat,* July 26, 1995 (*FBIS,* July 27, 1995).
102. *Washington Post,* September 30, 1998. See, for example, *New York Times,* January 14, 1996.
103. Washington Post, December 1, 1998; Reuters, December 2, 1998.
104. White House Office of the Press Secretary, "Remarks by the President to the Members of the Palestinian National Council and Other Palestinian Organizations," December 14, 1998.
105. *PR,* December 11, 1998.
106. See Appendixes 2 and 3 on the PLO Executive Committee and Fatah Central Committee for a full analysis of their membership.
107. *PR,* January 16, 1998. Results of polls conducted by the JMCC and the Tami Steinmetz Center for Peace Research during late November and early December 1997.

9. Recognizing Facts, Creating Facts

1. Interview in *Ha'aretz,* November 6, 1998. Compare the conclusion to a statement by Abdallah Hijazi, deputy minister of tourism, who had spent almost thirty years in exile, mostly as a PLO ambassador. He mused, "I dream about bringing to Palestine all the beautiful things I've seen in Europe, the clean streets, the greenery and all that." *PR,* March 27, 1998.
2. On these points, see Chapters 3 and 4.
3. *Al-Wasat,* January 9–15, 1995 (*FBIS,* January 13, 1995).
4. *PR,* September 18, 1998.
5. Reuters, August 19, 1998.
6. Interview with *PR,* September 13, 1996.
7. *Al-Hayat,* September 12, 1995 (*FBIS* September 13, 1995).
8. Ibid.
9. Associated Press, September 6, 1998.
10. *Al-Wasat,* January 9–15, 1995 (*FBIS,* January 13, 1995).
11. *PR,* September 11, 1998.
12. Associated Press, September 6, 1998.
13. "Standing Orders of the Palestinian Legislative Council," Article 3 (*PR,* August 9, 1996).
14. *PR,* November 22, 1996.

15. Arafat's speech at the signing of the 1994 Cairo agreement, in Laqueur and Rubin, *The Israel-Arab Reader*, p. 645.
16. *PR*, July 5, 1996.
17. *PR*, June 28 and July 26, 1996.
18. Article 6, paragraph 2 of the Israel-PLO agreement of May 4, 1994; see Laqueur and Rubin, *The Israel-Arab Reader*, p. 634.
19. United Nations Report A/52/1002, August 4, 1998, and UN Resolution A/RES/52/250, July 7, 1998, Fifty-second Session, Agenda Item 36.
20. Asya Abdul Hadi, "All Dressed Up with No Place To Fly," *Jerusalem Report*, January 31, 1997.
21. *PR*, January 17, 1997; Agence-France Presse, December 22, 1998.
22. *PR*, November 14, 1997.
23. Interview with *Ha'aretz*, November 6, 1998.
24. *Al-Majalla*, November 16, 1997.
25. On PA-PLO relations, see Chapter 5; on PA-Palestinian diaspora relations, see Chapter 7.
26. Quoted in *Jerusalem Post*, November 19, 1997.
27. For a discussion of these processes, see Barry Rubin, *Modern Dictators* (New York, 1987).
28. Abu-Amr, "Pluralism and the Palestinians," p. 85.
29. *Al-Ayyam*, January 17, 1998.
30. For projections on the nature and situation of a Palestinian state, see Mark Heller, *A Palestinian State? The Implications for Israel* (Cambridge, Mass., 1983); M. A. Heller and Sari Nusseibah, *No Trumpets, No Drums: A Two-State Solution of the Israeli Palestinian Conflict* (New York, 1991); and George Abed, *The Economic Viability of a Palestinian State* (Washington, D.C., 1990).
31. See Chapter 7.
32. *PR*, September 11, 1998.
33. Voice of Palestine, August 22, 1995 (*FBIS*, August 23 1995).
34. Interview with *PR*, September 13, 1996.

GLOSSARY

CC	Fatah Central Committee, its highest decision-making body. Under it is the Revolutionary Committee.
CPRS	Center for Palestine Research and Studies
DFLP	Democratic Front for the Liberation of Palestine. Radical nationalist group, member of PLO, opposed Oslo agreements.
EC	PLO Executive Committee, its highest decision-making body. Under it is the Central Council.
FIDA	The Palestine Democratic Party, a breakaway from the DFLP led by Yasir Abd Rabbu, which participated in the PA, though sometimes criticizing its policies.
Insiders	Palestinians who lived wholly or mostly in the West Bank or Gaza Strip between 1967 and 1993.
JMCC	Jerusalem Media Communications Center
LAW	Palestinian Society for the Protection of Human Rights and the Environment
NISP	National Islamic Salvation Party
Outsider	Those Palestinians who spent most of the time between 1967 and 1993 outside the Gaza Strip and West Bank because they were refugees or had left to join the PLO.
PA	Palestinian Authority, used here specifically to designate the executive branch.
PBC	Palestine Broadcasting Corporation

PECDAR	Palestinian Economic Council for Development and Rehabilitation, originally intended to handle incoming aid funds and development projects.
PFLP	Popular Front for the Liberation of Palestine. Radical nationalist group, member of PLO, opposed Oslo agreements.
PFLP-GC	Popular Front for the Liberation of Palestine–General Command, Syrian-backed anti-Arafat group which opposed the Oslo agreements.
PHRMG	Palestinian Human Rights Monitoring Group
PICCR	Palestinian Independent Commission for Citizens' Rights
PLA	Palestine Liberation Army
PLC	Palestinian Legislative Council, the PA's legislative branch.
PLO	Palestine Liberation Organization
PNA	Palestinian National Authority
PNC	Palestine National Council, the PLO's legislative branch.
PPP	Palestine People's Party, the Communist party, which participated in the PA though sometimes criticizing its policies.
UAE	United Arab Emirates
UNRWA	United Nations Relief and Works Agency

BIBLIOGRAPHY

Books

Abdallah, Samir. *Palestinian Economic Council for Development and Construction (PECDAR)* [Arabic]. Nablus, 1994.

Abdo-Zubi, Nahla. *Family, Women, and Social Change in the Middle East: The Palestinian Case.* Toronto, 1987.

Amnesty International. *Report, 1995.* London, 1995.

Awartani, Hisham, Bassam Makhul, Samir Abdallah, Atif Alawna, and Omar Abd al-Raziq. *Evaluation of Paris Agreement: Economic Relations between Israel and the PLO* [Arabic with English text of the agreement]. Nablus, November 1994.

Bar, Shmuel. *The Muslim Brotherhood in Jordan.* Tel Aviv, 1998.

Barghouthi, Mustafa. *Palestinian NGO's and Their Role in Building Civil Society.* Jerusalem, 1994.

Barghuti, Bashir. *The Development of the Palestinian National Movement* [Arabic]. Nablus, 1996.

Center for Palestine Research and Studies, Parliamentary Research Unit. *Committees in the Palestinian Legislative Council: Proposals for Their Development and Restructuring.* Nablus, 1997.

―――― *Comparative Analytical Study of Presidential Veto Power.* Nablus, 1997.

―――― *Evaluation of the Palestinian Legislative Council's First Year, 1996.* Nablus, 1997.

―――― *Palestinians inside Israel and the Peace Process* [Arabic]. Nablus, 1994.

Hamami, Jamal. *Islamists and the Next Phase* [Arabic]. Nablus, 1994.

Hamarneh, Mustafa, Rosemary Hollis, and Khalil Shikaki. *Jordanian-Palestinian Relations: Where To? Four Strategies for the Future.* London, 1997.

Hareven, Alouph. *Retrospect and Prospects: Full and Equal Citizenship?* Tel Aviv, 1998.

Al-Hasan, Hani. *The Relationship between the PLO and PA Institutions* [Arabic]. Nablus, 1996.

Abu Hilal, Ali, and Walid Salim. *National Opposition and National Elections* [Arabic]. Nablus, May 1995.

Jadallah, Muhammad. *Opposition and the Palestinian National Authority* [Arabic]. Nablus, 1994.

Ja'fari, Mahmud. *The Palestinian-Jordanian Trade Agreement* [Arabic]. Nablus, 1997.

Jarbawi, Ali, Ziyad Abu-Amr, Ibrahim Abu-Lughod, and Khalil Shiqaqi. *Palestinian Opposition: Where To?* [Arabic]. Nablus, 1994.

Kazziha, Walid. *Palestine in the Arab Dilemma*. London, 1979.

Khamaysa, Rasim, Basim Makhul, and Adnan Awda, eds. *Conference on Palestinian-Egyptian Economic Relations* [Arabic]. Nablus, 1995.

Landau, Jacob M. As'ad Ghanem, and Alouph Hareven. *The Arab Citizens of Israel towards the Twenty-first Century*. Tel Aviv, 1995.

Laqueur, Walter, and Barry Rubin. *The Israel-Arab Reader*. New York, 1995.

Luft, Gal. *The Palestinian Security Services: Between Police and Army*. Washington, D.C., 1998.

Makhul, Basim. *Cement Trade in the West Bank: A Preliminary Evaluation* [Arabic]. Nablus, 1997.

Al-Malki, Riyad. *Palestinian Opposition: Analysis of Alternatives* [Arabic]. Nablus, 1993.

Mansur, Jamal, and Jamal Salim. *Islamists and Elections* [Arabic]. Nablus, 1995.

Maoz, Moshe. *Palestinian Leadership on the West Bank: The Changing Role of the Mayors under Jordan and Israel*. London, 1984.

Palestinian Economic Research Institute. *Poverty in the West Bank and Gaza Strip*. Jerusalem, 1995.

Palestinian Independent Commission for Citizens' Rights. *Third Annual Report. 1998*. <http://msanews.mynet.net/gateway/piccr/reports.html>.

Plotkin, Lori. *Jordan-Israel Peace: Taking Stock, 1994–1997*. Washington, D.C., 1997.

Qasim, Abd al-Sattar. *The Islamic Movement and the Future of the Opposition* [Arabic]. Nablus, 1996.

Rabbu, Yasir Abd. *Analytical Review of the Reality and Nature of the Palestinian National Authority* [Arabic]. Nablus, 1995.

Al-Rahman, Asad Abd. *Relations between Palestinians and Jordan after the Palestinian-Israeli Declaration of Principles Agreement* [Arabic]. Nablus, 1994.

Rashad, Ahmad. *The Truth about Hamas*. <http://www.iap.org/politics/misc/truth.html>.

Rekhess, Elie, ed. *The Arabs in Israeli Politics: Dilemmas of Identity*. Tel Aviv, 1998.

——— ed. *Arab Politics in Israel: At a Crossroads*. Tel Aviv, 1996.

Robinson, Glenn E., *Building a Palestinian State: The Incomplete Revolution*. Bloomington, Ind., 1997.

Rubin, Barry. *The Arab States and the Palestine Conflict*. Syracuse, N.Y., 1981.
—— *Assessing the New Middle East: Opportunities and Risks*. Tel Aviv, 1995.
—— *The Palestinian Charter: Prospects for Change*. Tel Aviv, 1996.
—— *Revolution Until Victory? The Politics and History of the PLO*. Cambridge, Mass., 1994.
Rubinstein, Danny. *The Mystery of Arafat*. South Royalton, Vt., 1995.
Sahliyeh, Emile F. *In Search of Leadership: West Bank Politics since 1967*. Washington, D.C., 1988.
Said, Nazir Izat, and Rima Hamami. *Research into the Political and Social Trends in Palestine* [Arabic]. Nablus, 1997.
Sayigh, Rosemary. *Too Many Enemies: The Palestinian Experience in Lebanon*. London, 1994.
Sayigh, Yezid. *Armed Struggle and the Search for State*. Oxford, 1997.
Sela, Abraham. *The Decline of the Arab-Israeli Conflict: Middle East Politics and the Quest for Regional Order*. Albany, N.Y., 1997.
Al-Sharq al-Awsat. *Palestinian Elections*. Cairo, 1996.
Shehadeh, Raja. *The Declaration of Principles and the Legal System in the West Bank*. Jerusalem, 1994.
Shiqaqi, Khalil, ed. *Palestinian Elections: Political Environment, Electoral Behavior, Results* [Arabic]. Nablus, 1997.
—— *Transition to Liberal Democracy in Palestine: The Peace Process, the National Reconstruction, and Elections*. Nablus, 1996.
Sullivan, Denis J. *NGO's and Freedom of Association: Palestine and Egypt, a Comparative Analysis*. Jerusalem, 1995.
Ta'amari, Salim. *Political, Economic, and Social Dimensions of the Reintegration of Refugees* [Arabic]. Nablus, 1995.

Articles

Abu-Amr [Abu Amr], Ziyad. "Hamas: A Historical and Political Background." *Journal of Palestine Studies*, Vol. 22, No. 4 (1993), pp. 5–19.
—— "Pluralism and the Palestinians." *Journal of Democracy*, Vol. 7, No. 3 (1996), pp. 83–93.
—— "The Palestinian Legislative Council: A Critical Assessment." *Journal of Palestine Studies*, Vol. 26, No. 4 (Summer 1997), pp. 90–97.
Abu Awda, Adnan. "Jordanian-Palestinian Relations" [Arabic]. *Al-Siyasa al-Filastiniyya*, Vol. 4, No. 14 (Spring 1997).
Abu Bakr, Tawfiq. "The Impact of Netanyahu's Victory on Diaspora Palestinians" [Arabic]. *Al-Siyasa al-Filastiniyya*, Vol. 3, No. 11 (Summer 1996).
Abu Nizar, Sakher [Sakr]. "The Role of Fatah Movement in Shaping the Palestinian Future." April 1994. <http://www.fateh.org>.
Abu Toameh, Khaled. *Jerusalem Report*, January 8, 1998.
—— "Letting His People Go." *Jerusalem Report*, March 5, 1998.

Al-Agha, Zakariyya. Interview in *al-Siyasa al-Filastiniyya,* Vol. 5, No. 19 (Summer 1998).

"Agreement between the Hashemite Kingdom of Jordan and the Palestine Liberation Organization." January 7, 1994. *Palestine-Israel Journal,* Spring 1994.

Arafat, Yasir. Interview in *Journal of Palestine Studies,* Vol. 11, No. 2 (Winter 1982).

Bahatia, Shiham. "Arafat's Torturer's Shock Palestinians." *Guardian Weekly,* September 24, 1995.

Center for Palestine Research and Studies. "Special Poll Voting Behavior of al-Najah University Students: Election Day Poll." Nablus, July 19, 1996.

—— "Voting Patterns to Student Unions in al-Najah and Bir Zayt Universities" [Arabic]. *Al-Siyasa al-Filastiniyya,* Vol. 2, No. 7–8 (Summer–Fall 1995).

Center for Strategic Studies (Amman), "Jordanian-Palestinian Relations: Domestic Dimension" [Arabic]. *Al-Siyasa al-Filastiniyya,* Vol. 3, No. 12 (Fall 1996).

Dajani, Mohammed S. "The Palestinian Authority and Citizenship in the Palestinian Territories." PNA Official Website, <http://www.pna.net/reports/mcitizen.htm>.

Darbub, Leila. "Palestinian Public Opinion and the Peace Process." *Palestine-Israel Journal,* Vol. 3, No. 3–4 (1996), pp. 109–117.

—— "Palestinian Public Opinion Polls on the Peace Process." *Palestine-Israel Journal,* No. 5 (1995), pp. 60–63.

Darwish, Marwan. "The PLO Policy toward the Palestinians in Israel" [Arabic]. *Al-Siyasa al-Filastiniyya,* Vol. 3, No. 9 (Winter 1996).

Efrat, Roni Ben. "The Telltale Silence of the Post-Oslo Palestinian Press." Paper delivered at the conference "A Twenty-first–Century Dialogue: Media's Dark Age?" Athens, May 24–28, 1998.

Finkel-Shlosberg, L. "The Palestinian News Game." *Columbia Journalism Review,* May–June 1996.

Foley, Michael. "Democracy Courtesy Thomas Cook." *Index on Censorship,* 1996.

Gedal, Zoe Danon. "The Doha Summit: A Virtual Conference." Peacewatch No. 147, November 11, 1997.

Gerges, Fawaz A. "Egyptian-Israeli Relations Turn Sour." *Foreign Affairs,* Vol. 74, No. 3 (May–June 1995).

Ghosheh, Ibrahim. "The 1948 Nakba: Facts and Lessons." *Palestine Times,* May 1998.

Habash, Sakr. Interview in *al-Siyasa al-Filastiniyya,* Vol. 5, No. 19 (Summer 1998).

Al-Hajj, Majid. "The Day after the Palestinian State: Arab and Jewish Attitudes in Israel." *Middle East Focus,* Vol. 13, No. 4 (1991), pp. 23–26.

—— "State, Territory and Boundaries: Attitudes and Positions in the Palestine National Movement." Israeli-Palestinian Peace Research Project, *Working Paper Series,* Vol. 2, No. 12 (1991).

Hamami, Rima. "Palestinian NGOs: The Professionalization of Politics in the Absence of Opposition" [Arabic]. *Al-Siyasa al-Filastiniyya,* Vol. 3, No. 10 (Spring 1996).

Abd al-Hamid, Muhammad. "Terrorism: Violence, and 'Suicide Operations.' "
[Arabic]. *Al-Siyasa al-Filastiniyya*, Vol. 5, No. 18 (Spring 1998).
Harb, Ahmad. "Cultural Impact of the Declaration of Principles" [Arabic]. *Al-Siyasa al-Filastiniyya*, Vol. 1, No. 1–2 (Winter–Spring 1994).
Hassassian, Manuel S. "The Transformation in the Political Attitudes in the National Movement" [Arabic]. *Al-Siyasa al-Filastiniyya*, Vol. 2, No. 7–8 (Summer–Fall 1995).
Hilal, Jamal. "The Elections of the Palestinian Legislative Council: A Preliminary Reading of the Results of the Election" [Arabic]. *Al-Siyasa al-Filastiniyya*, Vol. 3, No. 10 (Spring 1996).
——— "Features of Poverty in Palestine" [Arabic]. *Al-Siyasa al-Filastiniyya*, Vol. 3, No. 12 (Fall 1996).
——— "The PLO and the PA: The Upside-Down Equation" [Arabic]. *Al-Siyasa al-Filastiniyya*, Vol. 4, No. 15–16 (Summer–Autumn 1997).
Hummami, Rema. "NGO's: The Professionalization of Politics." *Journal of Race and Class*, 1995.
Hussari, Ruba. "Arafat's Law." *Index on Censorship*, March 21, 1996.
——— "The Position of Palestine Islamists on the Palestine-Israel Accord." *The Muslim World*, Vol. 84, No. 1–2 (1994), pp. 127–154.
Islamic Jihad—Al-Aqsa Battalions. "Presentation of Candidacy for the Elections to the PLC" [Arabic], 1996.
Jad, Islah. "Palestinian Women's Movement and the Elections" [Arabic]. *Al-Siyasa al-Filastiniyya*, Vol. 3, No. 10 (Spring 1996).
Jarrar, Naja. "Palestinian Refugees and Civil Rights" [Arabic]. *Al-Siyasa al-Filastiniyya*, Vol. 4, No. 13 (Winter 1997).
Jarbawi, Ali. "Separation: Israel's Palestinian Ghettos" [Arabic]. *Al-Siyasa al-Filastiniyya*, Vol. 2, No. 5 (Winter 1995).
Khouri [Khuri], Rami. "A View from the Arab World," June 16, 1998. <http://msanews.mynet.net/ Scholars/Khouri/>.
Kuba'a, Taysir. "The Relations between the PLO and PA" [Arabic]. *Al-Siyasa al-Filastiniyya*, Vol. 4, No. 15–16 (Summer–Autumn 1997).
Laskier, Michael. "The Israel-Maghreb Connection: Past Contacts, Future Prospects." *Jerusalem Letter/Viewpoints*, No. 355, April 1, 1997.
Palestinian Society for the Protection of Human Rights and the Environment (LAW). Human Rights Annual Report, 1997, March 29, 1998.
——— "Palestinian Legislative Council Basic Law Draft Resolution, Third Reading Passed October 2, 1997."
——— Report of the Monitoring Unit on the Elections for the PLC, January 23, 1996.
Litvak, Meir, and Elie Rekhess. "Palestinian Issues." In Ami Ayalon, ed., *Middle East Contemporary Survey*, Vol. 17. Boulder, Colo., 1993.
——— "Palestinian Affairs." In Ami Ayalon and Bruce Maddy-Weitzman, eds., *Middle East Contemporary Survey*, Vol. 18. Boulder, Colo., 1994.

———— "Palestinian Affairs." In Bruce Maddy-Weitzman, ed., *Middle East Contemporary Survey*, Vol. 19. Boulder, Colo., 1995.

———— "Palestinian Affairs." In Bruce Maddy-Weitzman, ed., *Middle East Contemporary Survey*, Vol. 20. Boulder, Colo., 1996.

———— "Palestinian Affairs." In Bruce Maddy-Weitzman, ed., *Middle East Contemporary Survey*, Vol. 21. Boulder, Colo., 1997.

Malki, Majdi. "Characteristics of the Palestinian Student Movement: Bir Zayt University Elections" [Arabic]. *Al-Siyasa al-Filastiniyya*, Vol. 3, No. 11 (Summer 1996).

———— "Student Elections at Bir Zayt University" [Arabic]. *Al-Siyasa al-Filastiniyya*, Vol. 4, No. 14 (Spring 1997).

Al-Malki, Riad [Riyad]. "The Palestinian Opposition and Final-Status Negotiations." *Palestine-Israel Journal*, Vol. 3, No. 3–4 (1996), pp. 95–99.

Mamdu, Nufil. "The Growth and Development of the Relations between the PLO and the PA" [Arabic]. *Al-Siyasa al-Filastiniyya*, Vol. 4, No. 15–16 (Summer–Autumn 1997).

Masri, Majida. "Palestinian Women's Movement" [Arabic]. *Al-Siyasa al-Filastiniyya*, Vol. 4, No. 14 (Spring 1997).

Masria, Norma. "Reasons for the Failure of Plans to Resettle Refugees" [Arabic]. *Al-Siyasa al-Filastiniyya*, Vol. 4, No. 13 (Winter 1997), No. 355 (April 1, 1997).

Moughrabi, Fouad, and Elia Zurayiq. "Palestinians on the Peace Process." *Journal of Palestine Studies*, Vol. 21, No. 1 (1991), pp. 36–53.

Al-Natsha, Rafiq. Interview in *al-Siyasa al-Filastiniyya*, Vol. 5, No. 19 (Summer 1998).

Othman, Ziyad. "The [Women's] Model Palestinian Parliament: Gender and Legislation between Renewal and Stereotyping" [Arabic]. *Al-Siyasa al-Filastiniyya*, Vol. 5, No. 19 (Summer 1998).

Palestinian Legislative Council. "Self-Evaluation Report," October 30–31, 1996.

Palestinian National Authority. "1998 Second Quarterly Monitoring Report of Donors' Assistance," June 30, 1998. PNA Official Website, <http://www.pna.net/reports/mcitizen.htm>.

Qadamani-Darwish, Basma. "The Palestinian Authority and the Opposition" [Arabic]. *Al-Siyasa al-Filastiniyya*, Vol. 2, No. 6 (Spring 1995).

Qatamish, Ribhi. "The Crisis of the Palestinian Opposition" [Arabic]. *Al-Siyasa al-Filastiniyya*, Vol. 5, No. 19 (Summer 1998).

Rahman, As'ad Abdal-. "The Evolution of Palestinian-Jordanian Relations" [Arabic]. *Al-Siyasa al-Filastiniyya*, Vol. 3, No. 10 (Spring 1996).

Al-Raziq, Umar Abd. "Analysis of the Results of Al-Najah University's Student Elections" [Arabic]. *Al-Siyasa al-Filastiniyya*, Vol. 4, No. 13 (Winter 1997).

Rekhess, Elie. "Arabs in a Jewish State: Images vs. Realities." *Middle East Insight*, January–February 1990.

Robinson, Glenn E. "The Growing Authoritarianism of the Arafat Regime." *Survival*, Vol. 39, No. 2 (Summer 1997), pp. 42–56.

Ross, Lauren G. "Palestinians: Yes to Negotiations, Yes to Violence." *Middle East Quarterly*, Vol. 2, No. 2 (1995), pp. 15–24.

Roy, Sara. "U.S. Economic Aid to the West Bank and Gaza Strip: The Politics of Peace." *Middle East Policy*, Vol. 4, No. 4 (October 1996).

Rubin, Barry. "External Influences on Israel's 1996 Election." In Dan Elazar and Shmuel Sandler, eds., *Israel's 1996 Election*. London, 1998.

—— "Is the Arab-Israeli Conflict Over?" *Middle East Quarterly*, Autumn 1996.

—— "Notes on Turkey-Israel Relations." *Middle East Review of International Affairs (MERIA) News*. No. 1997/7 (July 1997). <http://www.biu.ac.il/ SOC/ besa/meria.htm>.

Rubinstein, Danny. "Bio Sketch: Faruq Qaddumi, the PLO's #2." *Middle East Quarterly*, March 1996, pp. 29–32.

Saydam, Jamila. Interview in *al-Siyasa al-Filastiniyya*, Vol. 5, No. 19 (Summer 1998).

Sayigh, Yezid. "Fatah: The First Twenty Years." *Journal of Palestine Studies*, Vol. 13, No. 4 (Summer 1984).

Schulz, William F. "Palestinian Abuses: The Amnesty Report." *The New York Review of Books*, February 6, 1997.

Abd al-Shafi, Haydar. "Excerpts from His Letter of Resignation" [Arabic]. *Al-Siyasa al-Filastiniyya*, Vol. 5, No. 17 (Winter 1998).

Shiblak, Abbas. "The Peace Process and Its Implications for the Refugees" [Arabic]. *Al-Siyasa al-Filastiniyya*, Vol. 2, No. 6 (Spring 1995).

Shiqaqi, Khalil. "The Future of Democracy in Palestine" [Arabic]. *Al-Siyasa al-Filastiniyya*, Vol. 4, No. 15–16 (Summer–Autumn 1997).

—— "Jordanian-Palestinian Relations and the Process of National Reconstruction" [Arabic]. *Al Siyasa al Filastiniyya*, Vol. 3, No. 10 (Spring 1996).

—— "The Peace Process, National Reconstruction, and the Transition to Democracy in Palestine." *Journal of Palestine Studies*, Vol. 25, No. 2 (Winter 1996).

Al-Siyasa al-Filastiniyya. Panel Discussion, "The Palestinian Opposition: Where To?" [Arabic]. *Al-Siyasa al-Filastiniyya*, Vol. 5, No. 19 (Summer 1998).

Sourani [Surani], Raji. "Human Rights in the Palestinian Authority: A Status Report." *Peacewatch* No. 168, June 10, 1998.

Al-Tal, Tarik. "Myth and Misunderstanding in Jordanian-Palestinian Relations" [Arabic]. *Al-Siyasa al-Filastiniyya*, Vol. 3, No. 12 (Fall 1996).

Tamimi, Azzam S. "The Legitimacy of Palestinian Resistance: An Islamist Perspective." Paper presented to the Seventh Annual Conference of the Center for Policy Analysis on Palestine, Washington, D.C., September 11, 1998.

United States Information Service. "The Wye River Memorandum Signed at the White House." Washington, D.C., October 23, 1998.

UNSCO. "Report on Economic and Social Conditions in the West Bank and Gaza Strip," Fall 1996, April 1997, October 1997, and Spring 1998. <http:// www.arts.mcgill.ca/mepp/unsco/unfront.html>.

Zuhira, Kamal. "Relations between the Executive and Legislative Branches: The Expectations and the Realities" [Arabic]. *Al-Siyasa al-Filastiniyya,* Vol. 5, No. 17 (Winter 1998).

Periodicals

al-Akhbar
Amnesty International Reports
Associated Press
al-Ayyam
al-Bilad
Bir Zayt University Homepage <http://www.birzeit.edu>
Christian Science Monitor
CPRS Public Opinion Polls
Davar
Filastin al-Muslima
Financial Times
Foreign Broadcast Information Service (FBIS), Daily Report
Globes
Ha'aretz
al-Hayat
al-Hayat al-Jadida
Jerusalem Post
Jerusalem Report
JMCC Public Opinion Polls
Joint Publications Research Service (JPRS)
Journal of Palestine Studies
Ma'ariv
The Middle East
The Middle East Review for International Affairs (MERIA)
Mideast Dispatch
Mideast Mirror
New York Times
The Official Palestinian Authority Website <www.pna.net>
Palestine Report (PR)
Palestine Times
Palestinian Independent Commission for Citizens' Rights Newsletter The Palestine Human Rights Monitor
Palestinian Society for the Protection of Human Rights and the Environment (LAW) news releases and Annual Reports
Peacewatch reports
al-Quds

Reuters
al-Sharq al-Awsat
Wall Street Journal
Washington Post
Yediot Ahronot

INDEX

al-Abadla, Qusay, 67

Abbas, Mahmud (Abu Mazin), 21, 23, 27, 97–98, 112, 164, 168–169, 172, 173, 176, 200–201; corruption and, 40–41; on peace process, 188, 190

Abd al-Aziz, Ali Shahin, 19

Abd al-Aziz al-Rantisi, 60, 117, 121, 167, 264n91

Abd al-Fatah Hamid, 180

Abd al-Hadi, Nasir, 74

Abd al-Hakim Zurayqi, 82

Abd al-Hamid al-Qudsi, 180

Abd al-Jawad Salah, 4, 17, 20, 39, 90, 179; elections and, 28, 30

Abd al-Khadir, Hatim, 197

Abdallah, Samir, 174

Abd al-Latif Ghayth, 116

Abd al-Majid Dudin, 60–61, 62

Abd al-Qadir, Asad, 28

Abd al-Qadir, Hatim, 75, 110

Abd al-Rahim, Tayyib, 21, 28, 29, 130–131, 171–172, 173

Abd al-Rahman, Ahmad, 21

Abd al-Rahman, Asad, 84, 97

Abd al-Rahman Zabin, 62

Abd al-Raziq, Hisham, 106, 107

Abd al-Razzaq Yahya, 21

Abd al-Sala'am, Amin, 66–67

Abd al-Saud, Salim, 124

Abd al-Shafi, Haydar, 28, 30, 36, 43, 90, 115, 117, 188

Abd Rabbu, Yasir, 17, 19, 22, 92; corruption and, 41; on PA goals, 101–102; on peace process, 141; on Arab states, 254n13

Abu Akar, Nidal, 102

Abu Ala. See Khuri, Ahmad

Abu al-Nada, Hashim, 40

Abu Amr, Ziyad, 137, 168, 247n24; on elections, 27; on opposition, 29, 30–31; on Arafat, 34, 36, 49, 197; on PLC, 35–36, 43, 51; on legislature, 39, 229n5, 229–230n6; on pluralism, 48; on Islam, 52; on PA transition, 54, 55, 93; on security forces, 109

Abu Arrous, Nasir, 60

Abu Ayyash, Radwan, 21

Abu Ghazala, Hatim, 5

Abu Marzuk, Musa, 116, 182

Abu Midayn, Frayh, 18, 28, 29, 33, 67, 120, 128; Basic Law and, 36; on opposition groups, 116–117; on Arab states, 138; on United States, 182

Abu Musama, Sa'id Salam, 59

Abu Nidal, 146, 152

Abu Rahma, Fayiz, 60, 67

Abu Sabha, Musa, 69
Abu Salam, 180–181
Abu Wardah, Muhammad, 135–136
Abu Zayida, Sufyan, 1, 6, 120, 164–166, 171
Abu Ziyad, Ziyad, 5–6
al-Agha, Zakariyya, 22, 23, 90, 98
Ahmad, Tallal, 124
al-Ahmad, Azzam, 50
al-Alami, Mahir, 77
Ali Mash'al, Sharif (Abbas Zaki), 23, 28
Amal militia, 158
al-Amayra, Khalid, 80
Amira, Hanna, 138
Amr, Nabil, 17, 29, 98, 146, 183
al-Aqsa Battalions, 124, 249n65
al-Aqsa mosque, 15, 43, 80, 81, 150
Arab Hotels Company, 74
Arab Journalists' Union, 146
Arab League, 95, 140, 141–142
Arab Liberation Front, 97
Arab states, 254n13; Arafat and, 138, 144, 148; PLO and, 139–141; Israel and, 140, 141–142, 145; financial aid and, 141, 143–145; peace process and, 141–142, 143; Gulf states, 142, 144; summits and, 143, 145; PA rivals and, 145–146; United States and, 146–147, 148; Dropout states, 147, 154–155; Radical states, 147, 151–154, 198–199; Peace Camp states, 147–148; Fatah and, 155, 157, 158; state-building and, 198–200. See also individual countries
Arafat, Musa, 103
Arafat, Suha, 196
Arafat, Yasir, 1, 8, 12, 16, 25; leadership style, 4–7, 13, 21, 23–25, 46, 47, 93, 192–194; Hamas and, 13, 58, 81, 116–117, 124, 130, 181; Netanyahu and, 14, 175, 176; cabinet and, 16–20, 32, 38; PLC and, 28–30, 32–33, 230n17; no-confidence vote and, 33; on democracy, 34; Basic Law and, 36; supporters, 47, 49; human rights and, 58, 59, 65; corruption and, 69; on economy, 71; media and, 75, 77, 78; Christians and, 82; popular support for, 85–86; elites and, 88; Outsiders and, 88–89; on PLO, 92–93; PLO Charter and, 96; Executive Committee and, 97; Fatah and, 97, 98–99; security forces and, 108, 109, 110; opposition and, 124, 129, 137; Islam and, 124–125; Insiders and, 126–127; Outsiders and, 126–127; on Arab states, 138; Arab states and, 144, 148; Iraq and, 153; refugees and, 157; Israeli view of, 166; on peace process, 170, 175, 191; on terrorism, 170; on Israel, 172–173; United States and, 181–182; state-building and, 187–188; successors, 194–196
Arikat, Sa'ib, 18, 28, 29
al-Asad, Hafiz, 146
Asfur, Hasan, 21, 29, 36, 176, 191
Ashrawi, Hanan, 20, 30, 90
Awadallah, Adil, 136
Awadallah, Imad, 136
al-Awda, 68, 77
Awni, 107
Ayn al-Hilwa camp, 158
al-Ayyam, 78
Ayyash, Yahya, 103, 110, 135
al-Azhar University, 63
Azzam, Nafidh, 116, 117

Baba, Yusuf Isma'il, 62–63
Bahr, Ahmad, 131
al-Bahr Company, 40
Balata refugee camp, 103
Bal'awi, Hakim, 23, 29
Balusha, Zakariyya, 69
Banks, 74
Barak, Ehud, 173
al-Bardawil, Salah, 125
al-Barghuti, Bashir, 19
al-Barghuti, Hafiz, 80, 182
al-Barghuti, Marwan, 23, 30, 33, 51, 66, 90, 91, 153; as Insider, 102–103, 106

Basic Law, 28, 30, 33, 36–39, 195
Bayt Lid, 134, 174
Ben Baruch, Shmuel, 60
Ben-Gurion, David, 165
Bethlehem University, 114
al-Bilad, 67, 80
Bir Zayt University students, 66, 67, 102, 114
Bishtawi, Mahmud, 60
al-Bitawi, Hamid, 179–180
Buwayz, Faris, 158

Cabinet, 16–20, 32–33, 38
Cairo agreement, 11
Center for Palestine Research and Studies (CPRS), 44
Central Council (PLO), 156
Central Intelligence Agency (CIA), 184
Charter (Hamas), 120–121, 122
Charter, Palestinian National, 10, 94, 96, 152–153, 242n38
Charter (Hamas), 120–121, 122
Checkpoints, 2, 31
Chirac, Jacques, 181
Christians, 27, 81–82, 114
CIA (Central Intelligence Agency), 184
Citizenship, 71, 236n1
Civil police, 110
Civil society, 54, 82–83, 229–230n6
Clinton, Bill, 182, 184
Closures, 12, 58, 72–74, 95, 134, 135
Communist Party, 161
Constitution, 6–7
Corruption, 39–41, 67–69
Counterterrorism, 54
Court system, 43, 63, 66, 67
CPRS (Center for Palestine Research and Studies), 44

Dahlan, Muhammad, 108, 110–112
Dahlan, Nahid, 64
Dajani, Muhammad, 2
Darwish, Abdallah Nimr, 131, 161
Darwish, Marwan, 161

Darwish, Muhammad, 260n124
al-Dassuki, Mahir, 180
Declaration of Independence, 192
Democracy, 28, 34, 52, 91, 106, 107, 168, 197; pluralism, 48–49, 112
Democratic Front for the Liberation of Palestine (DFLP), 19, 20, 24, 50, 97, 124
Demographics, 72
DFLP. See Democratic Front for the Liberation of Palestine
District Court, 66
Dome of the Rock, 150
Dropout states, 147, 154–155

East Bank, 159–160
East Jerusalem, 10, 11, 14–15, 147, 191; PA activities in, 21, 83; elections and, 27; restrictions on travel, 72
Economic Committee (PLC), 40
Economy, 71–74, 127
Egypt, 48, 139–140, 143, 147–148, 172, 180, 199
Election Law, 32, 49–50
Elections: Palestinian Legislative Council, 6, 11, 27–28, 227n44; Israeli, 14, 177; Fatah and, 27–31, 50; independents, 29–30, 35, 50–51; Arafat's leadership and, 47, 98; media coverage, 50–51; student groups, 114–115; Hamas and, 135–136
Elites, 17–18; peace process and, 90, 91, 104, 105; leadership and, 91–94; democracy and, 107; institutional roles, 112–113. See also Insiders; Outsiders
Elscint, 149
Employment, 73, 74
Europe, 69, 181
Executive branch, 21, 31–32, 38–39
Executive Committee (PLO), 16, 17, 20–22, 92, 94; Oslo II and, 95–96, 185

Fahd, King, 139
al-Faluji, Imad, 19, 78, 123, 124–125

Fatah, 4, 6–7; Outsiders and, 17–19, 185; elections and, 27–31, 50; civil society issues and, 54; in Gaza Strip, 89–90; Arafat and, 97, 98–99; peace process and, 99; discipline, 104; Insiders and, 107, 185; students and, 114–115; Arab states and, 155, 157, 158. *See also* Fatah Central Committee; Palestine Liberation Organization

Fatah Central Committee, 6, 16, 17, 21–23, 32, 92, 97, 99

Fatah Hawks, 64, 101

Fatuh, Rawhi, 225n9

FIDA. *See* Palestine Democratic Party

Finance Ministry, 68

Financial aid, 12, 72, 141, 143–145, 184

Fityani, Rashid, 62

Force-17, 110

France, 181

Franji, Abdallah, 22

Garoudy, Roger, 17

Gaza Bar Association, 60

Gaza Community Mental Health Program, 63

Gaza International Airport, 193

Gaza Strip, 1, 2, 8, 10; elections and, 27; closures, 58; Islamic groups and, 89–90

General Monitoring Commission, 68

Ghawsha, Ibrahim, 120, 122, 126, 132, 139, 167, 259n102

Ghawsha, Samir, 17, 19, 20

al-Ghusayn, Jawad, 21

Giacaman, George, 53

al-Gol, Adnan, 61

Gold, Dore, 32, 142

Gulf states, 142, 144

Habash, George, 85, 99–101, 119

Habash, Sakr, 112

Habbal, Khalid, 62

Hadaya, Ibrahim, 64–65

Hadaya, Jamil, 65

al-Hakawati Theater, 193

Hamad, Ghazi, 125–126

Hamas, 24–25, 31, 50, 262n44; terrorism by, 12–13, 46, 58, 59–62, 65, 111, 127–128, 130–137; Arafat and, 13, 58, 116–117, 124, 130, 181; cabinet and, 17, 19; arrests of members, 32, 80, 130–132; popular support and, 85–86, 114; in Gaza Strip, 89–90; security forces and, 109–110; students and, 114–115; Charter, 120–121, 122; ideology, 120–124, 178; PLO and, 122–124, 126; defectors, 124–125; dialogues with PA, 129–131, 250n103; elections and, 135–136; Arab states and, 146; Jordan and, 150; United States and, 153, 182, 264n91

Hammami, Jamal, 131

Har Homa, 5

Hasan, Crown Prince, 149

al-Hasan, Hani, 9, 90, 99, 156, 254n13

Hawwa, Jamal, 193

al-Hayat al-Jadida, 77, 78, 79, 80, 173, 178, 179; on United States, 182, 183

Hebron, 11, 12, 14, 15, 43, 114

Hebron negotiations, 15, 16

Hebron University, 115

Higher Fatah Committee of the West Bank, 65, 102

Higher State Security Court, 59

Hijazi, Abdallah, 265n1

Hilal, Jamal, 94

Hirsch, Moshe, 177

Hizbullah, 158, 159

Holocaust, 178, 179

Human rights: repression, 25, 45–46; security forces and, 47, 56–59, 69; PLO and, 47–48; Israel and, 53–54, 58–59, 180, 234n90, 260n2; women's issues, 54–56; arrests of opposition groups, 54–67, 62–63, 166; activists, 63–65; media and, 66, 78–79. *See also* Terrorism

al-Hurani, Abdallah, 21, 180

Husayn, King, 142, 148–149, 150, 160

Husayn, Saddam, 10, 152, 153

al-Husayni, Faysal, 20–21, 22, 23, 90, 98, 112; as Insider, 105, 195
Hussari, Ruba, 76

Id, Bassam, 79
Independents, 29–30, 35, 50–51, 224n68
Insiders, 18, 20, 23, 33, 82, 87; intifada and, 89, 100, 102, 103–105; criticism of PA, 89–90; occupation, view of, 91–92; Executive Committee and, 97; disillusionment, 102; leadership, 126; Arafat and, 126–127. *See also* Outsiders
Interim Autonomy Agreement, 11, 27
Interior Ministry, 17
International Federation of Airports, 193
Intifada, 10, 19, 22, 64, 65; refugees and, 84; Insiders/Outsiders and, 89, 100, 102, 103–105; leadership and, 107–108
Iran, 146, 152, 158–159
Iran-Iraq war, 140
Iraq, 10, 141, 144, 151, 152–154
Isa, Bassam, 61
Isa, Shawqi, 64, 66
Islam, 36–37, 52, 81; pro-Arafat parties, 124–125. *See also* Hamas; Islamic Jihad
Islamic Conference Organization, 146
Islamic Group, 115
Islamic Jihad, 24, 25, 32, 50, 249n65; terrorism in Israel, 59, 61, 134; students and, 114–115; opposition to PA, 117, 118; popular support for, 119; Arab states and, 146
Islamic Resistance Movement. *See* Hamas
Islamic University of Hebron, 115
Isma'il, Nidal, 67–68
Israel, 49; Soviet immigrants to, 10; withdrawal from occupied territories, 10–12; closures and, 12, 58, 72–74, 95, 134, 135; Jewish extremists, 14;

parliament, 43; human rights and, 53–54, 58–59, 234n90, 260n2; security forces and, 57–58; terrorism against, 58–62, 118, 127–128, 134; supporters, 62; corruption and, 69; economy and, 72–73; Arab states and, 140, 141–142, 145; economic boycott against, 145; Iraq and, 153–154; Palestinians in, 160–161; PLO view of, 162; PA view of, 163–164; view of Arafat, 166; PA opposition to, 178; human rights and, 180
Israeli Supreme Court, 43
Israel Radio, 81
al-Istiqlal, 78, 117
Iyad, Abu, 156
Izz al-Din al-Qassam brigades, 115, 116

Jabali, Ghazi, 61, 64, 110, 187, 195
Jabr, Haj Isma'il, 154
Jalayita, Sulayman Musa Ata, 64
Jericho, 10–11, 12
Jerusalem. *See* East Jerusalem
Jerusalem Media Communications Center (JMCC), 14, 41–42
Jews, historical context, 178, 179, 260n1, 263n63
Jihad, Abu, 19
Jihad, Muhammad, 99, 100
JMCC (Jerusalem Media Communications Center), 14, 41–42
Jordan, 48, 142, 148–151, 199; media and, 77, 80–81; refugees in, 159–160, 197
Jordan-Israel peace treaty, 78, 150
Jordan-PLO agreement (1994), 149–150
Jum'a, Nasir, 101
Jumayyil, Mahmud, 64, 101

Kamil, Ibrahim, 143
Kanafani, Marwan, 32, 118, 127–128, 197
Kan'an, Said, 83
Kar'in, Ibrahim, 98

Khadir, Husam, 30, 65, 103–105, 106
Khalaf, Salah (Abu Iyad), 159
Khalifa, Kamal, 61
Khalil, Samiha, 50–51
Khalil al-Wazir Secondary School, 75
Khamena'i, Ayatollah Ali, 146
al-Khatib, Ghassan, 42, 53, 79, 184, 194
al-Khatib, Umar, 139
Khayan, Ali, 75–76
Khomayni, Ayatollah Ruhollah, 119
Khuri, Ahmad (Abu Ala), 1, 16, 17, 20, 23, 72, 159; Arafat and, 6–7, 20, 24, 34–35, 90, 91; elections and, 28, 30, 51; corruption and, 41; on peace process, 190–191; as possible successor, 194–195
Khuri, Rami, 70
Khutab, Daud, 42
Koor Corporation, 143
Kuwait, 10, 141, 144, 154, 155

Lahham, Rana, 82
LAW. See Palestinian Society for the Protection of Human Rights and the Environment
Leadership: top-down, 49; elites and, 91–94; intifada and, 107–108. See also Arafat, Yasir; Democracy
Lebanon, 140, 151; refugees in, 157–158, 197
Legislation, 31–33; Islamic Doctrine and, 36–37. See also Palestinian Legislative Council
Levitzky, Nomi, 164–166, 171
Lewinsky, Monica, 182
Libya, 144
Likud Party, 14, 32, 171, 172, 177
Local Committee Councils Election Law, 33

Makda, Munit, 158
al-Masri, Hani, 127
al-Masri, Mahir, 18, 28, 29
Media, 38, 42–43, 75–76, 180–181; re-
pression of, 42, 57, 76–77; election coverage, 50–51; human rights and, 66; newspapers, 77–78; human rights and, 78–79; propaganda, 79–80; credibility, 80–81; opposition and, 125–126
Military, 109, 196
Ministry of Sports and Youth, 41
Ministry of Waqf and Religious Affairs, 81, 179
Mish'al, Khalid, 120, 121–122, 182
Mordechai, Yitzhak, 143
Mubarak, Hosni, 139, 142, 143, 145, 148
Muhsin, Samih, 64
Musallami, Abu Nidal, 124
Muslih, Azzam, 64
Muslim Brotherhood, 117, 119
al-Musmar, Khalid, 182

Nablus, 83, 101, 103
al-Nahar, 77–78
al-Najah University, 61, 114
al-Nashashibi, Muhammad Zuhdi, 17, 18, 68
Nasr, Maha, 54
National Dialogue Office, 124–125
National Islamic Salvation Party (NISP), 125, 249n71
Nationalism, 8, 71, 122, 192
al-Natsha, Rafiq, 17, 99
Naveh, Danny, 153
Nawfal, Mamduh, 156
Nazis, 178, 179, 263n63
Nazzal, Muhammad, 115–116
Negotiations Directorate, 21
Netanyahu, Benjamin, 11, 14–16, 58, 86, 111, 127; Arab states and, 142, 143, 148; Hamas and, 167; peace process and, 171, 173, 175, 176, 190
Neteuri Karta Jewish sect, 177
NISP. See National Islamic Salvation Party
Nizar, Abu, 99
No-confidence motions, 32, 33, 66

Non-government organizations, 55, 231n40
Norway, 144

Occupied territories, 10–12. *See also* East Jerusalem; Gaza Strip; West Bank
Opposition groups, 3, 12–13, 24–26, 50; arrests of, 62–63, 166; popular support for, 114–116, 118–119; state-building and, 116–117, 128–129; Islamic radicals, 118–119; Arafat and, 124, 129, 137; media and, 125–126. *See also* Hamas; Islamic Jihad
Organization for African Unity, 95
Orient House, 21, 105
Oslo agreements, 1–2, 5, 10–11, 15, 38, 143, 149, 157–158, 176
Oslo II agreement, 85, 86, 95–96, 185
Outsiders, 20, 22, 47, 82, 87; Fatah and, 17–19, 185; corruption and, 69; Arafat and, 88–89; intifada and, 89, 100, 102, 103–105; criticism of PA, 89–90; occupation, view of, 91–92; leadership, 126; Arafat and, 126–127. *See also* Insiders

PA. *See* Palestinian Authority
Palestine: as partial state, 3, 6; economy, 71–72; demographics, 72; independence day, 192
Palestine Broadcasting Corporation (PBC), 75
Palestine Democratic Party (FIDA), 17, 19, 119, 124
Palestine Liberation Army (PLA), 109
Palestine Liberation Front, 97
Palestine Liberation Organization (PLO), 1, 2, 118, 129, 249n65; leadership style, 4–5; splits within, 7; worsening circumstances, 9–10; Executive Committee, 16, 17, 20–22, 92, 94–96, 185; Basic Law and, 36; refugees and, 83–84; structure, 92–93; popular view of, 93–94; Charter, 96; Hamas and, 122–124, 126; Arab states and, 139–

141; Central Council, 156; view of Israel, 162; United States and, 181–182. *See also* Fatah
Palestine National Council (PNC), 9, 28, 94, 96–97; Declaration of Independence, 192
Palestine People's Party (PPP), 19, 51, 119
Palestine Report, 14
Palestinian Airlines, 193
Palestinian Authority (PA): transitional epoch, 1–2, 7–9, 51–55, 93; critics of, 3, 12–13; internal politics, 5–6, 16; cabinet, 16–20; advisers, 21; executive branch, 21, 31–32, 38–39; repression and, 25; Election Commission, 27; president, 38–39; corruption and, 39–41, 67–69; expectations of, 51–54; financial aid to, 72; popular support for, 84–86; leadership, 91–93; stability, 101; local politics and, 107; state-building and, 128–129; dialogues with Hamas, 129–131, 250n103; view of Israel, 163, 178; view of United States, 182–183. *See also* Executive Committee; Fatah Central Committee; Palestine National Council; Palestinian Legislative Council
Palestinian Center for Human Rights, 53, 74
Palestinian Civil Aviation Authority, 193
Palestinian Company for Trade Services, 40
Palestinian Economic Council for Development and Rehabilitation (PECDAR), 6
Palestinian High Court, 63
Palestinian Human Rights Monitoring Group (PHRMG), 80
Palestinian Independent Commission for Citizens' Rights (PICCR), 56–57, 63, 66
Palestinian Journalists' Union, 146
Palestinian Legislative Council (PLC), 1;

Palestinian Legislative Council (*cont.*) elections, 6, 11, 27–28, 227n44; cabinet, 16–20, 32–33; executive branch, 21, 31–32, 38–39; elections, 27–28; Arafat and, 28–30, 32–33, 230n17; divisions within, 29–31; legislative proposals and, 31–32, 36–37; achievements, 34–35; criticism of, 35–36; poll ratings, 41–42; resolutions, 42–43

Palestinian Model Parliament on Women, 55

Palestinian National Authority, 192

Palestinian National Charter, 10, 94, 96, 152–153, 242n38

Palestinian National Fund, 21

Palestinian National Theater, 193

Palestinians: expectations of, 51–54; refugees, 83–84, 91, 103, 108, 155–160, 191–192, 197; in Israel, 160–161. *See also* Insiders; Outsiders

Palestinian Society for the Protection of Human Rights and the Environment (LAW), 36, 53, 63, 64

Palestinian Supreme Court, 66, 67

Palestinian Women's Federation, 54–55

Pan-Arab ideology, 8, 37, 95, 192

Parliament, 31, 96

PBC (Palestine Broadcasting Corporation), 75

Peace Camp states, 147–148

Peace Now, 166, 167

Peace process, 13–16, 164–169; sovereignty and, 31, 188–189; popular support for, 84–87; Palestinian reinterpretation of, 86–87, 168–169; elites and, 90, 91, 104, 105; Fatah and, 99; Arab states and, 141–142, 143; Syria and, 145, 146, 148, 152, 199–200; Arafat on, 170, 175, 191; progress of, 189–190; concessions, 191–192. *See also* Oslo agreements; Wye agreement

PECDAR (Palestinian Economic Council for Development and Rehabilitation), 6

People's Rights, 64

Peres, Shimon, 14, 15, 166, 174–175

Petrol Board, 39, 40

PFLP. *See* Popular Front for the Liberation of Palestine

PHRMG (Palestinian Human Rights Monitoring Group), 80

PICCR. *See* Palestinian Independent Commission for Citizens' Rights

Planning Ministry, 1, 8

PLC. *See* Palestinian Legislative Council

PLO. *See* Palestine Liberation Organization

Pluralism, 48–49, 112

PNC. *See* Palestine National Council

Polytechnic College, 114–115

Popular Front for the Liberation of Palestine (PFLP), 20, 24, 31, 50, 61, 97, 119

Popular Front for the Liberation of Palestine–General Command (PFLP-GC), 124

PPP. *See* Palestine People's Party

Preventive security, 61, 62, 64, 77, 80, 110–112, 196, 245n96

Protocols of the Elders of Zion, The, 80, 121

Public opinion, 41–42, 45–46

Qaddumi, Faruq, 94–96, 146, 185, 194–197, 242n34

Qadhafi, Muammar, 156

Qatar, 144

Qawasma, Ali, 41

al-Qazzaz, Yusuf, 169

al-Qidra, Khalid, 63, 64, 66

al-Quds, 77, 79, 179

al-Quds hospital, 158

al-Quds University, 42

Qumayl, Muhammad, 60

Quraysh, Salman, 62

Rabin, Leah, 168, 174

Rabin, Yitzhak, 10, 13, 95, 100, 118, 174; peace process and, 164, 169, 171

Radical states, 147, 151–154, 198–199
Radio Monte Carlo, 81
al-Rajjub, Jibril, 64, 69, 108, 110–112, 116
Ramallah, 83
Ramallah Appellate Court, 66–67
Ramat Gan, 134
Ramlawi, Nabil, 180
al-Rashidiyya camp, 158
Real estate dealers, 62–63
Reformers, 51–52
Refugees, 83–84, 91, 103, 108, 155–157, 191–192; in Lebanon, 157–158, 197; in Jordan, 159–160, 197
Reporters sans Frontières, 51
Resettlement, 83–84
Revolutionary Punishment Law, 60
al-Risala, 125–126
al-Riyad, 144
Robinson, Glenn, 45, 46
Ross, Dennis, 183, 184
Rubinstein, Amnon, 263n63

Sabri, Ikrama, 81, 179, 182–183
Sadir, Tallal, 19, 41, 125
Salah, Hashim Daraghma, 107
Salama, Dallal, 104
Salama, Jasir, 60
Salama, Shaykh Yusuf, 193
Samara, Adil, 73
Samaritan Jewish sect, 27
Sanwar, Mahmud, 61
Sarraj, Iyad, 63
Saudi Arabia, 139, 144, 154–155, 257n81
Schools, 74–75
Security forces, 31, 38, 108–109; human rights violations, 47, 56–59, 69; Preventive security, 61, 64, 77, 80, 110–112, 196, 245n96; Hamas and, 109–110; civil police, 110
Shahid Filastin, 159
Shallah, Ramadan Abdallah, 119, 121, 132

Shallah, Umar, 134
Shanab, Isma'il Abu, 125
Shaq'a, Bassam, 115
Shaq'a, Ghassan, 22, 64, 101
Shaqura, Fakhri, 28
al-Sharafi, Kamal, 35
al-Sharq al-Awsat, 52, 160
Sha'th, Nabil, 17, 18, 22, 41, 116, 118; elections and, 28, 29; human rights and, 59; on state-building, 129; on Arab states, 138; on Israel, 172; on United States, 183–184
Shatila camp, 158
al-Shawwa, Mansur, 107, 109
al-Shawwa, Rawiya, 27–28, 29, 30, 39, 168
Shihah, Iman, 63
al-Shiqaqi, Fathi, 80, 119, 134
Shiqaqi, Khalil, 48, 50, 88–89, 137, 149, 241n19
Shkirat, Khadir, 53
Shu'aybi, Azmi, 35
Siftawi, Asad, 146
Soviet Union, immigrants to Israel, 10
Standing Orders, 28, 30, 31, 38, 192
State-building, 3, 11–12, 93, 187–189; opposition groups and, 116–117, 128–129; national identity and history, 192–193; successors to Arafat, 194–196; Hamas and, 195–196; exiled Palestinians and, 196–197; Arab states and, 198–200
Students, 66, 67, 75, 85, 102, 114–115, 151
Subuh, Fathi, 63
Suicide bombings, 59, 60, 61, 62, 85, 133–134, 135, 169, 173
Supreme Command Council, 124
Supreme Court (Israel), 43
Supreme Court (Palestine), 66, 67
al-Surani, Jamal, 4, 97
al-Surani, Raji, 53, 54, 74
Syria, 95, 119, 140, 144–146, 148, 151–152, 199–200, 257n69; refugees in, 157, 197

Ta'amri, Salah, 30, 32, 33, 43, 66, 188, 226n25
Tabuk, Ahmad, 101
Tahbub, Hasan, 179
Tanzim, 103
al-Tarifi, Jamal, 28, 29, 41, 103, 170–171
al-Tarifi, Wasim, 103
Tawil, Raymonda, 68
Tenet, George, 184
Terrorism, 12–13, 24–25, 58–62, 173–174; by Hamas, 46, 58, 59–62, 111, 127–128, 130–137; counterterrorism, 54; punishment of, 58–61; by Islamic Jihad, 59, 61, 134; suicide bombings, 59, 60, 61, 62, 85, 133–134, 135, 169, 173. See also Human rights
Tibi, Ahmad, 161
Tulkarm jail incident, 130
Turkman, Fakhri, 32

al-Umma, 77
United Arab Emirates (UAE), 144
United Nations, 120
United Nations General Assembly, 193
United Nations Relief and Works Agency (UNWRA), 43, 72, 75, 158
United States, 8, 141, 145; Arab states and, 146–147, 148; Hamas and, 153, 182, 264n91; Iraq and, 153; Arafat and, 181–182; media view of, 182, 183; Congress, 184; financial aid, 184
Universities, 75, 114–115
UNWRA. See United Nations Relief and Works Agency

Veto power, 38–39
Voice of Palestine, 42, 66, 78, 79, 81, 155, 169

Wachsman, Nahshon, 133
al-Watan, 78, 125
al-Wazir, Intisar, 17, 18–19, 23, 29, 54–55
Weizman, Ezir, 164–165
West Bank, 1, 2, 8, 10, 15, 83; divisions, 11; elections and, 27; Iraq, support for, 153
Women's issues, 54–56
Wye agreement, 11, 14, 16, 58, 124, 137, 183, 184, 190, 193

Yaghi, Ala' al-Din, 104–105, 138
Yakhlaf, Yahya, 179
Yasin, Ahmad, 85, 111, 115, 116, 119–123, 125, 127, 137; Arab states and, 146, 158; on Israel, 167; United States and, 182
Yasin, Badr, 116
Yasir Arafat Center for Social Activity, 158
Yediot Ahronot, 164
Young Men's Muslim Association, 125
Yusuf, Nasir, 23, 108, 109–110, 131, 133

al-Zahar, Mahmud, 77, 116, 117, 121, 126, 167
Zaki, Abbas, 92, 99, 101, 168
al-Za'nun, Riyad, 18, 29, 154
al-Za'nun, Salim, 28, 99, 100, 101, 197–198
Zidam, Jamila, 180
Zionism, 120–121, 178–179, 182